Carbine & Lance

Carbine & Lance

THE STORY OF OLD FORT SILL

BY COLONEL W. S. NYE

UNIVERSITY OF OKLAHOMA PRESS : NORMAN

By W. S. Nye

Carbine & Lance: The Story of Old Fort Sill (Norman, 1937, 1942, 1969)
(with Jason Betzinez) *I Fought with Geronimo* (Harrisburg, 1959)
(with Edward J. Stackpole) *The Battle of Gettysburg: A Guided Tour* (Harrisburg, 1960)
Bad Medicine & Good: Tales of the Kiowas (Norman, 1962)
Here Came the Rebels (Baton Rouge, 1965)
Plains Indian Raiders: The Final Phases of Warfare from the Arkansas to the Red River, with Original Photographs by William S. Soule (Norman, 1968)

Library of Congress Catalog Card Number: 79–13137
ISBN: 0–8061–1856–3

15   16   17   18   19   20   21   22

To Elleane

PREFACE

LIVING TODAY within a few miles of Fort Sill are human beings who, in a single life-span, have passed from the Stone Age to the era of the eight-cylinder motor car and the low-wing monoplane. Here are men who in fierce exultation have torn reeking scalps from their enemies. Here are women who, while their village moved to evade soldiers, have known the anguish of childbirth on horseback.

Kiowas and Comanches!

The United States government never was able to ignore the Indians of the southwest plains, numerically insignificant though they were and are. On account of them Fort Sill was established. Because of them and them alone it was maintained for the first four decades of its existence. The story of their rise from barbarism would be utterly incomplete without a full exposition of the part played therein by Fort Sill and the Army. The stone walls of the Old Post stand as an everlasting monument to the cunning of the red dwellers of the prairie, to their perversity and valor, and to the memory of those blue-clad troopers who wrote the final chapter of their primitive life.

CONTENTS

Part II : The City of Refuge

Part III : The Last War

Part IV : The Last Tepee

Part V : Appendices

ILLUSTRATIONS

xiii

MAPS

(All maps follow page 10)

INTRODUCTION

TO THE THIRD EDITION

IN 1933 I was a lieutenant in the 1st Observation Battalion at Fort Bragg, North Carolina—a field artillery unit devoted to the study and practice of locating enemy guns by sound and flash ranging. That spring I was ordered to attend the advanced course of the Field Artillery School at Fort Sill, Oklahoma, starting in the fall. Several of my friends who had taken the course warned me: "You are required to write a theme. It may well be the hardest part of the course. We urge you to start on it as soon as you get there."

I thought I could do better. Several months intervened before I was to move to Fort Sill, and in that time I could draft a paper on military acoustics, in which I fancied myself as an expert. Perhaps none of the instructors at Sill would know enough about this rare specialty to criticize what I might submit; they would have to give me a good grade. I resolved to write the monograph at once, and did so. It was in my pocket, all neatly typed, when I arrived at Fort Sill in September.

The Assistant Commandant, General (then Lieutenant Colonel) Charles S. Blakely, whom I had known at Fort Bragg, sent for me. "Nye," he said pleasantly, "as you know, you must write a theme while you are a student. We generally give you your choice of subjects. You may write either a 'Fort Sill History' or 'The History of Fort Sill.' "

"Yes, sir," I replied.

General Blakely went on to explain that a project was being launched to preserve the history of the post both in writing and in the establishment of a museum. Lieutenant Harry C. Larter, Jr., would set up the museum and I would write the history.

I didn't take the sound-ranging theme out of my pocket, but started within hours to collect material for the history. I wrote to General Hugh L. Scott, former Chief of Staff of the U.S. Army, whose memoirs (that

xvii

I had recently read) dealt with frontier and Indian history, with some emphasis on Fort Sill in the 1890's. He was most generous in the resulting correspondence, both in supplying me with data and in putting me in touch with a Kiowa Indian, George Hunt, who could help with the Indian lore.

Mr. Hunt, who also had heard from General Scott, wrote to me during the week before Christmas when classes at the school were suspended. I drove out to Rainy Mountain to see him. He was friendly and interested in my project, but the old Indians he took me to interview were reserved and uncommunicative. Then an emergency occurred in the Hunt family. His mother-in-law, "Mrs. Goombi," was a white woman who had grown up as a Kiowa; she had been captured in Texas about 1868 and only recently had discovered that she was probably Millie Durgan. The aged woman, who had many descendants among the Kiowas, was sick in the government Indian hospital near Fort Sill; but believing that her "die day" was near, she wished to be taken home. I was able to secure an ambulance from the post for this purpose, and my action was deeply appreciated by the Indians. On the death of Mrs. Goombi a little later, Fort Sill sent a bugler to blow taps at the graveside and an American flag to drape over the casket—as the widow of a former U.S. Indian scout she was entitled to this honor. Two officials of the school attended the funeral. The Kiowas were greatly impressed, and word of this attention spread through the tribe and to other tribes. From then on I had no difficulty. The door was opened to me for many interviews of old Indians, and much valuable source material was obtained.

George Hunt became my guide, interpreter, and close friend. He spoke several tongues as well as being adept in the sign language. He was intensely interested in Indian and frontier history, and knew all the old Indians of several of the Plains tribes who either had been participants in events or had learned of them from their parents. He was familiar with the country—as far north as the site of the Medicine Lodge Treaty and as far west as the battlefield in Palo Duro Canyon. Together we made many field trips and had innumerable interviews, over a period of four years, with Kiowa, Comanche, Apache, and other Indian veterans of the exciting days when the redmen were wild, free corsairs of the prairies. I filled many notebooks with what must be regarded as source material—information no longer available from such sources.

It was also my great good fortune to secure the assistance of Master Sergeant Morris Swett, veteran librarian at the Field Artillery School. He was an old friend of the Indians and of many white pioneers as well as officers and men who had been attending the school for years. He had voluminous notes on the history of the area and the post, and had an amazing memory concerning the books that had been written on the history of the Southwest. Best of all, he had collected and preserved documents that constituted all that is left of the official records of early Fort Sill and its parent post, Fort Arbuckle. Had it not been for "Mike" Swett these would have been destroyed. One day a member of the post guard had hastened to the library to tell Mike that a detail of garrison prisoners were burning old papers at the dump. Some misguided official, having noted boxes of yellowed documents in the basement of head-quarters had said to the Officer of the Day, "Get rid of all this old junk!"

Much priceless material had already been burned when Swett reached the scene, and papers were blowing all over the prairie. But he was able to save most of the heavy, leather-bound books in which were entered the correspondence, orders, and reports from 1869 (1867 in the case of Arbuckle) on into the 1890's. These records are now in the Fort Sill Museum.

In addition to this source material I had the good fortune of being sent to Washington to research documents in the Adjutant General's Office—then in the old State, War, and Navy Building—and in the Division of Manuscripts, Library of Congress. In the former I dug into original records which I cite as "Old Files, AGO" and "Old Records, AGO." They are now in the National Archives. In the Manuscripts Division I examined the papers of General Philip H. Sheridan. At that time they were dust covered and stacked in old packing boxes, apparently as they had been stored after the General's death. Today they are in excellent shape, collated and catalogued.

Some secondary sources, chiefly published books that in 1935 were so rare they were accessible only with special permission in the Hunting-ton Library in California, have since been reprinted. A noteworthy ex-ample is Gregg's *Commerce of the Prairies*. I spent several weeks in the Huntington Library and in the library of the Command and General Staff School at Fort Leavenworth, which had a valuable collection of old books and periodicals.

It was difficult to obtain maps of portions of Texas and Oklahoma, for in the 1930's very little mapping had been done except in making modern road maps. I was able to fill this need in two ways: first, from old maps then in the files of the Adjutant General, accompanying reports of expeditions; and second, in the files of the Interior Department. Here again research is much easier today, for such documents have been as-sembled in the National Archives. Where old maps did not exist or were too inaccurate, I obtained official assistance: The aero squadron at Fort Sill flew a number of photographic missions for me in Texas and along the North Fork of Red River, supplying air mosaics from which the school cartographers made maps.

Of course, I interviewed many non-Indians who had personal knowledge of the early history of Fort Sill and the Southwest. These included ranchmen and cattlemen in Texas and pioneer settlers in Oklahoma. Probably my best informant was Mr. William H. Quinette, who came to Fort Sill in 1878 and was post trader to 1915. I lived at his home during the summer of 1934, and we spent the long summer evenings on the porch of his home in Lawton while he reminisced about his experiences at Fort Sill. We also made many trips over the area to enable him to point out historic spots. He had been well acquainted with Horace P. Jones, the post interpreter for many years, who had given him much first-hand information. During the summer of 1935 I was on temporary duty in Washington performing research in the government repositories and became well acquainted with Captain R. G. Carter, who had served in Mackenzie's 4th Cavalry at Fort Sill and in Texas during the 1870's. Although he was then ninety years old, his memory had been kept sharp by more or less constant writing of articles and books.

I also had the privilege of becoming acquainted with General William J. Snow and other senior officers who had served at Fort Sill when the school was in its infancy.

The photographs used in this book are chiefly from the William S. Soule collection, made in Kansas and at Fort Sill during the period 1867–75. I first obtained them from an original Soule album in which Soule himself had written in ink the identifications; this album was lent to me by Mrs. Charles Cleveland of Anadarko. Her husband, a prominent trader, had been a clerk in the post trader's store while Soule was post photographer at Sill. Other photographs have been given to me by Indians and by the late Claude Hensley of Oklahoma City, who obtained them from the Soule album owned originally by Neal Evans, of the firm of Evans Brothers, early traders at Fort Sill. Other sources of these photographs have since been discovered, but in 1934 were unknown. In 1965 I visited Soule's daughter, Miss Lucia Soule, in Boston, and she gave me a few other photographs made by her father, which I had not previously seen. The pictures in this edition are from all these sources, plus others furnished by Gillett Griswold, director of the Field Artillery Center Museum, who has made a long study of them and obtained identifications previously in doubt. Some of the pictures from sources other than Soule are so labeled.

I am most grateful to the many persons who have furnished information and other assistance. In addition to those already mentioned herein and in the footnotes, I must salute the last two Chiefs of Field Artillery, Major Generals Upton Birnie and Robert M. Danford, who gave official support to the project, and to the Commandants of the school, Generals William Cruikshank, H. W. Butner, and Augustine McIntyre, and to Generals Charles J. Blakely and Frederick W. Black. My long-time friend Major General Ray W. Barker, who in the 1930's was instructor in tactics at the school, generously gave a critical reading of the manuscript and accompanied me and old Indians on field trips where we studied historic events on the ground. Harry Larter contributed the jacket and frontispiece painting and gave much sound advice. And for recent support and assistance, especially relating to the post-World War II history, I am indebted to Major General Charles P. Brown, commandant; and to Miss Anne Powell and Mrs. Jerry McClung, of the Public Information Office, and above all to my old friend Gillett Griswold, director of the Museum, for data and permission to use (and I have used them liberally) their writings on recent post history.

IT SEEMS STRANGE that Fort Sill should have such a fascination for all who have served there or who live in its environs. Yet this is so. There is an old saying in the Army that those who have been stationed at Fort Sill always return at least once. Since the first world war the post has steadily grown as the Field Artillery center of the U.S. Army and has exerted profound influence on the careers of successive generations of our country's defenders. In recent years it has changed so tremendously that visitors who have not seen it in the interim will scarcely be able to find their way around. Yet the Old Stone Post, established a century ago and built by the 10th Cavalry, is still there and the buildings are still in use.

In my introduction to the Second Edition, published in 1942, I said: "The Field Artillery and the Sill graduates will be heard from again [in World War II.]." That prophecy was realized magnificently, and in the succeeding years the sons of Fort Sill are continuing to help forge the Nation's destiny. The influence of the Old Post will endure and grow as time rolls on.

WILBUR STURTEVANT NYE

Wormleysburg, Pennsylvania

PART I

THE TROOPER AND THE INDIAN

CHAPTER ONE

THE DRAGOON

MASSACRE OF CUTTHROAT GAP—THE DRAGOON EXPEDITION—
THE VILLAGE OF GRASS HOUSES

O NE of the landmarks of the great war trail which led south from
Arrow-Point River (the Arkansas) into Texas and Old Mexico
was a detached hill which stood in a mesquite-dotted plain north
of the Wichita Mountains. It is a tradition among the Kiowas that whenever one of their roving bands camped near this peak a rainstorm descended; therefore they named it Rainy Mountain.

A little creek, rising near Rainy Mountain, meanders north for fifteen
miles to empty into the Washita River at the present site of Mountain
View, Oklahoma. Along this creek valley the grass once remained green,
even in the wintertime. Buffalo and antelope were to be found there
throughout the year; there was ample grazing for the Indian ponies;
there was an abundance of firewood and sweet water. For these reasons
the mouth of Rainy Mountain Creek was a favorite camp ground of the
Kiowas and Comanches.

In the late spring of 1833 the entire Kiowa tribe was camped in this
locality.[1] There was color and jollity—yet industry—in that great village
of skin lodges. A successful hunting party had just come in. Throughout
the encampment strips of drying meat hung over saplings supported by
forked sticks thrust in the ground. Women were scraping fresh hides
pegged to the ground, cooking buffalo meat in brass buckets suspended
from crude tripods, or baking tortillas made of mesquite-berry meal.
Young girls clad in long buckskin garments, and wearing moccasins that
reached halfway to their knees, were cutting firewood and carrying water
from the stream. Small boys were frolicking naked, wrestling with each

[1] James Mooney, "Calendar History of the Kiowa Indians," *Seventeenth Annual Report*
(Washington: Bureau of Ethnology, 1898), pp. 257-60. Considerable data on the Cutthroat
Massacre was given to the author by the following Kiowas: Hunting Horse, Andrew Stumbling Bear, Tonemah, and Guitone. Several of them had parents or grandparents who were
present at the massacre.

3

other furiously, or shooting at marks with bows and arrows. Little girls were playing quietly with toy tents and buckskin dolls. Older children were harnessing a miniature travois to an embarrassed camp dog.

Ancient warriors sat in the sun smoking kinnikinic. Infants, strapped upright in their wood-and-leather carriers, dozed in the warm limpid atmosphere, while wolfish dogs, with the corners of their mouths drawn down grimly, scratched elusive fleas.

Through the air drifted innumerable bits of down blown from the cottonwoods which shaded the riverbank. Bluejays and squirrels scolded in the elms, swelling the babel rising from the great barbaric encampment. The tepees showed light grey or buff against the trees; their tops were blackened from the smoke of many campfires. A few of the lodges were distinguished by the weird and colorful designs painted on them. From one of these dwellings came the fragrance of cedar chips and sage grass smouldering on the embers of a ceremonial fire. Within the dim interior a medicine man reclined on a pile of buffalo robes, crooning falsetto melodies and softly shaking a pear-shaped rattle made of rawhide.

In one part of the camp a group of men were beating tom-toms and shouting war songs; one of the chiefs was recruiting a war party to ride west against the Utes. On the outskirts of the village youths were practicing warlike feats, preparing for the day when they too could join a band of raiders. Some were exercising with lance and bow, others riding their ponies at breakneck speed, hanging over the sides of their mounts, with only a hand and foot exposed to the "enemy." Others were galloping in pairs, reaching down to rescue comrades supposed to be wounded and dismounted in battle.

Elsewhere gambling games were attracting crowds: Here an awl-game (like parchesi), there the favorite hand-stick guessing game. On the flats along the creek a score of braves were horse racing, wagering everything they possessed on the outcome of a single heat.

Beyond the camp an immense herd of horses grazed in the deep meadows, tended by a few boys. Some of the animals were frisking in rough play, others rolling contentedly in the dust of dried buffalo-wallows. On all sides the gentle folds of the prairie stretched afar to the rim of the sky. At this season of the year it presented the appearance of a vast carpet of indescribable beauty. On the background of chrome green were massed in bright confusion millions of wildflowers—gold with wine centers, azure, white, scarlet, purple, salmon.

The village had been here only a few days when a party of buffalo hunters, riding north of the Washita, came upon the carcass of a freshly slain bison from which protruded an arrow. The markings on the shaft showed that it was of Osage manufacture. At once the Kiowas returned to camp. The whole tribe was aroused. On the south side of the river adobe works were thrown up for defense.[2] The Osages, being armed with flintlocks secured from white traders on the Missouri, were feared by the Kiowas.

Several days passed but no enemy appeared. The alarm subsided. The big war party which had been planning the expedition against the Utes departed, leaving the camp guarded mostly by old men and young boys. The people who were left decided to divide the village into several groups and disperse. One part moved south toward the present site of Mountain Park, on Otter Creek. Here this portion subdivided, one band remaining on Otter Creek, the other going northwest to the mouth of Elk Creek. The purpose of this maneuver was to get as near as possible to the range of wild horses. The Kiowas planned to liberate their brood mares, hobbled, near the wild herds so as to breed them to wild stallions. In this way the endurance and hardiness of the domestic stock would be increased.

A few days later the remainder of the tribe which had stayed on the Washita split into two divisions. One of these went to a camp site four miles southwest of Rainy Mountain. The other group traveled southeast to Eagle Heart Springs, near the head of Cache Creek. Ah-da-te, principal chief of the tribe, was in charge.

They stayed in this locality for only a day or two, then moved to Saddle Mountain Creek, about a half-mile from the site of Saddle Mountain Post Office. Still not satisfied, they made a final move westward, through that gap known today as Cutthroat Gap, to a glen at the head of the west branch of Otter Creek. Here they pitched their tepees and prepared to await the return of the war party. They were unaware that a large band of Osage warriors, traveling on foot, had followed their plain trail from the Washita.

Before the sun appeared over the eastern crags a Kiowa youth went up the canyon to gather the ponies belonging to his family. In the dim light his startled gaze fell on the shaven head of an Osage, who was bobbing behind the rocks. The boy ran to give the alarm.[3]

Old Ah-da-te sprang up shouting, "To the rocks! To the rocks!"

Women and children swarmed from the lodges. They scrambled up among the boulders atop the little butte lying south of the camp site. But the Osages were upon them with long knives, searching them out to cut their throats. There was no attempt to stand; it was simply a butchery of panic-stricken noncombatants.

[2] The remains of this earthen fort are still clearly visible on the south bank of the Washita River, about a half-mile west of the mouth of Rainy Mountain Creek. They are on the farm formerly owned by Quitan.

[3] Ay-tah (Mrs. Toyebo) and Frank Given to author, 1935. Ay-tah's grandfather was the boy who ran to give the alarm. Frank Given, a son of Satank, received his information from Calf Mountain, a survivor of the massacre.

Some of the people escaped by fleeing west. The Tai-me Keeper (custodian of the great medicine) abandoned one of the sacred idols to the Osages. An elderly warrior named An-zah-te ran away without his war shield. Kiowa law brands this as inexcusable cowardice, and it indicates the terror which the Osage attack inspired. The refugees continued their flight until they arrived at the camp of the band which had gone to hunt wild horses. The panic was communicated to them. Many of the frightened Indians attempted to dig hiding places in the bare rocks of the little hill which stands a mile or so northwest of the mouth of Elk Creek. From this incident the knoll thenceforth was known to the Kiowas as "Scratching Rock."

There were, however, a few feats of individual heroism at the Massacre of Cutthroat Gap. Some of the Kiowas were killed defending their children. Tai-on paused to snatch up the cradle containing his infant son. As he fled he stopped several times to shoot arrows at his pursuers. As he did so he held the top of the cradle in his teeth. The Kiowas say that if all the warriors had been present the whole story would have had a different ending.

After the affair was over the Osages decapitated their victims, and placed each ghastly trophy in the Kiowa camp buckets. These buckets later were found standing in rows in the midst of the litter of the camp.[4] This was a sacrificial rite peculiar to the Osages, who were accustomed to offer the heads of their victims to propitiate the gods and to facilitate the passage of deceased relatives into the spirit world.

Two children—brother and sister—were taken away as captives. A woman also was captured but later escaped. The Osages found in the camp a number of silver dollars, which they carried to Fort Gibson. This was part of the loot taken the preceding year by the Kiowas in an attack on a party of traders returning from Santa Fe.[5]

The Kiowas were thrown into great consternation by this Osage invasion of their territory. The alarm extended to their allies the Comanches, who promptly commenced assembling for common defense. Nearly all of the Comanches who lived north of Red River—the Kotchatekas, or Buffalo-eaters, the Yapparikas, or Rooteaters, and the Noyika or Noconee (Antelope Band)—gathered together at the east end

[4] One of these same brass buckets is now in the Fort Sill museum. It was presented by George Hunt, who received it from the wife of Stumbling Bear.

[5] Mooney, *op. cit.*, pp.254-57. See also Josiah Gregg, *Commerce of the Prairies* (reprint ed.; Dallas: Southwest Press [now Turner Co.], 1933), pp. 242-44. Mooney's work, published in 1898, apparently started rumors of buried treasure. The Kiowas told Mooney that some of the silver was buried at the site of the massacre; they were not aware of the exact location. During the last three decades, thousands of people have dug into Mr. Haley's pasture, vainly seeking this treasure. Some of these earnest diggers have brought witching rods or queer boxes filled with radio tubes and nests of wire; most of them, however, rely on picks and shovels.

6

of the mountains. This was unusual. The Comanches spoke a common language, had common customs, and were associated with each other in war. But the various bands rarely assembled in one place, as the Kiowas did for their annual sun dance.

Tribal organization among the plains Indians was loose. Discipline or authority, aside from that imposed by the bare necessities of primitive camp life and religious taboo, was almost non-existent. The so-called principal chief of a tribe or subdivision thereof was little more than a sort of billeting officer who decided when the village would move, and to what place. A war chief was an individual who had organized a raid and had made several *coups* against an enemy; to use modern terms, he was a man who had made his major varsity letter. However, his advice might be sought on account of his proved courage and experience, and he was "looked to in time of danger." There might be a number of these petty chiefs in each band.

It was the custom of the Indians to spread out their encampments along watercourses. They disliked being crowded, and required considerable pasturage for their vast horse herds. Consequently the Comanche village which lay east of the Wichita Mountains in 1834 extended along Cache Creek from Medicine Bluff north to Chandler Creek and south to Wolf Creek. The principal part was in the center, with tepees located as far west as Signal Mountain.

Sentry duty was purely voluntary; and, as nearly a year had elapsed without a reappearance of Osage invaders, the Comanches had relaxed their vigilance. A party of warriors had gone east toward the Keechi Hills to hunt the wild horses which abounded in that area.

On July 16 the rays of the sun clutched the valley of Cache Creek with the usual summer ferocity. The Comanches lolled indolently under brush arbors built in front of the tepees. The afternoon stillness was broken only by the rhythmic hum of locusts in the fields. Suddenly a cry of alarm went up from one of the camps, repeated, as if in waves, from band to band.

A column of dark-clad horsemen had appeared on the high ground three miles east of the camp. They had stopped on the knoll later known as Dodge Hill, and seemed to be studying the Indian camp. The sunlight flashed from their weapons and uniform ornaments. American soldiers had arrived, for the first time, in the heart of the Comanche country.

The Comanche camps were thrown into immediate and violent commotion. Warriors ran around to catch up their war ponies. Women yelped shrilly as they packed camp gear for flight. Disturbed infants bawled lustily; a thousand dogs barked and howled.

Into the midst of all this rode calmly the party of horse hunters. They assured Chief Sequi-to-tori[6] that there was no danger. They had met the strangers two days ago at Keechi Hills and had guided them to the village. The newcomers were white soldiers, but they came to shake hands and to make peace.

The Comanches were relieved and pleased. At this early day they believed what the white man told them, and in this case it happened to be true. The soldiers were a part of the dragoon regiment, mobilized at Fort Gibson for service on the western frontier. They had been sent out under Colonel Henry Dodge to contact the wild Indians and to bring some of them back to Fort Gibson for conference and treaty. The purpose of the government was to secure protection for the Santa Fe trail, for hunters, trappers, and traders who desired to enter the plains, and for the Five Civilized Tribes who were being settled in the eastern part of the territory.[7]

Sequi-to-tori called for a piece of whitened buffalo hide, which he fastened to a stick as a flag. He mounted a hundred of his braves and led them off at a gallop to meet the soldiers. The Indians formed in line and "dressed up" their ranks like cavalry, no doubt in imitation of Mexican lancers with whom they had fought. Opposite them were two hundred and fifty dragoons formed in columns of twos, with three columns abreast. If the Comanches displayed a colorful spectacle with their gay trappings and flowing war bonnets, so did the dragoons. Judged by present-day standards, the latter were attired in costumes better suited to comic opera than to summer field service in Oklahoma.

At the head of the regiment was the commander and his staff, with a white flag planted in the ground in front of them. The Indians placed beside it their "flag." The chief greeted Colonel Dodge warmly, taking him to his breast and giving him a hearty hug. Fortunately an interpreter was available. This was a Mexican captive member of the Comanche tribe who had been present at the first meeting with the dragoons at Keechi Hills. He had not forgotten all his Spanish, and among the officers was one who spoke this language brokenly. The interpreter had told Colonel Dodge that his name was Hi-soo-san-ches, no doubt a phonetic variant of Jesus Sanchez.

[6] The Comanches today state that the two head chiefs of the village were Sequi-to-tori (Splashing-the-Mud) and Poy-weh-neh-parai (Buffalo Leaf-Fat). Catlin, Wheelock, and other contemporary writers give the name of the chief as Isha-coly (Isaconee—Wandering Wolf) ; this is the name appended to the treaty of 1835. Likely it was the same man. The Kiowas and Comanches, because of an old superstitious custom, frequently changed the name of deceased tribesmen.

[7] Excellent accounts of the dragoon expedition are given in George Catlin, *North American Indians* (Philadelphia: Leary, Stuart and Co., 1913) ; and in "Journal of Hugh Evans" (edited by F. S. Perrine), in *Chronicles of Oklahoma* (published by the Oklahoma Historical Society), III (1925), 175-215.

After the chief greeted the colonel, the whole troop of Comanches rode down the columns shaking hands with each grinning dragoon. This ceremony consumed nearly an hour, after which the Indians invited Colonel Dodge to cross Cache Creek and camp with them.[8]

The good colonel declined. He preferred to keep the stream between himself and the savages. He made his camp in the form of a hollow rectangle, pitching it in on the flat ground just north of where the remains of the first stone bridge now stand, near Magazine 19.[9] It was called Camp Comanche. The bend of Cache Creek, with its precipitous banks, afforded protection against mounted attack from the front and from the south flank; a tributary protected the rear. A chain of sentinels was posted about the encampment. Strict orders were issued prohibiting any member of the command from visiting the Indian village after dark. Indian tepees were directly across the creek; Colonel Dodge was astonished to see an American flag hoisted over the lodge of the chief![10]

The following day Colonel Dodge held a conference with the headmen of the Comanche village, while the lesser Indians gathered about staring in curiosity at the troops and their camp. At first there was some trouble with the interpreter; the rascal seemed to have lost his sense of hearing. Colonel Dodge presented him with a fine *yauger* (jaeger) rifle. His hearing magically was restored. The powwow proceeded without further difficulty.

Colonel Dodge told the Comanches that he had with him two captive Indians whom the Osages had taken from the Pawnee Picts. The Comanches made no reply. They had seen these captives in the soldier camp, and recognized one of them as a Wichita and the other as a Kiowa girl. Colonel Dodge went on to explain that the soldiers had come to restore these captives to their own people. He desired to know where the Pawnee Picts lived.

The Comanches shook their heads dubiously. The only Pawnees known to them lived far to the north, on the Platte River. Colonel Dodge attempted to clarify matters by saying that Pawnee Pict was what the Americans called all of the wild Indians of the southwestern plains; he understood that the Pawnee Picts tattooed their faces and lived in peculiar grass houses.

[8] The Comanche account of the meeting with the dragoons was given to the author by the following old Comanches: Quasiah, Timbo, Poafebitty, and Hoy-koy-bitty. Quasiah is the son of Pah-kah, who was present when the dragoons arrived, and who signed the treaty of 1835. The account furnished by these Indians agrees remarkably well with that of Catlin, yet none of them have ever heard of Catlin's book.

[9] Quasiah states that his father pointed out this spot very definitely to him.

[10] *Dragoon Campaigns to the Rocky Mountains,* by "A Dragoon" (1st ed.; New York: Wiley and Long, 161 Broadway, 1836), p. 157; Lieutenant Wheelock's official journal of the expedition, in *American State Papers,* Class V, V, 373; letter from C. S. Stambaugh in *Niles Register,* August 8, 1835.

9

This was sufficient identification for the Comanches. They knew the Pawnee Picts as *Towyash* (Wichitas). They stated that the Towyash village was about three days' march to the west. They agreed to furnish a man who could guide the soldiers there.

Official matters now being concluded, and friendly relations established with the Comanches, the dragoons spent the following two days visiting the big Indian camp, and in bartering cheap trade knives for good horses. Artist George Catlin had an umbrella which the Indians coveted. But Catlin, being ill, used the device as a sunshade and would not part with it. Years later, when traders were established in the Fort Sill country, every Indian equipped himself with an umbrella.

On July 18 the dragoons packed up and marched south of the mountains toward the Wichita village.[11] The first day, after making only a few miles, they camped on Blue Beaver Creek. Thirty soldiers were sick, and could go no farther. Since leaving Fort Gibson the dragoons had suffered from acute dysentery and malaria. A number had died. On Blue Beaver they built a fortified camp of logs, roofed over with brush. Here the sick were left, attended by a small detachment commanded by Lieutenant Izard. It is to the credit of the Comanches that they did not disturb this little group, though it would have been easy for them to destroy it.

On July 21 the Dragoon expedition arrived at the Wichita village, which nestled in the mouth of Devil's Canyon, at the foot of a group of rugged granite peaks which lies a few miles northeast of the junction of Elk Creek with the North Fork of Red River. The North Fork is a broad, shallow stream which changes its course every year or two. At the time of the dragoon visit it was more distant from the mountains than it is today. Extensive fields of corn, pumpkins, beans, and melons occupied what is now the river bed, and beyond that was the village of some eighty igloo-like grass houses. On recent airplane photos the traces of a few of these houses can still be identified.

The Wichitas were accomplished agriculturists; in this they differed from the more numerous and powerful Kiowas and Comanches, who were strictly a carnivorous people. As is so frequently the case, the latter were much more warlike and aggressive.

Though frightened at first by the arrival of the soldiers, the Wichitas quickly became friendly. It was fortunate for the dragoons that the village was well supplied with food, especially fresh vegetables. The white men were hungry, and suffering from their steady diet of fresh buffalo meat. One of the dragoons writes: "Our arrival at the Wichita village

[11] Major General H. L. Scott to Brigadier General William Cruikshank, December 13, 1933. General Scott's uncle, Captain David Hunter, was a member of the dragoon expedition. In 1889 Scott also received much information from Pah-kah, who was then a very old Comanche living with Quanah Parker.

MAPS

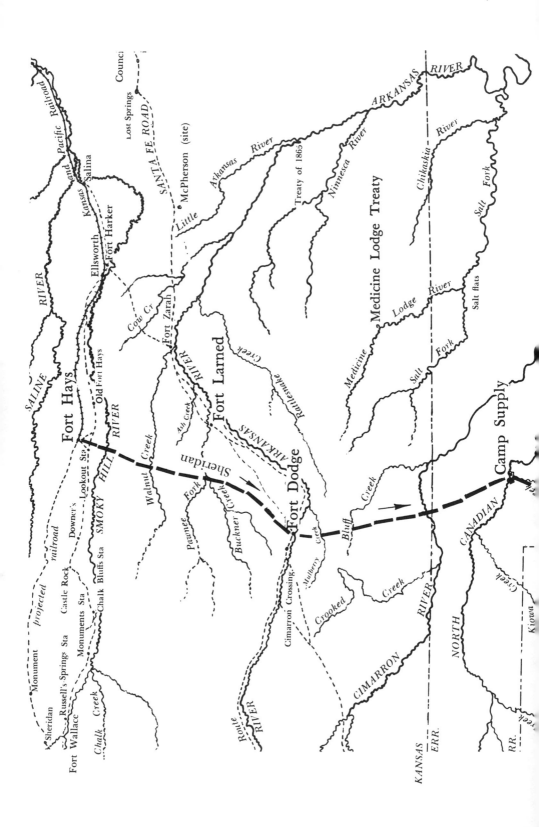

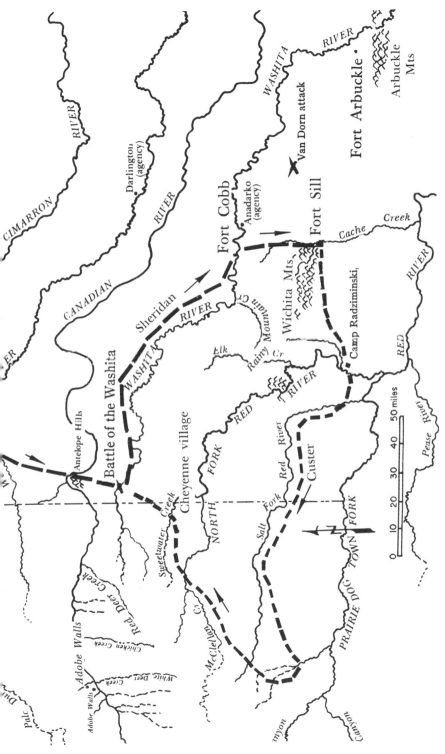

Portions of Kansas and Indian Territory in 1868–69, showing Sheridan's route from Fort Hays to Fort Sill and Custer's route to the Cheyenne village of Medicine Arrow. See Chapter Five.

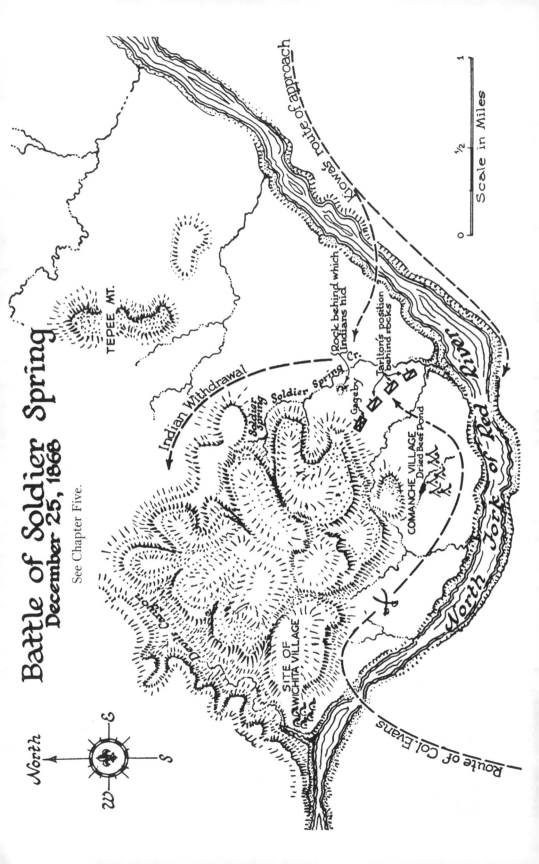

Battle of Soldier Spring
December 25, 1868

See Chapter Five.

North

Scale in Miles

0 ½ 1

Kiowa's Route of approach

Route of Col. Evans

North Fork of Red River

TEPEE MT.

Indian Withdrawal

Soldier Spring

Soldier Spring

Rock behind which Indians hid

Tarlton's position behind rocks

Gageby

COMANCHE VILLAGE
Dried Beef Pond

SITE OF WICHITA VILLAGE

Gageby Creek

FORT SILL AND VICINITY
AS IT EXISTED IN 1871

Topography from modern map
Roads and buildings from map drawn in 1871

Scale

See Chapter Six.

CADDO ROAD

FORT ARBUCKLE ROAD

Caddo Crossing

Indian Commissary

E. D. Smith Trader's Store (site of Tonecei's store)

Hazen's adobe house

Kiowa-Comanche Agency buildings

Corral

Satank killed here, 1871

FORT RICHARDSON ROAD

Evan's Trading Store

Grierson House

Trader's Store

ROAD TO FORT COBB

Red Creek

Beef Creek

Medicine Bluff Creek

Medicine Bluff

Wolf Hill
Frank Lee killed here, 1872

Craig Hill

White Wolf Mt.
(Rabbit Hill)

Hoyl's Hole
Cattle Herder killed here, 1870

Four Mile Crossing

Mt. Hinds

White man killed by Indians, 1874

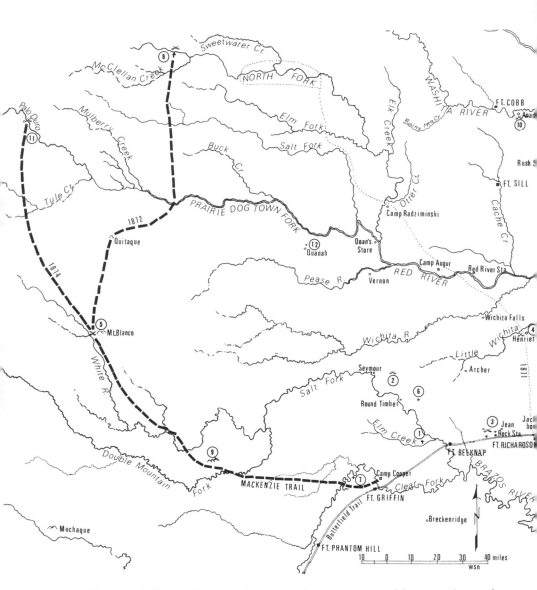

Kiowa and Comanche depredations and engagements with troops in northern Texas in 1870–74, and punitive expeditions of Colonel R. S. Mackenzie. The encircled numbers indicate the following events: (1) Elm Creek raid, October, 1864; (2) Kicking Bird–McClellan fight, July 12, 1870; (3) Salt Creek prairie, site of numerous killings, including Warren wagon train massacre and Lost Valley fight; (4) Lieutenant Boehm attacked Kiowas, May 20, 1871; (5) Mackenzie's Mt. Blanco fight, October 10, 1871; (6) surveyor killed, May 19, 1872; (7) Abel Lee massacre, June 9, 1872; (8) Mackenzie attack on village, September 29, 1872; (9) Buell attack, January 28, 1874; (10) Anadarko fight, August 22–24, 1874; (11) Mackenzie Palo Duro attack, September 27, 1874; (12) Joe Earle killed, April 12, 1878. See Chapter Six.

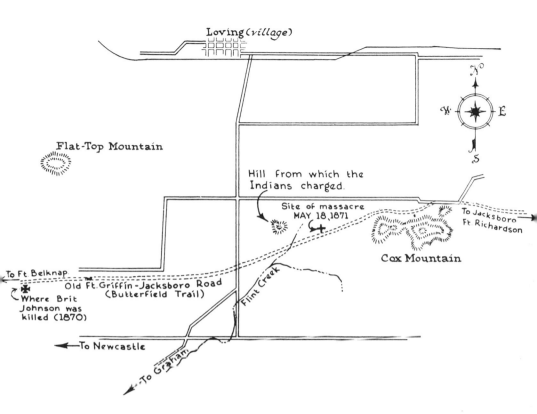

Massacre of Captain Henry Warren's Wagon Teamsters. See Chapter Seven.

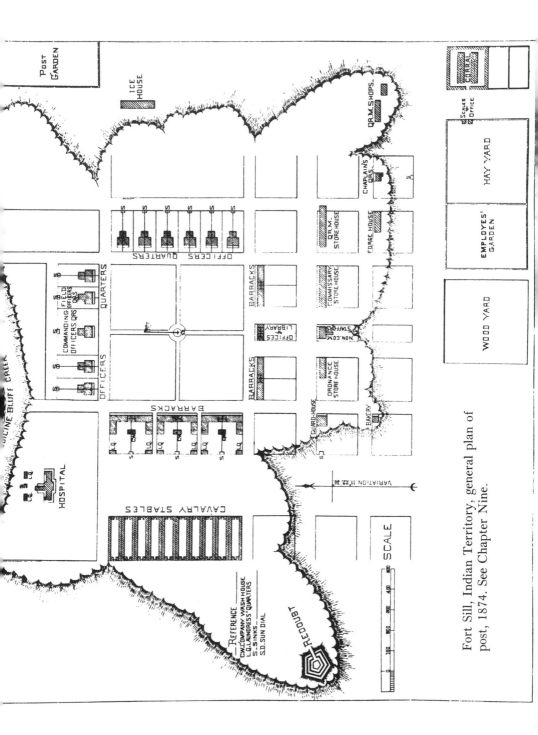

Fort Sill, Indian Territory, general plan of post, 1874. See Chapter Nine.

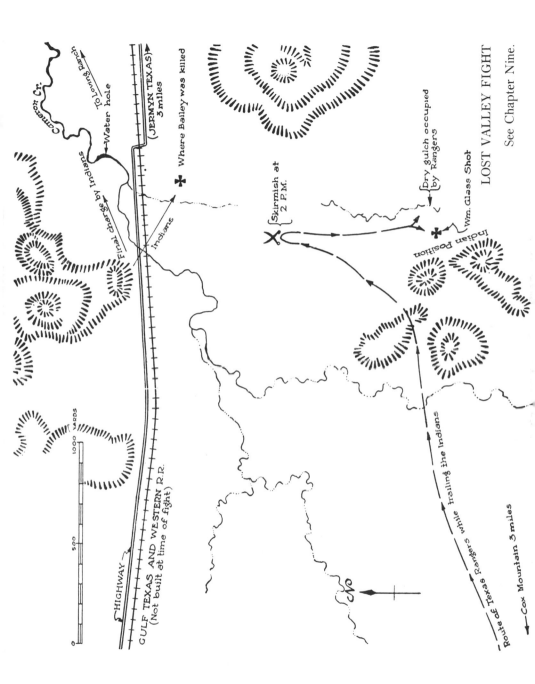

Cameron Cr.

To Loving Ranch

Water hole

Final charge by Indians

(JERMYN TEXAS)
3 miles

Where Bailey was killed

Indians

1000 YARDS

500

0

HIGHWAY

GULF TEXAS AND WESTERN R.R.
(Not built at time of fight)

Skirmish at
2 P.M.

Dry gulch occupied
by Rangers

Wm. Glass Shot

Indian position

Route of Texas Rangers while trailing the Indians

Cox Mountain 3 miles

LOST VALLEY FIGHT

See Chapter Nine.

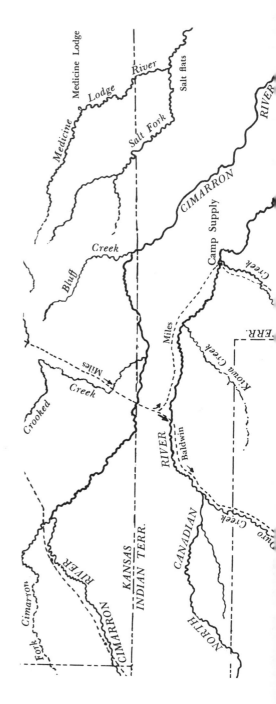

Campaign of 1874, showing the converging of columns from several directions, according to Sheridan's plan. See Chapter Ten.

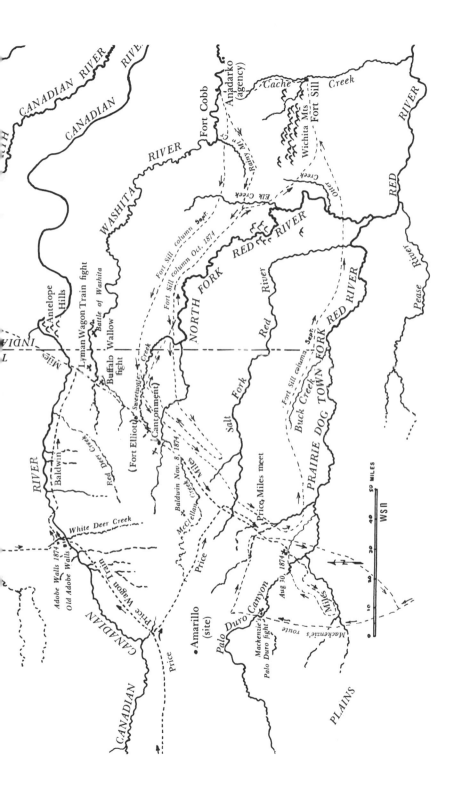

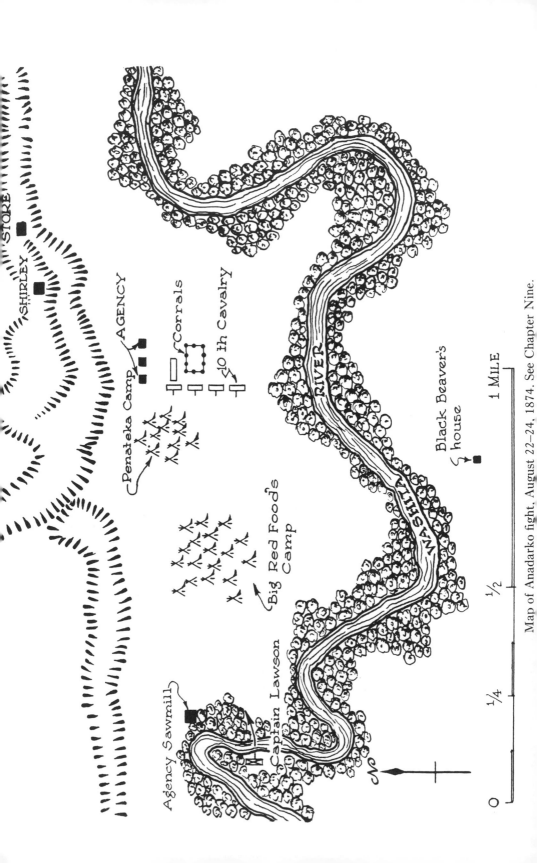

Map of Anadarko fight, August 22–24, 1874. See Chapter Nine.

was timely; for we were hungry and had nothing to eat. They had plenty of corn just in good eating order, pumpkins, squashes, water- and muskmelons, together with dried buffalo and horse meat. For these supplies we gave them tobacco, tin cups, buttons, the yellow stripes from our pantaloons, etc., but when we offered them money they laughed at us, for these unsophisticated beings knew not its value. They call themselves Towea Indians and appear amiable and industrious. The women are beauties. . . . ."[12]

Colonel Dodge opened negotiations with the Wichitas on July 22. The conference began inauspiciously, for the colonel made certain demands upon the Indians. He asked them to turn over to him two white captives. A mounted ranger named Abbay and a small boy named Martin had been captured by Indians in the southeastern part of Indian Territory. The Wichitas replied that the ranger had been captured by some other tribe, and that he was dead. They claimed to have no knowledge of the Martin boy. Colonel Dodge thought he knew better, having inside information from the Comanches, but tactfully changed the subject until a better opportunity should present itself.

Next he inquired concerning the American flag which he had seen in the Comanche camp. He was informed that it had been obtained from the Pawnees on the Platte River. On asking whether the Spaniards (from Santa Fe) came to trade with the Wichitas, he was told that they did. They had been in the village recently.

"The Americans will give you better and cheaper goods than the Spaniards do," said the business-like colonel briskly.[13]

Colonel Dodge had with his party a number of Indian scouts from Fort Gibson. A few of these were Osages. While the conference was in session the Osages were snooping about the village. Presently they discovered that the Martin boy was concealed in a near-by cornfield. They hurried to the colonel with this information. Colonel Dodge, in turn, was just commencing to tax the Wichita chief with this knowledge when an exciting interruption occurred.

A group of strange Comanches and Kiowas arrived to investigate the cause of the unusual gathering at the Wichita village. They spied the Osage scouts. Full of rage the Kiowas dashed into the council lodge. The Cutthroat Massacre was fresh in their minds.

For a moment the situation was dangerous. The Kiowas were numerous, well armed, and wore determined scowls. They were quieted temporarily, but the atmosphere remained tense.

[12] *Niles Register,* August 8, 1835. Evidently some money was given to the Wichitas, because Mrs. Lee Winters, who now lives on the site of the village, has a United States dime minted in 1827 which she found among the rubbish, together with dragoon buttons and other similar items.

[13] "Journal of Hugh Evans," *op. cit.,* p. 189.

The stout-hearted American officer repeated his demand that the Wichitas release the Martin boy. They did so with reluctance. The old buck who had the child in charge had grown fond of the small captive and was loath to part with him. He shed copious tears when forced to do so.

Colonel Dodge then brought in the Wichita girl and the Kiowa girl and gave them back to their people. The Indians were quite overcome, especially the Kiowas. There was a most affecting scene in which the relatives of the released captives embraced Colonel Dodge repeatedly and wept on his shoulder. The whole tone of the conference changed like sunshine appearing after a shower. Broad smiles were seen on all sides.

The wild Indians were told that the soldiers had come especially to make peace between the various Indian tribes. The Osage, Delaware, Seneca, and Cherokee scouts made speeches of friendship toward the Kiowas, Comanches, and Wichitas. The latter responded suitably. Then the principal chief of the Kiowas arose to talk. He was a young man named To-hauson, who had been elevated to principal chieftainship as successor to Ah-da-te. The latter had been deposed after the Cutthroat Massacre. To-hauson was a man of magnetic personality, with great natural ability as a leader. He remained principal chief of his people until his death in 1866. The whites called him Little Mountain, Little Bluff, or Over-the-Mountain, but the correct translation of his name is "Overhanging Butte." He had one request to make: That the Osages restore to the Kiowas the great tribal medicine idol, the *Tai-me*, which had been captured at the massacre. The following year this was done.

In the cordial atmosphere established by the restoration of the prisoners, Colonel Dodge was able to persuade the wild Indians to send representatives to Fort Gibson for treaty and conference. As a result of these conferences a treaty was signed with the Comanches and Wichitas in 1835, and with the Kiowas in 1837.

THE VILLAGE OF GRASS HOUSES

The Wichita Indians are the first people definitely known to have lived for any length of time at the site of Fort Sill. Formerly this tribe was divided into the following bands: Waco, Tawakoni, Ioni, Nadarko, Keechi, Wichita proper, and perhaps others. They spoke a common language and were one people. Ethnologists claim that they spring from Caddoan stock, but the Wichitas themselves deny this. They say that their language contains no words similar to those of the Caddoan tongue.

First historical mention of the Wichitas occurs in 1541, when they were visited by the Spanish explorer Coronado, who found them living in villages of distinctive grass houses located in what is now central Kansas. He called them *Quiviras*. Two hundred years later Spanish colonists in the province of Louisiana found the Wichitas settled at the site of Spanish Fort, Texas (near Ringgold), on Red River. They now were called *Towiache,* or *Towyhash;* living with them were a few French trappers and traders.

These early French voyageurs knew the Wichitas as *Panee Pique,* or Pawnee Picts. They intermarried with them to such an extent that many present-day Wichitas boast of French blood. It may be that the French were the first people to give them the name *Wichita,* although the Indians themselves state that it is derived from two archaic words of their own language: *Weets,* which means man, and *ee-taw,* which signifies "of the north."[14] Their more recent name for themselves is *Kiddykadish.*

About 1770 the fierce Osages and Pawnees of La Platte began harassing the Wichita villages along Red River. As a consequence the Wichita bands moved to escape this menace. One of the villages went to the site of Wichita Falls, Texas, another traveled north on Cache Creek to the mouth of Medicine Bluff Creek. The people of this band erected their grass houses on the present site of the Fort Sill polo field. They had a custom of concealing supplies of corn, dried pumpkin, and jerky, in pear-shaped holes sunk in the sod along the banks of Cache Creek. The creek was named by the French, who found many of these caches in the area; *cache* is a French word meaning "place of concealment."

Toward the close of the eighteenth century a renewal of the Osage attacks caused the Wichitas to move once more. The village near Medicine Bluff, and the one at the site of Wichita Falls reunited and traveled up Red River to a place they call Twin Mountains—perhaps Double Mountain, Texas. Part of the tribe remained in the interior of Texas and settled along the Brazos River. Another portion went to the North Fork of Red River and built a village at the place where Colonel Dodge found them in 1834.

The peace made with the Osages as a result of the Dragoon expedition permitted this band of Wichitas to return to Medicine Bluff. They were anxious to do so because the soil was more fertile there than along the North Fork. Furthermore the water of North Fork was impregnated with gypsum and salt, whereas Medicine Bluff Creek flowed only through hills of granite and limestone. Also there was an ancient spring (Ambrosia Spring) on the north bank of Medicine Bluff Creek, which never had failed to produce a copious supply of clear, good water.

This time the Wichitas built their village on the exact spot where Fort Sill was established thirty-five years later. The Wichita grass houses on Medicine Bluff Creek were substantial affairs, built to exclude weather

[14] Burgess Hunt (Wichita Indian) to author, 1935. At this time the author held a lengthy conference north of Anadarko with about fifty of the oldest Wichitas. Ut-see-ah (Mrs. Pickard), a woman of over ninety years of age, and Mr. Hunt were the principal informants.

and to last for many years. The framework of each lodge was made of trimmed cedar poles imbedded in the ground at the bottom and lashed together at the top, forming a curved dome. The outer covering was a thatch of dried reeds or grass, neatly and securely tied to the frame in the fashion of shingles, so as to shed water. The completed structure was about fifteen feet high, and fifteen or twenty feet in diameter at the base. It was shaped exactly like a gigantic beehive. There were no windows and no chimney; the only opening was a low, narrow door. In the center of the floor was a circular pit about eight inches deep, used as a fireplace. Around the walls were two or three tiers of benches, utilized for storage and sleeping accommodations. Fifteen or twenty persons lived in each hut.

The interiors of the grass houses were dark from lack of windows and from the accumulation of soot on the walls. For this reason the Comanches called them *Dokana,* which means "dark houses." The Comanches called the western part of the mountains (where the old Wichita village was) the Dokana, or Wichita Mountains. The main or eastern part of the range they called, simply, "The Mountains." The Kiowas called them *To-guat,* which also means "Mountains."

The Wichitas say that three years after the stars fell (there was a notable shower of meteors in 1833), a drifting band of Pawnee horse thieves visited the village on Medicine Bluff Creek. The Pawnees, traveling on foot as was their custom, approached from the north. They climbed Medicine Bluff, where they concealed themselves.

"We will stay here until nightfall," said the leader of the Pawnees. "After the Wichitas are asleep we will go down and steal their horses."

Five of the raiders, with typical Indian lack of discipline, slipped away before dark. They thought to get ahead of their fellows in securing booty. They sneaked southeast under cover of the timber lining Sitting Bear Creek until they reached the vicinity of where the polo club house stands now. In the meadows east of the woods they saw the Wichita horse herd, guarded by two boys.

One of the Wichita youths noticed that the animals were alarmed by something in the brush. Peering intently, he caught a glimpse of the roached scalplock of a Pawnee disappearing behind a tree. With studied nonchalance he mounted a pony and rode up the hill to the village. His shrill whoop brought the warriors of the tribe running to the edge of the plateau. Fifty of them mounted horses which were kept tethered near at hand against emergencies. They galloped in the direction indicated by the boy.

The Pawnees, hearing the commotion in the village, attempted to escape west along the creek. But the Wichita chief saw them flitting single file through the woods, and wheeled his force to cut them off. There followed a short, furious pursuit below the site of the old guardhouse. Fifty angry bowstrings were plucked as in the sudden pizzicato of a symphony orchestra. A chorus of yells and screams broke out. Five quivering Pawnees lay scalped on the grass.[15]

In 1837 those great Franco-American traders—the Chouteaus—sent an agent to establish a trading post on Cache Creek. This store was located on the west bank, a few hundred yards south of where Highway 277 now joins the road leading from Post Field. There is no record of how long it remained; probably not long, since the attitude of the wild Indians was too uncertain to make the post a safe one. The Kiowas, who have superior memories for these matters, and are able to recall events and names, and to fix dates with great accuracy through reference to their pictograph calendars, still speak of this trader, whom they call "To-me-te."[16]

Two or three years after the advent of To-me-te an American named Abel Warren built an independent trading post near where Cache Creek empties into Red River. His establishment consisted of a house surrounded by a picket stockade. Here he conducted a lucrative but somewhat perilous business with various wandering bands of Indians. After a few years he too abandoned the locality.[17]

The Wichitas were visited in the Fort Sill locality once more by white men. In the summer of 1843 an expedition headed by J. C. Eldredge was sent north by President Sam Houston of Texas to make a treaty with the Comanches. Eldredge reports that the Wichitas gave him a cordial welcome and treated him kindly. After a brief visit they directed him to the Comanche camp, which was situated west of the mountains.

During their occupancy of the Fort Sill area the Wichitas moved twice. Elementary camp sanitation forced them to transfer their village upstream to that little vale just north of Medicine Bluff, known today as "The Punchbowl." Afterwards they returned to the previous site on the plateau now occupied by the Old Post. About 1850 they left the area, never to return. They had been bothered by malaria and most of the game had been driven away. So they moved east thirty miles to Rush Springs. The site of the future Fort Sill remained deserted for many years thereafter.

[15] Wichita informants.
[16] Mooney, *op. cit.,* p. 172.
[17] W. H. Clift, "Warren's Trading Post," *Chronicles of Oklahoma,* II (1924), 129-40.

CHAPTER TWO

FIRST ARMY POSTS

ACTIVITIES OF CAPTAIN MARCY—CAMP RADZIMINSKI—BATTLE OF
WICHITA VILLAGE—FORT COBB—DESTRUCTION OF FORT
COBB AND TONKAWA MASSACRE

ALTHOUGH the Kiowas and Comanches were close allies, and roamed the entire southwestern prairie promiscuously, the Wichita Mountains constituted a quasi-boundary between their respective domains. The Comanches lived generally south of the mountains and occupied themselves with annoying the inhabitants of Texas and Mexico. The Kiowas also raided to the south, but their principal range was north of the mountains. They had little contact with white men except for an infrequent encounter with travelers along the Santa Fe Trail or a meeting with a few trappers and traders at Bent's Fort, on the Canadian River. For a number of years subsequent to the Dragoon expedition the government sent no official representatives into this section.

In the fall of 1845 the War Department detailed Lieutenant J. W. Abert to survey Purgatory Creek, the Canadian River, and the Washita. During the course of these explorations Abert's camp on the Canadian was paid a friendly visit by a party of Kiowas under To-hauson. In this band was a rising young chief named Set-ankeah (Sitting Bear), who in later years was well and unfavorably known at Fort Sill under the name of Satank, or Setank.[1]

The discovery of gold in California in 1849 brought a rush of prospectors and emigrants through the Indian country, but the principal transcontinental routes lay considerably north or south of the Wichita Mountains. Some of the caravans required military protection. Captain Randolph B. Marcy led one such party west along the Canadian River, over the Rockies to California. Part of the way his trail followed the divide between the Canadian and the Washita. The road thus made was still visible in 1868.

[1] Report of Lieutenant J. W. Abert, Senate Document 438, Twenty-ninth Congress, first session, pp. 50-51 (Washington, 1856).

16

A tragic by-product of the gold rush was the introduction of Asiatic cholera into the plains. The disease spread to the Kiowas and Comanches. They say that 1849 was the most terrible period which they can remember. More than half of them perished, and the survivors were utterly terrified. Since that time the total population of these two tribes has been less than three thousand souls.

Fort Washita was established on the lower Washita in 1842 to assist Fort Gibson and Fort Towson in protecting the civilized tribes from wild Indians to the west and white meddlers from the south. But the post was too far east of the actual frontier to afford the necessary protection. Therefore in 1851 the War Department ordered Captain R. B. Marcy with his company of the Fifth Infantry to march south from Fort Gibson into Texas, building a chain of frontier posts along the way.

In April Marcy founded Fort Arbuckle, on Wild Horse Creek, near the site of Davis, Oklahoma. From there he went southwest, laying out what later was called the Fort Arbuckle Road. He crossed Red River at the mouth of Beaver Creek and continued into Texas. Fort Belknap was established on the Clear Fork of the Brazos, a mile south of the site of Newcastle, Texas.

The following year Captain Marcy was directed to explore the country north of Red River, and to locate the source of that stream. He left Fort Belknap May 2, 1852, accompanied by Captain George B. McClellan, topographical engineers, and a company of the Fifth Infantry. The entire expedition was conducted in a scientific manner. The Wichita Mountains and their environs were examined, specimens of flora and fauna were collected, and geological formations were noted. Two of the meridians were marked by monuments or by marks on trees, and a map was drawn.[2] The courses of Red River and its principal tributaries were charted, and the source of the river was visited. Several creeks, including Otter Creek and Elk Creek, were named, as well as Mount Webster, which was named in honor of Daniel Webster.[3]

In July Marcy turned east again. He passed north of the mountains and camped (July 18) at the foot of the highest peak, which he named Mount Scott in honor of Lieutenant General Winfield Scott, commanding the army. The following day the expedition moved down the north bank of Medicine Bluff Creek (then unnamed), and camped opposite Medicine Bluff Number 3. During this day's march Marcy noticed the remains of the old Wichita village in the Punchbowl. On July 19 the officers climbed Medicine Bluff from the south side, after which they rode to the knoll where Fort Sill now stands. The Wichitas had abandoned

[2] He placed the hundredth meridian one degree too far east.
[3] R. B. Marcy, *Exploration of the Red River*, Senate Executive Document 54, Thirty-second Congress, second session, pp. 72-74 (Washington, 1853).

the place two years before, but the lodge frames were still standing. In the surrounding flats the brown cornstalks stood amidst a rank growth of weeds.

Captain Marcy thought well of the site; he recommended that it be occupied as a military post, but the government did not see fit to take any action at the time.

From Medicine Bluff the Marcy expedition marched east, visited the Wichita village near Rush Springs, then returned to Fort Arbuckle.

CAMP RADZIMINSKI

The establishment of Forts Arbuckle and Belknap did not decrease permanently the amount of raiding done in Texas and Mexico by the Kiowas and Comanches. The Great White Father in Washington resorted to treaty. Thomas Fitzpatrick was commissioned agent and empowered to negotiate with the Comanches, the Kiowas, and the Kiowa-Apaches. On July 27, 1853, a treaty was signed at Fort Atkinson, in southern Kansas.

The first provisions of this document were similar to those of former treaties: They proclaimed perpetual brotherly love between the Indians and the whites. The Indians agreed to leave the Santa Fe Trail alone, and to cease bothering the Mexicans and Texans. For the next few years they did respect the Santa Fe Trail, but to the agreement concerning Texas and Mexico they paid no attention whatever.

The right of the United States to build military posts in the Indian country was affirmed. Since posts already had been built and others planned, this proviso was superfluous. The Indians did not like the idea, but they had seen so few American troops that they were not greatly worried. To-hauson told Fitzpatrick that he had been looking for some time for all these soldiers with which he had been threatened, and had come to the conclusion that "Washington" was bluffing.

Washington *was* bluffing. Few soldiers appeared in the Indian country north of Red River either for peace or war until 1858. By that time the raids in Texas had increased in destructiveness until the Federal government could scarcely ignore the screams for help that were arising in Texas. The Kiowas and Comanches did not realize that they were violating a treaty by making war in Texas. They had no idea that Texas was a part of the United States; they considered the Texans and the Mexicans to be their natural enemies.

In 1858 General Twiggs, the portly, profane commander of the United States troops in Texas, obtained authority from the headquarters of the army, at West Point, to abandon the passive defense measures which heretofore had been in force. His plan was to send an expedition into the Comanche country, which would keep the Comanches busy protecting their families, and thus give Texas a breathing spell.[4]

A punitive force was organized at Fort Belknap, consisting of several companies of the Second Cavalry (later redesignated the Fifth Cavalry), which had been stationed on the Texas frontier since 1855. Captain (Brevet Major) Earl Van Dorn (later Major General, C.S.A.), an active, wiry little cavalryman, was placed in command. Lawrence "Sul" Ross, son of an Indian agent in Texas, came home on summer vacation from Alabama Wesleyan College to organize a force of 135 friendly Indians to accompany the soldiers. These Indians were of the Waco band of Wichitas under Nasthoe and Towakani Jim, and Caddoes and Tonkawas from the Texas Indian Reserve. While Van Dorn was making ready at Fort Belknap, Captain Prince, the commanding officer at Fort Arbuckle, was in the midst of that popular American pastime—making a treaty with the Indians. The Indians with whom he was conferring were the same band of Comanches against whom Van Dorn was preparing to march. Neither officer knew what the other was doing. It was before the day of the telegraph.[5]

Captain Van Dorn marched from Fort Belknap September 15, 1858, with four companies of the Second Cavalry, one company of the Fifth Infantry, and Ross's Indian scouts. A base of operations was established on the southeast bank of Otter Creek, in what is now Tillman County, not far from the present site of Tipton. It was named Camp Radziminski, in honor of Lieutenant Charles Radziminski of the regiment, who had lately died from tuberculosis.[6] While a picket stockade was being constructed to protect the mule teams and supplies, the Indian auxiliaries roamed the country looking for hostile Indians.[7]

Two Wichita scouts, Nasthoe (Shot-in-the-Foot), and his son, Wau-see-sic-an, went east to the Wichita village near Rush Springs.[8] They were startled to find a large Comanche village near the Wichitas. It was a camp of mixed bands. Quo-ho-ah-te-me (Hair-Bobbed-on-One-Side) was in general charge, with several other chiefs present, including Ho-to-yo-ko-wot (Over-the-Buttes) and Buffalo Hump.[9] Buffalo Hump

---

[4] *Report of Secretary of War, 1858,* pp. 258-59.

[5] *Ibid.*

[6] G. F. Price, *Across the Continent with the Fifth Cavalry* (New York: D. Van Nostrand, 1883), pp. 68, 469; see also testimony of veterans who had served at Camp Radziminski, in *United States, Complainant,* v. *State of Texas,* Supreme Court of the United States, October term, 1894 (Washington: Judd and Detweiler, 1894), pp. 682-99 (hereinafter referred to as the Greer County case).

[7] Letter from L. S. Ross, quoted in John Henry Brown, *Indian Wars and Pioneers of Texas* (Austin, Texas: L. E. Daniel, 189[?]), p. 1112.

[8] Poafebitty to author, 1935.

[9] "Buffalo Hump" is the polite name by which he was known to the whites. The correct translation of his name, Pochanaw-quoip, has to do with priapism.

was well known in Texas, where he had been in several scrapes with the citizens and troops.

These Comanches, having concluded their conference with the officers from Fort Arbuckle, were trading and gambling with the Wichitas. The two Wichita spies from Camp Radziminski waited in the brush until after dark, when they made their way to the huts of the Wichita chiefs, How-its-cahdle and Esadowa. They warned them that the soldiers were coming to attack the Comanches.[10]

The Comanches also received notification that the soldiers were camped at Otter Creek. Two Comanche warriors, Auti-toy-bitsy (Brown Young Man), and one other whose name is forgotten, while returning from a raid into Chihuahua, Mexico, saw the camp at Otter Creek. Chief Quo-ho-ah-te-me directed them to ride west again and keep an eye on the soldiers.[11]

Nasthoe and his son reported back to Sul Ross on the afternoon of September 29. Ross immediately informed Van Dorn. Officers' call was blown. Company commanders hastened to Van Dorn's tent for instructions. Wagons, spare animals, and supplies were moved inside the unfinished stockade. The four cavalry companies and the Indian scouts prepared for a short campaign, with spare ammunition and rations for two days in their saddle bags.[12]

An hour later the column rode eastward under the shadows of the purple hills. The last rays of the sun glinted on gutta percha cartridge boxes, and on scabbard and carbine. Through the night, with scarcely a halt, the troopers marched along the southern base of the mountains. Van Dorn expected to attack at daylight; but when that time arrived he learned that the Comanche village was nearly one hundred miles from Camp Radziminski instead of the forty miles reported by the scouts. The march continued during the next day. Auti-toy-bitsy and the other Comanche warrior observed the column from a distance.

Toward sunset on September 30 the troops arrived at White Wolf Ford, on the south bank of Medicine Bluff Creek.[13] While the horses were eating their meager allowance of corn the dragoons boiled coffee. Auti-toy-bitsy watched from a nearby hilltop. When he saw the cavalry resume the march he raced ahead into the gloaming to warn his chief that the soldiers were coming to attack.

[10] Ut-see-ah to author, 1935. This old Wichita woman was in the Wichita village, a child of about ten years, when Van Dorn attacked.

[11] Comanche informants: Poafebitty, Mumsukawa, Timbo, and Penateka. The latter was present as a very small child at the time of the battle; he states that his mother concealed him in the brush.

[12] "Report of Captain Van Dorn," in *Report of Secretary of War, 1858-59*, pp. 272-74.

[13] Comanche informants. This is verified by the map of Van Dorn's route to the battlefield, as shown on the map of the leased portion of the Choctaw and Chickasaw Nation, Bureau of Topographical Engineers, August 26, 1859.

20

Quo-ho-ah-te-me considered this information for a time in silence. Then he ordered a camp crier to summon the people for a council. The warriors said that they were ready and anxious for a fight. Mexican lancers never had whipped them. What could these bluecoats do? The chief advised the people to abandon the village. A female medicine prophet consulted her oracle. The omens were good. There was no danger. Furthermore the troops were friendly. Had not the soldier chief from Fort Arbuckle assured them that it was so? Reassured, the Comanches went to bed. Only a few apprehensive old men and women slept in the brush.

But Captain Van Dorn knew nothing of Captain Prince and his private treaty. He had been ordered to punish the Comanches and he intended to do so thoroughly. His plan was to surprise the village at daybreak and destroy it.

All through the night the weary troopers plodded over starlit prairie, or felt their way gingerly through black creek bottoms and treacherous prairie-dog towns. Toward morning they plunged into a chill blanket of fog, which hung motionless in the autumn air, clinging close to the billows of the plains. The Wichita scouts under Nasthoe and Towakani Jim ranged far to the front. Soon they sent word that the enemy village was near. Five hundred ponies grazed on its outskirts.

Van Dorn told Ross to move his Indians out to the right of the cavalry so as not to be mistaken for hostiles when the assault was made. Low-voiced orders were passed along the column. The companies took up the approach march in columns of twos, all four companies abreast with intervals of a hundred yards. When the trumpeter sounded the charge the companies were to deploy to the front and advance on the village at a gallop.[14]

Four successive ridges were crossed before the hostile camp was discovered. Then, as the sun came up to sweep aside the fog, the Comanche tepees were seen dimly through the trees in the valley beyond the creek. The stirring notes of the bugle sounded through the frosty air. The cavalry deployed and took up the charge.

[14] J. W. Wilbarger, *Indian Depredations in Texas* (Austin, Texas: Hutchings Printing House, 1889); *Annual Report of Secretary of War, 1858–59*, pp. 272-74.

For many years past the site of this battle has been in dispute. It is definitely located, however, on two maps made in 1859. One of these maps is of the leased district, already referred to. The other is a map dated August 25, 1859, bearing the following notation: "Drawn by Lt Stanley Commander of the Escort to Major Elias Recter [sic] Supt Indian affairs." These maps place the battlefield about five miles southeast of Rush Springs, on Rush Creek. This agrees with information furnished the author by Mrs. J. A. Slaton, a Choctaw resident of Rush Springs, who was born at Fort Arbuckle. Mrs. Slaton locates the battlefield on the old Huntley farm.

See also Greer County case, pp. 605, 640-41.

Although the Comanches were still asleep when the clamor of Van Dorn's attack broke upon them, they sprang to their feet with weapons ready. The warriors ran to catch their ponies. But the Tonkawas already were driving the herd away. Two hundred blue-clad troopers were almost in the village. The Comanches rushed to the shallow ravine in front of the camp and commenced shooting arrows to cover the withdrawal of their families.

The Indian camp was spread out along the creek for a distance of several hundred yards. Thick brush and a maze of little gullies broke up the impact of the assault. In a few moments the fighting became individual. Sabers flashed. Feathered shafts flicked through the chill air. Pistols and carbines sounded like corn popping in a skillet. Above the tumult rose the high tremolo whoops of the Indians and the deep-toned cheers of the soldiers.

Three companies led by Van Dorn in person engaged the Comanches on the left, at the upper part of the village. Captain Nathan G. Evans, with the fourth company and the friendly Indians, fought in the lower part of the camp. In a few moments the white clouds of powder smoke so thickened the mists in the creek bottom that the antagonists were almost invisible to one another. Sul Ross, peering through the fog, saw a group of Indians escaping down a branch about one hundred and fifty yards below the camp. Shouting for assistance he rode to head them off.

But the confusion was so great that only Lieutenant Cornelius Van Camp, a private soldier named Alexander, and a Caddo scout joined him. The fugitives were women and children. Ross told the Caddo to grab a little captive white girl who was with the Comanches. Then he saw about twenty-five braves bearing down to rescue their families. He and his two companions were cut off. They wheeled their horses to meet this threat. Van Camp aimed his double-barreled shotgun. The hostiles loosed a shower of arrows. The lieutenant and Private Alexander fell to the ground. Ross's Sharps rifle misfired. Mohee, a Comanche, caught up Alexander's carbine and shot Ross in the side. Ross tried to draw his pistol, but his side was paralyzed. Mohee advanced on him with drawn scalping knife. At that moment Lieutenant James Majors galloped up and killed the Indian. A squad of troopers with him drove the other Comanches away.[15]

In the ravines and brush in front of the upper part of the camp was the main body of hostiles. Mounted attack could not dislodge them. The Indians fought with absolute desperation. They were covering the re-

[15] L. S. Ross, *loc. cit.*; J. B. Thoburn, "Indian Fight in Ford County, 1859," *Kansas Historical Collections*, XII, 312-29; J. W. Wilbarger, *op. cit.*, p. 330.

treat of their women and children. But they could not understand why the white soldiers kept charging in. The Mexicans never had been so persistent.

The soldiers dismounted and commenced sniping at the Comanches. Superior fire power soon decided the issue. The Indians lost heavily. At long range their bows and arrows were no match for firearms. Their horses were gone. Several of their bravest warriors, including Auti-toy-bitsy, Arikarosap (White Deer), and Tanowine (father of Nahwats) were dead. It was hopeless to remain longer. Finally they broke and fled. But they had held long enough to permit most of the noncombatants to escape. When the break came the cavalrymen went after the Indians like tigers. Many fugitives were cut down as they ran. Lieutenant James Harrison saw eighteen Comanches driving a small herd of horses over a distant ridge. He pursued them for miles, killing several and capturing the horses. Then he turned back to the battlefield conscious of a good fight won. To his consternation he saw the troops lined up to receive him with a volley in the face. They thought that his detachment was a body of Indian reinforcements. Fortunately they recognized him before the order to fire was given.

The Comanche camp was empty and in disorder. The excitement was over. As the soldiers set to work to destroy the tepees they realized their weariness. They had been in the saddle for thirty-six hours, had been fighting for three or four. Captain Charles Whiting found himself in command. Van Dorn was on the ground with an arrow through his abdomen near the navel, and another between the bones of his wrist. It seemed certain that he would die. Cornelius Van Camp lay where he had fallen, his sightless eyes staring up at the murky October sky. Fastened to his wrist was the leathern loop of his bare saber. In his hand was the arrow which had pierced his heart, and which he had withdrawn in a last convulsion.[16] Sergeant P. E. Garrison was mortally wounded. Two other enlisted men were dead, and nine wounded, some dangerously. Sul Ross and a medical officer were wounded.

Fifty-six dead Comanches were counted. Other bodies discovered later brought the total to seventy. Unfortunately, some of these were women. Captain R. W. Johnson says they fought with the warriors and were not distinguishable from them. The Wichitas reported that one of their young men, who had been visiting in the Comanche camp, was missing, and probably was dead.

Captain Whiting sent an "express" rider to Fort Arbuckle requesting a surgeon, an ambulance, and rations for the command for four days. Captain Prince sent these things at once. When the doctor arrived he cut the arrow point from the shaft which had passed through Van Dorn's

16 G. F. Price, *op. cit.*, pp. 70-71.

body, and pulled out the arrow. Van Dorn was forced to remain on the field for five days, until he was strong enough to be moved. Then the soldiers fastened a litter between two horses hitched in tandem, and took the wounded officer to Camp Radziminski. The other wounded were sent to Fort Arbuckle. The dead soldiers were buried on the field. Lieutenant Van Camp's body was sent home to Lancaster, Pennsylvania.

The action and the subsequent occupation of the battlefield destroyed the cornfields of the Wichitas. The latter thus were deprived of their supply of food for the winter. Also they were alarmed lest the Comanches consider that they had betrayed them to the troops. So they fled to Fort Arbuckle for protection. Captain Prince fed them for several weeks, but finally they drifted away and rebuilt their village on the Washita between the sites of Verden and Chickasha. Some of them eventually joined the Waco band in Texas.

Captain Van Dorn was invalided home to Mississippi. He was cited in War Department orders and was feted by his friends and relatives at home. For a brief period he was the most prominent man in the cavalry, if not in the army. He recovered from his wounds so rapidly that within five weeks he was back at Radziminski. He hoped to follow up his initial blow against the Comanches with a further expedition, but his wounds forced him to turn this duty over to Captains Whiting and Evans. These officers scoured the country for hostiles, but came to the conclusion that the Comanches had fled to Mexico. As a matter of fact they had joined the Kiowas on the Arkansas River. While at the Kiowa camp they sold to the Kiowas a small Mexican boy who had been captured in Arikarosap's expedition into Chihuahua. This captive, who remembers that his Mexican name was Esteban, became well known in later years, under the name Quitan, as a warrior and medicine man of the Kiowa tribe.

In November Van Dorn moved his Otter Creek camp several miles upstream. By March the grazing in this new locality had become exhausted, necessitating another move. This time Van Dorn crossed to the west bank and marched north to the point where Otter Creek runs through a gorge between two granite peaks, four miles northwest of the present site of Mountain Park. Here he found a cove sheltered from the "northers," with plenty of timber and grass near-by. All three of these camps were called Camp Radziminski, but the last or upper camp was the best known and the most permanent. The officers constructed several small huts from pickets set upright in the ground, chinked with sod and roofed with canvas. The ruins of the makeshift stone chimneys which they built may be seen today a few yards from the base of the rocky hill. While the command was at Radziminski a new type of conical tent called the Sibley was received from Fort Belknap to provide shelter for the enlisted men. These tents were pitched on the flat ground about a hundred yards south of the officers' line. Between the two portions of the cantonment a well was dug, the remains of which are still visible. Uniform buttons and brass belt buckles, marked with the designation of the old Second Cavalry, have been found within the last three years in the cotton field which today covers the site of the enlisted men's camp.

During the winter one of the soldiers' tents caught fire, burning two of the occupants fatally. These men, and three others who died from other causes, were buried on a low ridge about a half-mile southwest of the camp. The graves were undisturbed until 1933, when the authorities at Fort Sill moved the remains to the National Cemetery at Fort Gibson.

Regular communication with Fort Belknap was maintained by messenger and wagon train. The road which resulted from this traffic became known as the Van Dorn or Radziminski road; it was visible for a number of years after the Civil War, and was used occasionally by Mackenzie in his expeditions against the Indians. Evidently life at Radziminski during the winter of 1858–59 was not all hardship, for recently while poking among the ruins the author picked up several marble poker chips and parts of champagne bottles. The enlisted men were kept partially busy with "extra duty," the training of their mounts, and hunting buffalo for food. Some of them climbed the adjacent hills; in the canyon north of camp they found a bear's den, where they amused themselves by throwing rocks at the supposed occupant of the cavern. By midwinter the Indian situation was so quiet that it was safe to send up from Belknap a number of recruits to fill up gaps in the ranks caused by sickness or death. Also a few of the officers were permitted to visit the settlements in Texas. Lieutenant Harrison went to Fort Belknap to marry the daughter of Mathew Leeper, Texan agent for the Penateka Comanches.

At Camp Radziminski were several soldiers who later were associated with the history of Fort Sill. Among these were Phillip McCusker, famous as a scout and interpreter, John Coyle, and others. A man named Bunger was orderly at the officers' mess. One day Van Dorn told Bunger that he ought to save out enough food for himself before serving the officers.

"Oh, that's all right, Major," said Bunger, airily. "I always eats first. You gents only get what is left."[17]

The garrison at Radziminski was reinforced during the spring. An additional battalion under Major W. H. Emory also was sent to Fort Arbuckle. It was planned that vigorous measures would be taken against the Indians as soon as the horses were in shape to take the field.

By the end of April, when the grass was green, Van Dorn set forth

[17] Mrs. John Coyle to author, 1935. Mrs. Coyle, a resident of Rush Springs, is the widow of one of the early pioneers of southwestern Oklahoma who was an enlisted man in the infantry of Van Dorn's command at Radziminski.

toward the north. On May 30 he again attacked the Comanches. They were camped in southern Kansas, fifteen miles south of the ruins of Fort Atkinson. In the desperate, bloody action which followed, fifty Comanches were killed and thirty-six captured. Van Dorn was so handicapped by his wounded and prisoners that he was forced to return to his base at Otter Creek. He arrived the last day of May, having covered four hundred miles. Among the wounded were Captain E. Kirby Smith and Lieutenant Fitzhugh Lee, who became Confederate generals a few years later. Lee carried an arrowhead embedded in his chest the rest of his life.

FORT COBB

Captain Van Dorn's expeditions did not settle the troubles with the Comanches. The focus of infection was, as usual, in Texas. Several years before the government had settled the Penateka Comanches, the Wacoes, the Caddoes, and the Tonkawas on two reservations in the northern part of the state. But the raiding continued. The reservation Indians were blamed for depredations which should have been charged to their wild brethren from north of Red River, but doubtless they carried on a bit of horse stealing themselves. At any rate the Texans were determined to get rid of them.

For over a year the United States had been considering leasing land from the Choctaws and Chickasaws on which to settle the Texas Indians. In the summer of 1858 Douglas Cooper, agent for the Chickasaws, reconnoitered west of Fort Arbuckle. He visited the area around Medicine Bluff, which he reported as suitable for the proposed agency.[18]

In 1859 the Texans became so inflamed against the Indians that it became necessary to move the reservation people at once. Major Emory, the commander at Fort Arbuckle, rode to the Wichita Mountains to select a place to build a new post for the protection of the agency. The site of the old Wichita village at Medicine Bluff seemed admirable to him. However, the duty of making the final selection rested with Elias Rector, superintendent of the southern superintendency. For this purpose Mr. Rector journeyed from his headquarters at Fort Smith to Fort Arbuckle. He received Major Emory's recommendation that the Medicine Bluff area was suitable, but decided to inspect the site personally. He asked the headmen of several of the reservation bands to accompany him. Major Emory furnished an army wagon to carry the supplies for the expedition, and an escort of fifteen soldiers under Lieutenant David Stanley. The agent of the Wichitas, Samuel A. Blain, and Horace P. Jones, farmer-

---

[18] "Journal of Douglas Cooper" (edited by Grant Foreman), *Chronicles of Oklahoma*, Vol. V, No. 4 (December, 1927), p. 385.

instructor of the Penateka Comanches, were included in the party, as well as Caddo and Wichita chiefs.

Rector's expedition left Fort Arbuckle June 18, 1859, and arrived at Medicine Bluff June 22. Every previous explorer had been pleased with the place. Marcy had been delighted with it; so had Emory and Cooper. Not so Elias Rector. He found the scenery disappointing. He did not agree with Marcy that the place was "admirably suited for defense." He noted that the creeks were apt to overflow in the spring, leaving stagnant pools from which the breezes would "waft foul malarial emanations"; the Indians had reported that the locality was unhealthy. Rector did not even like Marcy's name for Mount Scott. He renamed it Blue Mountain.

Horace Jones gives various reasons for Mr. Rector's dissatisfaction: The ride from Arbuckle had been unusually hot and uncomfortable. Immense herds of buffalo had cropped off the grass, leaving the ground dry and dusty. The supply of whisky was exhausted long before the party reached Cache Creek. Rector was unable to see good in anything. He marched north to the Washita. Cobb Creek looked better than Medicine Bluff Creek. The Indians liked it. Mr. Rector decided to build the agency there.

On his return to Fort Arbuckle Rector conferred with Robert Neighbors, superintendent of the Texas Indians, and with a number of Penateka chiefs. They concurred in Mr. Rector's decision. The wild Kiowas and Comanches, who occupied the proposed reservation, were not considered nor consulted.

On August 1 the work of removing the Indians from Texas began. As upon other occasions when a people have been deported from their native land, it was a sad affair. There was so much haste to get the Indians away before the Texans attacked them that the Indians were unable to round up their cattle. Mr. Neighbors was in charge, and he was assisted by Agents Blain, S. P. Ross, and Mathew Leeper. A military escort of two companies of cavalry and one company of infantry under Major George H. Thomas, the future "Rock of Chickamauga," accompanied the long column. Horace P. Jones, Phillip McCusker, and several other civilians came along as interpreters, employes of the agency, and the like.[19]

In the middle of August the picturesque cavalcade arrived at the bluffs overlooking the Washita west of the site of Anadarko. Peacefully feeding in the bottom lands were countless numbers of buffalo. The Indians became greatly excited. Bison near their reservation in Texas had

[19] Scott to Cruikshank, December 13, 1933; W. H. Quinette to author, 1934. Mr. Quinette was a close friend of Horace Jones for many years. For Rector's report see *Report of the Commissioner of Indian Affairs, 1859.*

become scarce, and with their cattle gone, they were nearly starving. Permission was given for a big buffalo hunt. The soldiers seated themselves around the rim of the valley while the Indians slaughtered buffalo to their hearts' content.

August 16, the agency was established four miles northeast of the site of the present town of Fort Cobb. The post was to be built later. In the meantime there was considerable argument among the civilian officials over who should sign for the property. Major Thomas did not propose to mark time while this discussion proceeded, so with his troops he departed for Texas. Finally Mr. Blain agreed to assume responsibility. Mr. Neighbors promptly appointed him in charge of the consolidated Wichita, Caddo, Tonkawa, and Penateka agencies.

This left Leeper and Ross without jobs. They went back to Texas with Neighbors. On his return to Belknap Neighbors was murdered by Ed Cornett, a stranger to him, who resented his partisanship to the Indians in the troubles between the redskins and the settlers.

The military post of Fort Cobb was established October 1, 1859, by two companies of the First Cavalry (formerly the First Dragoons) and one company of the First Infantry, under Major W. H. Emory. It was built of pickets and adobe, on the high ground east of the present townsite. Camp Radziminski then was abandoned by the army, but immediately was reoccupied by a regiment of Texas Rangers. The latter remained at Radziminski for a year, patrolling the border and skirmishing with the wild Indians. In the late summer of 1860 they marched north, accompanied by some Tonkawas, Caddoes, and Wichitas. They attacked a camp of Kiowas and Comanches near the head of the Canadian, in the country now known as the Panhandle of Oklahoma.

Tabananica (Hears-the-Sunrise) and Isa-habbit (Wolf-Lying-Down) were in charge of the Comanches. The Comanches say that a number of their people, including some women and children, were killed. One of the Caddoes killed a prominent Kiowa named Bird-Appearing, which led to subsequent bad feeling between the Caddoes and Kiowas. A ranger named James Pike states that after the fight the Tonkawas indulged in their well-known flair for cannibalism by roasting and eating some of the slain Comanches.[20]

When the Civil War broke out, the garrisons of Forts Washita, Arbuckle, and Cobb retreated north into Kansas. This did not mean the end of Fort Cobb, however. The agency continued to be administered under the Richmond government. Mathew Leeper, who had succeeded S. A. Blain as agent, was in charge; Horace Jones was interpreter; J. J. Sturms, who had married into the Caddo tribe, was also an employe.

[20] James Pike, *Scout and Ranger* (Cincinnati: J. R. Hawley and Co., 1865), pp. 101-11; Mumsukawa to author, 1935.

Several other white men were permitted to settle in the vicinity as traders, or as contractors to furnish corn and other foodstuffs to the agency. Among these were the Shirley brothers, Joseph Chandler, and the ex-mess orderly from Radziminski, Bunger.

Albert Pike, a well-known explorer and writer, was commissioned brigadier general by the Confederate government, and sent to Fort Cobb to make treaties with the Kiowas and Comanches. Pike arrived in 1861, made preliminary arrangements with the Indians, and promised to return in 1862, after the Confederate authorities had approved the terms of the treaty. He wrote enthusiastic letters to his superiors concerning his work, even sending letters to Jefferson Davis himself.

In spite of General Pike's efforts, things did not go well at Fort Cobb. Tosawi (Silver Brooch) and Asa-Havey were first and second chiefs of the Penateka Comanches. They were friendly to the whites and gave no trouble. The third chief, however, was Buffalo Hump. His disposition had not improved since the troublesome times in Texas. He told Mathew Leeper that he wanted a house because he intended to settle down. Leeper did not intend to build a house for any Indian, and told Buffalo Hump so in undiplomatic terms. Buffalo Hump thereupon allowed his young men to create mischief around the agency and himself quarreled with Horace Jones.

Leeper also was a contrary soul. He had differences with his subordinate, Sturms, and with his superior, Elias Rector. Mr. Rector rebuked him. So did Pike. They even placed Leeper in arrest, although they later released him. Then Rector quarreled with Pike and Pike with the department commander, General Hincnan.[21]

All this had a bad effect on the Indians. The Caddoes and the Tonkawas showed signs of shifting their allegiance to the Federals. The Delawares already sympathized with the Union. The Penatekas did not care who won the war, as long as they were fed. The wild Indians continued to raid in Mexico undisturbed.

DESTRUCTION OF FORT COBB AND TONKAWA MASSACRE

During September of 1862 there were rumors around the Fort Cobb agency that Shawnees, Osages, Delawares, and others who sympathized with the Union or hated Leeper were coming south to wipe out the Tonkawas and kill all the Confederate officials at the agency. Mr. Leeper, who had just returned from a business trip to Texas, promptly departed again with his family. He intended to return when he had established them in a safe place. Horace Jones was left in charge. Jones paid little attention

---

[21] *Official Records of the Rebellion*, Vol. XIII, Series I, pp. 854, 860-64, 964.

to the disquieting reports, believing that his Indian friends would give him timely warning of attack. He did not even become alarmed when he noticed that the Caddoes were having secret meetings.[22]

But Jones was too complacent. One day a young Caddo, while hunting deer near the site of Anadarko, was murdered by two Tonkawas. Another Caddo youth, hiding near the Tonkawa village, saw the cannibals return with portions of the dismembered body, and heard them direct the women to cook the meat for supper. He ran to report to his own people what he had discovered. Parties of Caddoes went out and located what was left of the dead Caddo boy.[23]

The Indians always had known that the Tonkawas were cannibals, and felt a great abhorrence toward them. The Kiowa name for the Tonkawas is *Kia-hi-piago*, which means "Eaters of human beings"; the Comanche name for them is *Neuma-takers*, which means the same thing. Both of these tribes were glad to coöperate with the Caddoes in exterminating the Tonkawas.

Meantime the Caddoes kept assuring the whites that no trouble was brewing. Agent Leeper, either not being informed that the local Indians wanted him relieved from office, or not caring, sent word that he was returning to the agency. He arrived at Fort Cobb on the afternoon of October 23, 1862. That night the agency was attacked and destroyed.

Horace Jones thought later that the Caddoes had watched Leeper's approach across the prairies and timed the attack to occur shortly after his arrival. They deny this; they claim that they had no part in the affair and that the raid was made by a party of Indians from the Kansas agency which included Osage, Shawnees, Delawares, and probably Indians of other tribes. An Indian named Ben Simon was the leader. There is little doubt, however, that the Indians around Fort Cobb joined in the fun. Many of them disliked Leeper, and favored the United States. Ben Simon was known to have stopped that day at the Caddo settlement, and Caddo spies had been at the agency during the afternoon.

Two hours after sunset, when the employes were closing up for the night, Simon's raiders swooped down on the agency. Many of the whites were shot down in the first rush. Their bodies were thrown into the buildings, and these were burned to the ground. Among those killed was Bunger. Ben Simon reported, when he returned to Kansas, that Leeper had been killed, but this was a mistake. Leeper was still alive in 1875, and writing letters to Fort Sill. What happened was that he escaped by climbing from the rear window of his house, and fled into the timber in

22 J. B. Thoburn, "Horace P. Jones, Scout and Interpreter," *Chronicles of Oklahoma*, Vol. II, No. 4, December, 1924, pp. 383-85.

23 Timbo (son of Parra-o-coom) and Poafebitty to author, 1935.

his nightshirt. Old Tosawi found him and gave him a horse on which he rode to Texas.[24]

Horace Jones was warned by the barking of his hounds that Indians were stealthily approaching his cabin. He sprang out a rear window and escaped, but a companion was killed. Jones then rode three miles north to warn Dr. Sturms. Sturms was living with the Caddoes, and could not be convinced that an attack had been made without his knowledge. Jones had to lead him to the top of a hill and show him the burning buildings. Together with the Shirleys and Phil McCusker they escaped into Texas.

At this time the Tonkawas were living along the Washita, south of the agency. Hearing the uproar they abandoned most of their belongings and fled east. Before daylight they halted and camped in a valley southeast of the site of Anadarko, near the site of the present Catholic mission. They thought they were safe. But the other Indians had trailed them there, and had surrounded the camp. A merciless attack was made. The Tonkawas were almost exterminated. Among those slain was the chief of the band, Placido. The few who escaped found refuge at Fort Arbuckle, then later went to Fort Griffin, Texas. The bones of their people lay bleaching for many years in what is now called Tonkawa Valley.

The Confederates never reoccupied Fort Cobb. The semi-tame Indians who had been attached to the agency were left to shift for themselves.

---

[24] Mathew Leeper to Colonel R. S. Mackenzie, Sherman, Texas, June 18, 1875, *Letters Received Book,* old files of Fort Sill, 1875. The letter was in reply to an inquiry from Fort Sill concerning persons captured in Texas about 1834 or 1835. Apparently Quanah was making inquiries through the post commander to former Indian agents in an effort to learn details concerning his mother, Cynthia Ann Parker. Mr. Leeper replied that he knew nothing regarding the matter. At this time Leeper's son, Mathew, Jr., was a second lieutenant in Mackenzie's regiment at Sill. Horace Jones also told Mr. Quinette that Leeper was *not* killed in 1862.

CHAPTER THREE

THE PRAIRIE WAR OF 1863-64

KIOWA AND CADDO—INDIANS AND WHITES

THE SUMMER of 1863 marked the beginning of a general "war" on the plains. Most of the fighting was between the Southern Cheyennes, Arapahoes, Kiowas, and Comanches, on one side, and the white men on the other; some of the strife however was between the Indians themselves. Most historical writers have supposed that this Indian uprising was caused wholly by the Indians' indignation against the ever increasing white encroachment into their country. This is a mistake. While the Indians did resent the flow of immigration across their country, they made no concerted effort to stop it. They did not possess that characteristic of the white man—the ability to organize against a common danger. Their restlessness came merely, or at least in large part, from their fondness for raiding. It was aggravated by the absence of troops from the area.

The Indian made war to increase his prestige among his fellows. It was the only way in which he could make a name for himself. He could not be a captain of industry, a statesman, an artist, or a scientist. He could only be a warrior. The Kiowas and Comanches made forays against any enemy opportunity offered. Sometimes it was the Mexicans, the Texans, the Utes, or the Navajos. During the Civil War the Caddoes happened to be convenient.

Enmity between the Kiowas and Caddoes commenced in 1860 with the killing of Bird-Appearing. It was as certain as sunrise that some member of the slain Kiowa's family would make an effort to avenge this death. The following winter Crow-Bonnet, the brother of Bird-Appearing, led a small war party south from the Kiowa headquarters on Arrow-Point River (the Arkansas). They went to the Caddo camp on Sugar Creek, a few miles north of the site of Anadarko, where they caught an incautious Caddo, killed, and scalped him

This success encouraged Tone-tsain (Stray Horse) to make a similar raid. He was unable to enlist volunteers until the summer of 1863.

By that time Fort Cobb had been destroyed, and the whites driven away from the area, so that Tone-tsain was able to convince his tribesmen that they would not be interfered with in their foray.

The Kiowas were preparing for their annual Sun Dance. One of the rules of this ceremony was that no war parties should leave camp from the time the assemblage was called until after the dance was over. Tone-tsain announced that he was going anyway. The people were unable to dissuade him from taking so sacrilegious a course. Only ten of the war party he had recruited agreed to go with him. Six of these were Kiowas and four were Kiowa-Apaches.

They left camp on the Arkansas, rode south for several days, and crossed the Washita River without seeing any Caddoes. When they had reached a point fourteen miles north of Medicine Bluff Creek they encountered a lone Caddo. The Caddo was on foot hunting deer, and was unable to get away before the Kiowas surrounded him. Badly frightened, he tried to ingratiate himself by inviting them to dinner.[1]

The Kiowas conferred in their explosive, guttural tongue. Some of them were in favor of killing the Caddo at once; he had a fair-looking scalp. But Tone-tsain said no. They would go to the Caddo's camp and enjoy his dinner. Then they could kill him at their leisure, and his family as well, after which they would take his stock and depart. The brilliance of this plan commended it to the rest of the party.

But when they reached the high ground north of the valley of Chandler Creek they realized that they had been led into a trap. Spread out along Cache Creek, below the mouth of Chandler Creek, was a large encampment of Caddoes and Penateka Comanches. With them was a company of Confederate soldiers from Fort Arbuckle. They had escorted the Indians to this locality on a buffalo hunt. It was too late to withdraw; the Kiowas put on a bold front and went to the Caddo's tepee. They unsaddled their horses and stretched out at ease while waiting for the meal to be prepared. An Indian never refuses an invitation to eat.

Presently the Kiowas noticed unusual movements in the lower part of the camp—men mounting their horses, stirring about. At once they dashed for their own mounts. But they were too late. The firing commenced. Two of the band were forced to abandon their ponies and flee on foot. They were taken up behind comrades. Thus delayed, the fleeing Kiowas got no farther than the grove of trees where Highway 277 now crosses Chandler Creek before they were overtaken by the enemy. Several were killed there.

Tone-tsain, bringing up the rear, crossed the creek to the north side, and tried to escape into the timber. But his horse stumbled in a gully covered with weeds, throwing him to the ground. One of the Confederate

[1] George Hunt and Yee-goo (son of Tone-tsain) to author, 1935.

33

soldiers charged him with a saber. Tone-tsain gathered up his scattered arrows, and fitted one of them to the bowstring. The soldier's horse fell in the same gully. The Kiowa ran forward and pinned the white man to the ground with an arrow. As Tone-tsain tried to escape, a Caddo shot him in the back of the head.

The survivors attempted to win clear by fleeing west along Chandler Creek. Only two succeeded in doing so, and they were separated. One of these was a young man without previous war experience. He was on foot and weaponless except for a bow and three arrows; he was in a hostile country, and two hundred miles from home. He continued to walk north until he reached the site of Clinton. Here he found an abandoned horse grazing on the prairie. He was unable to get close enough to the animal to catch it, but with a blunt arrow he managed to lame the animal temporarily, and succeeded in capturing it. He then used his bow-string as a bridle and rode home, to find his family in mourning for him, thinking him dead. They had killed his horses and burned his property.

The following spring seven Kiowas came south to kill Caddoes in revenge for the defeat of Tone-tsain. They left their blankets at a place they call Tall Timbers, near the site of Sentinel, then went toward Keechi Hills. Here they were seen by a superior force of Caddoes, who tried to surround them. But they got away and went west along the Washita River. The next morning at daylight they were four miles west of the mouth of Rainy Mountain Creek, still fleeing. The Caddoes, who were tracking them with hounds, had lost the trail and were about to turn back. One Caddo climbed a knoll to take one last look. He saw the Kiowas disappearing into the timber.

Both parties were on foot, but the Kiowas did not know that the Caddoes were keeping up the pursuit until the latter were within close rifle range. The Caddoes were considered the best marksmen with the rifle of any of the southern plains tribes. They opened fire at short range, killing four of the Kiowas immediately and wounding one other. His unhurt companions concealed him in the tall reeds until the Caddoes had gone, when they made their escape. Relations between the Caddoes and Kiowas lack cordiality to this day.

INDIANS AND WHITES

In 1863 and 1864 the white men were too busy fighting each other to pay much attention to the Indians, who, thus unrestrained, commenced raiding in Texas, Colorado, New Mexico, and Kansas. A number of outrages occurred along the Santa Fe Trail. Wagon trains and stage stations were attacked. The Comanches killed five Americans attached to Allison's train at Lower Cimarron Springs. Two boys were scalped alive in eastern New Mexico.[2]

The Kiowas had an encounter with United States volunteer troops at Fort Larned, Kansas. They were camped outside the post, holding a scalp dance in honor of a successful raid made by Set-tain-te (White Bear), commonly called Satanta, near Menard, Texas, in which he had killed several whites and captured Mrs. Dorothy Field. After the dance was over Set-ankeah and another Indian approached the entrance to the fort, probably wishing to go to the sutler's store. They were warned away by the sentry. Not understanding his words they continued to advance, whereupon the sentry raised his gun in a threatening manner. At once Set-ankeah pumped two arrows into him and the Indians fled.[3]

In the excitement which followed, the garrison was turned out to defend the post against a supposed attack. The Indians raced away, driving with them most of the soldiers' horses, which were grazing near-by. A few days later Satanta sent word to the post commander that he hoped the quartermaster would provide better horses in the future, as the last lot which he had received were inferior in quality.

The authorities considered that a general Indian war was in progress. They began making preparations to chastise the redskins. Meanwhile the Kiowas had moved south to the Staked Plains, and had camped at a place called Red Bluff, on the Canadian River. Here, also, was a camp of Comanches. While camped together the Comanche chief, Little Buffalo, recruited the largest war party that ever had been sent out by these two tribes.

In October of 1864 Little Buffalo's raiders rode across Red River to Young County, Texas. They swept through the countryside sixty miles south of the site of Wichita Falls, attacked Fort Murray, a Confederate outpost near Fort Belknap, killed five troopers, then ravaged the settlements on Elm Creek, sixteen miles west of Belknap. Eleven whites were killed, seven women and children were carried into captivity.

A brave Negro named Brit Johnson, who had been orderly to officers at Fort Belknap before the war, and was one of the best shots on the frontier, volunteered to visit the Indian country to ransom the captives. He went to the friendly Penateka camp on the Washita, where through

[2] Carleton to Steck, Santa Fe, October 29, 1864, *Official Records of Rebellion,* Vol. XLI, Series I, Part IV, pp. 319-22.

[3] James Mooney, *op cit.,* pp. 313-14; see also Curtis to Blunt, September 22, 1864, *Official Records of the Rebellion,* Vol. XLI, Series I, Part III, p. 314.

It was never learned what happened to Dorothy Field, although her relatives were still inquiring for her at the Fort Sill agency in 1872. The agent from 1872 to 1878 was James Haworth, whose efforts to recover white captives were inadequate. There are a number of members of the Kiowa tribe living today whose mothers were captured in Texas during this time. None of these people, with the exception of Millie Durgan's descendants, know the true names of their parents.

the assistance of Asa-Havey (Milky Way) he traded horses for the captives. All of these who still were alive were secured except one, an infant of eighteen months named Millie Durgan. Millie was adopted by Au-soant-sai-mah, a noted warrior and member of the Ko-eet-senko.[4] The captive white girl grew up among the Kiowas, and never learned to speak English. Not until three years before her death did she learn her true identity. When she died at her home near Mountain View, Oklahoma, in February, 1934, her funeral was attended by two representatives of the army, from Fort Sill—Colonel C. S. Blakely and Captain F. H. Black. Several aged Texas pioneers who were present at the time of Millie's capture also came up from Newcastle to attend the funeral.

It was high time for another treaty. The Federals were not interested in what was happening in Texas, but the outrages in Kansas and Colorado aroused them to a war of reprisal. There was nobody on hand to make a treaty; the military people were in charge in the West, and they thought that the Indians ought to be disciplined rather than rewarded for their forays. In Kansas the war schemes did not mature, as the available troops were diverted in a vain attempt to catch the Confederate raiders Quantrell and Shelby. In Colorado the government sent Colonel J. M. Chivington, with the First Colorado Volunteer Cavalry, against the Cheyennes. In New Mexico General J. H. Carleton sent Colonel Christopher (Kit) Carson to attack the Kiowas and Comanches.

Carson's force consisted of three hundred volunteer cavalrymen and a hundred Utes and Jicarilla Apaches. It was planned to strike the hostiles in their winter camp, which was thought to be in Palo Duro Canyon. Carson left Cimarron, New Mexico, on November 3, 1864. With snow on the ground two feet deep, it was difficult for Carson to persuade his Indian allies to make the march. When the weather is cold the wild Indian loves nothing so much as the warmth of his lodge fire. On November 24 the troops found the Kiowas and Comanches camped along what is now called Kit Carson Creek in the Panhandle of Texas, near Bent's old post of Adobe Walls. They attacked the upper part of the village, killing several ancient braves, who, blind from the prevalent trachoma, could not escape. Then they set to work destroying the camp.

To-hauson, great chief of the Kiowas—at that time an old man—galloped downstream to warn the rest of the tribe. When he arrived, on his steaming and blood-flecked horse, the women and children set up an awful uproar of frightened wails. The warriors tied up their horses' tails and galloped out to protect the camp. While they were riding upstream the women and children fled in the opposite direction. The white captive,

4 The Ko-eet-senko was a warrior society of the Kiowas, the members of which were supposed to be the ten bravest men in the tribe. Mooney spells the name *Ka-it-senko*.

Millie Durgan, was concealed in the brush but later was rescued by her foster mother.

Hundreds of warriors arriving from the adjacent camps forced Carson to abandon his attack and retreat. If he had not been covered by the fire of Lieutenant Pettis' platoon of mountain howitzers he would have been cut to pieces.

On the Indian side To-hauson and Stumbling Bear were the heroes. To-hauson had a horse shot under him. Stumbling Bear made so many reckless charges that his small daughter's shawl, which he wore for good luck, was pierced by a dozen bullets. Stumbling Bear was not wounded.[5] The battle ended with the troops retiring, closely followed by the Indians, who set fire to the brown grass and harassed the soldiers by shooting and charging from the cover of the smoke.

Colonel Chivington's campaign against the Cheyennes was more successful than that of Carson.[6] But it culminated in an affair so disgraceful that it brought upon Chivington the condemnation of the entire country. Black Kettle, a Cheyenne chief, had brought his village to Fort Lyon, Colorado, in compliance with orders of the agent that all well-disposed Indians should come in for roll call. While camped near the fort, with an American flag flying over his tepee, Black Kettle was attacked by Chivington. One hundred and twenty Indians were slaughtered. Women and children were butchered in cruel and inhuman ways. A wave of horror swept over the United States when the details of this attack became known. The feelings of the Indians may well be imagined.

As a result of the Chivington massacre at Sand Creek, the hostility of the Cheyennes and Arapahoes increased toward the whites, until finally, in 1868, General Sheridan was forced to drive them to a reservation, the eventual result of Sheridan's campaign being the establishment of Fort Sill.

[5] George Hunt and Andrew Stumbling Bear to author, 1935.
[6] J. M. Chivington was a Methodist minister who held a commission in the Colorado volunteer forces.

CHAPTER FOUR

THE TREATY CHIEF

TREATIES OF 1865—COLONEL LEAVENWORTH'S "PEACE"—MEDICINE
LODGE TREATY—THE CRY FOR PROTECTION

F OR A few months subsequent to the campaigns of Colonels Carson
and Chivington the Indians in Kansas and along the Santa Fe trail
remained fairly quiet. The Kiowas camped along the Canadian and
the Cimarron. The Comanches were farther south and west. Twelve
years had elapsed since they had been invited to sign a treaty, and no
annuities had been issued for some time. The civilized Indians decided
that since neither the Confederate nor the Federal governments were
going to make a treaty, they might as well draw up one of their own.

On May 26, 1865, an impressive powwow was held at Camp Napoleon
(now Verden, Oklahoma) between the confederated tribes from the
eastern part of the territory and the plains Indians. An agreement was
reached and signed, the keynote of which was that "an Indian shall not
spill Indian blood." Few of the Kiowas or Comanches were there. They
knew that no presents or annuities were available.[1]

Before the war had come to a close both the North and the South
had been on the point of making overtures to the wild Indians. For the
Confederacy, Albert Pike was called back in harness. He was instructed
to get in touch with General Douglas Cooper, former Indian agent at Fort
Washita, with a view toward enlisting the Kiowas and Comanches to
fight the Yankees. It was thought that the latter were preparing to
invade Texas from the north.

Pike did not progress far with his scheme before the Civil War came
to a close; but the energetic Cooper made such a stir that word was
carried to Kansas concerning his warlike activities.

The Federals did not immediately send a treaty-maker among the
Indians. In fact they showed signs of getting ready to fight them. General
G. M. Dodge, at Fort Leavenworth, proposed to follow up Kit Carson's

[1] *Official Records of Rebellion*, Vol. XLVIII, Part II, Series I, pp. 1102-3.

38

effort by subjugating the Indians once and for all. On April 23 he was startled to hear that Douglas Cooper, with three hundred Indians of the Civilized Nations, was on the point of riding west via the Wichita Mountains to plunder the Santa Fe trail. At once he ordered three columns south to circumvent Cooper and punish the Indians. Only one small column under Colonel J. H. Ford got under way before an order arrived from Washington staying General Dodge's hand. A treaty man was afield.

The new emissary was one J. H. Leavenworth, a self-appointed dove of peace.[2] Leavenworth was on the prairie trying to assemble the chiefs of the Kiowas and Comanches for a treaty conference. In this he was aided and abetted by a commission of eastern politicos, which was investigating Indian affairs in general and the Chivington outrage in particular. This delegation met Leavenworth thirty miles south of Fort Zarah, in southern Kansas. They applauded his efforts and encouraged him to write to Washington in an effort to stop General Dodge's warlike preparations. The result was General Halleck's letter to Dodge. But the latter made such a convincing reply that on April 29 the Secretary of War told him to go ahead regardless of Leavenworth. The Secretary of the Interior, under whose charge was the handling of Indian affairs, concurred.

On this same day the Indians stole all of "Colonel" Leavenworth's mules, and nearly killed him as well. The treaty chief's pacific attitude underwent an immediate change. He became vociferously bellicose and commenced writing letters to everyone, wanting to know how long the authorities were going to permit the unspeakable savages to commit forays on the frontier.

But the mania for treaty-making would not be denied. During May everything was quiet; Leavenworth's ruffled feathers subsided. He took up once more his efforts to assemble the chiefs. He even gained adherents among the military. On May 31 General McCook wrote to the department commander, General John Pope, recommending that Ford's "puny" expedition against the Indians be stopped, and that Colonel Leavenworth be allowed to go ahead with his work of making a treaty with the Indians and putting them on a reservation.

This was referred to General Dodge for rebuttal. He replied that the Indians had fooled McCook as well as Leavenworth. "They have congregated around Fort Cobb," he said, "and are using it as a headquarters to send out raiding parties." He recommended that an expedition consisting of three powerful columns be sent toward Fort Cobb to punish the Indians for past depredations and to force them to cease marauding along the Santa Fe trail.

"I have attempted to get these expeditions off twice," he continued.

[2] Leavenworth was the son of General Henry Leavenworth, for whom Fort Leavenworth, Kansas, was named.

"The first time they were stopped by General Halleck on Colonel Leavenworth's representations. He started to make peace; the Indians stole all his stock, and very nearly got his scalp. He came back for a fight and wished to whip them, but now has changed again and it is possible he may get the chiefs together; but even if he does they will only represent a portion of each tribe."

In spite of these misgivings General Dodge decided to oppose Leavenworth no further. "I have concluded," he said, finally, "to wait and see the effects of Colonel Leavenworth's mission."

In the meantime the Civil War ended. Colonel Ford sent word that Jesse Chisholm had informed him that some Texas officer [Douglas Cooper?] had told the Indians that the war had been won by the North, and that they had better make their peace with the United States.

This gave Leavenworth a clear track. A treaty was signed with the Cheyennes and Arapahoes on October 14, with the Kiowa-Apaches on the seventeenth, and with the Kiowas and Comanches on the eighteenth. On the last day old To-hauson, the great chief of the Kiowas, made a speech in which he protested having his ancestral domain parceled out to him by the white man. Nevertheless, he and the other chiefs signed the treaty, the terms of which moved the two tribes south of the Arkansas to a reservation which consisted roughly of what is now the Panhandle of Texas and that part of southwestern Oklahoma lying south of the Canadian River. The Indians also agreed to surrender white captives and to stay away from the Santa Fe trail.

This treaty had several peculiar features, chief among which was the fact that a powerful nation of many millions of inhabitants should treat with a group of less than three thousand persons living within her borders, as with a separate nation; and second, that she should present to the Indians a large slice of the sovereign state of Texas, without consulting that state.

But no harm was done. The Indians had no intention of remaining on the reservation.

COLONEL LEAVENWORTH'S "PEACE"

Colonel Leavenworth's treaty lasted less than two years. During the first part of 1866 the Indians remained fairly quiet. Then To-hauson died —the last chief who had strong influence over the whole Kiowa tribe. He was succeeded by Gui-pah-go (Lone Wolf), a man who did not have enough force of character to restrain or command all of his people. Each separate subchief did as he saw fit. Among these was the redoubtable Satanta, a large, muscular man of middle age who was well known to the army officers stationed at the border posts on account of his great love for whisky and fondness for oratory. Satanta was of that type which today makes gangster leaders. He was brazen and impudent, shrewd at times, yet naïve, addicted to violence and boasting. In August he had led a war party into Texas, killed James Box, and carried Mrs. Box and her four children into captivity.

A little later Satanta took his prisoners to Fort Larned for ransom. Agent Leavenworth told him sharply that he had violated the recent treaty, and that he must release the captives without remuneration. Satanta promptly disappeared. A few days later he bobbed up at Fort Dodge, where the post commander took pity on the Box family and paid a large sum for their release.[3]

It was apparent that the United States owed a duty to Texas. The army posts along the southern border would have to be reoccupied, to control the raiding Kiowas and Comanches.

In the southern part of Indian Territory Fort Arbuckle alone was regarrisoned. Forts Towson, Washita, and Cobb remained in ruins. Fort Arbuckle was destined to become the "mother" post of Fort Sill. Its troops and materiel were moved to Fort Sill when that post was built. So it deserves more than a passing mention.

Two companies of the Sixth Infantry and two of the Tenth Cavalry (colored) arrived at Fort Arbuckle toward the close of 1866. It was an isolated place. The Tenth Cavalry had just been organized. There were only about two hundred men present for duty. Many of these were recruits—mostly former slaves—and had to be trained as soldiers. The post itself had to be rebuilt and enlarged. As a consequence, few troops were available for the duty of patrolling the border. A force of about twenty Caddo scouts was maintained for the purpose of keeping the post commander apprised of the movements of the wild Indians, but they were not able even to prevent their own horses from being stolen. The Comanches were beginning to bother the near-by Chickasaws again. But by the time news of these raids reached Fort Arbuckle it usually was too late to follow the marauders.[4]

Thus the little post stood alone in the great expanse of wilderness, wrapped in its own troubles, letting the tide of outside events flow past unnoticed. The commanding officer's attention was occupied in handling the routine problems of garrison life. For instance, in December he noticed that the stock of fresh reading matter in the post library was unaccountably low. A close investigation resulted in the publication of the following momentous order: "First Lieutenant C. D. Lyon, Sixth Infantry, having been notified, shortly after having been relieved from duty as Post Treasurer, that the Commanding Officer desired him to have the papers and periodicals, for which he had subscribed with the Post

[3] Old Files, Fort Arbuckle (preserved at Fort Sill).
[4] *Ibid.*

41

Fund for the Post Library, addressed to the Post Library instead of himself personally, and having again been reminded a second time, he is hereby *ordered* to direct the publishers of the *Army and Navy Journal, The Cavalry,* and the *Washington Chronicle,* to address these publications to the Post Library."

The coming of spring (1867) did not provide relief from petty annoyances: On May 22 Captain T. H. Baldwin wrote from Fort Smith, complaining that he had furnished Lieutenant P. L. Lee a horse to ride to Fort Arbuckle. He had not heard from the horse since. He requested that it be returned. Lieutenant Lee replied by indorsement: "When the horse was turned over to me the request was made that he be returned direct, lest an inferior one be returned by the Quartermaster Department. No opportunity has occurred to return the horse."

With the approach of summer weather there appeared to be no excuse for the men not bathing. The post commander issued this somewhat ambiguous order: "Company Commanders will require their men to bathe in Garrison Creek, at least three times a week, at such places as are not exposed from the rear."

Cleanliness did not produce godliness, however, for we find that when Private John Kelly, who had been detailed on special duty as a teamster in the Quartermaster Department, was ordered to get some salt for the mules, he replied: "To hell with the mules," or words to that effect. For this careless statement he was fined ten dollars, though there is no record that the mules took offense.

Private William Keating was detailed on kitchen police, but he broke a china plate purposely, announcing that he would "break many more in order to get relieved from this damned place." This remark cost Keating five dollars. Furthermore he was required to carry a thirty-pound log on his shoulder six hours a day for fifteen days.

Corporal James Smith, while assisting in watering the horses of D Company, "did leave his proper place in column, and cause the government horse he was riding to leap over logs, ditches, a fence, and run a race or gallop at the top of his speed, all this to the prejudice of good order and military discipline."

Private William Alexander unlawfully sold his overcoat to a teamster for five dollars, with which he presumably purchased a jug of whisky. For this crime he was sentenced to "stand on the head of a barrel from 9 o'clock A.M. until 4 o'clock P.M. each day for ten days, and forfeit fourteen dollars of his pay."

The wild Indians, too, felt the touch of spring. They annoyed the civilized tribes, took scalps and horses in Texas, and interfered with the mail service between Fort Arbuckle and Fort Gibson to such an extent that it became impossible to get a white man to contract to carry it. The mail service was maintained then by the Indian scouts, who established relay stations fifty miles apart, and rode in pairs.

During the summer, wandering parties of prairie savages visited the post, activated by curiosity and a desire to trade. On one occasion the post commander availed himself of the opportunity to practice the time-honored custom of impressing the wild men with the power of the whites. Several twenty-four-pound siege guns had been sent to the post together with large quantities of ammunition. The adjutant improvised a gun squad from some cavalrymen. Through the interpreter, Horace Jones, he explained to the Indians how the fuse was cut to make the shell burst in the air, or on the ground, as desired. A couple of shots were fired. For a wonder, the fuses functioned properly. The shells burst more than a mile away, greatly astonishing the savages, and killing a cow belonging to the post dairyman.[5] This demonstration cost the government seven dollars, paid to the irate owner of the cow.

During one of these visits the post commander was able to effect the release of a white child captive, Theodore Adolphus (Dot) Babb, captured by the Comanches in Texas in 1866. Two hundred and ten dollars in cash, and twenty dollars worth of uniform clothing was turned over as ransom money to the Penateka chief Asa-Havey, who acted as contact man to the wild Indians. Post Adjutant R. H. Pratt thought that this method of obtaining the release of white captives furnished the Indians with an incentive to continue their raiding. With the approval of the commanding officer he wrote a letter to the division commander, General Sherman, recommending that the practice be discontinued. In a short time a reply was received, in General Sherman's own handwriting, directing Captain Walsh to assemble the Indians, inform them that the raiding must cease. Otherwise the whole army would be sent to enforce compliance.

Having heard that large bodies of Indians were congregating near Cottonwood Grove (site of Verden, Oklahoma), Captain Walsh sent word that he desired to meet them in council. With the surgeon, the adjutant, twenty men from Company D, and the twenty Caddo scouts, he proceeded to the site of Verden, where hundreds of tepees lined the banks of the Washita.

General Sherman's letter was read and explained to the Indians. Some of them were inclined to be ugly. For a time the situation was tense, for the soldiers were greatly outnumbered. But the older chiefs—Little Raven for the Arapahoes, Black Kettle for the Cheyennes, and Tosawi for the Comanches—were more conciliatory. Through the offices of Dr. J. J. Sturms, Louella Babb, sister of Dot Babb, was ransomed. In spite

[5] R. H. Pratt, "Some Indian Reminiscences," *Journal of the U.S. Cavalry Association,* October, 1905, pp. 200-5.

of General Sherman's letter it was necessary to pay $333 dollars for this child. The principle was wrong, and the officers knew it, but no white man close to the situation had the heart to allow captives to remain with the savages. There was no other sure way of recovering the captives alive.

The Indian troubles around Fort Arbuckle were trivial compared with what was going on in Kansas. The inroads of white settlement, the activities of the buffalo hide-hunters, and above all else the building of the transcontinental railroads had so enraged the Indians that a general outbreak appeared imminent. General W. S. Hancock, commanding the Department of the Missouri, held a council with the Kiowas on April 24 at Fort Dodge. Into the Sibley tent in which the powwow was held were crowded: White chiefs Hancock, A. J. Smith, Wyncoop, Leavenworth, Mitchell, and Douglass, seated on camp stools; Kiowa chiefs Kicking Bird and Stumbling Bear, seated on the ground. Kicking Bird and his cousin Stumbling Bear represented the peacefully inclined portion of the Kiowa tribe. On May 1 near Fort Larned a similar conference was held with Satanta. The Kiowas promised peace; but on May 4 the hostile Cheyennes, with whom councils also had been held declared "war to the knife." General Hancock's answer was, "You shall have it, until every warrior cries enough." Immediately afterwards he put the troops in motion. The Indians scattered into the plains.[6]

General Sherman himself went out to inspect the movements of Hancock's forces. He inquired into the causes of the disorders, finding that there was something to be said on each side. The Indians had a real grievance. They were being crowded out of the country which they had regarded as their own. Impartial observers reported that for several years certain classes of whites had sought every opportunity to start a war. On the other hand many innocent citizens were in real and immediate need of protection. The average frontier farmer was not always the bold, hardy, independent fellow pictured in popular fiction. Sherman returned on May 19, remarking sagely, "We can have an Indian war or not, as we choose."

Apparently the Indians did the choosing. A number of skirmishes were fought between Indians and small detachments of troops. Not always did the redskin come off second best. For example, on June 26 three hundred Cheyennes, led by Roman Nose, made an attack on Fort Wallace, Kansas. Captain Albert Barnitz went out to meet them with Company G, Seventh Cavalry. After a severe fight the troops were driven back into the post, suffering a loss of seven men. Among the killed was a young Englishman, a graduate of Eton, and a candidate for a commission —Sergeant Frederick Wyllyams.[7] What the Cheyennes did to Wyllyams,

---

[6] *Harper's Weekly*, May-June, 1867.   [7] *Harper's Weekly*, July 27, 1867.

44

and many other similar spectacles, were in the minds of the men of the Seventh Cavalry when they attacked Black Kettle's village a year later.

The war against the Indians in the northern plains was deplored by the people in the eastern part of the United States. Congress appointed a commission to establish a lasting peace with the Indians, the plan being to place the tribes on reservations where they would be undisturbed by the whites and would thereafter cease to molest the frontier settlements. A treaty was to be made—a treaty to end treaties. The commissioners met the Kiowas, Comanches, Kiowa-Apaches, Cheyennes, and Arapahoes in October, 1867, near the site of Medicine Lodge, Kansas.

It was a colorful gathering. At least five thousand Indians were there. A squadron of the Seventh Cavalry under Major Joel Elliott was present as protection for the whites. While waiting for the council to begin, Major Elliott and some of his friends went on a buffalo chase, killing numbers of the beasts for sport alone. This angered the Kiowa chief Satanta. On his complaint several of the officers were placed in arrest.

The council consisted of a series of speeches by various white men and Indians, following which the treaty was drawn up and explained to the Indians. Phillip McCusker acted as interpreter. McCusker spoke only Comanche. Some members of the other tribes understood this language, others did not. It is doubtful how much of the whole proceedings was intelligible to the Indians. Most of them had come out of curiosity, and because they had been told that the soldiers were going to provide them with free food.

The commissioners demanded that the Indians retire to assigned reservations, cease depredating, and permit railroads to be built through the plains. In return for these concessions the Indians were to be given protection against white hunters who were invading the buffalo range; they were to be issued certain annuities, to be provided with schools, churches, farming implements, and be taught how to walk the white man's road.

When it came their turn to speak, various Indian chiefs responded with the best oratory of which they were capable. As usual, the Kiowas were the most talkative. A Kiowa orator makes an excellent impression. The language is unmusical, but forceful and full of emphasis. The Indians are dignified, yet freely use graceful and expressive gestures. Satanta stated the case for his people in part as follows:

"All the land south of the Arkansas belongs to the Kiowas and Comanches, and I don't want to give any of it away. I love the land and the buffalo and will not part with it. I don't want any of the medicine lodges (churches) within the country. I want the children raised as I was.

45

I have heard that you want to settle us on a reservation near the mountains. I don't want to settle. I love to roam over the prairies. There I feel free and happy, but when I settle down I grow pale and die. A long time ago this land belonged to our fathers; but when I go up the river I see camps of soldiers on its banks. These soldiers cut down my timber; they kill my buffalo; and when I see that it feels as if my heart would burst with sorrow."

A little later he said:

"This building of homes for us is all nonsense. We don't want you to build any for us; we would all die. Look at the Penatekas! Formerly they were powerful, but now they are weak and poor. I want all my land, even from the Arkansas south to Red River. My country is small enough already. If you build us houses the land will be smaller. Why do you insist on this? What good will come of it? I don't understand your reason. Time enough to build us houses when the buffalo are all gone. But you tell the Great Father that there are plenty of buffalo yet, and when the buffalo are gone, I will tell him. This trusting to agents for food I don't believe in."[8]

When the commissioners heard Satanta's words they were nonplused. The things which he said he did not want were the very things they intended to force on the Indians. They expected to civilize the Indians without delay, and the best way they could think of to accomplish this was to make farmers of them, coop them up in houses, make them wear white men's clothing, and send them to school and to church.

What the Indians desired most was to be let alone, provided, of course, that they be permitted to raid in Texas and Mexico. But this was not to be. The white man would not be content until he had killed every bison, antelope, and bird, fenced in every plot of grass, chopped down every tree, and plowed up every acre of prairie. The Indians and the white commissioners alike were powerless to hold back the great flood of immigration which even then was surging across the plains. Into the treaty were written the very things which the Indians did not want as Satanta had pointed out: Provision for reservations, houses, schools, plows, instruction in agriculture.[9]

THE CRY FOR PROTECTION

Colonel Leavenworth was chosen as agent for the Kiowas and Comanches. He went to Fort Cobb full of hope and enthusiasm in his plan to civilize the Indians and make farmers of them. He established an

[8] Mooney, *op. cit.*, pp. 207-8; photostatic copies of Satanta's speech furnished by librarian, Office of Indian Affairs, Washington, D.C.

[9] The older Indians know the Medicine Lodge treaty as Timber Hill treaty, because there was a prominent timbered hill near the council grounds.

agency at a place called Eureka Valley. The same crowd of employes, farmers, and traders who had been at Fort Cobb in the old days joined him; all except Horace Jones, who was interpreter at Fort Arbuckle.

Leavenworth was one of those idealists who believed that the Indians could be lifted from savagery by purely peaceful methods, without the application of discipline. His viewpoint was destined to undergo a radical change. He was about to collide with a people who responded only to their own desires, a race who did exactly as they chose except when compelled by superior force to do otherwise.

There was nothing in the Medicine Lodge agreement which specifically bound the government to feed the savages. Nevertheless the obligation was implied. Indian agents and military officials alike realized that this must be done if the Indians were to be weaned away from their nomadic habits and taught to settle down as farmers. No race is so adaptable as to be able to change overnight its established mode of living.

Early in 1868 the Indians began to congregate around Colonel Leavenworth's agency begging for food and presents. No provision had been made by the Indian department to furnish these. The Indians grew surly, even threatening. The young bucks began to depredate: they intimidated the peaceful Wichitas who were located at Cottonwood Grove, and stole horses and food from them. At first Leavenworth was discouraged. Then he became alarmed. He wrote to Fort Arbuckle requesting military support. Captain J. W. Walsh made a forced march with two companies of the Tenth Cavalry to suppress the depredators. But when he arrived they had vanished.

The Kiowas and Comanches did not confine their attention to the Wichitas and Caddoes. Cyrus Harris, governor of the Chickasaws, reported outrages visited on his people by the wild Indians. He requested authority to raise a force of sixty rangers or militia for the defense of his borders. This request was forwarded by the commanding officer to the War Department. In due course of time a reply was received, approving Governor Harris' proposal, if it meant no expense to the government![10]

Bitter March winds whistling down from the Colorado snowfields did not improve the attitude of the Indians at Eureka Valley. Agent Leavenworth sent another galloper to Fort Arbuckle, asking military assistance.

Captain Joseph B. Rife, Sixth Infantry, was now in command at Fort Arbuckle. Knowing that his predecessor was familiar with the situation at the agency, he sent the letter to him for remark. Captain Walsh promptly penned the following indorsement: "I am of the opinion that it would be utterly useless and of no benefit to the public to send any troops to Colonel Leavenworth's assistance. The whole command at this post

[10] Old Files, Fort Arbuckle.

would be insufficient to carry out his object. It is not his intention to have trouble right or wrong. I am convinced that his only desire is the assistance of troops as a camp guard for his personal safety as well as that of his party, and that alone prompts him to call upon the military authorities. Let him come to this post with his party, where he will be properly protected, or within a reasonable distance; and when he is properly prepared to meet the requirements of the Indians, I anticipate not the slightest trouble. There is not sufficient grass for the subsistence of the horses. The last expedition cost the Government four of the best horses of the command caused by want of grass."

Captain Rife referred the matter to higher authorities. Before reply was received Agent Leavenworth wrote again. This time he was greatly agitated: "A large body of Indians are expected daily near the agency. Request the assistance of all the troops that can be spared."

Captain Rife forwarded this note to department headquarters, remarking sourly that all the troops in the post would not be sufficient if there were as many Indians as Leavenworth indicated. A few days later an order came from department headquarters, in response to Leavenworth's previous request, directing the commanding officer at Fort Arbuckle to march to the agent's relief with his entire command. Before the force could be set in motion a third letter was brought in from Leavenworth, stating calmly that the previous letters were based on false information. The agent was confident, now, that the only thing the Indians desired was peace.

A brief interlude of quiet settled down over Fort Arbuckle. Captain Rife was able to turn his attention to the more engrossing matter of interior grievances. He had opportunity, to cite a typical case, to attend to Captain Robert Gray. Gray had written him a letter complaining that the cavalrymen were getting a raw deal in the matter of post fatigue and special duty, being discriminated against by the infantry. This question was hardly settled before Gray wrote again, protesting that when his men were sent to the post hospital as patients, the surgeon retained them there as kitchen police and orderlies, long after a reasonable period for convalescence had elapsed. In addition to this, Rife had to do something about the troublesome matter of relative rank among the officers. Veterans who had served through the Civil War as captains were now submerged, being forced to take orders from young fellows recently commissioned in higher grades. There was considerable bickering over this subject.

Colonel Leavenworth's estimate of the pacific intention of his red charges proved inaccurate. In May a party of Comanches raided the Wichita agency (located west of the site of Anadarko), robbed the agent and the trader's store. They set fire to the buildings and told the official in charge that they did not propose to have him build any more houses or cut down any more timber. The white men in the vicinity moved out, some of them going to Pauls Valley, others to Texas. Colonel Leavenworth also had seen enough of the wild Indians. He took his departure from the Indian country, not stopping to turn over his property. S. T. Walkley was left in charge, without official authority from anyone.

These developments made it obvious that a military post would have to be established for the protection of the agency. Fort Arbuckle was too far east to render timely assistance when need therefor arose. The authorities recognized that there should be a military post in the center of the Indian reservation, where the movements of raiding bands could be observed and prevented. The Wichita Mountains were in the heart of the Indian range. It was recalled that previous explorers had recommended that a post be built near Medicine Bluff. Department headquarters ordered that a reconnaissance be made into that area for the purpose of selecting a site for a new post.

Brevet Major General Benjamin H. Grierson, colonel of the Tenth Cavalry, came from Fort Gibson to make the reconnaissance. He brought with him two companies of his regiment as escort. Two more companies of cavalry were added at Fort Arbuckle, as well as a wagon train and a train guard consisting of a company of the Sixth Infantry. Horace Jones went along as guide and interpreter.

Colonel Grierson's force left Fort Arbuckle the latter part of May, 1868, and marched west over Marcy's old road. They had not gone many miles before they encountered boggy ground. It was necessary to corduroy long stretches of the trail.[11]

Then it rained.

It rained for two weeks. The troops struggled through mud by day and slept in puddles of water at night. The heavy prairie sod clung to the wagon wheels. It formed in huge balls on the horses' feet. Every man wished that he were back in Fort Arbuckle.

Finally the sun reappeared. Far away in the blue hilly distance the summits of the Wichitas showed above the billows of the prairie like islands at sea. The spirits of the men rose. A few hours later the column passed over Arbuckle Hill and approached Cache Creek. A broad, cool wind streamed pauselessly up the valley, laden with summer perfume. The cottonwoods were in full leaf. Scarlet and purple wild-flowers gleamed in the meadows. Cicadas throbbed in the trees. The sparkling waters of Medicine Bluff Creek ran through shady groves of elms and pecans.

Colonel Grierson was delighted. He rode to the top of the hill where

[11] R. T. Jacobs, "Military Reminiscences," *Chronicles of Oklahoma*, Vol. II, No. 1 (March 1924), pp. 12-14.

Marcy, Rector, and Emory had been before him. Horace Jones told him that the Wichita Indians formerly had a village on the site. Grierson sat and looked at the scenery for a few moments. He noted from the marks on the trees that the place was above high water in flood season. There were ample supplies of wood, water, and pasturage. Limestone hills near-by would provide rock for building. High peaks to the west were fine places for outposts and block houses.

Why look farther? The colonel removed his saddle, threw it on the ground, and said, "We will build the post here."

The troops camped on the flat ground where the trader's store was built later. The site of the post was staked out at this point.[12] Adjutant Samuel L. Woodward was directed to kill some buffalo to supply the command with fresh meat, and the chase extended over the Adams Hill-Arbuckle Hill area. Over fifty buffalo were killed in two hours, and wagons had to be sent out from the camp to collect the meat.

After a few days the expedition marched westward, passing along the south side of the mountains to Otter Creek. While in camp there they were visited by a band of Comanches. That evening the chiefs were invited to dinner, in return for which courtesy they staged a scalp dance, displaying several scalps which Interpreter Jones thought might have been taken in Texas.[13]

The following day, June 27, 1868, a conference was held with these Indians, as a result of which several captive children, including four whites and two negroes, were ransomed.[14]

While at this place Colonel Grierson visited the ruins of Camp Radziminski, several miles to the north, where Otter Creek emerges from the gap in the hills. In fact, nearly everyone who went near it succumbed to some unknown fascination and paid it a visit. Possibly it was because of the persistent tales of buried treasure there.

The troops marched north around the west end of what is now the Wichita Forest Reserve to the valley of the Washita. Immense clouds of grasshoppers appeared in the sky. At first the men thought that a belated blizzard or snowstorm was approaching, so great was the size and density of the insect cloud. Soon the prairie was covered with them. They ate every bit of vegetation—grass, leaves, shrubs. They even devoured the nap from the blankets. This year became known to the Wichita and Caddo Indians as "the year the grasshoppers ate our crops."

The expedition marched east along the Washita past the site of Fort Cobb, then returned to Fort Arbuckle, where it was disbanded. The

[12] Annual Report of the Surgeon, Fort Sill, 1893, Old Files Section, Adjutant General's Office, Washington, D.C.

[13] *Ibid.*

[14] Reminiscences of John Thomas, late of Troop L, Tenth Cavalry, in *Winners of the West* (St. Joseph, Mo., May 30, 1934).

troops returned to their proper commands and Colonel Grierson went to Fort Gibson. It appeared that the military post at the eastern end of the Wichita Mountains was to be built at last. There had been many postponements. Yet it was not to be accomplished even now; not until another Indian war had been fought and one more reconnaissance had been made to Medicine Bluff.

INDIAN ACTIVITIES

Colonel Leavenworth deserted his post on May 26. Shortly thereafter the acting agent noticed that the Indians were in possession of considerable liquor. Investigation indicated that "Caddo George" Washington was hauling it in for Shirley and Sturms. The Indians, inflamed by whisky, and unrestrained by the presence of their regular agent, departed on the warpath.[15]

Nearly all of the Comanches, except the Yapparikas, were camped at Eureka Valley. The Yapparikas, together with the Kiowas, were following the buffalo north so as to arrive at Fort Larned in time for the first issue of annuities promised under the Medicine Lodge Treaty. This issue did not take place until August, so that the Indians found time hanging heavily on their hands.

The Kiowas escaped boredom by celebrating their annual Sun Dance, following which Poor Buffalo organized a team to go west and attack the Utes. Nearly two hundred bucks made the varsity; they elected Heap-of-Bears as captain. A number of Comanches went along to swell the cheering section.

On July 10 the Utes were encountered. In the ensuing scrimmage Heap-of-Bears was killed and his aggregation was given a thorough whipping. Even worse, the Utes captured one of the two Tai-me idols, most sacred medicine of the Kiowas. This was an appalling disaster.[16]

When the defeated warriors straggled into the main camps near Fort Larned, the whole tribe went into mourning. Ghastly wails rose night and day from the tepees. The women cut great gashes in their flesh. Some lopped off one or two fingers. Kicking Bird and Stumbling Bear were sent west to collect and bury the remains of the defeated braves. It would take a mighty fine annuity to smooth out this sorrow.

Meanwhile Satanta consoled himself by going on a raid in Texas.[17]

Satanta was not the only Indian who was observing the Medicine Lodge Treaty by raiding in Texas. On June 10 a party of Comanches, consisting of Kotchatekas and Noconees, returned to the Eureka Valley

[15] Walkley to Hazen, October 10, 1868, MS paper of General P. H. Sheridan, Library of Congress, Manuscript Division.
[16] Mooney, *op. cit.,* pp. 322-25.
[17] Report of Captain H. E. Alvord, Sheridan Papers, *loc. cit.*

agency from a raid into Montgomery County, Texas, bringing one scalp —that of a young white man about eighteen years old—three children named McElroy, and a number of horses.[18] On July 14 a number of Noconees came in from the Brazos River country, proudly displaying the scalps of a family of four settlers whom they had murdered.[19]

On September 1 a party of Noconees, Penatekas, and Wichitas appeared at Spanish Fort, Texas, just south of Red River. The following day they returned to the agency with eight scalps and a large number of horses and mules. The Indians were not at all adverse to telling the acting agent what they had done at Spanish Fort:

"The raid was made by Tosawi's son-in-law," says Mr. Walkley. "I will give their own account of the raid. They said they came in sight of a fine house, put out their sentinels—one reconnoitered. He said that the windows had curtains which were put back on each side; he saw a woman through the window, sitting in a rocking chair. He signaled to his comrades that all was right, and thirteen entered the house with a whoop —some through the windows and some through the doors. The woman was afraid and fell on the floor. The thirteen ravished her, Tosawi's son being the first, and Horseback's son the last, who killed her by sticking his tomahawk into her head. Tosawi's son-in-law then scalped her, and killed three or four of her children. The party then started up the river —killing and stealing as they went. They also say that they had two white squaws whom they ravished as much as they pleased, and then threw them away."[20]

Several other raids were made during the fall by Comanches and Wichitas.

Similar things were happening in Kansas and Colorado. Acting Governor Hall of Colorado reported: "The Indians have again attacked our settlements in strong force, obtaining possession of the country to within twelve miles of Denver. They are more bold, fierce, and desperate in their assaults than ever before. It is impossible to drive them out and protect the families at the same time, for they are better armed, mounted, disciplined, and better officered than our men. Each hour brings intelligence of fresh barbarities and more extensive robberies. We have been impoverished of horses by the frequency and success of these attacks. The prospect was never so dark as now. Is there no way to bring the Government to a proper realization of our terrible condition? Many outlying districts are being abandoned, entailing untold loss to the country."[21]

The plight of Kansas attracted even more attention. Included in the annuity issue at Fort Larned, which had been promised by the Medicine

[18] One of the McElroy captives is still living, near Warren, Oklahoma.

[19] Walkley, *loc. cit.* [20] *Ibid.* [21] Sheridan Papers.

Lodge Treaty, were rifles and ammunition. There had been considerable dispute as to whether this was wise. At first the Indians were informed that no arms would be issued. Such a howl arose that later the arms were given out, much to the disgust of General Sherman.

But before this change in the original decision was made several bands of Cheyennes and Arapahoes went on the warpath, claiming that they were angry because the arms had been refused them. The authorities were not immediately aware of this and went ahead with the issue.[22] The Indians were well aware of it. Promptly they moved their camps south of the Arkansas, where they were supposed to be safe, under the terms of the treaty.[23]

The raiders were members of the bands of the Cheyenne chiefs Black Kettle, Medicine Arrow, Little Rock, and Bull Bear. They went to the Solomon and Saline rivers in Kansas, where they perpetrated crimes which brought on the War of 1868 and resulted in the establishment, finally, of Fort Sill.

Many good people throughout the East claimed that there never was sufficient justification for attacking the Indians. Perhaps not. But to show how the Kansans felt, the following letter written by the governor to President Johnson is quoted.

"TOPEKA, KANSAS, August 17, 1868.

"To His Excellency Andrew Johnson, President:

"I have just returned from Northwestern Kansas, the scene of a terrible Indian massacre. On the 13th and 14th inst. forty of our citizens were killed and wounded by hostile Indians. Men, women, and children were murdered indiscriminately. Many of them were scalped and their bodies mutilated. Women after receiving mortal wounds were outraged, and otherwise inhumanly treated in the presence of their dying husbands and children. Two young ladies, and two little girls were carried away to suffer a fate worse than death. . . . .

"The settlers, covering a space of sixty miles wide, and reaching from the Saline to the Republican, were driven in, and the country laid in ashes, and the soil drenched in blood. How long must we submit to such atrocities? Need we look to the government for protection, or must the people of Kansas protect themselves? If the government cannot control these uncivilized barbarians, while they are under its fostering care and protection, it certainly can put a stop to the unbearable policy of supplying them with arms and ammunition. . . . . The savage devils have become intolerable, and must and shall be driven out of this state. General

[22] *Report of Secretary of War, 1868*, pp. 51-52. *See also* P. H. Sheridan, *Personal Memoirs* (New York: Charles L. Webster, 1888).

[23] E. S. Godfrey, "Reminiscences of Medicine Lodge," *Cavalry Journal*, January, 1928, pp. 112-15.

Sheridan is doing and has done all in his power to protect our people, but is powerless for want of troops. . . . .

"S. J. CRAWFORD, *Governor of Kansas.*"

Strong words, these. And they must have had some effect. Washington turned the Indians over to the army for punishment.

The task was assigned to Major General P. H. Sheridan. He immediately began to lay groundwork for a winter campaign. He ordered vast stores of supplies to be concentrated at key points—at Fort Gibson for forwarding to Forts Arbuckle and Cobb, at Fort Larned to go with the column of troops from that point. Four hundred wagons were collected to move the supplies.

General Sheridan planned to invade the Indian country from three directions: One column to move east from Fort Bascom, New Mexico, another to march southeast from Fort Lyon, Colorado, while the third body of troops was to operate south from Fort Larned. This last force was the largest, and Sheridan planned to accompany it in person. It was to consist of the Seventh Cavalry, to be recruited up to full strength for the purpose, and a regiment of volunteer Kansans under Governor Crawford.

While Sheridan was engaged in these preparations, Brevet Brigadier General Alfred Sully led several troops of the Seventh Cavalry across the Arkansas River in pursuit of the hostile Indians. This march was conducted in a dilatory manner, being held up several times by skilful rear-guard actions fought by the Indians. When Sully reached the confluence of Beaver Creek and Wolf Creek, in Indian Territory, he turned around and marched back to Kansas, escorted part of the way by savages who rode on the flank of the column, just out of rifle range, thumbing their noses at the cavalry and making other insulting gestures. One morning, just after camp was broken, two loitering "strikers" were seized by the Indians, and carried off screaming. Sully would not permit Major Elliott to pursue.[24]

On his return to Fort Larned, General Sully recommended that Lieutenant Colonel George A. Custer be assigned to command the Seventh Cavalry. Custer had been in semi-retirement for several months under sentence of suspension from command. Through Sheridan's influence he was restored.

Sheridan, in his preparations for the punitive expedition, was embarrassed by the presence of the Kiowas and Comanches, who continued to loiter about Fort Larned. These two tribes were not officially listed as hostile, and it was earnestly desired to move them onto their reservation, in order to avoid embroiling them in the coming conflict.

[24] E. S. Godfrey, "Some Reminiscences of the Washita Battle," *Cavalry Journal,* July, 1927, pp. 417-25. A "striker" is an officer's orderly.

Colonel W. B. Hazen, Sixth Infantry, had been loaned to the Indian department, and placed in general charge of these Indians. Sherman wrote to him concerning this matter:

"I want you to go to Fort Cobb and make provision for all the Indians who come there to keep out of the war, and I prefer that no warlike proceedings be made in that quarter. . . . . The object is for the War and Interior Departments to afford the peaceful Indians every possible protection, support, and encouragement, whilst the troops proceed against all outside the reservation, as hostile; and it may be that General Sheridan will be forced to invade the reservation in pursuit of hostile Indians; if so I will instruct him to do all he can to spare the well-disposed; but their only safety now is in rendezvousing at Fort Cobb."[25]

Consequently Colonel Hazen and General Sheridan held a conference with the chiefs of the Kiowas and Comanches, in which it was arranged for the tribes to go to Fort Cobb with the new agent. General Sheridan realized that in all fairness to the Indians it would be necessary to issue them rations, in order to keep them congregated at one place. If they were allowed to wander around hunting buffalo they might run afoul of the troops. Therefore he agreed to furnish them military rations, to be drawn from Fort Arbuckle and forwarded to Cobb, sufficient in quantity to last until the end of October. By that time it was hoped that the Interior Department would take over this function. The latter branch of the government had enough money, but in view of the demands of the military for the campaign, could not secure the necessary transportation.

This arrangement was satisfactory to the agent, and to the Indians. However it was discovered that there were not sufficient supplies on hand at Fort Larned to subsist the Indians in their move to Fort Cobb. While these supplies were being secured the Indians were allowed to go on a buffalo hunt, it being understood that they were to report in at Larned at the end of a week, draw their rations, and depart for Fort Cobb.

Movements of troops and hostile Indians in the area had driven the buffalo so far south that the Indians continued their trek to Cobb, not bothering to return to Fort Larned. This alarmed Sully and Sheridan, who thought that the Indians had played them false. Hazen waited a reasonable time, then decided to proceed to Fort Cobb to meet the Indians. In making this trip he was forced to make a wide detour to the east in order to avoid being scalped by the Cheyennes, so that he did not arrive at the agency until two weeks after the leading bands of savages.

Captain Henry Alvord, Tenth Cavalry, was sent from Fort Arbuckle to act temporarily for Hazen. He organized an intelligence force of white scouts and friendly Indians, which enabled him to keep his superiors

[25] W. B. Hazen, "Some Corrections to Custer's *Life on the Plains,*" *Chronicles of Oklahoma,* III (1925), 303.

informed as to the movements of the doubtful Kiowas and Comanches. On October 30 he wrote that these tribes had not joined the hostiles. The Comanches were camped on the Canadian, but were expected to arrive shortly. The Kiowas had arrived, but being hungry, had gone up the Washita, to the Antelope Hills area, to hunt buffalo.[26]

It was recognized by this time that the agency at Fort Cobb could not exist without military protection. Acting under instructions from higher authority, a force consisting of Company M, Tenth Cavalry and Company E, Sixth Infantry was sent October 5 from Fort Arbuckle. On their arrival at Fort Cobb the troops found that most of the wooden buildings had been burned during the Civil War. The ruins of several adobe huts and one stone house still remained. The soldiers repaired these, constructing thatched roofs which darkened the interiors and filtered the rain water a bit before it leaked through to the inhabitants and government property beneath. Work was commenced on a log storehouse, with rude picket shelters for the personnel.

Colonel Hazen arrived November 7. The Indians began drifting in shortly afterward. The semi-tame Penatekas under Tosawi and Asa-Havey maintained a friendly attitude, but the Yapparikas and Kiowas were so saucy and arrogant that the post was in continual trepidation. Double guards were kept on duty day and night. A stockade was built on the high ground, east of the present town of Fort Cobb, inside which it was intended to move the whites if attacks developed. The animals were kept in a corral surrounded by a trench. This latter precaution probably saved the stock, because Gotebo, a Kiowa, had been planning to steal all of them. When he found out about the trench he gave up the idea.[27]

Colonel Hazen shook his finger at the Indians, telling them that they had better watch out; a big war chief was coming from the north to punish them. Gray-haired Indians laughed when they heard this. They said that they had been told that since they were children, but nothing came of it.[28]

The Indians continued to browbeat Hazen until he sent to Fort Arbuckle for more troops. Major Kidd's squadron of the Tenth Cavalry came. They were met near Cottonwood Grove by large bodies of Kiowa and Comanche warriors, who roughly ordered them back to Arbuckle. Major Kidd paid no attention to this, but went on into Fort Cobb. When this matter was reported to General Sheridan, the general remarked, "I will take some of the starch out of them before I get through with them."[29]

[26] H. E. Alvord's report, *loc. cit.*   [27] George Hunt to author, 1935.
[28] Hazen to Sherman, November 10, 1868, Sheridan Papers.
[29] Sheridan to Sherman, December 19, 1868, Sheridan Papers.

On November 20 several chiefs belonging to the hostile Cheyennes and Arapahoes came to Fort Cobb for a conference with Colonel Hazen. Their young men had finished the summer raiding and they thought that it was time for a winter truce. This had been customary in the past; they were upset by reports that a no-treaty chief was coming right down into their country to fight them in the winter time.

Black Kettle made the principal address: "I always feel well while I am among these Indians—the Caddoes, Wichitas, Wacoes, Keechi—as I know they are all my friends, and I do not feel afraid to go among the white men, because I feel them to be my friends also. The Cheyennes, when south of the Arkansas, did not wish to return to the north side, because they feared trouble there, but were continually told that they had better go there as they would be rewarded for so doing. The Cheyennes do not fight at all this side of the Arkansas, they do not trouble in Texas, but north of the Arkansas they are almost always at war. When lately north of the Arkansas some young Cheyennes were fired upon and then the fight began.[30] I have always done my best to keep my young men quiet, but some will not listen, and, since the fighting began, I have not been able to keep them all at home. But we all want peace, and I would be glad to move all my people down this way. I could then keep them all quietly near camp. My camp is now on the Washita, forty miles east of Antelope Hills, and I have there about 180 lodges. I speak only for my own people."[31]

Big Mouth, an Arapaho, made a similar speech, in which he asked Hazen to stop the soldiers from coming down to fight them.

Colonel Hazen responded: "I am sent here as a peace chief. All here is to be peace, but north of the Arkansas is General Sheridan, the great war chief, and I do not control him, and he has all the soldiers who are fighting the Cheyennes and Arapahoes. Therefore you must go back to your country, and if the soldiers come to fight you must remember that they are not from me, but from that great war chief, and it is with him that you must make your peace. . . . . I cannot stop the war, but will send your talk to the Great Father, and if he gives me orders to treat you like the friendly Indians I will send out to you to come in; but you must not come in unless I send for you, and you must keep well out beyond the friendly Kiowas and Comanches. . . . . I hope you understand how and why it is that I cannot make peace with you."[32]

In explaining his stand to his superiors, Colonel Hazen wrote: "Big Mouth was accompanied by Spotted Wolf, and Black Kettle by Little Robe. To have made peace with them would have brought to my camp

[30] This is Black Kettle's explanation of the murders on the Saline and the Republican.
[31] Hazen to Sherman, November 20, 1868, Sheridan Papers.
[32] *Ibid.*

most of those now on the warpath south of the Arkansas, and as General Sheridan is to punish those at war, and might follow them in afterwards, a second Chivington affair might occur, which I could not prevent. . . . . The Kiowas and Comanches are all of the opinion that the suit for peace by the Cheyennes and Arapahoes is not sincere beyond the chiefs who spoke, who were without doubt in earnest.

"The young men who accompanied these chiefs expressed pleasure that no peace was made, as they would get more mules, and that next spring the Sioux and northern bands were coming down and would clean out this entire country."[33]

Satanta reported in on November 10 from the raid which he had been enjoying along the Brazos near Fort Griffin. Colonel Hazen fed him because he was hungry after his recent exertions and out of supplies. By the twentieth the principal Kiowa chiefs, including Lone Wolf, Satank, and Eagle Heart, were in the vicinity of Fort Cobb, with their camps stretched up the Washita as far as Rainy Mountain Creek. Kicking Bird, Big Bow, and Woman's Heart still were absent. Kicking Bird was near Antelope Hills, but was known to be friendly. Woman's Heart was with the Cheyennes and Arapahoes, as was Big Bow, an intractable savage who had not participated in the Medicine Lodge agreement. The Quohada Comanches were on the Staked Plains. Mow-way and the Kotchatekas were in the same region. The Noconees were camped near the west end of the mountains.

On November 26 Colonel Hazen issued rations to the Indians at Fort Cobb. They went back to their camps grumbling because they could not have everything in the place.[34]

[33] *Ibid.*
[34] *Ibid.*

CHAPTER FIVE

THE NO-TREATY CHIEF

BEGINNING OF SHERIDAN'S CAMPAIGN—THE RED MOON—THE MARCH
TO FORT COBB—FINAL RECONNAISSANCE TO MEDICINE BLUFF
—BATTLE OF SOLDIER SPRING—ANNUITY DAY—ESTAB-
LISHMENT OF CAMP WICHITA—SATANTA AND LONE
WOLF RELEASED—A CONFERENCE WITHOUT A
TREATY—THE CLOSE OF THE CAMPAIGN

EARLY in November Custer's Seventh Cavalry was ready to march south against the hostile Indians. The Nineteenth Kansas Volunteer Cavalry, not being fully mobilized, was ordered to join Custer later, at the junction of Wolf Creek and Beaver Creek, in the northern part of Indian Territory. This was where General Sully's recent expedition had turned back from its pursuit of the Cheyennes. General Sheridan ordered Sully to build a supply base at that point, from which mobile columns could be sent in search of hostiles.

Under command of General Sully the Seventh Cavalry, followed by a long wagon train with its infantry escort, moved south from Fort Larned. On the way they crossed the path of a large Indian war party, headed north. Custer wanted to back-track on this trail and attack the village from which it had come, but Sully would not consent. It was learned later that the Indians had come from Black Kettle's camp, from which after being supplied with flour and ammunition by William "Dutch Bill" Griffenstein, a trader, they set forth to raid the settlements. They killed one of Sheridan's mail couriers between Fort Dodge and Fort Larned, and ran off the mules belonging to Clarke's wagon train. Then they moved to the vicinity of Fort Dodge, where they killed and scalped two civilians, one of whom was a hunter named Ralph Morrison.[1]

On their arrival at the rendezvous on Beaver Creek the men of Sully's command set to work building a stockade fort which was called Camp Supply. Here occurred one of those trivial incidents which illus-

[1] Sheridan Papers; George Hunt to author, 1935.

trates how the course of events often is influenced by the personality of the participants. General Sully was disturbed over the fact that Governor Crawford soon would arrive with the Kansas Volunteers. Crawford was a full colonel of militia. Being on active duty he would rank Sully, whose permanent rank was only lieutenant colonel. Sully sought to avoid this embarrassment by issuing an order assuming supreme command by virtue of his rank as brevet brigadier general. Lieutenant Colonel Custer, not to be outdone where brevet rank was concerned, issued an order assuming command as a brevet major general.[2]

In a few days General Sheridan arrived. He confirmed Custer's order. Sully was sent back to Kansas.

As the month wore on, Sheridan became increasingly impatient and anxious over the non-arrival of the Kansas Volunteers. Attached to the expedition were a number of civilian scouts, including Ben Clark, California Joe, Romeo, Jack "Broken Hand" Fitzpatrick, Jimmy Morrison, and others. They knew full well where the Cheyennes and Arapahoes were camped, and they told Sheridan about it repeatedly.[3] A blizzard swept across the plains from the north, burying the grass under a blanket of snow. Now was the time to strike. The Indians would be lying close in their winter camps. They would not dream that the soldiers would attack in such weather. Appreciating these facts, Sheridan ordered the Seventh Cavalry to march against the hostiles on November 23, prepared for a campaign of two weeks.

The snow continued to fall on November 22, and all through the night.

THE RED MOON[4]

Reveille on November 23 sounded two or three hours before daybreak. The snow was still drifting down in large, lazy flakes. The adjutant of the Seventh Cavalry poked his head out of his tent and surveyed the landscape doubtfully.

"Fine weather for a campaign," he remarked with heavy sarcasm.

[2] General E. S. Godfrey, "Some Reminiscences of the Washita Battle," *Cavalry Journal,* October, 1928, p. 487.

[3] General Custer had a fair idea of the general location of Black Kettle's village before he left Camp Supply. Colonel Hazen had been sending frequent reports from Fort Cobb as to where the Cheyennes were camped (Sheridan Papers).

[4] Principal authorities for description of Washita battle: Official report of Colonel G. A. Custer, Sheridan Papers; G. A. Custer, *Wild Life on the Plains* (St. Louis: Excelsior Publishing Co., 1891); Report of Phillip McCusker, Sheridan Papers; General E. S. Godfrey, "Some Reminiscences of the Washita Battle," *Cavalry Journal,* October, 1928, pp. 481-500; James A. Hadley, "The Kansas Cavalry and the Conquest of the Plains Indians," *Kansas Historical Collections,* X, 428-56; Charles J. Brill, "The Battle of the Washita," *Sunday Oklahoman,* November 10, 1935; information furnished in sign language by Ute and Henry Little Bird, Arapahoes, 1934.

"Certainly," replied Lieutenant Colonel Custer. "Just what I like. It will keep the Indians from moving around."

It was still dark when the column formed. When the order to march was given the little mounted band struck up the familiar Civil War marching air, "The Girl I Left Behind Me." The tune was jolly but the words were without significance. There was not a woman in the camp.

The Osage guides confessed that they could not distinguish landmarks through the storm. The white scouts were equally at a loss. Custer himself set the course by means of a pocket compass.

Three days later, November 26, the regiment reached the Canadian River. The sun was out, and across the dazzling white plain the low buttes of Antelope Hills stood outlined against a clear sky. Major Joel H. Elliott was sent with three companies of cavalry and a few scouts to search upstream for signs of hostile Indians. The other companies and the wagon train spent the morning floundering through the slush, ice and quicksand to the south bank of the river.

About noon Scout Jack Corbin returned with the intelligence that Elliott had found the abandoned camp of a large Indian war party. The pony tracks leading from this place pointed south; in the fresh snow it was easy to determine that the trail had been made within the past twenty-four hours. Custer surmised it was that of the band which had gone north some two weeks previously.

The young commander made a quick decision. He sent orders that Elliott should follow the trail until dark, then halt and await the main column. A bugle assembled the officers at the head of the column. They listened eagerly to what the colonel had to say. All realized that the scent was warm. All felt that the game soon would be flushed.

Custer directed that the supply train be left on the Canadian, guarded by eighty men under the officer of the day. Seven wagon-loads of ammunition and one ambulance were to accompany the column. Each trooper was to carry one hundred rounds of ammunition, hard tack and coffee for one day, and a ration of grain for his mount.

Captain Louis McLane Hamilton, a grandson of Alexander Hamilton, was officer of the day. He came to Custer in great distress. Might he not be allowed to go with his troop? The colonel was sympathetic, but would not establish precedent by changing the detail. If Hamilton could get some other officer to exchange places with him it would be all right.

Lieutenant E. G. Mathey, suffering from snow blindness, agreed to take Captain Hamilton's post with the wagons. No presentiment of any kind came to either young officer. For Louis Hamilton it was the final fork in life's trail. And there were others for whom "Boots and Saddles" had sounded for the last time.

It was nine o'clock at night before Elliott was overtaken. The men

61

had been in the saddle since four that morning, so fires were made in a sheltered draw, and the men were allowed to boil coffee. They unsaddled and unbitted the horses, and fed them a meager allowance of corn. Then the march was resumed.

No loud talking was permitted, no smoking nor lighting of matches. The bugle was stilled; commands were transmitted softly and passed from troop to troop. Two Osage trailers led the advance, followed at a little distance by Custer and a few scouts. The rest of the auxiliaries were strung out as connecting files to the main body, a half-mile to the rear. During the day a slight thaw had melted the surface of the snow; but with nightfall came zero weather, forming a crust. Through this the horses' hoofs crunched and squeaked, the sounds being carried for hundreds of yards on the still night air. A great golden moon rolled up over the eastern curve of the earth, casting long shadows beyond the writhing black serpent of troops sliding across the white breast of the prairie.

Shortly after midnight the point halted. Custer hurried forward to investigate.

"What's the matter?" he asked.

"Me don't know, but me smell fire," whispered Little Beaver.

The colonel sniffed the air skeptically. He directed two of his staff to do the same. They could detect nothing. The advance continued cautiously. Within a half-mile they came upon the smoldering embers of a small fire, evidently left by pony herders. A ripple of excitement went down the column as the news was passed along. In a few moments the guide stopped again at the crest of a little rise. He shaded his eyes from the glare of the moon on the snow.

Custer dismounted. "What now?"

"Heap Injuns down there!"

Indistinctly the commander could make out a large body of animals huddled together in the bottom of a long valley which sloped away from his feet. He expressed the opinion that it might be buffalo.

"No buffurow. Ponies," insisted the Osage. "Me heard dog bark."

At that moment Custer also heard the faint barking of a canine sentinel. Then through the sharp air came the distant tinkle of a bell as a bell-mare moved restlessly in the sharp air.

"That settles it," Custer decided. "Buffalo are not equipped with bells." And the next instant he heard the wail of an infant, far down the valley.

The officers were sent for. They were directed to remove their sabers, lest an incautious clanking be carried to the supposed village. Then they joined the commander on the crest, where he explained the situation as he conjectured it to be, and issued orders for the attack. He divided the command into four attack groups of about two hundred men each. Two were to charge the village frontally. A third commanded by Major Elliott was to circle to the east; a fourth under Captain Thompson was to make a circuit to the right for several miles and take the Indians in reverse from the southwest. Custer and his staff, the scouts, the band, and Lieutenant Cook's group of forty selected sharpshooters were to charge with the left center column.

This plan involved an advance over unexplored terrain against an enemy of unknown strength, culminating in a double envelopment. Such a maneuver implies overwhelming superiority of numbers. Custer had no information as to his relative strength. As it turned out, the village which he was about to assault consisted of only fifty-one lodges, with perhaps two hundred warriors under the ill-fated Cheyenne chieftain, Black Kettle. But below this camp, for a distance of fifteen miles, extended the entire winter encampment of the Cheyenne and Arapaho tribes, together with small bands of Kiowas under Woman's Heart, Big Bow, and Kicking Bird. Thus there were present in the immediate vicinity hostile reinforcements numbering into the thousands.

The danger inherent in a plan calling for such a wide dispersion of forces, especially since no reserve was held out, is quite apparent. It reflected, however, the impetuous nature of its author. This time luck was with General Custer. But on another field, eight years later, his famous star of fortune was to be blotted out. It may well be that his decision on that later field was influenced largely by the favorable outcome of the action of this winter morning on the Washita.

Apparently Custer and his men were not bothered with any disturbing thoughts as they huddled in the bitter cold awaiting the time of attack. Hard Rope and his Osages were full of misgivings, but said nothing. Not only were they doubtful of the wisdom of attacking on such incomplete information of the enemy, but also they feared that in the confusion they might be taken for Cheyennes and shot down by the troops. They determined to stick close to Custer—a prudent decision.

Custer notified Lieutenant James Bell to wait with the ammunition wagons until he heard the opening fire. Then he was to come forward with the extra ammunition. On the way he was to pick up the overcoats and haversacks which the men were removing and piling in heaps on the snow.

As the eastern sky began to lighten, the center columns moved forward slowly, picking their way over the uneven ground, to reach a closer position from which to launch the charge. As he approached the village, Custer could see the untended Indian pony herd drifting away to the south. A furious barking of dogs came from the village. Gray forms of tepees showed here and there through the leafless timber, with wreaths of smoke rising from two or three of the conical tops. Not an Indian was in sight. Could it be that the camp was deserted after all, that the quarry had taken alarm during the night?

Suddenly the morning quiet was ruptured by a single rifle shot from the edge of the village. A scattering rattle of carbines answered from Cook's sharpshooters. The trumpeters sounded the stirring notes of the charge. At a signal from Custer the band began to play his favorite fighting air, "Garry Owen." After a few bars the instruments froze; but already eight hundred troopers were thundering into the vortex of battle.

From sundown until just before midnight on the twenty-sixth of November the war drums had throbbed in the village of Black Kettle. A large band of braves had just returned from a successful raid on the Kansas settlements. The Cheyennes were celebrating the scalp dance around the flickering fire. Among the dancers was Eonah-pah (Trailing-the-Enemy), a Kiowa who had turned back from a recent expedition against the Utes and who, with a companion, had reached the Cheyenne village at dusk. On the way they had crossed a broad trail made by shod horses. When they arrived at the Cheyenne camp they told the Cheyennes about the trail which they had seen, but the Cheyennes only laughed at them. The other Kiowa thought that they ought not to stop at this place; it was too dangerous. Eonah-pah ignored his companion's fears. He had been reassured by the nonchalance of the Cheyennes. Besides, there was going to be a big scalp dance in Black Kettle's village. He could see several very pretty Cheyenne girls making ready for it. He intended to get a partner and participate.

And so the dance went on. The dancers, alternately young men and women, tied themselves together with rawhide ropes. It was the custom that no one could disengage himself until the dance was over.

Black Kettle and Little Robe did not take part in the dance. They were extremely uneasy. They sat in the chief's tepee, smoking thoughtfully and discussing the unfavorable result of the visit to Colonel Hazen. Black Kettle thought perhaps it would be safer to move the camp the next day.

"But before we move we will take other precautions," said Black Kettle.

"It does not seem possible that soldiers will come so far, or travel in such weather, to attack us. Neither do I think they can find us. But lest so incredible a thing should happen, we will fasten this piece of white cloth to a pole. If soldiers approach it will be the duty of the warrior on guard over the camp to raise the cloth above my lodge, in token that we are peaceful."

Late into the night the tom-toms boomed. Finally the dance was ended and the weary Indians rolled themselves in their robes and slept.

Double Wolf went forth to relieve the man who had been on watch since sundown. Everything was still. The bright moon illuminated the surrounding hillsides. A papoose wailed for a moment and was quiet. Soon the insistent, bitter cold penetrated the sentinel's blanket. He stole inside a lodge to warm himself over the dying embers of the fire. In a few moments he too was asleep.

Early in the morning a Cheyenne woman, troubled with rheumatic pains, went out to get firewood. She saw something shining on the hillside, something moving. Soldiers! Hastily she roused her children, sent them scurrying down the creek. Then she followed, afraid to shout lest the soldiers see her and shoot.[5] The savage barking of camp dogs aroused the negligent Double Wolf. He seized his rifle and went to the edge of the frozen river. A woman ran from the timber where she had gone to get her horse.

"Soldiers!" she cried.

Double Wolf listened intently, all faculties alert. Unmistakably there came the noise of many hoofs breaking through the snow, crackling the underbrush. The head of a white man appeared over a fallen tree. Thoughts of the Sand Creek tragedy raced through the Indian's mind; orders about raising the white flag were forgotten. He lifted his gun and fired.

From the distinctive black tepee of the chief came the old leader, shouting to arouse his people. With trembling fingers he strove to untie his pony, tethered close at hand. He was on its back, with his squaw up behind. As Black Kettle rode to the banks of the Washita a volley of carbine shots rang out from the woods across the stream. Double Wolf fell dead. Black Kettle slithered from his mount and flopped in the icy waters, his body half awash. More shots. The woman dropped dead beside her chief.

Two minutes after the sounding of the charge Custer, with Hamilton's and West's squadrons, was in and through the village. With him, boot to boot, rode Scout Ben Clark. The troopers fired at every blanketed fleeing figure, hacked savagely at every topknot. Many Cheyennes plunged waist deep in the icy waters of the Washita and then from the shelter of the river bank fired at the soldiers. Others ran south across the sand dunes. Thompson and Meyers drove these back into the village, or chased them south and east along the stream. Women and children cowered within the tepees, taking refuge under piles of buffalo robes; yelling Osages dragged them out by the heels. The snow became stained with blood.

Captain Meyers' column, impeded by brush and fallen timbers, moved to the right and crossed the river over a little pony ford. They charged through the west side of the village, saw no hostiles, emerged

[5] George Hunt to author, 1935.

65

on the sand bluffs to the south and engaged in individual fights with scattered warriors. Two platoons under Lieutenant E. S. Godfrey were detailed to round up the Indian horse herd.

The Indians who were not shot down in the village fled east along the Washita, wading the chill waters, or dodging along the bank. Some took refuge in gullies or behind logs and trees. With these the sharpshooters kept up a continuous exchange of shots. Seventeen Cheyennes were found dead in one of these hollows.

Troopers motioned the women and children back into the village. Some obeyed. Others ran east along the river bank.

While the turmoil was at its height, Major Elliott, seeing a group of Indians escaping down the valley, called for volunteers to make pursuit. Sergeant Major Walter Kennedy and eighteen other men responded. As the detachment moved away Elliott turned to Lieutenant Hale, waved his hand, and called cheerily:

"Here goes for a brevet or a coffin!"

The Kiowa visitor, Eonah-pah, was one of those who fled down the river. As he ran he saw little geysers sprouting up all around him in the snow where the bullets were striking. Cheyenne women and children were panting along on either side of him. Now and then one of them would fall in a heap.

"Scatter out!" shouted the Kiowa. "Don't bunch up so much."

A squad of blue-clad riders dashed to intercept the fugitives. One of them charged Eonah-pah with drawn saber. The Kiowa stopped short, fitted an arrow to the string, loosed it at the cavalryman. The arrow missed its mark. Dodging the flashing blade, Eonah-pah drove a shaft into the horse. The wounded beast reared abruptly, threw its rider. The Indian was able to gain many yards on his pursuers.

More of Meyers' and Thompson's men appeared. The low bluffs on either side of the Washita resounded with gun shots, yells, shrill whoops. Women and children screamed in fright and pain. Dogs barked and howled. The valley was a bedlam of noise.

Soon Eonah-pah's quiver was empty. But he had assisted twenty Cheyenne women to escape the uniformed terror. He ran to the river bank. Down the stream came Little Rock (second in command to Black Kettle), and She Wolf, accompanied by a number of other women. Eonah-pah joined them. Before the fugitives lay a deep pool in the stream. They must climb the bank to avoid it. As they emerged into view they were spied by Elliott and his volunteers. At once the troopers turned that way.

Pistol shots hurtled into the little group of Indians. The chief fell dead. Eonah-pah seized the Cheyenne's full quiver. He fired several arrows in quick succession, then ran. Soon he was safe in the timber which lay two miles east of Black Kettle's village.[6] Other refugees, farther east, were not so fortunate. Buffalo-Woman fell exhausted in the snow. Elliott detailed a near-by soldier to lead her back to camp. This man was Sergeant Major Kennedy. His horse was lame. Kennedy dismounted and motioned the woman to walk back to the village. The rest of the soldiers continued east in pursuit of a group of young Indian boys.

Suddenly from the river bank to the north appeared a group of Indians, riding hard. Straight at Kennedy they came. He fired once. One of the horses swerved. Then his carbine jammed. Frantically he worked with the mechanism. Bob-tailed Bear led the charge. His hatchet rose and fell. The soldier's body slumped to the ground; his skull was broken in bits. A few yards to the east of where he lay a little creek trickled unheeding on its way to join the Washita. From that day on it has been called Sergeant Major Creek.

East of this creek Elliott was pursuing several half-grown Cheyenne boys. He had not reached the timber when there emerged to his front a swarm of mounted Indians—Cheyennes and Arapahoes arriving from the lower camps. Their scarlet-and-white war bonnets gleamed in the light of the winter sun. It seemed that there were hundreds of them. Elliott's detachment stopped short. Then they turned to withdraw to the main command.

Too late! Other warriors, fresh from killing Kennedy, appeared in Elliott's rear, on the east side of the tributary. Elliott was cut off. More hostiles were arriving every moment. They were circling the little band of soldiers, riding closer and closer, whooping shrilly, shooting as they flashed past.

The soldiers moved back slowly until they were within pistol range of the little creek. From its banks could be seen feathered heads bobbing, brown arms signaling to other savages. There were more Indians than eighteen men could handle. Elliott had to make a quick decision. He dismounted his men and turned the horses loose. He ordered his men to lie down in a thicket of tall grass.

It was the worst thing Elliott could have done. He violated thus the basic principle of defensive combat. He sacrificed a good field of fire. His men could not see out of the thicket; the high banks of the opposite stream dominated the position and furnished shelter to the dismounted Indian riflemen.

Touching-the-Sky found a place from which he could look right down into the thicket. There in its very center he saw the soldiers lying in a circle with their feet to the inside. Little piles of cartridges lay ready beside each man. The whites were not far away; he commenced shooting

---

[6] George Bent to Robert Peck, in article by James Hadley, *loc. cit.*, pp. 441-42.

at them. It was very easy. He motioned some of his friends to join him.[7] The swelling horde rode round and round the beleaguered cavalrymen, sending showers of arrows and bullets into the weeds. Few shots replied from the thicket. Elliott's ammunition was running low. He only hoped now to hold out until reinforcements came.

The fight did not last long. Probably not much over an hour. The shots from the tall grass grew more and more infrequent. The yelling, revolving mass of Indians drew closer and closer. At length a belated brave arrived from the lower village; he was freshly painted and feathered. It was Smokey (or Tobacco), an Arapaho. He had taken too much time with his ceremonial toilet. Was he too late to win a coup?

With an earnest yell Smokey thrust himself through the circle of Indians and charged into the thicket. The whole horde followed like flotsam sucked into a whirlpool. There was a brief, terrific tussle; a chorus of shots, thuds, groans. When the heap was untangled, Smokey was found lying at the bottom. He was dead.

The bluecoats too lay still. The Indians turned them over. There was the young major. Most of them had seen him many times before, at the treaty grounds at Medicine Lodge. Those who had not made coup deliberately fired arrows or bullets into the unresisting bodies. It was good medicine. Then She Wolf led the squaws up from the creek bottom where they had been resting after the pursuit. With knives and hatchets they completed the ghastly work. No enemy must be left in such condition that his spirit could follow the Indians into the night.

Did Custer know what was happening to Elliott? No one can say for sure. The commander was busy mopping up the village—burning tepees, examining evidences that the Indians had participated in the Kansas raids. Stolen albums of daguerrotypes, unopened mail, household implements from murdered settlers' cabins—all testified to the guilt of the Cheyennes. While this was going on, four soldiers carried Captain Hamilton's body in and laid it tenderly on the ground before the colonel. Hamilton had died instantly from a shot through the heart. He had fallen at the head of his squadron, in the first rush to the village. Captain Barnitz too was wounded—seriously. They thought he would die. A number of enlisted men were down. Elliott had not been seen since his detachment rode away to the east.

Lieutenant Godfrey had rounded up the herd of seven hundred Indian ponies against the bluffs south of the village. After completing this task he led his platoon to the north bank and pursued fleeing Cheyennes east along the ridges. Two miles away he topped a high hill and made an alarming discovery. In front of him in the river valley were hundreds of tepees, in front of which, and to either side as far as his vision extend-

[7] *Ibid.*

ed, were groups of mounted, circling warriors. It was the Indian signal for combat.

Godfrey retired at once. But the Indians had seen him. They rode to attack. The platoon retreated by successive rushes, the odd-numbered files halting to cover the withdrawal of the even-numbered, and vice versa. On the south side of the river Godfrey could hear continuous heavy firing. But the thick timber screened from his sight the tragedy which was being enacted there. At length he reached the safety of the village.

Custer stood thoughtfully in the center of the ruined camp. Godfrey told him of the big villages which he had seen to the east. Custer was interested immediately. The lieutenant also described the firing which he had heard; he thought that it might be where Elliott was.

The colonel pondered for a moment, then replied slowly, "No, I don't think so. Colonel Meyers has been down there all morning, and probably would have reported it."

Increasing numbers of Indians began to appear on the ridges surrounding the valley. Custer became alarmed. The day was growing shorter. Ammunition was running low. He was worried about his wagon train, which had been left on the Canadian, many miles to the north. What if the Indians should learn that it was there, inadequately guarded? Lieutenant Bell had brought the ammunition wagons safely through the hostile ring, but he had been unable to save the overcoats and haversacks.[8] These had fallen into the hands of the Indians. The command was alone in a hostile wilderness, in subzero weather, without food, overcoats, or shelter. They would perish if they lost the wagon train.

Then there was the question of what to do with the captured horses. Custer would have preferred to take them with him. But the animals were too wild to be managed. The Indians must be punished thoroughly; Custer knew full well that the horse herd represented their principal wealth. So he gave orders to have the animals destroyed. This was a painful duty for the men, but they went to work with pistols. The horses, after being shot, broke away and ran bleeding in all directions. In this way the snow on the great bend of the river was made red with blood. For this reason the Indians call it the "Red Moon."

The watching Indians were wild with rage and grief. But they could do nothing. They dared not fire into the village for fear of striking their women and children held captive there. They could only press anxiously forward, closer to the camp. Custer detailed a squadron to drive them back. The skirmishing continued until late in the afternoon.

Toward evening the regiment was formed in column to withdraw. There was no time to search for the missing Elliott; it seemed certain

[8] Information given by Captain James Bell to W. H. Quinette.

69

that he and his men were dead. There was only slight hope that they had broken through and would join the column on the Canadian.

Custer moved east, feinting as if to attack the other villages. The surprised Indians withdrew before him. Suddenly they vanished into the woods along the great bend of the river. Perhaps they were preparing an ambush. But Custer did not make an effort to follow; he turned abruptly north into the gathering darkness. Long after midnight he halted to rest the horses. The keen frosty air bit through the shoddy blue tunics of the men. They were numb with cold and fatigue. But after a brief rest the march was resumed.

In the morning Custer found the wagon train safely corralled where he had left it. The next night Osage scouts, who had remained to watch the hostiles, came in with the story that Major Elliott and all of his men were dead. Soon the news reached the ears of the Cheyenne captives. Their hearts chilled. Which of them would be put to death in retaliation? They had no doubt that this would be done. It was the custom among the Indians.

Mahwissa, sister of Black Kettle, was deputized to approach the yellow-haired soldier chief on the subject. Accompanied by Ben Clark and Romeo she went up to where Custer sat. She asked how many of her people would be slain for Elliott. Custer covered his face with his hands in grief, and made no reply. A soldier started to drive the woman away. But the colonel raised his head and called her back. "Tell her that white soldiers do not kill captives," he said. When Mahwissa brought the answer to the huddled group of prisoners there was no outward rejoicing. But the captives built a big fire, and accepted meat for the first time. The medicine man said that the smoke rose straight to the sky as a symbol that the Great Spirit was with them, and would lead them safely back to the tribe.

THE MARCH TO FORT COBB

Custer's command returned jubilantly to Camp Supply, reporting that they had killed one hundred and three Cheyennes and had taken fifty-three prisoners. General Sheridan was anxious to follow up this victory by an immediate thrust with the entire column. But the Kansas regiment, which had just arrived, was not in shape for a campaign; the horses, in particular, were greatly fatigued, so that many of the Kansans were dismounted. Several days were spent refitting both regiments; then, on December 7, the whole force headed for Fort Cobb, from which point Sheridan planned to follow the Indians into the Wichita Mountains. The march was directed via Custer's recent battlefield; Sheridan was anxious to inspect it for some trace of Elliott.

Black Kettle's burned village was found in the condition in which

Custer had left it. Wolves and crows were feeding on the carcasses of the horses and on unburied Indian dead. Riding along the south bank of the river with a few of his staff Sheridan came upon the bodies of Elliott's detachment. They were naked, frozen, and horribly mutilated. Two wagons were sent to bring them in to camp. That night large fires were built, by the light of which comrades identified all but two of the pitiful remains. Then they were buried in a trench on the crest of a knoll overlooking the valley. Major Elliott's body was taken to Fort Arbuckle, thence sent to Fort Gibson.[9]

That evening the surgeon of the Nineteenth Kansas Volunteers found in an abandoned Indian camp the body of a white woman and that of a little boy about two years old. The woman had been shot in the forehead and the child killed by striking his head against a tree. The next morning the woman was laid on a blanket with the child on her arm. The frontier boys of the Kansas regiment were marched past to see if any could recognize her. The solemn-faced men saw the small figure of a young woman of unusual beauty, about twenty-two years old. Someone identified her as Mrs. Clara Blinn, who had been captured near Fort Lyon by Arapahoes. General Hazen had been negotiating for her release, but when Custer made his attack the Indians killed both the woman and her child. This sad discovery made General Sheridan and his men eager to strike the Kiowas a heavy blow; for they were under the impression that Mrs. Blinn had been the prisoner of Satanta. But that chief, accomplished kidnapper though he was, had been exercising his peculiar talents in Texas at the time Mrs. Blinn was taken.

On the march down the Washita the column followed for many miles the trace of an old wagon road. This was a surprising thing, for this part of the country was thought to be inhabited only by wild Indians who possessed no wheeled vehicles. It was Captain Marcy's old trail, made in '49 when he guided a party of immigrants to California.[10]

Drag-marks made by many Indian travois also were seen, all headed toward Fort Cobb. Sheridan surmised from this that the Kiowas and Comanches had been present at the Battle of the Washita, and that they had fled from there to the protection of the agency. The officers felt that one branch of the government—the Department of the Interior—was protecting the hostiles, while the War Department was fighting them.

Sheridan was mistaken, or at least partially so, in his estimate of the activities of the Kiowas and Comanches. The Kiowas had indeed been camped on the upper Washita, hunting buffalo. But, with the exception of the small bands previously noted, they had moved downstream before

[9] Old Files of Fort Arbuckle.
[10] Also followed in 1853–54 by Lieutenant Whipple. James McGranahan, who recalls seeing this road, was one of Custer's wagonmasters during the Washita campaign.

71

the fight took place. On the very day it was fought most of them were at the mouth of Rainy Mountain Creek. They learned of the affair through Big Bow and Woman's Heart. Immediately upon hearing of Black Kettle's fate the whole tribe stampeded and moved off toward the western terminus of the Wichita Mountains. Here they joined the Cheyennes and Arapahoes who had fled from Custer's battlefield.

On December 2 the consolidated Indian camps were at the mouth of Sweetwater Creek, a tributary of the North Fork of Red River. On that day a big powwow was held among all these Indians. The Kiowas and Comanches expressed sympathy for the Cheyennes and Arapahoes. There was much talk of joining them in a general war against the whites; but the advice of cooler heads prevailed.

Eagle Heart, a Kiowa chief, was the first to get over his fright. He returned to Rainy Mountain Creek, followed by Satanta. Here Captain Henry Alvord talked to the Indians, trying to reassure them. Lone Wolf also came in, so that by December 10 three-fourths of the Kiowa tribe were camped once more along the Washita, upstream from Fort Cobb. Most of the Comanches were in the immediate vicinity of Fort Cobb; only the Quohadas and a few other small bands remained out. The Quohadas were, as usual, in the Staked Plains; a band of Noconees was at Soldier Spring, and Woman's Heart's Kiowas were at Sheep Mountain, five miles east of Soldier Spring.[11]

On the sixteenth the Kiowas who were on Rainy Mountain Creek heard from their scouts that a big body of soldiers was approaching from the northwest. The skittish ones packed up their lodges and began to move. Several of the chiefs asked Hazen for some further guarantee of protection, but Colonel Hazen had seen so much of the insolence of the Kiowas, and had heard so much concerning their activities in Texas, that he was disinclined to shield them. Nevertheless, he had received the following positive instructions from General Sherman: "Every appearance about Fort Cobb should be suggestive of an earnest desire to afford a place of refuge where the peaceable Indian may receive food and be safe against the troops, as well as against hostile Indians who may try to involve them in the common war. If you have not already notified General Sheridan of the fact that some of the Kiowas are peaceful, get word to him in some way, lest he pursue them and stampede your whole family." Furthermore it was unthinkable to Hazen that he should permit a repetition of the Chivington affair; especially since the Indians were

---

[11] Soldier Spring derived its name during the eighties, from the fact that troops from Fort Sill and Fort Reno camped there while patrolling the cattle trail. It is at the base of the mountains southwest of Tepee Mountain. There is another spring of the same name farther north. Sheep Mountain, named by the Kiowas for their fraternity of warriors called the "Society of Wild Sheep," is a short distance east of the junction of the North Fork and Elk Creek.

under his official protection. Consequently, he wrote the following letter, which he sent out by two mounted orderlies:

"FORT COBB, 9 P. M., Dec. 16, 1868.

"To the officer commanding troops in the field:

"Indians have just brought in word that our troops today reached the Washita some twenty miles above here. I send this to say that all camps this side of the point reported to have been reached, are friendly, and have not been on the warpath this season. If this reaches you, it would be well to communicate at once with Satanta or Black Eagle, chiefs of the Kiowas, near where you now are, who will readily inform you of the positions of the Cheyennes and Arapahoes, also of my camp.

"Respectfully, W. B. HAZEN."

Colonel Hazen's couriers were captured en route by the Kiowas, and held as hostages. On the seventeenth the Indians made contact with the troops on the high ground west of where Mountain View now stands. Satanta and Lone Wolf rode forward to parley with Colonels Custer and Crosby, offering to shake hands. The officers, who fancied they could see innocent blood dripping from the brown fingers, refused the civility.

Custer was in favor of attacking at once. But Sheridan restrained him. The letter from Colonel Hazen was received and studied.

Here was a puzzle. After the army had been thrown against the Indians in an announced effort to punish them and drive them to the reservation, another department of the Federal government interfered to halt the campaign, just when success seemed assured. Should the Department of the Interior be obeyed, or should the war continue? Sheridan decided that though he personally was sure that the Indians were hostile, he would give them the benefit of the doubt. But he insisted that they give proof of their pacific intentions by accompanying him to the Fort Cobb agency. The short reception accorded the chiefs, and the scowling attitude of the officers convinced Santana and Lone Wolf they were not among friends. Perhaps they were not properly understood.

"Where is that fellow who speaks English?" yelled Satanta at some of his warriors who were hanging back coyly. A buck named Walking Bird was shoved to the front.

"Now, Walking Bird, let us hear you use some of the white man's language. Go ahead talk to them," the chiefs ordered.

Walking Bird puffed visibly at being thrown into the limelight. He once had loafed around Fort Dodge, and had what he thought was a perfect command of the English language.

"Gimme blat," he announced.[12]

[12] George Hunt to author, 1935. Years after this occurrence the discredited Walking Bird still insisted that he spoke perfect English, the trouble being that nobody understood it properly.

The officers looked bewildered.

"Por-dodge" was the next bit of "English," likewise bringing no response from the soldiers.

As a last resort Walking Bird attempted a bit of what he thought was flattery. He had heard the soldiers at Fort Dodge address their horses in what sounded like a term of endearment. So he went up to the great white chief, patted him affectionately on the arm and said, "Heap big nice sonabitch. Heap sonabitch!"

The officers understood this perfectly, but their reaction was not all that the Indians desired. Lone Wolf and Satanta thought it best to withdraw, and acted accordingly. The members of Sheridan's staff drew their pistols and made prisoners of them.

Satanta's eldest son, Tsa'l-au-te, impressed into service as messenger between the two chiefs and the rest of the tribe, was sent to inform the Kiowas that they must come in at once, and accompany the troops to Fort Cobb. But the Kiowas, who already were in motion in a southwesterly direction, when they heard that Satanta and Lone Wolf were forcibly restrained, accelerated their gait. They did not slacken in their headlong flight until they reached Elk Creek, twenty miles away.

The Indians at Fort Cobb also were alarmed by the approach of the formidable body of soldiers. They stayed where they were, but their sensitiveness and fright were beyond description. Hazen says that they did not go to bed, but sat up all night, showing the whites of their eyes. They kept their ears cocked, and their ponies saddled for immediate flight.

Custer's force went into camp just west of the stockade, about where the town of Fort Cobb now stands. They were glad to arrive; but the contingent from Fort Arbuckle was even happier to see them. They had been greatly humiliated, they said, by the overbearing attitude of the savages. Everything would be different now. And so it was. Satanta and Lone Wolf were kept in close confinement in a guarded tent. Each day they promised that their people would arrive. Each day came and went without sign of the Kiowas. Finally General Sheridan's short Irish patience was exhausted.

"Tell those Indians," he said to Custer, "that if their villages are not here by sundown tomorrow I will hang them both to the nearest tree."

Colonel Custer delivered the ultimatum in person. Satanta and Lone Wolf did not lose their stoicism. But in a few moments their heads were together and a great deal of hasty jabbering went on. Soon Satanta's heir was seen galloping across the prairie to the southwest. Shortly after noon on the following day the Kiowas commenced to arrive. In a few hours all were present, as nearly as could be determined. Actually Woman's Heart's band was still out, camped at Sheep Mountain.

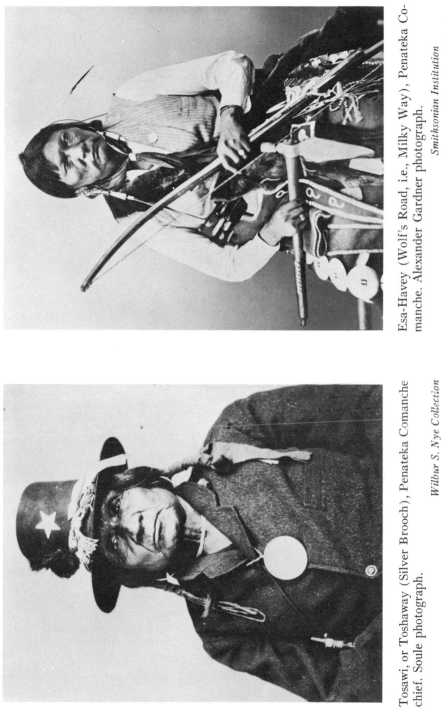

Tosawi, or Toshaway (Silver Brooch), Penateka Comanche chief. Soule photograph.

Wilbur S. Nye Collection

Esa-Havey (Wolf's Road, i.e., Milky Way), Penateka Comanche. Alexander Gardner photograph.

Smithsonian Institution
Bureau of American Ethnology

Buffalo-skin tipis of Plains Indians about 1869. Note brass bucket for water and cooking and buffalo meat drying on rack. Soule photograph.

Smithsonian Institution
Bureau of American Ethnology

Wichita grass house near Anadarko, photographed by Soule about 1874. This is the type seen by the Dragoon expedition in 1834.

Set-ankea or Set-angia (Sitting Bear) usually
called Satank by the whites. Soule photograph.

Wilbur S. Nye Collection

Set-tain-te (White Bear), commonly called
Satanta, a Kiowa chief. This is one of Soule's
earliest Indian portraits, made at Fort Dodge
about 1867.

Wilbur S. Nye Collection

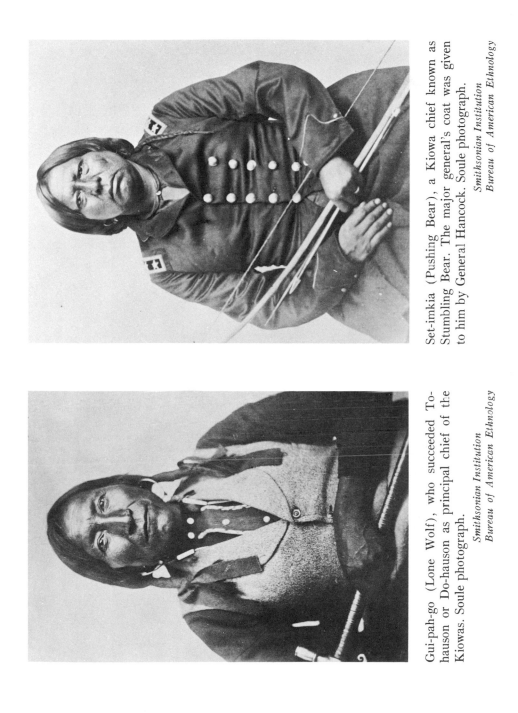

Gui-pah-go (Lone Wolf), who succeeded To-hauson or Do-hauson as principal chief of the Kiowas. Soule photograph.

Set-imkia (Pushing Bear), a Kiowa chief known as Stumbling Bear. The major general's coat was given to him by General Hancock. Soule photograph.

Tay-nay-angopte (Eagle-Striking-with-Talons), known as Kicking Bird, prominent Kiowa chief and leader of peace faction. Soule photograph.

Smithsonian Institution
Bureau of American Ethnology

Zepko-ette (Big Bow), Kiowa war chief. Soule photograph.

Smithsonian Institution
Bureau of American Ethnology

Ts'al-aute (Cry of the Wild Goose), usually called Saloso by the whites, oldest son of Satanta. Soule photograph.

Smithsonian Institution
Bureau of American Ethnology

Mamay-day-te (Medicine Standing Bundles), who succeeded Lone Wolf as principal chief of the Kiowas and took his name. Soule photograph.

Smithsonian Institution
Bureau of American Ethnology

Tabananica (Hears-the-Sunrise), a Comanche chief.

Towakani Jim, Wichita scout, with Van Dorn in 1858. Soule photograph, about 1874.

Pacer, head chief of the Kiowa-Apaches. Soule photograph.

Man-yi-ten (Woman's Heart), Kiowa chief. Soule photograph.

Esse-too-yah-tay (Striding-along-in-the-Dusk), Penateka Comanche. Soule photograph.

Tir-ha-ya-quahip (Sore-backed Horse), known as Horseback, a Nokoni (or Noconee) Comanche chief, signer of Medicine Lodge Treaty. Soule photograph.

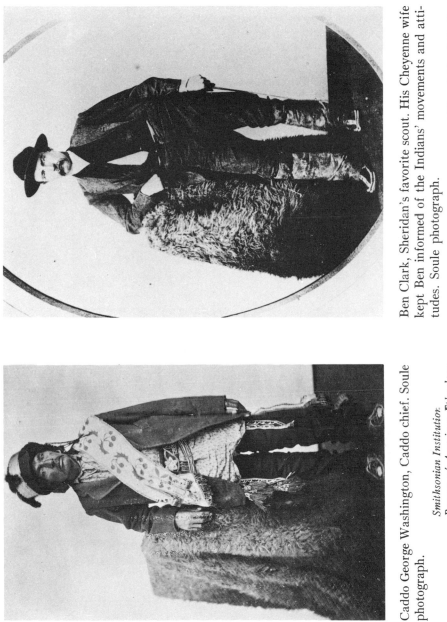

Caddo George Washington, Caddo chief. Soule photograph.

Smithsonian Institution
Bureau of American Ethnology

Ben Clark, Sheridan's favorite scout. His Cheyenne wife kept Ben informed of the Indians' movements and attitudes. Soule photograph.

Wilbur S. Nye Collection

Addo-ette (Big Tree), Kiowa raider. Soule photograph.

Tsain-tainte (White Horse), Kiowa chief. Soule photograph.

Mow-way, or Mowi (Push Aside), known as Shak-ing Hand, a Kotchateka Comanche chief. Soule photograph.

Wilbur S. Nye Collection

Ho-wea (Gap-in-the-Woods), Nokoni Comanche chief. Soule photograph.

Wilbur S. Nye Collection

Gui-tain (Young Wolf's Heart), nephew of Lone Wolf, killed with Tau-ankia. Soule photograph.

Kobay (Wild Horse), second chief of the Quohada Comanches. Soule photograph.

Kicking Bird's village, perhaps near Rainy Mountain Creek. Soule photograph.

Fort Sill Museum

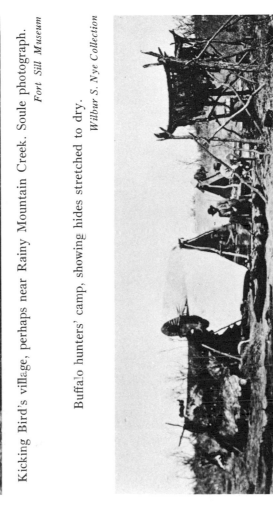

Buffalo hunters' camp, showing hides stretched to dry.

Wilbur S. Nye Collection

Parra-o-coom (Bull Bear), head chief of the Quohada Comanches, in his camp near Fort Sill in the winter of 1872, when he was trying to secure the release of his women and children. Soule photograph.

Brevet Major General Benjamin Grierson, Colonel, 10th Cavalry.

U.S. Army

Grierson's reconnaissance to the site of Fort Sill. This Soule photograph shows Grierson, in foreground, and his party at Medicine Bluffs on December 28, 1868.

U.S. Army

John S. Evans (second from left), early post trader at Fort Sill, with party of hunters visiting Horseback's camp near Fort Sill. Soule photograph.

Fort Sill Museum

Fort Sill under construction—officers' quarters on the east line. Soule photograph.

Wilbur S. Nye Collection

Old cavalry stables at Fort Sill. In background is trader's store (left) and
Grierson's first house, later Fort Sill "Hotel."

Wilbur S. Nye Collection

North line of officers' quarters, 1872. The house where Sherman stayed in 1871 is in center.

Fort Sill, looking east from the guardhouse. Soule photograph.

Blockhouse on Signal Mountain, familiar Fort Sill landmark.

Wilbur S. Nye Collection

Stone corral built in 1870 to prevent Indians from stealing quartermaster mules.

U.S. Army

Cell under barracks where Indians were held prisoner. Soule photograph.

Kiowa-Comanche agency headquarters, northwest of Quarry Hill. This was one of two issue warehouses, built side by side, and also contained the agent's dwelling and office. The rest of the agency buildings were located east of the air field at Fort Sill. Left to right: Geo. Smith, clerk; Mrs. Smith; Henry Lamb, cook; Mrs. Tatum; Lawrie Tatum, first agent. Soule photograph.

Gay house party at Fort Sill in the 1880's.

Captain S. R. H. "Tommy" Tompkins, 7th Cavalry, entertaining children of Captain Hugh L. Scott, post quartermaster.

Philip McCusker, scout and interpreter, and Buffalo Good (or Goad), Wichita chief.

Camp of U.S. Indian scouts (Troop L, 7th Cavalry) at Fort Sill.

Wilbur S. Nye Collection

Apache village north of Medicine Bluff.

Fort Sill Museum

Fort Sill in the 1880's.

The Old Post in 1969.

Fort Sill in 1877, from a water color by Brigadier General S. B. Holabird.

Sunday morning inspection.

General Ranald S. Mackenzie.

Fort Sill Museum

Simpson E. "Jack" Stilwell, noted plainsman and U.S. scout.

Fort Sill Museum

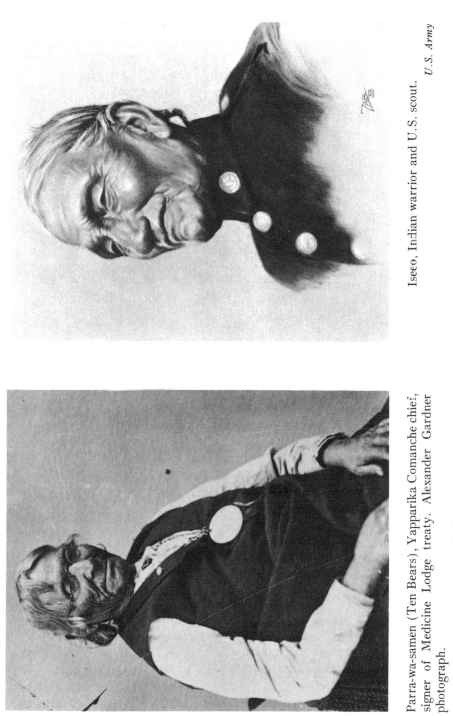

Parra-wa-samen (Ten Bears), Yapparika Comanche chief, signer of Medicine Lodge treaty. Alexander Gardner photograph.

Smithsonian Institution
Bureau of American Ethnology

Iseeo, Indian warrior and U.S. scout.   *U.S. Army*

Isa-tai and his family, Quohada Comanche.

The Kiowas state today that the message delivered by Satanta's son contained no reference to the fact that the two chiefs were threatened with hanging. They were told that if they arrived at Fort Cobb by sundown they all would be given large quantities of free rations. They state that if they had known that Satanta and Lone Wolf would be hanged, they would not have come in at all. Satanta and Lone Wolf remained in confinement, pending decision as to what was to be done with them.

The soldiers did not know how long they would have to remain at Fort Cobb. Sheridan wrote to Sherman that he intended to stay there until his horses were in better shape, then he might go to Fort Arbuckle for supplies. In view of this the men decided to make themselves comfortable for the winter. They dug little three-man pits, with a sod fireplace in the end of each, and shelter tents for roofs.

Presently it commenced to rain. The water came down intermittently but in heavy showers. The downpour softened the whole landscape. Little rivulets trickled into the dugouts. The men were not required to shave. Bathing was unpopular. In a few days the soldiers looked and smelled like tramps. Horses were dying on the picket lines. Forage ordered from a contractor named Shirley had not been delivered. The Indian horses had cropped off the prairie grass for miles in every direction. Cottonwood trees were cut down and the animals were allowed to browse on the tender tops, but it was a poor substitute for grain and hay.

"This is a hell of a place," Sheridan snorted. "Grierson, how about that camp of yours at Medicine Bluff?"

Colonel Grierson replied that it was ideal.

"The grass may have burned off since you were there last summer," the General pointed out. "I want you to take an escort and inspect the place once more. See if there is sufficient grazing for all the animals. I want a complete report on its suitability as the site of a permanent post to replace Forts Cobb and Arbuckle."

FINAL RECONNAISSANCE TO MEDICINE BLUFF

Colonel Grierson made up a reconnaissance party consisting of himself, Colonel Hazen, Colonel Forsythe of Sheridan's staff, Captain Clous, Lieutenant S. L. Woodward, and Mr. Randolph Keim, a journalist. The escort was composed of forty cavalrymen from the Tenth, commanded by Lieutenant Doyle. The interpreter was Phillip McCusker, and the guide was Asa-Toyeh (Gray Leggings), a Penateka Comanche.[13]

The expedition left Fort Cobb at nine o'clock on the morning of December 27, 1868. At eleven the following morning they arrived north of Medicine Bluff. Here they paused to admire the scenery. It was a

[13] De B. Randolph Keim, *Sheridan's Troopers on the Borders* (Philadelphia: David McKay, 1885), pp. 231-51.

damp, misty day, with a biting chill in the air which portended an approaching storm.

Medicine Bluff had been known for years to the Indians as a semi-sacred locality. It was the custom for young braves, before undertaking any warlike feat, to climb to the top of the hill for a period of meditation and fasting. Visions and hallucinations caused by this fasting were described to the medicine men, whose interpretation thereof was followed scrupulously. It was considered beneficial also to carry sick or ailing members of the tribe to a low rock altar built on top of the bluff. Here they were left to recover or perish according to the will of the Great Spirit. It was on account of these associations that the peculiar cliff formation became known as Medicine Bluff. Medicine meant anything supernatural—pertaining to religion—as well as to medicinal cure as the white man thinks of it.

Grierson's party amused themselves in the manner of the white man by firing shots at the cliff to listen to the echoes set up. The Comanche guide, Asa-Toyeh, was scandalized. When it was proposed to cross the intervening stream and scale the medicine hill he obstinately refused to go along, exclaiming, "Me no sick!"

The officers crossed Medicine Bluff Creek at the place known later as White Wolf Ford. Leaving the escort in the little gorge at the eastern base of Bluff Number 1, they ascended the slopes on foot. They collected specimens of a peculiar flowering cactus found clinging among the broken granite boulders. From the summit they admired the view. Eight miles to the northwest Mount Scott thrust its shoulders magnificently through a shroud of mist. On the slopes of Mount Hinds (then unnamed) was a small herd of buffalo, grazing peacefully, unaware of the presence of intruders. On the flats to the south they saw Asa-Toyeh galloping madly in pursuit of a single bison.

The distant crack of his rifle reminded them that it was time for lunch. They descended to the canyon where they had left their horses. Here were little springs of saline and sulphur oozing from the earth. The trampled condition of the ground indicated that animals of all kinds frequented the locality in search of salt. Several of the party wished to camp in the vicinity. The shooting should be excellent, they suggested. Grierson would not hear of it. He could smell a norther coming. He was anxious to finish the reconnaissance and return to Cobb.

The party mounted and rode east toward the camp site of the previous summer. It was plain that the area had been undisturbed. There remained plenty of good grass, and plenty of clear water. Near the site of the present Fort Sill Theater they came upon Asa-Toyeh's squaw cutting up the carcass of a buffalo which her lord had killed. The soldiers of the escort appropriated all of the meat not already packed by Madam

76

Asa-Toyeh. They went a little farther to the banks of the creek, near Quinette Crossing, where they built fires. Broiled buffalo steaks smelled good, and tasted better.

After lunch the party divided. Colonel Grierson sent the escort north to the place where they had camped on the previous night, approximately where the town of Apache now is. After an additional short inspection of the locality he too would turn north and meet them there. With Adjutant Woodward and Writer Keim he set out to locate some coal veins which he had heard of on his visit during the summer. If it were true that coal existed in the area, the site for a post was ideal. At Fort Arbuckle they had been required to haul it from Boggy Depot.

En route to the coal deposits the party crossed the little plateau where, a year later, Fort Sill was built. They saw again the remains of the old Wichita Indian village—circular fireplace depressions, heaps of trash, burned stubs of cedar frameworks—all covered with a scattered growth of vines. Then they forded Cache Creek and proceeded toward what is known now as Feigel Point. Here they examined a slaty deposit, with a trace of coal too slight to be of value. On top of Adams Hill they found some Indian "medicine," a heavy exudation of petroleum or asphalt. The Indians used it as salve on the sore backs of their animals. Years later, after they had been introduced to the refinements of civilization, they went there to gather it for use as chewing gum.

The clouds were settling over the face of the prairie. It would be dark soon. The explorers turned north. All along the creek beds they started game—deer, an occasional buffalo, furtive wolves and coyotes. Once Grierson rode too near the edge of the high banks along Cache Creek. His horse slipped and precipitated the colonel down the slope. The other two men rushed up, expecting to find a casualty. But Grierson puffed up the steep bank and climbed unhurt into his saddle. From his long black beard rumbled a vigorous sample of the language for which he was noted.[14]

Night came before the trio reached the rendezvous. And with night came cold rain, blown flat by a north wind. For a time they thought they were lost. Not a light showed through the darkness. Finally came the welcome challenge of a sentry. The members of the escort were huddled in their tents on wet ground. The rain-soaked firewood would not burn.

Since no one could sleep, they made an early departure for Fort Cobb. It was a dangerous trip. The rain had changed to sleet. The wind came with such force that the horses tried to turn their backs to it. It was with difficulty that the men kept them headed north. Eventually it became an endurance contest, each man for himself, each hoping to be one of those to get back before he froze. Luckily, all arrived safely at Fort Cobb, with no injuries except a few cases of frostbite.

[14] Data on Colonel Grierson furnished by Mrs. Charles Grierson, Los Angeles.

On December 30, the day following Grierson's return from Medicine Bluff, General Sheridan listened to reports of the officers who had accompanied the expedition. He decided, as a result of the recommendations made by Grierson and Hazen, to abandon Fort Cobb and move to the new site as soon as the incessant rains should subside.

During the day Indians in the surrounding camps received information from fugitives coming in from the southwest that a village of Comanches had been attacked by white men near the western end of the Wichita Mountains. They said that the whites were soldiers or Texans, they did not know which, and that they were driving a herd of cattle with them. Reports of this matter were made to General Sheridan. At first he was inclined to consider it a baseless rumor, but the white scouts insisted that the Indians were telling a straight story. At noon a staff officer, Lieutenant Edward Hunter, from Colonel Evans' Fort Bascom column, arrived at Fort Cobb. He reported that Evans had destroyed an Indian village on Christmas day, and was now camped near the mouth of Rainy Mountain Creek.[15]

Major A. W. Evans (brevet lieutenant colonel) left Fort Bascom, New Mexico, November 17, 1868, with six companies of the Third Cavalry, one company of the Thirty-Seventh Infantry, and a battery of mountain howitzers. He marched down the Canadian River for a distance of 185 miles to the mouth of Monument Creek. Here a small redoubt was constructed, in which Evans left his impedimenta, guarded by a small detachment. He left all his tentage behind, and took only three wagons to carry ammunition.

The march was continued through snow, sleet, and intense cold toward Antelope Hills. Near these hills Evans struck the broad trail made by the Cheyennes fleeing south after the Battle of the Washita. He crossed the Canadian River and followed this trail south until on December 23 he came in sight of Headquarters Mountains.[16] The North Fork of Red River runs southeast toward another group of rough, granite mountains. Evans' Mexican guides told him that these were the Sierra Jumanes (Wichitas). Evans could see that the trail of the Indians had turned southeast into the canyon formed by the North Fork. The water in the stream was impregnated with gypsum and salt; the grass in the surrounding plains had been burned off by the Indians. For these reasons Evans decided to pass south of the mountains in order to find forage for

---

[15] Lieutenant Edward Hunter, in *Army and Navy Journal* (Washington, D.C.), March 13, 1869; P. H. Sheridan, *Personal Memoirs*, pp. 336-37; Sheridan's official report, Vol. A 10, Old Records Section, AGO.

[16] Called *Cejas Sabinas* by the Mexican guides. The town of Granite, Oklahoma, stands today at the south end of these mountains.

his animals; he hoped to pick up the Indian trail on the other side of the canyon.[17]

Early on December 24 the column crossed the North Fork and marched south and southeast over an extensive prairie which sloped gradually to the south. During the day occasional Indians were seen hovering in the distance. Before long it was evident that the Indians had not emerged from the southeast end of the gorge. No trail was crossed. Evans halted for the night, making a dry camp on the bleak plains. The troops spent a Christmas eve devoid of cheer.

On Christmas morning Evans turned the head of his command northeast, hoping to strike the trail of the hostiles at the eastern exit of the gap. A biting wind drove thin snow in the faces of the men. The ground was white in patches. The soldiers grew colder as the hours passed. The horses were dying from exhaustion and lack of forage. Not an Indian had been seen. Evans decided to go into camp on the bank of the river under the shelter of the rough granite peaks, so as to permit the men to enjoy the remainder of the holiday as best they might.

The column approached the stream from the south, opposite the mouth of Devil's Canyon, where the dragoons had visited the Wichitas in 1834. Mexican scouts, who had been out on the right flank, came in to report that they had seen and conversed with two Indians. Colonel Evans determined to neglect these individual Indians no longer. They seemed to be watching his command. At the head of the column was Captain (Brevet Major) Tarlton's company of the Third Cavalry, thirty-four men. Colonel Evans ordered Tarlton to pursue the two Indians. The remainder of the command moved upstream and prepared to go into camp, while Tarlton crossed to the north bank and rode southeast between the hills and the river.

Nestled in a grove of trees situated about a mile and a half east of the site of the old Wichita village was a camp of sixty lodges of the Noconee Comanches. This was the same band from which had come many of the raiders who had participated in the murders near Gainesville and Spanish Fort during the summer and fall. The principal civil chief of this band was Horseback, a signer of the Medicine Lodge treaty. Horseback was friendly to the whites, and disapproved of the raiding done by his people. At this time he probably was at Fort Cobb with his immediate family group. A war chief named Arrow Point was in charge; chiefs Howea and Habby-wake likely were in the village also.[18]

The Indians had been watching Evans' column wandering around, and had hoped that he would not discover their hiding place. When it

---

[17] Official report of Major A. W. Evans, Sheridan Papers, Vol. V.

[18] Comanche informants: Poafebitty (son of Habby-wake), Yellow Fish, and Timbo; Kiowa informants: Toyebo and Doyeto.

was seen that some soldiers were coming toward the village Arrow Point hastily mounted his men and rode out to turn them back.[19] They met about one mile west of the village. The Comanches charged Tarlton vigorously, using lances, rifles, and pistols. At first Tarlton had more than he could handle. He sent for help. Soon Captain Monahan arrived with his company,[20] then Captain Hawley. Thereupon Tarlton took the offensive and pushed the Indians back slowly.

When the Comanches had fallen back to the open ground lying west of their village they increased their resistance, which forced the soldiers to halt. During this skirmish Chief Arrow Point suffered a gunshot wound in the mouth, the injury later causing his death. When he fell his comrades carried him away, but his war equipment fell into the hands of Tarlton's men. One of these captured weapons was a lance of ancient Spanish manufacture.[21]

Adjutant Edward Hunter now arrived with two sections of the mountain battery.[22] The small howitzers were placed in position and threw two spherical case shot into the Indian camp. The first round was a dud; the second exploded.

The Indians in the village were industriously engaged in trying to pack their property. The projectile burst in their midst, stirring them up like a nest of ants. The noise of the battle had stampeded the Indian horse herd east across the shallow river, but when the artillery shell burst in the camp the Indians departed in great haste, riding the few animals which had been left in the camp. Three or four were mounted on each horse. Those of the Comanches who could not obtain mounts commenced climbing the rocky mountain which rose abruptly at the northern edge of the village.

Tarlton charged into the village. He dismounted his men in the grove of trees; then, after leaving a few horseholders and sentries to guard the captured property, he pushed forward with the rest of the command to the high ground lying northeast of the camp. A broken line of large granite rocks juts out from the ridge at this point, forming a half-moon from the river bank on the right to the precipitous mountainside on the left. Tarlton's men lay down behind these rocks and commenced sniping at the Indian warriors, who were riding in half-circles across the front of the firing line in the manner of a typical western cinema. No one was hurt. The poor marksmanship of the Indians was matched by that of the soldiers.

[19] *Ibid.*

[20] In the sixties and seventies cavalry units were called either *troops or companies.* In 1880 the title was officially changed to troop.

[21] Major Evans' report; Indian informants cited above; also Mumsukawa, Millet, Ay-tah, and Tone-mah.

[22] Each gun was drawn by four mules. The sections were manned by infantrymen who had previous service in the artillery.

Tarlton lay happy in his snug position until he noticed that Indians were crossing the river in his rear and threatening to cut him off. These were mostly Kiowas from Woman's Heart's village at Sheep Mountain, who had been attracted to the scene by the sound of the cannon. Large numbers of them were riding in from the east, fording the river, and taking position on Tarlton's front and right rear. His squadron was in danger of being surrounded, but was saved by the timely arrival of Colonel Evans with the rest of the command. Evans threw two cavalry companies to the river bank to protect Tarlton's right and rear, and pushed Captain Gageby's company of infantry to the left to prevent the Indians from getting between Tarlton and the mountain.

The Indians had divided, part of them riding northwest along the tributary which rises at Soldier Spring, the others cantering southwest along the river bank. Several heavy volleys were fired at both groups of savages, and they commenced to fall back out of range. Those along the river bank took shelter among the sand dunes on the south bank; while the others hid among the trees south of Soldier Spring, or behind a large rock situated six hundred yards southeast of Soldier Spring.

Evans saw that it was useless to try to close with them. Their mounts were too fresh. He therefore ordered Tarlton to retreat to the village. The withdrawal was accomplished quickly, and without incident until all but one soldier had retreated to the grove. This man evidently had not heard the order to retire and, engrossed in watching the Indians, did not notice that he was alone. Suddenly, realizing that his companions had retreated, he too jumped up from behind his rock and started to run back. Mama-day-te, a Kiowa, galloped to cut off the lone trooper. He fired his pistol at the man in the blue overcoat, without apparent effect, then circled back to the shelter of Soldier Spring Creek. Next K'op-ah-hodel-te (Kills Enemy Near Mountain) made a charge. He overtook the soldier, and wounded him severely with a lance thrust. But the fire from the soldiers had begun again, so that the Kiowa was unable to make coup by touching his fallen enemy with his hand.

The infantry company had remained in position at the extreme left. Gageby sent word to Colonel Evans that he was pinned to the ground by fire coming from the Indians who had scaled the mountainside. He could not retire without exposing his men to severe loss. Accordingly Evans deployed three companies of cavalry forward under Tarlton to flank out these Indians. As Tarlton's men approached the sharp rock which juts out of the ridge immediately south of Soldier Spring Creek, a large number of savages flushed from in rear of the rock and fled west toward the woods bordering the mountain. Several volleys were fired at them at close range. Evans reports that a number of the Indians were seen to fall; but no bodies were found. The Indians claim that the only one of their men who fell at this point was Mama-day-te, whose horse bucked him off during the excitement; they say he was not hurt. To this day one may pick flattened lead balls from the rocks around Soldier Spring, fired by the soldiers at the retreating Indians.

By sunset all of the soldiers were back in the grove in which the Indian camp was located. The Indians, watching from rocks and sand dunes saw them lighting fires to cook their supper. Marveling at the nonchalance of the soldiers under fire, the Indians were afraid to renew the attack. They thought that the indifference of the troops implied overwhelming strength of numbers concealed in the grove.

Evans had his men establish a fortified camp, after which he put them to work destroying the Indian property. This task was not completed until nearly midnight. It was a rich village; the tepees were of the best Indian workmanship, nearly new. Evans burned everything, including a hundred bushels of corn, much flour, coffee, sugar, soap, cooking utensils, mats, parfleche (leather pouches), bullet moulds, weapons, and robes. He did not spare even the buckskin dolls, doll dresses, and other playthings left by the Indian children.

One of the principal items destroyed by the soldiers was several tons of dried buffalo meat, the entire winter food supply of the Noconee Comanches. At the head of the Indian village, where the mountain rises from the plain, is a small pond covered with lily pads, and fed by small bubbling springs. The Comanches drew their drinking water from this spring. Into this Evans threw all of the dried meat, and to this day, the Indians call it "Dried-Beef Pond."

No pursuit of the Indians was made. Colonel Evans says that he was out of supplies. This is a curious reason. Either the colonel was unreasonably fastidious in his diet or extremely shortsighted. According to his own report he destroyed enough food to have lasted him several weeks. The Indians fled in two directions. Some of them surrendered at Fort Cobb, the others went west to join the Quohadi on the eastern edge of the Staked Plains. Evans marched to the Washita, whence he sent to Fort Cobb for supplies. On January 18 he arrived back at Fort Bascom.

The Battle of Soldier Spring was a smaller affair than the attack made by Custer on Black Kettle's village. Only about two hundred soldiers, and perhaps an equal number of Indians (including Kiowas) were engaged. It was singularly bloodless, considering its duration and the amount of ammunition expended; the troops and the Indians each lost but one man killed, with a few wounded on each side.

Yet the fight was not without significance. It was a successful part of General Sheridan's plan to converge on the Indians from several directions. It showed the hostiles that they were not safe from the troops, no matter which way they might turn. It caused the surrender of a number, including Mow-way, who might otherwise have remained out and defied the government for several years. Nevertheless it was so overshadowed by the Battle of the Washita, which occurred three weeks before, that it has become lost in the annals of history, and is mentioned in only one place—Sheridan's memoirs—and there only briefly.

ANNUITY DAY

December 30 was Annuity Day at Fort Cobb. Articles of clothing promised the Indians by the Medicine Lodge treaty had arrived and were ready for issue. The goods were carried from the paulin-covered shacks where they had been stored, and were piled in heaps on the grass. On one side of the circle the women and children squatted on the ground, their unblinking eyes fixed on the fine things which they expected to receive. Opposite them were the bucks, not less eager, but a bit more stolid. Wolf-like camp dogs sat on their haunches with dripping tongues hanging out as if they too were to be issued annuities. To one side was a group of grinning army folk, gathered to see the fun.

For the Indian men there were black shoddy suits of clothing, practically worthless (but which had enriched some enterprising contractor), hats, red flannel shirts, knives, paint, pieces of red flannel, mirrors, and combs. The women were provided with cotton stockings, calico and flannel cloth, awls, combs, and needles. Both sexes were given tobacco.[23]

Asa-Havey and Tosawi were in charge. The former filled the role of Sunday school superintendent; Tosawi was Santa Claus. Asa-Havey loudly ordered everyone about, called each tribesman by name to receive his share. As each name was called out "Tosh" seized the goods and shied them at the recipient in a manner more reminiscent of an army supply sergeant than of St. Nicholas. The brave solemnly gathered the goods out of the dirt and resumed his seat. The women were treated with similar courtesy.

Whoever supervised the purchase of the various items must have had a profound sense of humor. The hats were of that high, puritanical pattern much later to be considered typical of Old Man Prohibition. Some of the older savages enjoyed the dignity of these headpieces immensely, but the majority of the Indians discarded them as soon as the novelty wore off. Old-timers among the whites declared that the principal way to distinguish a hostile aborigine from a friendly one was to observe whether he wore a hat. The amiable Indians wore hats, they said. It was a risky test.

The trousers were all of the same size, being fashioned for a man weighing 250 pounds. It was comical to see wizened bucks or women lost in the voluminous folds of these garments. The vests were welcome; all

[23] Keim, *op. cit.*, pp. 254-55.

Indians like vests. The coats were converted also into vests by cutting off the sleeves. The severed sleeves then were bestowed on the children, who wore them as leggings.[24]

These clothes were designed to further the noble work of civilizing the Indian. It would appear that someone had concluded that the main difference between a civilized man and an uncivilized one was that the former lived in houses and wore pants, whereas the latter lived out-of-doors and was attired in a breechcloth. Or if he did have pants, the shirt tail was left hanging down on the outside. Therefore, pants were issued to each and every Indian—man, woman, and child. What did the redskins do? Promptly they cut the seats out of the trousers, changing them into leggings. The few who did not so mutilate their pants left their shirt tails hanging outside. So the experiment was a failure. It was very discouraging.

THE ESTABLISHMENT OF CAMP WICHITA

Sheridan would have moved the troops to Medicine Bluff on the day following Grierson's return from the reconnaissance if the weather had permitted. But the command was marooned at Fort Cobb. The Wichita and its tributaries ran foaming from bank to bank. In the camps the soldiers wandered forlornly about in the rain, sucking their feet by main effort out of the pasty mud. The officers sat on their bunks with their feet up, swapping stories of the Civil War and warming themselves with liberal internal applications of Texas "corn." Gaunt horses drooped on the picket lines while flocks of crows fidgeted in the trees watching them expectantly.

On the sixth of January the weather turned clear and cold. Sheridan seized the opportunity to set the command in motion toward the mountains. A penetrating wind from the north flattened the brown prairie grass, quickly drying it so that when some lurking savage built a fire the flames were carried in waves over the countryside. The wind freshened to a gale. The trees roared. The deep grass in the valley raced ahead in whitening surges. Toward Keechi Hills the sea of fire rushed abreast of the troops, driving hundreds of wild animals before it in frightened herds. At night the folds of the plain were outlined in flame, as far away as the eye could see.

In the morning winter again pulled a gray curtain over the sky. A cheerless drizzle set in, increasing by noon to a business-like downpour. The long dark caterpillar of troops toiled south through the clinging mud. Sheridan, impatient, pushed ahead with his staff and light wagons.

Toward nightfall the mountains loomed up ahead, clothed in a veil

[24] George Hunt, Amo-tah, and Andrew Stumbling Bear describe this event with great amusement.

of mist. The general halted opposite the bluffs and made his camp. The next day the rain stopped sufficiently to permit him to look around. He approved the approximate site chosen, but decided to build the fort about three hundred yards southeast of where Colonel Grierson had staked it out. Instead of the stockade fort planned by that officer, Sheridan proposed to erect a permanent post. He therefore decided on this day, January 8, 1869, to stake out again the arrangement in which he wished the barracks and quarters built.

It was planned by the staff to have a short ceremony and some speech-making when the first stake was driven. But Sheridan was no orator. He drove up in his ambulance, climbed out with a merry grin and a joke for the officers gathered there. Then he knelt to hold the stake. Several officers started forward to drive it in.

"Hold on!" the general protested. "I want Johnny Murphy to drive it."

So the young Irish ambulance driver wielded the axe, and had the honor of driving the first stake to mark the site of Fort Sill.[25] Whether this was an example of racial solidarity, or whether Sheridan thought that the frontier youth was less likely to mash his fingers than one of the uniformed gentlemen is not known.

On this same day Sheridan wrote to General Sherman, making a report on his change of location, as follows:

"I have looked around, and fully agree with the report made (by Grierson and Hazen). There are numerous mountain streams of pure water, well timbered, with rich alluvial bottom lands, while the whole country is covered with nutritious bunch grass, which even at this season is very fair. . . . . I will enclose an application for the requisite authority from the Secretary of War, for the construction of a military post, for six companies of cavalry at this point. . . . . To speak generally of the country south of the Washita, and including the whole of the valley of the Washita, it is the best I have ever seen."[26]

That evening the Seventh Cavalry straggled in, covered with mud. They splashed across the creek and pitched their tents in neat rows on the flat ground between the present-day bungalow quarters and Medicine Bluff Creek. The two squadrons of the Tenth Cavalry stopped at Chandler's Creek for a few days, but finally moved to the plateau where in 1934 the new officers' quarters of the Academic area were built.[27] The

25 John Murphy, "Reminiscences of the Washita Campaign," *Chronicles of Oklahoma* Vol. I, No. 3 (June, 1923), pp. 266-67.

26 Sheridan to Nicholas, January 8, 1869.

27 David L. Spotts to author, 1934; H. L. Scott to author, 1933; Charley Ross (Comanche) to author; *Army and Navy Journal,* March 6, 1869.

Nineteenth Kansas Cavalry under Colonel Crawford camped four miles to the west near Heyl's Hole.[28]

On January 10 the weather cleared sufficiently to permit General Sheridan to move his headquarters nearer the site of the post. He pitched his wall tent in a nook below the bank, north of where the commanding general's quarters now stand. At the creek's edge was the headquarters mess. Sheridan had the orderlies lay stones in the mud, forming a walk from his tent to the mess tent at Quinette Crossing. This path, known in later days as "Sheridan's Walk," was visible for forty or fifty years, but recently has been destroyed by the construction of a road.[29]

Hazen's agency and the Indians were left at Fort Cobb until the soldiers were established in their new camp, when they too were brought to the vicinity of Medicine Bluff. A single company of the Sixth Infantry remained at Fort Cobb. Near Sheridan's headquarters Hazen put up a big tent, which he used as a storage place for the Indian supplies. Colonel Albert Gallatin Boone, a grandson of Daniel Boone, arrived to act as agent for the Kiowas and Comanches.

Sheridan planned to have Colonel Grierson and the Tenth Cavalry build the new post. It was impossible to predict how long the other troops would have to remain in the vicinity; that depended on how soon the runaway Indians would come in. Therefore Custer's veteran campaigners of the Seventh Cavalry set to work, as they had at Fort Cobb, to make their camp comfortable. The regiment was bivouacked in a column of troops, each company being in line. The men constructed little dugouts along these lines; the dugouts were roofed over with brush and with shelter tents, and each had a sod fireplace. They placed dry grass and leaves on the floors to make their beds comfortable. Although each man had but one or two blankets, there was plenty of covering, for three men slept together. When the weather was cold they lay nestled together under their blankets; if one man wanted to turn over during the night he cried, "Turn," whereupon all three flopped simultaneously. Sheridan was amused to see some of them poke their heads out and bark at the denizens of neighboring warrens in imitation of prairie dogs.[30]

Colonel Crawford's men at Heyl's Hole were not as comfortable as the regulars. They did not build dugouts because, as one of them remarked in his diary, they might be moved again and thus have all the work for nothing. In a few days the weather turned warm so that the lack of dugouts was not a serious matter. Though it was midwinter, the air was so balmy that overcoats were not needed. The Kansans spruced

[28] General H. L. Scott to author, 1934. General Scott states that the makeshift chimneys of the Kansans' camp were still visible in 1890.

[29] *Army and Navy Journal*, March 6, 1869; H. L. Scott to author, 1934. Several old Indians are familiar with the site.

[30] Sheridan's *Memoirs*, p. 339.

up the appearance of their camp by planting cedar boughs in the ground for ornamentation; they laid out neat little walks lined with stones, and "dragged" with branches the company streets each morning.[31] The habits of soldiers seem never to change.

Supplies were not coming through from Fort Arbuckle on schedule. The troops were living on bacon and hardtack, and such small amounts of fresh game as could be killed. But most of the wild animals had been frightened away from the vicinity of the camps, and it was considered unsafe on account of lurking Indians to allow the men to hunt at a distance; consequently not much fresh meat was obtained. It was noticeable that the faces of the men were beginning to take on a gaunt appearance. The horses too were in bad shape. The abundance of prairie grass did not compensate for lack of grain. In the winter the Indians were accustomed to go into camp, and wait until the fresh grass in the spring should make their ponies fat enough to travel. But the troops could not do that; their mounts must be kept in proper condition at all seasons. And Sheridan was anxious to finish the campaign.

Letters written to Fort Arbuckle to hasten the forwarding of supplies apparently had been without effect.[32] Sheridan knew that there was one sure way of getting action. He did not hesitate to take it. Accompanied by his quartermaster, Colonel McGonigle, and a woolly, unkempt scout named California Joe, he set out in his ambulance for Fort Arbuckle. He intended to build a bonfire under the lackadaisical supply personnel at the post. But when he arrived there he found that the officials were not entirely at fault. Swollen streams and the boggy condition of the trails prevented the stores at Fort Gibson from being moved to Arbuckle. Sheridan could not remedy this; but with his great authority he could do almost as well. He bought up all the local corn in Pauls Valley, and had it collected at Fort Arbuckle for forwarding to the command at Medicine Bluff.

When it came time to return Sheridan discovered that California Joe was dead drunk. After waiting overnight for this "guide" to sober up, the general loaded him, still unconscious, into the ambulance, and proceeded on his way west.

There now intervened a period of inactivity at Camp Wichita during the wait for the Indians to come in.[33] Colonel Hazen had successfully transferred the bands of Kiowas and Comanches at Fort Cobb to Medicine Bluff; some were camped near Mount Scott, some along Chandler Creek, and others were on Cache Creek, north of its junction with Medi-

[31] D. L. Spotts, *Campaigning with Custer and the 19th Kansas Volunteer Cavalry* (Los Angeles: Wetzel Publishing Company, 1928), pp. 101-24.

[32] Old Files, Fort Arbuckle.

[33] Also called "Camp Medicine Bluff."

cine Bluff Creek. The Cheyennes and Arapahoes were still out, though messages had been sent urging them to report in before forces were sent against them.

The soldiers were bored by the delay. At first the novelty of the locality, and the opportunity to go hunting and fishing, kept them amused. But finally they were forced to devise other forms of recreation. The Kansans organized intercompany baseball games, which provided great hilarity until the home-made balls were knocked to pieces. The officers staged horse races on the flat ground near Four-Mile Crossing, or played poker, "jawbone." Some of the enlisted men climbed over the hills east of the camp, catching horned toads, tarantulas, and other queer creeping things which they found hibernating in the rocks. They carried them back to the camp, placed them on exhibit, or prodded them into combat with each other. One day, while rolling stones down the face of Medicine Bluff, they found a rattlesnake den at the base of the cliff, a few feet above the water. Here reptiles in large numbers slept through the winter, rolled together for warmth in great slimy balls. The soldiers extracted over a hundred torpid rattlesnakes; these they gleefully killed and skinned. Snakeskin belts and hatbands became the order of the day at Heyl's Hole.[34]

Colonel Custer had a scheme for bringing in the recalcitrant Cheyennes. A large expedition would frighten them away, he told Sheridan. Therefore he proposed to go with only a small escort and a few friendly Indians to persuade the Cheyennes to come in and submit to governmental control. The idea seemed foolhardy to General Sheridan. He thought it unlikely that the Cheyennes would receive Custer, of all men, as a long-lost brother. He reluctantly gave permission for Custer to go.[35]

So Custer set out west from Camp Wichita on January 21, accompanied by a few soldiers, Little Robe of the Cheyennes, Yellow Robe of the Arapahoes, and two captive Cheyenne women. The expedition was not wholly successful. After traveling 180 miles Custer saw signs of the Cheyennes, but could not find their village. Little Robe, in whom he had placed great confidence, asked to be allowed to go on by himself to locate the Indians. This was the last he saw of Little Robe.

Lack of food forced Custer to return to Camp Wichita. On the return trip he encountered a band of Arapahoes under Little Raven who said they were on their way in, but were moving slowly on account of the poor condition of their animals. Custer arrived at Medicine Bluff on February 7.

On the following day Captain Weir, with two companies of the Sev-

[34] Spotts, *op. cit.*, pp. 106, 115.
[35] Sheridan to Sherman, January 20, 1869, Sherman Papers, Manuscript Division, Library of Congress. Photographic copy in Fort Sill library.

enth Cavalry, was sent out to accelerate the pace of Little Raven's Arapahoes. He found them, as they had claimed, in poor condition. They were as short of supplies as the soldiers. Even more so; the wild game having been frightened away, the Indians were reduced to the necessity of dining on their camp dogs. Barbecued canine was considered a delicacy by the Cheyennes and Arapahoes, but was not indulged in until all other food reserves had been exhausted.

While Custer and Weir were attempting to bring in the Cheyennes and Arapahoes, Sheridan and some of his friends were exploring the mountains near the camp. They scaled Mount Scott and the peak three miles northwest of it, which Mr. Keim named Mount Sheridan. In the gap between these mountains, where the road now runs north to Meers, they found an old Indian path which Asa-Toyeh told them had been made years ago by the Caddoes. In the valley near the present Cedar Planting the party sighted a large herd of elk. The officers enjoyed some excellent shooting.

SATANTA AND LONE WOLF RELEASED

For some time the Kiowas had been importuning General Sheridan to release Satanta and Lone Wolf from confinement, arguing that all of their people except one band which they "had thrown away," were now in. They claimed that they had complied with all of Sheridan's conditions. General Sherman had written to him in December, suggesting that he hang them. Sheridan's own inclinations were to do this, and to punish severely other Indians known to have been involved in murders and kidnappings. But, on sifting the matter, he discovered that if he commenced executing guilty Indians the two tribes would be almost exterminated. As he wrote in reply to Sherman, he was afraid that this was a little more than the success of the reservation system would stand. Therefore he determined to let them off with one more warning.[36]

His program was to bring Satanta and Lone Wolf to his tent for a private talk, then follow this with a similar conference with Horseback. After arriving at an understanding with these chiefs he would call in all the chiefs for a formal conference. He hoped that they would be influenced by the prior understanding with the principal leaders.

The first conference was held on February 15.[37] General Sheridan began by telling Satanta and Lone Wolf that he knew the names of all the chiefs who had been raiding in Texas lately, and that Lone Wolf's name was at the head of the list. He stated bluntly that he intended to

[36] Sheridan Papers. Satanta and Lone Wolf had been confined, since their capture, in a Sibley tent pitched in the center of the Seventh Cavalry camp.

[37] A verbatim account of Sheridan's conferences with the Indians is given in Vol. V of the Sheridan Papers.

stop this business, but that instead of hanging them and their compatriots he would give them another chance, provided that these two chiefs would give their pledge to be responsible for the future good conduct of the tribe. If they could not prevent outrages, at least they could inform him or some other responsible party as to who was guilty.

"I wanted to have this conversation today, before seeing the other chiefs tomorrow, when I shall have the other chiefs here and will tell them the same thing. . . . I will take the guards away from your tent, but would like to see you tomorrow when the other chiefs come," he concluded.

Satanta remarked: "The Kiowas and Comanches are here, but we are larger than any of them. I have nothing to say. Whatever you say, we will go by that."

Lone Wolf was more flowery in his reply: "The sun and earth will now witness what I say. All the blood that is here on the prairie will be wiped out. After this you will not see any more blood. We have thrown everything bad away from us. After this, everything which is to be said we will be spokesmen for; we will have nothing to say only what you tell us, and we will follow the road which you mark out for us. We want to lift up the road which you give us and travel on it. . . . After this the fires of the Indian and white man will all be one, and we will all eat as one people. . . . Now I have taken the white man by the hand, and it is strong, and our road will be white and pure and plain, until we are all old men and grow up and die. I will follow the same rule. If I hear anything wrong with any of my people, I will not hide it, but will come and tell you openly and plainly."

Sheridan was impressed in spite of himself. "That will be right," he agreed. The two Indians, noting the effect of Lone Wolf's oratory, continued to pour on the honey. Satanta said, "I am looking to you and General Custer because my heart is glad to look at you. When I first met you at Fort Larned my intentions were good, but since then they fell short, and I am in mourning for it. Whatever you tell us hereafter, we are going to lift that up and hold on to it until we get tired, and then we will still hold on to it. Today I am looking at you in truth as my father. . . . It don't [sic] alter my opinion a particle, if you take me by the hand now, or take and hang me. My opinion will be just the same. What you have told me today has opened my ears, and my heart is open also. All this ground is yours to make the road for us to travel on. After this, I am going to have the white man's road, to plant and raise corn. You can send the same reports to Washington."

Sheridan: "Yes, that is right. Yes, I will."

Satanta: "Now my heart is glad. I have cut off fighting. I hope you and General Custer will cut off fighting. All the time I have been held here as a prisoner, I have been talking and giving good advice to my people. Today my heart is big. You can look at us. We are each poor and have no clothing, nor shirts, nor anything to wear. We are not going to war any more."

The Indian was intimating that, as usual, he would be glad to receive presents or annuities as a reward for the promise to be peaceful. This was the customary conclusion to a peace talk. Sheridan did not take the hint. He merely repeated that he did not want to hear of any more murders or horse stealing.

The conference with straightforward old Horseback was much shorter. The general said to him: "I want to tell you the reason why I have not allowed goods to be issued to you. After I came down here I found that a portion of your people had been in the habit of going into Texas and murdering our people and stealing horses. I have the names of those who committed those depredations. That will have to be stopped . . . But I have been led to believe from your good conduct that if I let them off this time they would stop in the future, and I have concluded to do so, and to let you have your goods; but it will be only on the condition that you pledge to me that you will notify General Hazen or the commanding officer in case any depredations of this kind occur hereafter. If you are willing to make this pledge to me, I am willing to settle this affair. . . ."

Horseback replied quietly, "I agree to that. I am willing to do as you say."

General Sheridan waited a moment to listen to the flow of native metaphor which he had been led to expect, through his dealings with Satanta and Lone Wolf. When it did not come he said, "That is all I have to say to Horseback. If he has anything to say, I am ready to hear it."

But the Comanche merely answered, simply and sincerely, "I have nothing to say. I have heard your talk, and I agree to it, and shall be willing always to do anything you or General Hazen tell me." "I am glad to get the goods," he added.

A CONFERENCE WITHOUT A TREATY

The Indians were delighted when they heard that they were to assemble at the tent of the great soldier-chief for a conference. Now they were sure that the recent unpleasantness was about to end, that a new treaty was to be made. They could see with half an eye that the big tent standing near Sheridan's headquarters contained presents for them.

They were doomed to disappointment if they expected a treaty. Sheridan emphatically was not a treaty man. He gave it as his opinion that the Indians had been consulted too much.

It was a warm, clear day. Buds appearing on the trees foretold an early spring. Robins, cardinals, and woodthrush were uncommonly musical. Green grass was beginning to show in the meadows. General Sheridan sat at ease in a carpet-covered camp chair under an awning pitched in front of his tent. A half-dozen cronies of Civil War days were gathered there to share in the genial flow of reminiscence.

To this place came fifty or more invited Indian chiefs. They seated themselves majestically on the ground, while Goon-saudl-te, or Baa-o (Cat), who was self-appointed master of ceremonies, strode about full of importance, giving orders in guttural Kiowa. His cousin, Chief Stumbling Bear, had lent him the major general's uniform given him at Medicine Lodge by General Hancock. The magnificence of the blue raiment was marred somewhat by the fact that the pants were missing. A heavy cavalry saber banged against Chief Cat's bare brown legs as he stalked about, exhorting his admiring brethren. The officers with difficulty concealed their mirth.[38]

When Cat had finished, General Sheridan came forth from the tent and said, in part:

"Your people must now consider me their chief, just as much as I am the chief of the white people in this country. When white people do wrong—commit murder and robberies—we always punish them, and hereafter if you commit any crimes I am going to punish you just the same as the white people are punished.

"Since the treaty at Medicine Lodge Creek, in which you agreed to behave yourselves, you have committed a great many murders and robberies. I know, among you who are here, those who committed these crimes. At first I thought I would punish you as we punish white people, but I thought perhaps you did not fully understand these conditions, and I am willing now to give you another chance. . . . Our desire is to live at peace with you all, and we have taken a great deal of trouble to do as much for you as we can, and we have made up our minds now that these murders and robberies must stop. . . . Satanta and Lone Wolf have promised to do everything in their power to help keep their people here, and to prevent any of these crimes hereafter, and I expect all of the chiefs here today to promise the same thing. If you are willing to do so, I am willing to let you have your goods and be on good terms with you. . . . ."

Black Eagle, Kicking Bird, Stiff Neck, Lone Bear, Stumbling Bear, Timber Mountain, and the other chiefs who had not been present at the former interviews, all promised to be good. Lone Bear stated that his heart was so glad that he could hardly talk. Bear-That-Goes-into-

[38] Baa-o (Cat), or Goon-saudl-te, first came into prominence among his fellows as master of ceremonies when he acted as interpreter at Medicine Lodge. He interpreted Phil McCusker's Comanche into Kiowa (Kiowa informants: Mosaip [son of Baa-o], Andrew Stumbling Bear, George Hunt, and Amo-tai; *see also* Keim, *op. cit.*, pp. 275-76).

the-Timber, however, did not lose his voice. He snatched at the opportunity to be heard:

"I heard last night that these chiefs were set free, and I could not sleep for it, but sat up all night waiting for the morning's sun, and when the sun went up this morning I got on my horse and saw that what I heard was true. I saw these chiefs walking around free. . . ." He went on to declare that not only the Kiowas, but all the tribes, would be delighted to hear that Satanta and Lone Wolf had been liberated.

Then came the pay-off: Satanta asked, "When will we receive our annuities?"

SHERIDAN: "As soon as General Hazen can get them ready. In a day or two."

SATANTA: "But Colonel Boone told us that you would give us notice."

SHERIDAN: "I will."

SATANTA: "Our women and children are very poor. Their hearts will be glad and contented when they get the goods."

The Kiowa also had several complaints to make: "The Osages last fall killed two of my people," he said. "I want to know if you have anything to say about this?"

SHERIDAN: "Not now.

SATANTA: "The Utes also killed seven of my men last year, and my heart is burning about it now."

SHERIDAN: "I have nothing to say to you upon this subject now."

SATANTA: "One of my men got wounded at Fort Zarah last fall. Some of my men are big fools, and among the soldiers around here are some big fools. The man has got well, and I do not feel hard about it. I have the white man by the hand now. Speaking about our medicine, Heap-of-Bears was killed by the Utes. Their agent can get the medicine, and if only we can get it, I would make a lasting peace. We are looking strongly for that medicine."

SHERIDAN: "I have written to the agent about it, but have heard nothing. If you talk with General Hazen about it some time, perhaps he will write and get it."

The significance of this conference was that the Indians were made to realize that they were dealing with a man who would not temporize with them; he was a "no-treaty chief." The Indians understood this kind of treatment, and they had infinitely more respect for a man like Sheridan, who was firm but just, than they had for sentimentalists who permitted them to do as they pleased. Had Sheridan remained in control of the Indians, the succeeding five years of bloodshed and plunder would never have occurred. But he was soon promoted to the grade of lieutenant general and sent to Chicago. The management of the Indians then

93

was turned over to a group of Quakers who permitted the Indians to resume their marauding unrestrained.

THE CLOSE OF THE CAMPAIGN

General Sheridan had been absent from his duties as commander of the Department of the Missouri much longer than he had intended. Though he was anxious to remain in the field until all the Indians had been rounded up, he saw now that another expedition would have to be sent out. He could not accompany this in person, much as he desired to do so; therefore he ordered Custer to take charge, move west, locate the Cheyennes, and drive them in to Camp Supply. Custer's recent trip west of the mountains indicated the necessity for establishing an intermediate temporary base of supplies on the Salt Fork of Red River. Arrangements were made to have supplies forwarded from Camp Supply to that point, there to await Custer's arrival.

When he had completed these plans General Sheridan left for the north. On the day of his departure, February 23, 1869, he was tendered a farewell review by the Seventh Cavalry. This ceremony was held in an open field which lay on the site of the New Post parade ground. The troops were formed along the line occupied by the brick quarters. On account of this the Kiowas, to whom everything is symbolical, believe that the New Post was laid out according to the arrangement of Custer's troops for this review.

The Kansas Volunteers, not being schooled in close-order maneuvers, were lined up in the rear of the Seventh Cavalry, by dint of strenuous shoving and cursing, and were permitted to act as spectators.

It was a beautiful, fair morning. The air was clear and pure. The rays of the early sun flashed from guidon and saber blade. Custer's band played several stirring marching-airs. When the parade was finished the soldiers stood in ranks while Sheridan's ambulance trotted past. A tremendous cheer went up from the command, for the general was greatly admired by all ranks, not only on account of his great military reputation and genial personality, but also on account of his democratic manner, so dear to the hearts of American soldiers. One of the Kansas cavalrymen says of him at this time: "General Sheridan has been with us ever since we left Camp Supply and had his headquarters with us, camping in a tent when the weather was fair or foul, marching at our head in snow and rain, enduring all the hardships of wind and weather. He is not a young man either, between thirty-five and forty years old."[39]

The aged general was, in fact, thirty-seven.

On March 2 the Seventh Cavalry, followed in column by the Nineteenth Kansas Volunteers, part of them dismounted and acting as in-

[39] Spotts, *op. cit.*, p. 125.

fantry, departed from Camp Wichita. They marched west along the south bank of Medicine Bluff Creek, then turned south and skirted the slopes of Signal Mountain and Mackenzie Hill until they struck the old road leading to Camp Radziminski. This road no doubt had been made by Van Dorn or by Texas Rangers who had operated in the country before the Civil War. They camped at Radziminski on the third night, then pushed rapidly west to the North Fork of Red River, where they arrived on March 5. Here they found Captain Henry Inman's wagon train waiting for them with fresh supplies. Scouts reported fresh Indian signs in the vicinity. Custer at once made preparations for a rapid pursuit. The wagons, escorted by those of the Kansas troops who were dismounted, were sent north to a rendezvous on the Washita River. The remainder of the command, traveling light, set out after the Indians.

On the fifteenth of March, after an exhausting march in which everyone suffered great hardships, the Indians were found camped on Sweetwater Creek, west of the present boundary between Oklahoma and Texas. The soldiers were eager to attack. But Custer held back. He had learned that there were two captive white women among the Cheyennes and remembering what had happened to Clara Blinn when he attacked Black Kettle's village, he felt that it would be best to seek a conference with the Indians. He felt that it would be better to allow a thousand blood-guilty savages to escape than risk the sacrifice of two innocent girls. After considerable parleying with the chiefs of the village, which he followed with strong threats, Custer was able to secure the release of the prisoners. The chiefs were held by him as security that the tribe come in to Camp Supply for surrender.

The campaign now was finished. Most of the Indians were on their reservations. The Cheyennes had been punished. Yet several years were to elapse and many more white scalps to be lost before the Indians of the Wichita Mountain area were finally and completely pacified.

PART II

THE CITY OF REFUGE

CHAPTER SIX

THE PEACE POLICY

SOLDIER-HOUSE AT MEDICINE BLUFF—CONSTRUCTION OF THE STONE
POST STARTED—TATUM AND GRIERSON ARE HARASSED—THE
INDIANS RUN WILD—A COUNCIL WITH THE INDIANS
— CLOSE OF THE 1870 RAIDING SEASON—A
QUIET WINTER AT FORT SILL

GENERAL U. S. GRANT became President of the United States March 4, 1869. A few days after his inauguration he was visited by a delegation of Quakers, who desired a change in the Indian policy. They contended that the Indians had been chased here and there over the plains, harassed and mistreated by the army, swindled by civilian agents.

"Let us manage the Indians," they urged. "We are disinterested, and honest; we have no political axes to grind. We will treat the red men with kindness and justice. We will substitute brotherly love for the sword, and in a spirit of toleration will lift these wards of the nation from barbarity to Christian civilization." Grant pondered for a while. Then he said, "Gentlemen, your advice is good. I will accept it. If you can make Quakers out of the Indians, it will take all the fight out of them."

Thus was inaugurated the Peace Policy. The direct management of some of the Indian tribes was entrusted to the Society of Friends. No new treaties were to be made. The old ones would have to do. The army, through General Sherman, was instructed to give full support to the plan, and to the new agents.

Meanwhile the army officers who were temporarily on duty with the Indian office remained in active charge. General Hazen was superintendent of the tribes in Indian Territory; Colonel Boone was agent for the Kiowas, Comanches, Wichitas, and affiliated minor tribes, with headquarters at Camp Wichita. Colonel Grierson, commander at the new post, was an enthusiastic supporter of the Peace Policy. There seemed to be every reasonable expectation that things would go well on the reservation of the Kiowas and Comanches.

After Sheridan and Custer departed Colonel Grierson applied himself to the task of building the new fort. It was decided to erect permanent stone buildings rather than slab-and-mud affairs like those at Camp Supply and Fort Arbuckle. Grierson's command consisted of four companies of the Tenth Cavalry and two of the Sixth Infantry. Two companies of the Tenth Cavalry were at Arbuckle, and Rife's company of the Sixth Infantry remained at Fort Cobb. Later all these troops were brought to Fort Sill.

Camp Wichita at first was merely a collection of shacks, made of condemned tentage and wooden frames. As soon as the officers saw that it was to be their permanent station they had soldiers erect for them little log or slab quarters of one or two rooms each, similar to the type occupied by Washington at Valley Forge. For Colonel Grierson a more commodious picket house was built, near the creek, southeast of where General Sheridan's tent had stood.[1]

There had been considerable discussion over the selection of a name for the new post. The Seventh Cavalry wanted it called Fort Elliott, in honor of the young officer killed at the Battle of the Washita. The Nineteenth Kansas Volunteers suggested ironically that it be called Camp Starvation. The original occupants of the site—the Indians—were not consulted. The Comanches called it *Pu-hi-ti-pinab,* and the Kiowas knew it as *Tso-kada-hagya*—both of which names mean, "where the soldiers live at Medicine Bluff."

General Sheridan decided on *Fort Sill,* in honor of Brigadier General Joshua W. Sill, a West Point classmate who was killed leading the charge of a brigade of Sheridan's Division at the Battle of Stone River, Tennessee, December 31, 1862. Orders confirming this choice were issued at department headquarters July 2, and at Fort Sill on August 1, 1869.[2]

John S. Evans, who had been sutler at Fort Gibson and at Fort Arbuckle, obtained a license to operate a post trader's store at Fort Sill. As there could be but one post trader at each post, this was a juicy plum. Evans decided to invest considerable money in the business. During the summer he hauled lumber three hundred miles from the railhead at Fort Harker, Kansas, and built a barn-like store on the ground later occupied by the Field Artillery School library. Near-by he erected a comfortable

[1] Report of Acting Assistant Surgeon H. S. Kilbourne, September 24, 1870; *Army and Navy Journal,* April 3, 1869; R. H. Pratt, "Some Indian Reminiscences," *Cavalry Journal,* October, 1905, p. 207.

[2] G. O. No. 25, Hq. Dept of Mo., July 2, 1869 (Old Files Section, AGO); G. O. No. 1, Hq. Ft. Sill, August 1, 1869 (Old Files, Fort Sill).

two-story residence for himself and family. These buildings probably were the first permanent structures erected at Fort Sill.[3]

In addition to being post trader, Evans was a licensed Indian trader. Federal laws prohibited traders from dealing with Indians in establishments where liquor was sold. Regulations permitted wine and beer to be sold at army posts, the matter being regulated by the post commander. For this reason Evans built a branch store to handle the Indian trade. This establishment, called the "Lower Store," was located near Cache Creek, southeast of the present east entrance to Post Field. There was another Indian trader in the same locality, a man named William Mathewson. Mathewson, who was called "Buffalo Bill" (no relation to William Cody) because of his success as a buffalo hunter, traded blankets, knives, and other knicknacks for buffalo robes. He later sold out to E. D. Smith.

As long as Colonel Grierson was post commander, Evans was able to trade with the Indians at both the upper and lower stores; for Grierson kept the post bone dry. The trader's store at Fort Sill filled the combined functions of Post Exchange, officers' club, and enlisted men's service club. It was a general store, a post office, and loafing place for officers, soldiers, Indians, and civilian hangers-on.

The efforts of some of the veteran topers of that day to obtain spirituous beverages were ludicrous. Failing to wheedle a drink from hospital authorities by cajolery or bribery, they were forced to rely on several of the "tonics" stocked by the post trader. One favorite brand was Peruna, greatly admired for its flavor in plum puddings. Evans sold it by the case.[4]

Early in the spring of 1869 Colonel Grierson sent wagon trains to Fort Arbuckle for lumber, bricks, and tools. The quartermaster sawmill was dismantled and hauled to Fort Sill, where it was set up on the west bank of Cache Creek, east of the post. Major L. C. Forsythe, the constructing quartermaster, sent workmen to the vicinity of Mount Scott and Mount Sheridan, where there was a fine stand of oak and cottonwood timber. These trees were cut into logs and hauled to the sawmill, there to be converted into lumber for flooring and framing. At first no planing mill was available; the boards had to be dressed by hand. Bricks brought from Fort Arbuckle and Texas were used to build chimneys.[5]

In June Major Forsythe brought from Kansas two trains of twenty-five wagons each, loaded with tools, hardware, and civilian workmen.

[3] Reminiscences of Neal Evans, MS in the private collection of C. E. Hensley, Oklahoma City.

[4] W. H. Quinette to author, 1934.

[5] Old Files, Fort Sill; Old Files, Fort Arbuckle (files of Fort Sill); James McGranahan to author. Mr. McGranahan was a wagonmaster in the Seventh Cavalry in 1868; he remained at Fort Sill as a teamster in the quartermaster department.

These artisans, mostly key men, such as foremen, stonemasons, carpenters, and plasterers, were quartered with the teamsters in a canvas camp located near the site of Hoyle Bridge.

Winter came before much construction could be accomplished. The first requirement of the post was a quartermaster warehouse in which to store the supplies of food, clothing, and tools, which had been kept under paulins during the summer. To take care of this Forsythe put up a warehouse made of square-hewn cottonwood logs laid horizontally. This was the first building erected by the military at Fort Sill, except for the crude quarters occupied by Grierson and his officers. Later it was replaced by a stone warehouse.[6]

As long as the Indians remained under the military agent few arrangements could be made to erect agency buildings. Hazen and his assistants issued supplies to the Indians from tents located near Grierson's house. Pending the arrival of the new Quaker agent, Colonel Hazen awarded a contract to John Shirley to build two agency warehouses on the ridge immediately north of Quarry Hill. The site selected for the agency itself was farther south, in the neighborhood of the stores operated by Evans and Mathewson. Hazen constructed an adobe house for himself on the east bank of Cache Creek, opposite Mathewson's store.

Since, under the Medicine Lodge treaty, the Indians were to be trained as farmers, one of Hazen's first official acts was to hire a white man to plough up a tract of land near the agency and plant it to corn, melons, beans, and squashes. The carnivorous Kiowas and Comanches paid scant attention to these activities, but the Wichitas, Caddoes, and Delawares were delighted. With tender and solicitous care they watched the sprouting plants.

About the middle of the summer Lawrie Tatum arrived to relieve Colonel Hazen. Tatum was an honest Quaker farmer from Iowa who had had no previous experience in handling Indians, but was imbued with a sincere ambition to make a success of his work. With him came a staff of Quaker assistants—school teachers, clerks, artisans, and a physician. On July 1 all the agency property except the commissary was turned over to Mr. Tatum. The commissary remained under Colonel Boone until the following year.[7]

Agent Tatum was not satisfied with Colonel Hazen's adobe house. He saw that Cache Creek was subject to sudden rises during the rainy season. He reasoned correctly that a freshet would cut him off from Fort Sill. Therefore, having plenty of money allotted for the purpose, he let contracts for several stone buildings, to be erected on the west side of the creek near Evans' lower store. After he had attended to these matters

---

[6] Report of Surgeon Kilbourne, cited above.

[7] Lawrie Tatum, *Our Red Brothers,* pp. 25-27 (Philadelphia: John Winston Co., 1899).

Tatum departed for Chicago, where he purchased a steam engine, with attachments for a sawmill, a corn-grinder, and a shingle-maker.

Tatum, being a thoroughgoing farmer, was well pleased with the agency farm started by his predecessor. In order to encourage the Indians to make progress in the arts of husbandry he offered an annual prize of $500, to be divided among the ten Indians who raised the best crops. Under the provisions of the Medicine Lodge Treaty, army officers from Fort Sill supervised the awarding of these prizes, and also the periodic issues of rations and annuities. This was to insure that the Indians received what was due them and that the quality was as specified.[8]

The agricultural Indians—the Caddoes and Wichitas—set to work with vigor on their crops. But those congenitally predatory nomads, the Kiowas and Comanches, were not tempted. They thought that it would be an imposition to expect their women to do farm work in addition to their already onerous camp chores. Furthermore there were still plenty of buffalo on the plains. Why toil and sweat in the humorous fashion of the white men? Such ideas, however, did not prevent some of them from loitering around to watch the ripening vegetables. Soon they plundered the fields, eating the watermelons when they were about the size of cucumbers. As a result, the agency doctor was called upon to treat several cases of "Devil inside my belly." As Charlie Ross (Comanche) remarks, "Thus I lost my father."

The Wichitas and Caddoes were greatly annoyed by the thievery of the other Indians, but presently they were moved to an agency of their own, north of the site of Anadarko, where Friend Jonathan Richards was in charge.

The soldiers at Fort Sill did not have much better manners than the Kiowas and Comanches. Hucksters bringing fresh vegetables and fruit from the Chickasaw Nation, some forty miles to the east, were annoyed to such an extent that Colonel Grierson issued the following order: "The shameful, villainous, and criminal conduct of some of the enlisted men of this command in plundering and stealing from the market men who bring produce to supply the wants of this post, and in many instances stealing from the Post Trader, and other persons, will in the future be met with the most extreme and summary punishment which the law can impose."

Stealing vegetables was not the only mischief perpetrated by the Indians. Some of them had begun to recover from the fright occasioned by Sheridan's winter campaign, and thought that it would be fun to spend the summer raiding in Texas. The troops at Fort Richardson and Fort Griffin were considerably occupied pursuing raiding bands.

[8] Old Files, Fort Sill.

Not all the Indians had reported at the agency. Big Bow and his small band of Kiowas never came in for rations. The Quohada Comanches were still in the Staked Plains, and taunted those of their tribe who had settled near Fort Sill. They sent word that they did not intend to shake hands with the agent until the soldiers had come out and whipped them, and they doubted that the soldiers could do so.

Tatum had seen only one Quohada. This was Mow-way, who really was a Kochateka chief, but who had become associated, as had several others, with the wilder bands who inhabited the Staked Plains. Mow-way was one of those Indians who had surrendered at Fort Bascom following Colonel Evans' campaign. With several other Comanches he had been sent to Fort Leavenworth, from which, after a brief confinement, he had been released and forwarded under guard to Fort Sill.[9] His description of his journey is interesting as illustrative of the impressions of a true product of the stone age on being shown for the first time the works of the modern age:

"I supposed when we started (from Fort Bascom) that the soldiers were going to take us way off and then kill us. But we travelled on and on, day after day, in wagons, and were kindly treated. When one of the Indians was taken sick, I supposed that the white men would be glad for him to die. But instead they doctored him, and seemed to do all they could to cure him. But he died, and then they did not throw him out in the grass for the wolves to eat, as I expected they would, but the commanding officer had some of his men dig a grave for him. They made a box and put him into it with all of his clothing, his bows and arrows; everything he owned they gave him. The hole they dug was the nicest I ever saw. They made a little mound over him, smooth and nice. I could not understand why such mean people should be so kind to an Indian in sickness and after death.

"When we had traveled many days we came to where there was a new kind of road that I had never heard of. There was a very large iron horse hitched to several houses on wheels. We were taken into one of them, which was the nicest house I ever saw. There were seats on each side of it. As soon as we were seated the iron horse made a snort, and away it went, pulling the houses! Our ponies could not run half so fast. It only ran a little way, and then stopped at a white man's village. The iron horse kept running and snorting and kept stopping at villages, and the villages kept getting larger and larger. I had no idea the white men had so many villages and that there were so many white people. At length we reached Leavenworth which was the largest of any of the villages. There the people were so numerous and the land so scarce they built one house on top of another, two or three houses high. These

[9] *Army and Navy Journal,* July 3, 1869.

houses were divided into little houses inside. The houses were built close together on both sides of the road. They were full of people, and the roads between were full of people, I do not know where they all came from, but I saw them with my own eyes. I had no idea there were so many people in existence.

"After we were taken over to one of the houses built on top of one another, we were taken into another house down in the ground under the other one. There was nobody living in it, but there were barrels of foolish water in it. They offered some to us, but I saw that it made white men foolish who drank it, and I was afraid to do so.

"We were taken into a house that was built on the water, and it could swim anywhere. It made no difference how deep the water was, it could swim. That is where the sugar comes from. I saw men rolling big barrels of sugar out of the house to a platform on the land, and so many of them! Nobody need talk to me about sugar being scarce."[10]

On the way to Fort Sill from Fort Leavenworth Mow-way's guard got drunk, but the chief came on by himself and surrendered to Colonel Grierson. The latter, greatly surprised, turned him over to the agent. Mow-way soon wandered back to the plains to rejoin his band. From that time on he was convinced of the futility of opposing the white men; he had seen how many of them there were.

CONSTRUCTION OF THE STONE POST STARTED

Early in 1870 work was commenced on the permanent buildings at Fort Sill. Captain A. F. Rockwell superseded Major Forsythe as constructing quartermaster. Only a meager sum of money was allotted for the work and most of it went for hire of civilian artisans. Material had to be "rustled" locally, and all of the unskilled labor was furnished by the troops. A quarry was opened in the limestone hill southeast of the post, where rock was cut for the walls of the buildings. Crude kilns were made at the southeast side of the quarry to burn lime for cement and plaster. Sand was obtained from the bed of Cache Creek.[11]

The troops at Fort Sill were busy in those days. Not only were large details required for the construction of the post, but many of the soldiers themselves were recruits, and had to be given military instruction in preparation for the opening of the expected season of Indian troubles. In general, the first real training a recruit had was when he went into the field as a member of an expedition.

Officers had little time for recreation. Most of the colored troopers

[10] Tatum, *op. cit.*, pp. 74-75. Ti-so-yo, son of Mow-way, also told this story to the author, substantially as given in Tatum. Evidently Mow-way's family was greatly impressed by the story of his travels.
[11] James McGranahan to author, 1934; Old Files, Fort Sill.

were recent plantation hands from Arkansas; many of them were former slaves. Few could read or write. As a result the officers had to attend to much of the clerical and routine duty ordinarily performed by clerks or noncommissioned officers. Colonel Grierson, who was a violinist, personally organized the regimental band. On occasion he conducted it in concert. He also used to entertain the officers in his quarters by playing *Turkey in the Straw, Oh! Susanna,* and other barn-dance numbers.[12]

GRIERSON AND TATUM ARE HARASSED

Colonel Grierson, engrossed in building Fort Sill, paid little attention to the Indians. In April he reported optimistically that large parties of the bands which had failed to come in during the previous year were now camped near the farms on Cache Creek and the Washita, and were manifesting a desire to have their lands broken and fenced. He said that the Kiowas were beginning to realize that the buffalo were disappearing, and that they would have to raise their own food.

Grierson's estimate of the situation was completely erroneous. To have the prairie plowed and fenced was the last thing these Indians desired. They had no idea that the buffalo were being exterminated. Such a thing was beyond their comprehension. In May the Kiowas and Comanches left the reservation on a buffalo hunt. Grierson still was not alarmed. But he told Sheridan that on June 1 he intended to move west to "attend to" the medicine dance.[13]

The Sun Dance in itself was harmless. There was no reason for preventing it. But if the colonel had been conversant with Indian custom and superstition he would have known that raiding parties would go out from the Indian camps as soon as the dance was over. He was prevented from making his proposed expedition by troubles nearer home. White thieves and desperadoes were not affected by the Peace Policy. Probably they had never heard of it. The troops at Fort Sill began to be called upon to make trips to various parts of the territory and into Texas to recover stolen stock. On May 6 word was received from the north that a band of robbers had stolen a large number of government mules in Kansas. They were on their way to Texas with the booty.

Grierson sent out a second lieutenant to intercept the robbers. This officer happened to be William R. Harmon, one of the most energetic and successful thief-catchers the frontier produced. On this occasion he pursued the bandits eighteen miles after sighting them, killed one of them single-handed, captured eleven others alive, and recovered 127 government mules, three horses, and two wagons.[14]

[12] Major E. N. Glass, *History of Tenth Cavalry* (Tucson, Arizona: Acme Printing Co., 1921), p. 18; Captain R. G. Carter to author, 1935.
[13] Files 567M and 773M, Old Files Section, AGO.
[14] *Army and Navy Journal,* May 21, 1870.

If white desperadoes did not have to wait until the completion of the Sun Dance to begin raiding, neither did the irreligious Comanches. Consequently on May 28 Tabananica led off for the Comanches with a preliminary raid on Tatum's agency corral, bagging twenty horses and mules. Tabananica was the Indian who had sent word that he would like to have the soldiers come out and fight him. After his raid he notified Tatum that he had killed and scalped a man near the agency. A diligent search failed to locate the body, but it is unlikely that Tabananica's statement was an empty boast.[15]

The Kiowas thought they could do better than this. On June 12, the Sun Dance being over, they relieved the post quartermaster at Fort Sill of seventy-three mules. A young chief named White Horse was responsible for this insolent feat. White Horse was one of the foremost raiders of his tribe; he was a powerfully-built fellow, with a crafty face, heavily pock-marked.[16] His plan was a simple one. The quartermaster corral was a "stake-and-rider" rail enclosure located on the flats of Cache Creek east of the post. At night the mules were turned loose inside, hobbled to prevent them from straying away in case part of the fence was knocked down during the night. It was guarded by two sentries from the Tenth Cavalry. White Horse decided to drive away the guards under cover of darkness, and help himself to the mules.

The scheme proceeded without a hitch. One of the Kiowas slipped inside the corral with a blanket in his hand. At a prearranged signal the other Indians whooped loudly and shot at the Afro-American troopers. The latter discharged their carbines and reported, with a minimum loss of time, at the post guardhouse, distant one mile. Meantime, the Indian in the corral let down the bars of the fence, dashed about waving his blanket, and stampeded the mules out into the fields. The remainder of the party rounded up the frightened animals, cut their hobbles, and herded them rapidly west through the mountains.[17]

Early in the morning two troops of cavalry under Captain Walsh set out to recover the stock. Unfortunately the passage of a vast buffalo herd had obscured the trail. Walsh was obliged to return empty handed. For several months work at the post was seriously handicapped for want of teams to haul rock and lumber. To prevent a recurrence of such a disaster it was decided to build a more substantial enclosure for the mules.

The now familiar stone corral was built, in the summer of 1870, at

[15] Tatum to Hoag, June 30, 1870; Tatum, *Our Red Brothers*, p. 33; Report of Colonel B. H. Grierson, File 936, AGO, 1870.

[16] Report of Colonel Grierson, File 936. Tatum, in *Our Red Brothers*, p. 33, erroneously charges this to the Quohadas.

[17] Kiowa informants: Hunting Horse, George Hunt.

107

the foot of the hill on which the post was being erected. Although designed primarily as a corral, and not as a fort, it was loopholed for defense should the need therefor arise. Many romantic but erroneous notions have been current among later occupants of Fort Sill regarding this picturesque landmark. Old-timers snort scornfully when questioned about these stories. One of them gives it as his opinion that the loopholes were merely for ventilation; another states firmly that the holes were made so that the mules might be able to look out and view the surrounding landscape. But it is doubtful if the comfort and pleasure of the mules were considered in the planning of this corral.

Colonel Grierson was highly indignant over White Horse's raid. But he was helpless. He could not catch the raiders. He could not even prove who they were. And his instructions from the War Department did not permit him to make indiscriminate attacks on the Indians. He had to be content with sending a message to the Kiowas to come in to the post, or "he would drive them in."

When Colonel Grierson's ultimatum reached the Kiowas they were camped on North Fork of Red River, about eighty miles west of Fort Sill, where they had recently celebrated their annual Sun Dance. White Horse had been bragging about how easy it was to steal animals from Fort Sill, so some of the young men decided to accept Grierson's invitation. Big Tree (Addo-eta) enlisted eighty ambitious fellows, including a number of visiting Cheyennes, to make the trip. This chief, though yet in his early twenties, had won renown in Heap-of-Bears' Texas raid of 1868. Now he planned a foray which would completely eclipse that of White Horse.[18]

Big Tree's party rode past Mount Scott to that hill now known as Welsh Hill. On the eastern end of this hill Big Tree concealed his men among the rocks while he went forward on reconnaissance. For two or three days he watched the post and the activities of the troops, familiarizing himself with their routine. He noted that the soldiers habitually grazed their horses on the plateau now occupied by the buildings of Post Field. At noon each day they all rode into Fort Sill for dinner, leaving the horse herds in charge of two or three watchmen.

Big Tree conceived the bold idea of stealing every cavalry mount in Fort Sill.

On the following night—June 21, 1870—he sent ten of his bravest men, under charge of the accomplished White Horse, south along Cache Creek to the vicinity of Feigel Point, where Sitting Bear Creek joins Cache Creek. These men were told to remain there until the following day. Then, when the sun was directly overhead, they were to ride west along the dry bed of the tributary, attack the two sentries guarding the

[18] George Hunt obtained the details of this raid from Big Tree, who died in 1927.

108

horse herd, and drive the animals west toward Signal Mountain. The main band would wait under cover at the foot of the ridge north of Signal Mountain until they saw the dust of the approaching horses, when they would gallop to assist in herding the stolen stock through the mountains to the Staked Plains. Only ten men were sent to initiate the coup because a larger party would be observed. The soldiers, being completely dismounted, would be unable to pursue.

It was a brilliant scheme. The strategy was faultless. Only one thing militated against its success. That was the lack of individual discipline on the part of the Indians. The plan went according to schedule until about three o'clock on the morning of June 22, when one of the main party fired a premature shot which threw the whole affair out of gear.

A little north of Four-Mile Crossing, where the infantry rifle range house is now located, lived a white man named Joseph Chandler, who maintained a little farm for supplying vegetables and milk to the post. His wife Tomasa was a Mexican woman, a former captive member of the Comanche tribe. Through their contacts with the Indians the Chandlers were able to keep the authorities informed as to hostile tendencies on the part of the tribes. At this particular time Chandler had a suspicion that trouble was brewing, a suspicion which he passed on to the post authorities, but on the advice of interpreter Horace Jones the warning was given little credence.

On the south side of Four-Mile Crossing was a party of Texans who were on the reservation without authority. They had an ox train, and were busily engaged in cutting firewood. The evening before Big Tree's raid Chandler cautioned the Texan night-herder that Indians were prowling near-by. He told the man that he was taking a big risk to go unarmed.

"My trust is in the Lord," was the pious reply.[19]

It was a bright moonlit night. At about 2:30 in the morning the Kiowas left their hideout on Welsh Hill, and rode down Ketch Creek to Medicine Bluff Creek. They crossed the stream at Four-Mile Crossing, then moved out on the flat ground south of the ford. As they emerged from the shadows of the timber they spied the solitary guard dozing near his ruminating oxen.

Success of the plan demanded that they detour past unseen and unheard. But one of the young men saw a chance to win coup. There was a single shot and the white man fell over in the grass. The killer ran forward with drawn scalping knife. He made a circular incision around his victim's head. Then he grasped the short, thick hair, placed his foot on the man's chest, gave a jerk. The scalp came off with a loud pop.[20]

[19] George Conover, *Sixty Years in Southwest Oklahoma* (Anadarko, Okla.: N. T. Plummer, 1927), p. 19.
[20] Big Tree's account to George Hunt. Frank Given, a participant, to author.

A candle was lighted momentarily in the woodcutters' camp, revealing its position to the Indians. With their thirst for blood fully aroused some of them circled the camp calling taunts in a mixture of broken Spanish and Kiowa, trying to get some of the men to come out. But the woodcutters lay quiet, and after a time the Indians went away.[21]

Big Tree concluded that his plan was spoiled. He felt sure that the murder of the white man would lead to an investigation in the morning, which would arouse the post, so that the soldiers would be on the alert for further trouble. Therefore he sent a messenger to call in the detachment at Feigel Point. When these men arrived the whole party retreated west into the mountains. Colonel Grierson never knew how close he came to having to call for a board of survey on his entire herd of cavalry mounts.

About the same hour that Big Tree's men were testing the Peace Policy near Four-Mile Crossing a party of white desperadoes rode into Fort Sill and attempted to steal some horses from the cavalry picket lines. The guard halted them. They replied with a shot. Then they rode around back of the plateau and fired several times into the rear of the shanty in which Colonel Grierson was living. The post guard was turned out, but failed to catch the interlopers.[22]

The detachment which Big Tree had sent to Feigel Point made their way along Cache Creek until they came upon the cattle outfit of the beef contractor, a Mr. Buckley. The herders, being armed, were not molested. The Indians continued down the east bank of Cache Creek to a point opposite the agency settlement. Here they found the camp of a government ox train. The drivers were asleep in the grass.

Agent Lawrie Tatum and his wife were also asleep, in the adobe house near-by. Suddenly they were awakened by a gunshot. In a few moments two men came panting to the door, lugging the bleeding form of Levi Lucans, an employe of the quartermaster. While the Quakers were giving Lucans first aid another shot stabbed out in the night. This time it was on the west bank of the creek. The Quakers blew out the lamp. They stole to the windows to peer out. In the bright moonlight they saw several Indians cross Cache Creek and run horses out of the agency corral. Two or three of them were riding about the premises staring at the unfinished mill and schoolhouses. Presently they cantered off towards the mountains.[23]

The agency physician and the post surgeon were summoned. Lucans was badly wounded, but did not die. In the morning a dead Mexican was found near the corral. A squad of soldiers came to investigate. A

[21] Report of Colonel Grierson, File 937, AGO, 1870.
[22] *Ibid.*
[23] Tatum, *op. cit.*, p. 34.

troop went to Four-Mile Crossing, then rode through the Wichita Mountains in pursuit of the Indians. But the Indians had separated; the trail could not be followed. While at Four-Mile Crossing the soldiers talked to Mr. Chandler, who was greatly incensed because the post authorities had disregarded his warning, and refused to discuss the killing of the night-herder. Soon after these occurrences he moved back to his old farm on Chandler Creek, ten miles north of Fort Sill.[24]

While the troops, on the morning of June 22, were out west looking for the raiders, White Horse and his friends attacked a party of Texan cattle herders on the road a few miles south of Fort Sill. The harassed post commander sent out a detachment to rescue the frightened civilians. One man already had been killed and scalped.[25] The Peace Policy was not working out well.

The peace-loving employes of the agency were greatly perturbed. Mr. Tatum called them together and explained that he could not reasonably expect them to remain at such a dangerous post. They were free to return to their homes. However he hoped they would remain to assist in the worthy effort to civilize and Christianize the Indians. All of the hired help, except Schoolmaster Josiah Butler and his wife Lizzie, voted to depart at once.

These things were exceedingly distressing to Agent Tatum. Kindness was not having the desired effect on the Indians. The Quakers, in common with others engaged in Indian work, expected results too soon. Few realized that it would take at least a generation before the Indians would adopt the standards of conduct which the white men wished for them. Tatum, however, was a man of common sense. Though the Society of Friends did not approve the use of force, he was, at heart, a strict disciplinarian. He decided to go to Fort Sill for a talk with Colonel Grierson.

His relations with the latter were cordial. Grierson had assisted him on more than one occasion. Once, when the agency sawmill was about to shut down for lack of lubricating oil, the post commander sent lard from the post commissary to keep it running.[26] Furthermore, Grierson was kind to the Indians. Frequently he invited them to his house for meals. When they complained that their women and children were hungry, he gave them an order on the post bakery for bread. To this day old Indians come to Fort Sill to ask for "some of that good army bread."

After consulting with Colonel Grierson, the agent decided to discipline the Indians by withholding their rations until they returned the government stock which they had stolen.

24 Conover, *op. cit.*, p. 20.
25 Grierson's report, File 937.
26 Old Files, Fort Sill.

111

In a few days a representative of the Kiowas came in to ask when the rations for the Kiowas and Comanches would be ready for issue. He intimated that the Indians would be pleased also to receive special presents as an inducement to stop raiding. Such had been the custom in years past. On being informed that no presents would be given, nor rations issued, until the stolen animals were returned, the emissary departed. He wore a black scowl.

The next day Mr. Tatum's spirits were lowered even further. A mule train arrived from the north with supplies for the Indians. When it departed all the Quaker associates went with it except the Butlers. But Tatum was cheered somewhat by a visit made by two Friends from the Cheyenne agency at Darlington. They reported everything quiet at their establishment. Then they noticed a squad of soldiers stationed at the commissary to maintain order during the issue of rations to the "tame" Indians.

"What is this?" they asked, hoisting their eyebrows. "Dost realize that thou art violating the precepts of the Society by using armed force?"

Josiah Butler agreed that Tatum was tempting Divine Providence with an exhibition of little faith.

Lawrie Tatum pondered on the matter. His conscience told him that his friends were right and he dismissed the military guard. At once the Indians became quite boisterous. Unrestrained by the presence of soldiery they killed thirty more beeves than they were entitled to. When chided for this they laughingly ran off with all the provisions and cooking utensils belonging to the cattle herders.

THE INDIANS RUN WILD

As Lawrie Tatum's morale went down, that of the Indians rose. As far as they were concerned the Peace Policy was a howling success. White Horse visited Texas, killed Mr. Gottleib Koozer, and brought back Mrs. Koozer and her six children as captives. Kicking Bird led a hundred warriors south across Red River in one of the most important raids of the season. Kicking Bird made this expedition because he had been accused of cowardice. His tribesmen thought that he was consorting too much with the whites at Fort Sill. On account of this criticism he organized a foray for the purpose of recovering his lost "face." It was a war party pure and simple; the object was to have a fight. The braves rode their best racing ponies. They were painted and decorated in their finest costumes.[27] No one was supposed to leave the party to steal stock or to depredate. Nevertheless, shortly after crossing the river, several braves separated from the group and robbed a mail stage at Rock Station, near

[27] Hunting Horse to author, 1934.

112

the present town of Jermyn, Jack County. This episode aroused the troops at Fort Richardson. Captain Curwen B. McClellan, Sixth Cavalry, was sent with fifty-three troopers and one civilian scout to intercept the raiders.

McClellan located Kicking Bird at 10 o'clock on the morning of July 12, several miles east of the site of Seymour, Texas, and commenced an attack. He quickly changed to the defensive when he saw that he was outnumbered and that the Indian leader was throwing out flanking parties to cut off his retreat. Then Kicking Bird made an assault. Riding at the head of his warriors he personally impaled a trooper on his lance. The soldiers retreated all afternoon in the heat of the July sun. Kicking Bird used his men skilfully to harry the cavalrymen from all sides, forcing them to abandon their dead. Three troopers were killed and twelve wounded. McClellan made his men dismount and lead their horses, in order to prevent them from fleeing in disorder. Toward evening the Indians disappeared. The soldiers were reinforced by twenty cowboys who were camped near the site of Jean. In the morning the troop returned to Fort Richardson.[28]

Captain McClellan, in his report of the engagement, paid compliment to the Indian leader for his superior generalship during the fight. But it was the last time that Kicking Bird fought the whites. He expressed regret that he had been forced to lead the expedition. From that time on he devoted himself to promoting peaceful relations with the authorities. As a result he made powerful enemies among the war chiefs of the tribe. In the end he suffered martyrdom for his friendship with the whites.

In another raid made in Texas that summer the eldest and favorite son of Satank was killed. With several other young Kiowas he approached a picket farmhouse on the northern Texas frontier. The settlers fired from the shelter of the building. Young Satank sat down suddenly, mortally wounded. His companions fled without him. Then they recovered their pride and rode back to rescue the body. They concealed it among some rocks.

Old Satank went to the scene to recover the remains. Crows and buzzards had reduced them to a heap of bones. When the chief saw what was left of his beloved son, his friends had to tie him with a lariat to prevent him from committing suicide. Then they allowed him to gather the bones, wash them, and bundle them in a new blanket. Satank carried these bones with him wherever he went. It became a familiar sight in the Kiowa tribe to see the chief riding along in sorrow, leading a gentle horse laden with the skeleton of his son. When he camped he con-

---

[28] Associated Press dispatch quoted in *Army and Navy Journal*, July 30, 1870. J. B. "Bu" Terrell to author, 1935. Mr. Terrell was a member of the cattle "outfit" which reinforced the troops.

structed a special tepee for his son, with food and water placed therein for the spirit. Satank was inconsolable.[29]

Officers at Fort Richardson reported that the border was infested by Fort Sill Indians that summer. They said that the savages were armed with repeating rifles and carbines. The civilians in Texas, and even some of the army officers (who should have known better), were quite sure that these weapons had been furnished to the Indians by the Indian agent, or by the commanding officer at Fort Sill. The press at San Antonio was filled with scathing editorials directed against the authorities at Fort Sill.

But Tatum was innocent of these charges. So was the harassed Grierson. The latter kept most of his troops along the line of Red River all summer, but he could not catch a single Indian. Two hundred men mounted on horses had no chance to intercept the raiders, who knew the country perfectly, were acquainted with every ford and crossing, and could easily avoid the patrols. It would have required thousands, not hundreds, of soldiers to restrain the Indians by measures of passive defense.

The newspaper attacks stung Grierson into making reply: "Prohibited by order from interfering with Indians while on the reservation, and not even obliged to follow them beyond its limits unless called upon by the agent, the commanding officer of Fort Sill has, nevertheless, sent troops in pursuit of Indians and kept them patrolling the south side of Red River with orders to attack any Indians found off their Reserve, taking upon himself the responsibility of such action in view of the emergency. Notice has also been sent upon learning the departure of any raiding party of Indians from this reservation, to enable the military authorities and citizens of Texas to take steps to punish them. The commanding officer of Fort Sill has done all in his power to protect the Texas frontier from the depredations by both Indians and white marauders. He has returned upward of 50 horses and mules stolen from citizens of Texas by Indians, and during the last eighteen months his command captured and restored to the government upwards of 200 horses and mules stolen by persons of Texas, delivered to the civil authorities some twenty thieves and whiskey dealers, and killed a number who resisted the troops or attempted to escape."[30]

He could not resist taking a slam at the Texans: "Many of these desperadoes are disguised as Indians while engaged in this nefarious business. In view of these facts, the obvious suggestion presents itself that while the Legislature of Texas is taking measures to protect their borders from marauding Indians, they should also devise some means

[29] George Hunt to author. Mr. Hunt's first wife was a daughter of Old Satank.
[30] Old Files, Fort Sill, 1870.

114

for suppressing the organized bands of white thieves who infest their state, and steal alike from Indians, citizens, and the government."[31]

The question as to who was supplying the Indians with arms and ammunition was a sore one. Actually the redskins were obtaining them from Mexicans who came from New Mexico. Some of these smugglers conducted operations as close to Fort Sill as the northern entrance of Yapparika Canyon (now Gore Gap). Caddo George Washington, chief of the Caddoes, also bootlegged arms to the Kiowas and Comanches, meanwhile posing as a firm friend of the authorities.[32]

Actually the wild Indians did not have as many guns, nor as good, as they were credited with possessing. Most of their firearms were of an old pattern. Also the savages were execrable marksmen on account of not having enough ammunition for practice. They were much better shots with the bow and arrow. Still, they earnestly desired more and better guns and more ammunition. This was the burden of their unceasing complaint to the agent; they were forever trying to bargain with him for these things.

Their considerable success around Fort Sill and in Texas caused the Indians, in their visits to the agency for rations, to exhibit increasing impudence. Tatum's error in dispensing with the military guard permitted them to run completely wild around the place. Every night was Hallowe'en as far as the redskins were concerned. Each morning the distressed agency officials would discover their cattle standing disconsolately in the corrals, with arrows protruding from hips, backs, and necks—looking like so many grotesque porcupines. The Indians were accustomed to ride past the corrals at night and shoot at the animals just for devilment.[33]

Most of the Comanches were in the Staked Plains, annoying the Mexicans and Texans. Tabananica again sent word to Tatum that he wished the soldiers from Fort Sill would come out and give him a fight. Tatum and Grierson did not consider this amusing. They disdained to reply.

A COUNCIL WITH THE INDIANS

The Indians were shrewd. They realized by now that the commanding officer at Fort Sill was a different kind of man from General Sheridan, and that they could bargain with him. He was not prone to talk of hanging them as Sheridan had been. He did not put their chiefs in the guardhouse. The agent, too, was a man of peace. He was not even armed. They were not afraid of him or his scoldings. On August 7 they came to Fort Sill primed for a big powwow. They brought with them twenty-

[31] *Ibid.*
[32] Indian informants: Hunting Horse and Yellow Wolf.
[33] George Conover to author, 1934. Mr. Conover was employed at the agency.

seven of the mules which White Horse had stolen from the post corral. They also had the Koozers, whom they expected to trade for arms and ammunition. Tatum was informed that the Kiowas were ready to meet him in council.

There is no record of any American official ever refusing to have a powwow with the Indians, except Sheridan, and even he succumbed in the end. Mr. Tatum responded with alacrity. The conference was held in the council room of the Indian commissary, near Quarry Hill. No army officers were invited to attend except Colonel Grierson, who brought his interpreter, Horace Jones. Agent Tatum was accompanied by his issue clerk, George Conover, and Mathew Leeper, Jr., the agency interpreter.[34]

After the Indians had seated themselves comfortably on the floor Mr. Tatum rose to make the opening address. He reproved the Kiowas for their recent bad conduct, and advised them that it was poor sportsmanship to rob and kill their friends at the agency. Furthermore, he said, they ought to live at peace with the Texans, who now were citizens of the United States, and, like themselves, were children of the great white father in Washington. Both Washington and the Great Spirit felt very bad about the way they had been acting.

Lone Wolf took several minutes for rebuttal. He said that he had been looking and looking, but could see nothing for the agent to get mad about. It was true that a few Texans had been killed. So had a number of Indians. Things were now even. Why not dismiss the whole matter?

Colonel Grierson arose, and in an emphatic manner told the Indians that they would have to give up the warpath. Let them abandon their wild life and follow the road of the white man; they might as well realize this now as later, he roared.

The voluble Satanta, a strapping fellow with a face like an eagle, replied to this that the road he liked best was the scalping knife and the breech-loading gun. Look at the miserable Caddoes and Wichitas! They follow the white man's road and get nothing. We strong, warlike Kiowas are courted and fawned upon, invited to treaties and councils, given presents and annuities. Then he glanced keenly at Grierson, who was rumbling in his beard, and continued, insolently, "It is plain that Grierson is mad. Let's keep what we have, and see how much more we can get!" In the meantime the savages were flexing their bows, taking arrows out of their quivers and glancing along the shafts as if to select the best, snapping cartridges in and out of their guns. One mean-looking buck sitting near Tatum drew a butcher knife and commenced to whet the blade. But Tatum refused to be intimidated. He wiped the beads of perspiration from his square bald head and repeated his ultimatum: No

[34] Tatum, *op. cit.*, pp. 40-43; Conover, op. cit., pp. 23-26.

rations would be issued until the captives were released and the stock returned. Thrusting out his jaw obstinately he returned glare for glare with the Indians. Presently Lone Wolf came over and thrust his hand inside the agent's vest to see if there was any "scare." Finding Tatum's pulse apparently normal, he shook hands, and reseated himself.

The Kiowas then staged another show. They brought in White Horse, had him sit on a barrel in the middle of the room, and proudly pointed him out to Tatum and Grierson as the brave who had killed and scalped the two men near the agency on June 22. They also bragged that he was the one who had stolen the government mules and captured the Koozer family. He was, they said, the most dangerous man among them. Each Indian heartily shook the grinning White Horse by the hand and asked him to consent to make peace, for the poor white man's sake.[35]

They told Grierson and Tatum that they would not disturb Fort Sill or the agency any more that summer. The white people need not sit trembling in their tents, peeping out to see if the Kiowas were coming. They could now send their horses out to graze, and send men out to chop wood. These favors were granted by the Indians within a half-mile of a post where five hundred men were under arms, restrained by the Peace Policy.

Tatum and Grierson remained firm, for a few days, in their resolve not to issue rations to the Indians until the mules and the Koozers were given up. On the eighteenth the argument was reopened. A compromise was reached in which the mules were given up for nothing, and the Koozers ransomed for one hundred dollars apiece. Grierson then presented the Kiowas with some horses which had been found near the post and which Kicking Bird claimed were his.

The matter having been concluded in such a satisfactory manner, Tatum ordered his clerks to issue the rations. The Indians called loudly for powder and lead. They also wanted to have rations issued whenever they called for them instead of at regular intervals. In addition to this they demanded that the boundary lines of the reservation be wiped out. Of course Tatum could not comply with these requests. Some of the Indians thereupon refused to accept their rations. Others threw on the ground most of what they had received. They saved only the coffee and sugar, and howled for double rations of these.

In spite of all this Colonel Grierson remained a firm advocate of the Peace Policy. He announced to his officers that it was sure eventually to succeed; but meanwhile he did not want the newspapers to get wind of the atrocities which had been committed near the post during the summer.[36]

[35] *Army and Navy Journal,* September 17, 1870.
[36] *Ibid.*

Two weeks after Tatum's big council with the Kiowas the Comanche chief Isa-habeet came in with a white captive named Martin B. Kilgore, whom he offered for sale to Tatum. The agent said he would give one hundred dollars for the cowering miserable boy. Isa-habeet wanted more than that amount. During the bartering the Comanche glanced out the window and saw a troop of cavalry approaching from Fort Sill. He closed quickly for one hundred dollars.[37] Lawrie Tatum was not blind. He got the point. When the Indians came in for the next issue of rations he called again for a military guard. A basement was dug under the north end of the commissary building, where the soldiers could gather around a stove in the winter time, and thus be close at hand, yet not too obviously in view.

True to their word, the Indians did not raid around the agency or post any more that season. But they polished off with a few well-directed forays in Texas. The Quohada Comanches on September 5 attacked the home of Jesse Maxey on Denton Creek, Montague County. Mr. Maxey was not home when the Indians arrived. They killed his aged father and shot an arrow through the breasts of his wife, who was nursing an infant; the missile pierced the skull of the child, killing it instantly. The woman was scalped and left for dead, but she later recovered. Her two small children, a boy and a girl, were seized by the hair and carried off as prisoners. The first night the little girl cried so much that the annoyed Indians dashed her brains out and then impaled her naked body on the broken branch of a mesquite tree and left it hanging there. The small boy was not killed. He remained a captive for three years, forgot his name and mother tongue.[38] Eventually he was ransomed at the agency and restored to his relatives.

On September 30 a stage coach was attacked while en route from Fort Concho to Fort Griffin, near a place called Mount Margaret, or "The Mound." Two soldiers were on the stage as escort. When fifteen or twenty Indians suddenly appeared from the northeast the driver and one of the soldiers jumped from the vehicle and ran. Private Martin Wurmser, Company E, Fourth Cavalry, bravely remained at his post. Troops investigating later found the coach turned over, with the badly mutilated body of Wurmser inside. The mail was scattered all over the road. Even the seat cushions had been removed. This exploit was accomplished by White Horse. It was a revenge raid. One of the Kiowa girls of his band had been weeping because her brother had been killed

---

[37] Tatum, *op. cit.*, p. 45.

[38] Report of Captain D. Madden, Sixth Cavalry, Old Files, AGO, 1870.

in a raid. White Horse was persuaded to "wipe out" the death, as she had no near relatives of her own to do it.[39]

About the first of October Captain W. A. Rafferty, out on a scout from Fort Richardson, attacked a party of raiders on Cameron Creek, near Spy Knob. Two Indians were killed. One of them had a pass on his person signed by Agent Jonathan Richards, stating that he was a Wichita named Keesh-Kosh, and that he was a reliable man, to be treated well by all who met him.[40]

As cold weather came on the raids ceased. The Indians drew in closer to the agency to winter at government expense. The Fort Sill people and the Texans were given a breathing spell in which to recover from the effects of the second year of the Peace Policy.

But Agent Tatum's troubles were not over entirely for that year. The settlers of northern Texas, who had borne the brunt of the summer excursions of the Kiowas and Comanches commenced writing for redress and submitting big claims against the government. Some of them arrived in person to recover stolen stock. With understandable indignation they pointed out in the Indian camps animals which bore their brands. A few horses and mules were pried loose from the redskins and restored to their owners. But in general the Indians retained their loot. Smiling to themselves, they considered that they had done fairly well for one year. In this, however, they erred: unknown to the Indians, the government allowed settlement of many of the claims and large sums were deducted from the annuity money due the Indians, for which they had paid in land. The Texans had the last laugh after all.

Satank was the cause of one troublesome incident at this time. He was a wizened old chief of about sixty winters, with the habitual expression of a man who had just taken a large dose of raw quinine. One brisk autumn day he rode to the Fort Sill agency to see Tatum. The agent describes the encounter: "Satank was probably the worst Indian on the reservation. He rode a mule which was claimed by a Texan. The Texan proved that the mule had his brand, and the evidence further showed that the mule was his. Satank said that some time ago one of his sons went to Texas to steal a few animals without intending to hurt anybody, but while they were trying to get the animals the Texans were so mad that they shot his son. He afterwards went to the same vicinity and stole the mule he was riding and now he loved it as his son. For that reason he thought that he ought to be allowed to keep it."

When Mr. Tatum ruled otherwise, Satank proposed that the two of them—Indian and Quaker agent—should go out on the prairie and have

[39] Gillem to Wood, Fort Concho, October 2, 1870, Old Files, AGO; George Hunt to author, 1935.
[40] Report of Captain Rafferty, Fort Richardson, October 10, 1870, Old Files, AGO.

a finish fight. Whoever killed the other should keep the mule. Tatum did not accept this interesting proposal.

In the fall, when the Indians suspended raiding operations, the officers and men of Fort Sill were brought in from patrol duty on Red River. The troops resumed their duties of building the new post. The officers organized the Fort Sill Jockey Club. A one-mile track was laid out on the flat ground where the polo field is now. On October 1 was held the first of a series of race meets. Each meet consisted of three races of one mile each. Entry fees were thirty dollars for each horse. Fifteen officers of the Tenth Cavalry and Sixth Infantry entered private mounts. Captain Walsh won the main event on "Leather Lungs" in 1:59.[41]

Colonel Grierson did not succeed in completing the new barracks and quarters before winter set in. Some of the company commanders were given permission to move their units into the unfinished barracks, with the understanding that the assignments were only temporary. Permanent assignments were not to be made until all barracks and quarters were finished. As a result, several of the company commanders thought they were being discriminated against. The infantry commanders declared that preference was being given to the cavalry. The cavalrymen replied that they had been continuously in the field since before the Civil War, whereas the infantry, in general, had lived at ease in comfortable barracks. They thought it high time that the infantry be compelled to live in tents for several years. Grierson tried to smooth all this out, but the correspondence became quite heated and bulky.[42]

In addition to this the colonel was having an exchange of acrimonious letters with the officers left in charge of Fort Arbuckle. That post was scheduled for abandonment as soon as Fort Sill was well established. In the meantime a small force was maintained there to guard the public property and to assist in forwarding the material and records to the new post. The officers at Arbuckle apparently reveled in the rare opportunity to be post commanders.

Grierson found Captain Edward Byrne particularly trying. A sample of one of Byrne's letters sent to Fort Sill follows:

"All reasonable requests emanating from the commanding officer of Fort Sill will be cheerfully complied with; but Lieutenant Sherwood [one of Grierson's staff] is respectfully informed that these headquarters are not aware that the commanding officer at Fort Sill has the authority to issue peremptory orders directing the movements of these headquarters, in any case whatever, as he seems to think, by the tone of his letter.

[41] *Army and Navy Journal*, October 1, 1870.
[42] Old Correspondence file, Fort Sill.

. . . The condition, bad enough at any time, is rendered still worse by the unwarranted action of the Quartermaster at Fort Sill, who took all of the serviceable mules in two teams belonging to this post, and replaced them by others almost worthless. The action of the commanding officer at Fort Sill in attempting to give peremptory orders to the commanding officer at this post, and ordering him to report to the ACS at Fort Sill without clearly defined authority, is considered as being most extraordinary and without precedent in the History of this or any other post.

"E. BYRNE,
"Captain, 10th Cavalry, Comdg. Post."

It is entirely possible that Captain Byrne was correct in his interpretation of military history, but he was most impolitic in thus addressing his regimental and district commander. This was before the day of efficiency reports. Nevertheless, the following year when the strength of the commissioned personnel of the army was reduced by the operation of a "benzine board," one of the first officers mustered out of the Tenth Cavalry was one Captain Edward Byrne.[43]

By the end of August, in spite of strenuous efforts, the officers' quarters were not completed. Only the bare walls of two sets were up. Details of men were ordered out for every conceivable project. Captain George T. Robinson had one party afield surveying the military reservation; once he was called back to construct a sundial, to be placed just north of the flag pole. By the end of September the following buildings were completed: two quartermaster storehouses, a commissary, an ordnance building, the post headquarters building, one company barrack, the quartermaster stone corral, and two small buildings adjacent to the corral. The walls of the following were up: two barracks and six sets of officers' quarters on the east line. Foundations had been dug for five sets of quarters on the north line, and for the guardhouse. The hospital and bakery had not been established.

The winter was an unusually cold one. Two days before Christmas Captain Edward Byrne, now at Fort Sill, asked for some stovepipe for his barracks, where his company was shivering in subzero weather in an uncompleted building. Colonel Grierson told the quartermaster to take the stovepipe out of his quarters and give it to Byrne.

During Christmas week the water of Medicine Bluff Creek froze solid. Everyone, soldiers and civilians alike, was turned out to harvest ice. The cakes were stored in ice houses dug in the banks of the creek. One of these was near Medicine Bluff. The remains of another can be seen on the bank west of Rucker Park.

43 *Ibid.*

Drinking water was obtained in those days from the creek. The horses were watered in the old beaver pond back of where the present hospital stands. This is where Custer had watered his horses, and no one thought to make a change. The post surgeon complained bitterly and often over the practice of watering animals upstream from where drinking water for the post was obtained. He thought that the presence of manure in the water was a contributory cause in the prevalence of malaria at the post.

Concerning malaria, the doleful predictions made by Elias Rector in 1859 were now true. Over half the population of Fort Sill was afflicted with the disease. Even the Indians objected to camping in the vicinity.[44]

Colonel Grierson also had trouble getting mail and supplies through from the north. The roads at best were but trails, and after a heavy rain they were impassable. The streams were apt to rise suddenly and delay traffic for a week or more. Consequently efforts were made to purchase forage locally. In January of 1871 Grierson complained to department headquarters that the price of corn was exorbitant on account of contractors forming "combines" to raise the price.

As winter receded, construction work was resumed. By mid-spring of 1871 all of the troops and officers were in their permanent quarters. A stone blockhouse, to be used as a signal station and meteorological observatory, was built on the high hill (Signal Mountain) six miles west of the post. In April plans were made to commence the construction of a hospital. Ten thousand dollars had been appropriated for this purpose, but work was delayed on account of disagreement at the post between the commander and the surgeon as to the location and size of the building. Colonel Grierson thought that a twelve-bed hospital was ample; he said that the twelve beds would never be filled. The surgeon disagreed with this, and also desired a different site. He said that the one chosen by Grierson was too near the stables. Grierson replied that it was as near the barracks as it was to the stables, and that, besides, who ever heard that it was unhealthy to be near stables?

But these troubles were minor ones. The post commander realized that with the approach of summer Indian troubles would be renewed. Special duty was restricted. As many men as could be spared from construction work were returned to their organizations. The garrison was cautioned to be ready for field service.

[44] Medical History, Fort Sill, Station Hospital, Fort Sill.

CHAPTER SEVEN

THE BLOODY PEACE

THE INDIANS RESUME THEIR RAIDS—WARREN WAGON-TRAIN MASSACRE
—INDIAN ACCOUNT OF THE WAGON-TRAIN MASSACRE—ARREST
OF THE CHIEFS—"WE KO-EET-SENKO MUST DIE"—
DISPOSITION OF SATANTA AND BIG TREE—AU-
TUMN CAMPAIGNS, 1871—RAIDS OF 1872—
COUNCILS OF 1872—MACKENZIE
STRIKES THE QUOHADI

THE RAIDING season of 1871 opened unusually early. On January 24 a group of Kiowas under Maman-ti (Sky-Walker) and Quitan appeared on the Butterfield Trail two miles south of Flat Top Mountain, in Young County, Texas. Here they attacked four Negroes who were hauling supplies from Weatherford to their homes near Fort Griffin. One of these men was Brit Johnson, the hero of the Elm Creek Raid of 1864. Brit had his men kill their horses and use them as a barricade. Though the colored men defended themselves bravely, they all were killed and scalped.[1] On their way home the playful Kiowas amused themselves by throwing the kinky-haired scalps at one another. Finally they threw them away, as the hair was too short to be of value. They had little to show for their efforts when they arrived home, but bragged about the fight nevertheless.[2]

A few soldiers from Fort Richardson, under Lieutenant Borthwick, Sixth Cavalry, went out to bury Brit Johnson and his companions. They pursued the Indians and actually overtook them. They would have been better off if they had not ridden so rapidly. The Indians wounded Borthwick and drove his detachment back to the post.

On April 19 an unidentified white man, after being wounded, was scalped alive. This happened on Salt Creek, not far from where the Negroes had been killed. The following evening several citizens were

[1] *Army and Navy Journal,* May 13, 1871; James Mooney, *op. cit.,* p. 328.
[2] As told to George Hunt by Quitan.

123

attacked within sight of Fort Richardson; on the twenty-first other civilians were attacked and robbed of their horses within three miles of the post. Altogether fourteen persons were killed by Indians during the spring of 1871. The area between Fort Richardson and Fort Griffin was especially dangerous. The Indians seemed to strike due south from Fort Sill. Salt Creek prairie, halfway between Richardson and Belknap, was dotted with graves of victims of the Indians.[3]

WARREN WAGON-TRAIN MASSACRE

Persistent reports from Texas concerning the Indian depredations caused General Sherman to make a tour of inspection of the border posts. He was determined to discover from personal observation whether the reports were exaggerated. He also wanted to know whether the Indians committing the outrages were reservation Indians.

Accompanying General Sherman were Colonels Tourtelotte and McCoy of his personal staff, and Major General R. B. Marcy, Inspector General of the Army. They rode in a Daugherty ambulance, escorted by fifteen selected cavalrymen. Sherman risked his scalp by traveling with so small an escort, but he did not realize this until later. He saw no Indians; neither did the settlers along the way appear to be fearful of Indian attacks. "They expose women and children singly on the road and in cabins far off from others, as though they were safe in Illinois," Sherman wrote. "Of course I have heard other stories, but actions are more significant than words. If the Comanches don't steal horses it is because they cannot be tempted."[4]

General Marcy differed with Sherman. He could see that the country was less thickly populated than it had been when he traveled through it before the Civil War. "If the Indian marauders are not punished," he said, "the whole country seems in a fair way of becoming totally depopulated."[5]

Leaving Fort Griffin, Sherman's party journeyed along the Butterfield Trail. This was the same road which Marcy had laid out years before; later it was used by the Butterfield Stage Company, which operated a stage line to El Paso. The route was too expensive and dangerous to maintain, and had been abandoned since before the Civil War. On the evening of May 17 the officers reached Fort Belknap, which consisted of a few ruins and ghostlike chimneys standing in the wilderness of sandstone and mesquite. The place had been deserted for years, but, like Forts Chadbourne and Phantom Hill, was picketed by a few lonely and apprehensive soldiers. Sherman wrote to the department commander

---

[3] Mackenzie to Wood, File 1305, AGO, 1871.
[4] Sherman to Reynolds, May 10, 1871.
[5] R. B. Marcy, as quoted by J. S. Wilbarger, *op. cit.*, pp. 552-53.

recommending that these men be made more comfortable and confident. Still, there really seemed to be little danger. So far Sherman had found not a trace of Indians—he had only heard rumors.

The following day the general resumed his journey. About one o'clock in the afternoon he crossed the head of Flint Creek, and traversed the broad plain sloping gently eastward toward Cox Mountain. This was the area where so many white men had been killed within the last few years. The sun, which had been shining brightly, was suddenly obscured by clouds driving in from the south. Still no Indians appeared.

Sherman was met at Rock Station by a guard of honor under Lieutenant R. G. Carter. He arrived at Fort Richardson at sunset and went into camp near Mackenzie's rude quarters, preferring to sleep in a tent. After supper the officers of the Fourth Cavalry called to pay their respects, after which Sherman received a delegation of citizens who came to complain of Indian depredations. The general listened sympathetically, but still felt that the reports were embroidered considerably. He promised to investigate, when he arrived at Fort Sill, the charges that the Indians were receiving arms and ammunition at the post, and that they were allowed to bring stolen stock back to their camps with impunity.

Some time after midnight a civilian named Thomas Brazeal limped into the post and was admitted to the hospital. He was suffering from a gunshot wound in the foot. Sherman went to the hospital before daylight to hear his story. Brazeal told a pitiful tale; seven of his companions had been killed by Indians the previous afternoon two or three miles west of Cox Mountain. He, with four others, had escaped.[6] According to Brazeal's story, given more completely to a correspondent of the *New York Times,* a train loaded with corn, owned by the firm of Warren and Duposes, government contractors, was attacked by 150 Indians armed with carbines and revolvers. The train consisted of ten wagons, a wagonmaster, ten teamsters, and a night watchman. It was hauling supplies from the railhead at Weatherford to Fort Griffin. The train was about to go into camp at three o'clock in the afternoon when the Indians were discovered a half-mile distant, advancing rapidly.

The wagonmaster, Nathan S. Long, corralled the wagons for defense by forming them in a circle, with the mules turned to the center. The teamsters then prepared for a fight, and endeavored to build a breastwork of sacks of grain, but the fire of the Indians was so heavy they could not effect it. The wagonmaster and four teamsters were killed in the corral. The Indians then prepared to charge in front, whereupon the seven surviving white men left the wagons and ran for the woods, two

[6] File 1305, AGO. This is a general file covering all the correspondence and other papers relating to this affair.

miles to the east. The Indians pursued, and in the running fight which followed two more teamsters were killed and three wounded. The Indians broke off the pursuit at the edge of the woods and went back to plunder the train.[7]

After listening to Brazeal's story General Sherman called for the post adjutant and dictated several orders in rapid succession. Brevet Major General Ranald S. Mackenzie, colonel of the Fourth Cavalry, was directed to take a strong force of cavalry and thirty pack mules and proceed west to the site of the massacre. After an investigation to ascertain the truth of the report, he was to follow the Indians until he had caught and punished them, or had driven them to Fort Sill. He was to report to Sherman at Sill. Orders were sent to the Commander of Fort Griffin to coöperate with Mackenzie.

Mackenzie sent out at once an advance detachment under a sergeant, then followed with four troops of his regiment. The departure was made in a blinding rainstorm.

General Sherman, after collecting several citizens who agreed to accompany him to Fort Sill to identify stolen stock, departed north toward Red River.

It had been known to the military personnel at Fort Sill for several weeks that General Sherman was coming to inspect the post. William Tecumseh Sherman was the general of the army, the four-starred successor of George Washington and U. S. Grant. In addition to being internationally famous for his service during the Civil War, he was being mentioned as presidential timber. The army folk at Fort Sill were thrown into a flurry of preparation in anticipation of his visit. The troops were drilled and redrilled. Equipment was shined and polished. First sergeants and stable sergeants were prodded and harassed. Company records were brought up to date. The quartermaster lined up the cans on the shelves of the commissary in geometric precision. The police of the post was given minute attention. The ladies on the officers' line planned several brilliant social events.

INDIAN ACCOUNT OF THE WAGON-TRAIN MASSACRE[8]

Unaware of the advent of General Sherman the Indians also were planning brilliant affairs—though of a somewhat different nature. At their camp on the North Fork of Red River, near the present site of Granite, they were sitting around the council fire passing the war pipe from one brave to another. Kiowas, Kiowa-Apaches, and Comanches

[7] *New York Tribune,* quoted in *Army and Navy Journal,* June 10, 1871.

[8] The author obtained the Indian account principally from Yellow Wolf, who today is the sole survivor. Other interesting details were furnished by Hunting Horse, who was contemporary with the event but not a participant; by Ay-tah, whose husband, Set-maunte, was a participant; and by George Hunt, who obtained his information from Big Tree and others.

were invited to participate in a great raid against the *Tehannas*. A hundred chiefs and lesser warriors accepted the pipe.

At this point a sinister figure emerges from the obscurity of the past. It is Do-ha-te (Medicine Man), the Owl Prophet. This Kiowa war chief and medicine man was one of the strongest personalities the tribe produced. Though scarcely known to the whites, he was the secret instigator and directing spirit of nearly every major raid made by the Kiowas in the early seventies. Known vaguely to the authorities under his real name, Maman-ti (Touching-the-Sky, or Sky-Walker), this dread personality is scarcely mentioned in written history. But today ask any old Kiowa who was the leader of the great raid in 1871, when the wagon-teamsters were killed, and the answer is, invariably, "Do-ha-te!"

If you know your history you ask, "but wasn't Satanta the leader on that raid?"

Again the reply: "Oh, Satanta. Yes, he was there. He took a leading part. But Do-ha-te was the leader."

Maman-ti was not sinister to his own people. They saw him as a person of authority and wisdom—tall, straight, kindly, and generous. Through superior intellect he could influence the tribe, and pretend to foretell events by occult means; he was relied upon to bring to a successful conclusion any warlike effort.

About the middle of May, while Sherman was riding along the Butterfield Trail, skeptical of Indian peril, this great war party led by Maman-ti rode south toward the Texas settlements. The Indians crossed Red River between the sites of Vernon and Electra. Here at a place they call Skunk Headquarters, on account of the prevalence of skunks in the vicinity, they cached their saddles, blankets, and other unnecessary impedimenta. The spare horses also were left here, hobbled to prevent their straying away. A few young boys remained to guard the headquarters; the main body pushed rapidly toward the inhabited districts. Since they hoped to bring back many horses and mules, some of the men were without mounts. They rode double, or ran along holding to the tails of other animals. Extra bridles and lariats were taken along for the stock they expected to steal.

On May 17 the Indians entered Young County and headed for the Butterfield Trail, about halfway between Forts Belknap and Richardson. This was a favorite place. Sooner or later some white man would be sure to ride along the road, and the locality was remote from any town or military post.

After dark Maman-ti consulted his oracle. He sat apart on the side of a hill while the rest of the warriors crouched in silence listening for the voice of a dead ancestor. Soon it came in the cry of a hoot owl: "Hoom-hoom, hoom-hoom,"—several times repeated. The soft rustle of

127

wings was heard. Then all was quiet. The medicine man stood up, raised his arms, and, slowly intoning, interpreted the message of the owl.

"Tomorrow two parties of Tehannas will pass this way. The first will be a small party. Perhaps we could overcome it easily. Many of you will be eager to do so. But it must not be attacked. The medicine forbids. Later in the day another party will come. This one may be attacked. The attack will be successful."

At daybreak the Indians took position on a conical sandstone hill which commanded a long stretch of the stage road from where it crossed the head of the north branch of Flint Creek to a point some three miles east thereof, where it disappeared around the end of Cox Mountain. Between this hill and Cox Mountain was a broad open plain, sometimes called Salt Creek Prairie (though Salt Creek lies eight miles to the west). This field was at that time sparsely dotted with mesquite, with a few trees lining Flint Creek at the foot of the hill, and a heavier growth of scrub oak near Cox Mountain, where the timbered area begins. It was an ideal place for an ambush. The leader planned to allow the enemy to reach the middle of the plain, far from the shelter of the woods, then sweep down upon them from the hill.

Toward noon some of the scouts, who were peering through the brush on the north shoulders of the hill, saw a vehicle, preceded by a small group of mounted men, trot smartly through the trees near Flint Creek and head east across the plain. At once there was a great deal of excited whispering. The enemy were too far away to determine how strong they were. Some of the young braves wanted to attack. But the medicine man obstinately refused to permit it. Perhaps through experience or native cunning he was aware that white soldiers traveled with advance parties thrown out in front. Or maybe he had genuine faith in his powers as a prophet. At any rate the Indians allowed General Sherman (for it was Sherman's party they saw) to ride safely past, all blissfully unaware that a hundred pairs of savage eyes observed his passage.

Two or three hours passed. No other quarry appeared. Some of the young men became impatient. They had come for action, and were not getting it. They wanted to leave the band and set out for themselves. But Maman-ti held them there. Finally, toward mid-afternoon, a wagon train was seen approaching from the east. The Indians watched eagerly as ten lumbering, white-topped vehicles crawled around the north end of Cox Mountain and moved across the open plain toward them. With heels raised to prod their ponies they waited for the signal to charge.

Maman-ti waited until the wagons were in the center of the plain. Then he motioned to Satanta, who sat with a bugle in his hand. Satanta raised the instrument to give the signal. But even as it touched his lips the Indians were away at a mad gallop.

Down the slope they swept. It was a race to see who should win first coup. Second, third, and fourth coups counted also. To kill an enemy counted much. But to touch him first meant more. Several coups made a man a chief. A fast horse was a tremendous advantage. So was reckless daring.

Yellow Wolf had both. He was in the lead, closely followed by the renowned young chief, Big Tree. The rest of the horde thundered in the rear. The warriors were strung well out, with the old plugs and dismounted men toiling in the dust far behind. As the Indians emerged from the mesquite along the dry watercourse of Flint Creek the white men saw them coming. Hastily they turned off the road and began to corral their wagons.

The Indians commenced yipping shrilly and shooting off their guns at every jump. They were upon the wagon train before the corral was finished. Yellow Wolf rode between the last wagon and the others, cutting it off. The teamsters were on the ground, snatching at rifles carried in the leather boots fastened to the wagon bodies. Big Tree made a first coup. Yellow Wolf made second. Two Kiowa-Apaches were close after. Then as Yellow Wolf wheeled to the west again the firing commenced. Indians and whites were running here and there in the dust and smoke. Yellow Wolf saw a man jump off his horse and come running forward to engage in a hand-to-hand fight with the teamsters. It was Or-dlee, a Comanche. Suddenly, he dropped, shot dead. Red Warbonnet, a Kiowa chief, was wounded in the thigh. The whites were shooting "dangerously." Suddenly the Indians became wary. They pulled off and commenced whirling round and round the wagons in a yelling, shooting, pinwheel of color. Scarlet-and-white war bonnets mingled with cotton-like puffs of white smoke, yellow dust, and navy-blue loin cloths. Overhead black storm clouds were gathering across the sky. They held up the sun, whose divergent fingers reached down through gaps to touch as with a golden spotlight the fury below. It shone from polished bow, lance and carbine. It fell unheeded on desperate, frightened white men.

Three or four teamsters were killed in the first rush. The Indians did not know how many more there might be. As they rushed around and round the wagons they saw others kneeling on the grass firing from under the wagons, through the wheels. As Yellow Wolf made his second circle he saw Tson-to-goodle (Light-haired Young Man), a Kiowa-Apache, wounded in the knee. The Apache slipped from his horse and bounced in the dust. Two companions dragged him away. Several hundred yards to the west stood two women, Yo-koi-te, and another whose name is forgotten, lustily participating in the fight with shrill "tongue-rattling." Satanta may have been blowing signals on his bugle. Yellow

Wolf doesn't remember. But, he says, even if the bugle had blown, no one would have paid any attention to it.

Yellow Wolf, galloping around to the east, saw a little group of white men cut out of the corral on foot and start to run towards Cox Mountain. There happened to be an opening in the savage circle on the east; they broke through it. One was shot down after running a little way. Six more kept going. Only a few Indians pursued. They thought there were plenty more whites still in the corral. Near the timber one other white was killed. The remaining five disappeared in the blackjacks. The Indians turned back; they were afraid they would lose their share of the plunder. The Indians continued to circle, watching closely. No firing was coming from the corral. Maybe it was some kind of trap. Yellow Wolf saw one of the whites, the one who had been with the last wagon, lying in the open gap between that wagon and the corral. This was the one Big Tree had killed. The one Eagle Heart killed was lying close to the corral on the north side. Yellow Wolf also saw a dead man on the ground just inside the corral. Did he kill this man? Yellow Wolf does not say. In the excitement he did not see any other bodies. The Indians were using Spencer carbines, breech-loading rifles, pistols, and bows. Most of the firearms had been purchased from Caddo George, at his "store" near Anadarko. Yellow Wolf had a gun he had captured that year from a settler in Texas.

The sky was growing darker. A big storm was coming. The Indians were anxious to finish the work and get away. But no one dared approach the wagons too soon. Some of the whites might be waiting for them.

"Keep back! It's too dangerous!" shouted the older men. "Let's get them from behind."

Hau-tau (Gun-shot) would not listen. It was his first battle, his first chance to win a point in the race for chieftainship. He ran toward the wagons. No enemy appeared. He retired a few steps in indecision. White Horse and Set-maunte, more experienced, tried to hold him back. He evaded their grasp. He rushed to another wagon, touched it.

"I claim this wagon, and all in it, as mine!" he shouted in exultation.

At that moment a wounded teamster inside the wagon lifted up the canvas sheet and shot Hau-tau full in the face. The young Kiowa fell to the ground, horribly wounded. White Horse and Set-maunte were laying their hands on the mules to claim them. They ran to pick up Hau-tau. He was still breathing. They dragged him out of the way. At this point the Indian account breaks off abruptly. Yellow Wolf declines to say more except that the Indians, enraged by the shooting of Hau-tau, proceeded to "tear up everything." After the affair was over the Indians went back to the hill from which they had started their charge, driving with them the captured mules. They placed Or-dlee, the dead Comanche, in a crevice on the south side of the hill, and piled rocks over him. Then they tied the wounded men to horses and rode north. Soon a general storm broke. The heavy rainfall turned the streams into floods. The Indians made slow progress.

No white man survived to describe the last tragic moments of the massacre. What occurred must be pieced together from the descriptions of the scene written by Mackenzie and his officers. The advance detachment of soldiers arrived before dark on May 19. The rain was still coming down in torrents. The bodies of the teamsters, swollen and bloated beyond recognition, were lying in several inches of water. The place was a litter of opened grain sacks, broken wagons, pieces of harness, arrows, and bits of cloth.[9] Mackenzie's surgeon made the following report of what he found:

"Colonel R. S. Mackenzie,
"4th Cav
"SIR:
"I have the honor to report that in compliance with your instructions I examined on May 19, 1871, the bodies of five citizens killed near Salt Creek by Indians on the previous day. All the bodies were riddled with bullets, covered with gashes, and the skulls crushed, evidently with an axe found bloody on the place; some of the bodies exhibited also signs of having been stabbed with arrows. One of the bodies was even more mutilated than the others, it having been found fastened with a chain to the pole of a wagon lying over a fire with the face to the ground, the tongue being cut out. Owing to the charred condition of the soft parts it was impossible to determine whether the man was burned before or after his death. The scalps of all but one were taken.

"I have the honor to be, colonel,
                your obedient servant,
                    (signed) "J. H. PATZKI,
                        "Asst Surgeon, U.S.A."[10]

Mackenzie had the corpses placed in one of the wagon bodies and buried near the road. The soldiers set up two small stones over the grave, cut with seven marks to indicate the number of bodies. The grave may still be seen, a mile west of Monument School, in the field owned by Mr. James Barnett.

[9] J. B. Terrell to author, 1934. Mr. Terrell visited the scene a day or two after the massacre.
[10] Dr. Patzki mentions only five bodies. The other two were the men who were killed some distance from the wagons; their bodies were not found until several hours after Mackenzie arrived. The men who were killed were: N. S. Long, James Elliott, Samuel Elliott, M. J. Baxter, Jesse Bowman, John Mullins, and James Williams. Samuel Elliott was the man who was tortured; presumably he was the man who shot Hau-tau. The men who escaped were: Thomas Brazeal, Dick Motor, Hobbs Carey, Charles Brady, and R. A. Day.

131

The floods hampered Mackenzie in his pursuit of the Indians. Furthermore he was twenty-four hours' march behind them, and the trail had been obliterated by the rain. On the twentieth Mackenzie was on the south bank of the Little Wichita, waiting for the water to subside. The Indians were farther north, crossing the Big Wichita. They made crude boats from willow branches covered with canvas. In these they placed their guns, plunder, and wounded men. They propelled the craft across the swift river by swimming on either side and pushing.

Quitan and Tomasi, Mexican-captive members of the Kiowa tribe, were great buffalo hunters. Together with two other Kiowas they lingered behind the main body to kill some buffalo, which then were running in from the west and swimming the river. They had slaughtered twelve or more, and were engaged in cutting them up when they were surprised by twenty-five men of the Fourth Cavalry under Lieutenant Peter M. Boehm. Boehm was returning to Fort Richardson after a thirty-day scout.[11] In the sharp exchange of shots which followed, one trooper and two horses of Lieutenant Boehm's detachment were wounded. Tomasi and his horse were killed. The other Indians sprang on their ponies, mingled with the buffalo herd, and swam the river. When the main body of Indians heard the shots and saw the fugitives flying toward them they raced away. Quitan brought up the rear. The ground was soft and muddy. When the Indians stopped to catch their breath Quitan arrived, covered with mud thrown up by the flying hoofs. They gave him a big laugh and went on their way north.[12] Boehm's men scalped Tomasi. They took the scalp to Fort Richardson, where Boehm presented it as a souvenir to the regimental adjutant, Lieutenant Carter.[13]

Although the Kiowa raiders were burdened with the wounded Hautau, they moved rapidly across Red River and regained their village safely. A few days later Hau-tau died. "The screw worms got into his head," they explain. The death of Hau-tau brought the Indian fatalities to a total of three: Or-dlee, Tomasi, and Hau-tau. But the Indians were more than satisfied. They had killed seven whites, captured forty-one mules, and brought back much other plunder. They felt full of pride and importance.

ARREST OF THE CHIEFS

On the morning of May 23 the detachment in the blockhouse on Signal Mountain, searching the surrounding country through their field glasses, saw, twenty miles to the south, the dust stirred up by Sherman's party. They heliographed the news to the post, where a guard of honor

[11] File 1305, AGO.
[12] Quitan to George Hunt.
[13] File 1305, AGO; R. G. Carter to author, June, 1935.

was made ready to receive the distinguished visitor. Several hours later, after he had been made comfortable as a guest in the quarters of Colonel Grierson,[14] Sherman hastened to the Indian agency to make inquiries regarding the matter uppermost in his mind.

Lawrie Tatum sat in his office brooding over the misdeeds of his Indians. He had just written a letter to Enoch Hoag, head of the Central Superintendency at Lawrence, Kansas, expressing a view that patience and forbearance had been carried far enough. He recommended that in the future Indian murderers and kidnappers should be delivered to civil courts for punishment, in the same manner and to the same extent as if they were white criminals. "Will the committee sustain me," he asked, "in having Indians arrested for murder, and turned over to the proper authorities of Texas for trial?"[15]

Thus Tatum, independently of General Sherman, and prior to his knowledge that a massacre had taken place, decided that the Indians should be disciplined. In a few days he was to have opportunity to test out these ideas. But the committee did not sustain him. While he was yet thinking about the matter there came a rap on the door of his office. In walked Colonel Grierson, accompanied by a man Tatum had never seen, a tall, slender fellow with a stubble beard and reddish hair beginning to turn grey above a high forehead. His small sharp eyes seemed to take in everything, and though he was dressed in civilian clothing, Tatum realized that it was General Sherman. He seemed very much a man.[16]

Sherman plunged into an account of the corn train massacre. He asked the horrified agent if he knew whether any Indians were absent from the reservation during the past week. Tatum replied that he thought Satanta and a number of others were gone; the Indians would be in for their rations in a few days, when he would make inquiries.

Sherman spent the next few days inspecting the troops and the new buildings. He had not expected to remain so long, but no word had been received from Mackenzie, and the general was anxious to settle this Indian business before he departed. He felt that it was necessary to determine the question of the guilt of the Fort Sill Indians in the depredations in Texas. The citizens had told him that not only did the Indians come from the reservation, but that they were supplied with arms at Fort Sill. This was a serious charge, and one that required verification or complete refutation. It was apparent at once that no arms were being issued to the Indians at Fort Sill. The strict system of property accountability under which the army operated precluded the idea that Colonel

[14] In 1936, Quarters No. 135.
[15] Tatum, *op. cit.*, p. 116.
[16] Josiah Butler, "Pioneer School-teaching at the Kiowa-Comanche Agency School," *Chronicles of Oklahoma*, Vol. VI, No. 4 (December 1928), p. 504.

Grierson could give out arms, even if he had desired to do so. Sherman also saw the fallacy in the argument that Tatum, who did not believe that any person should carry arms, should issue them to the Indians. "That Genl. Grierson and the Indian Agent Mr. Tatum (a Quaker) should wink at or connive in this is simply absurd," he wrote on May 24.[17]

Sherman was well pleased with Fort Sill. "This is a magnificent military site," he wrote to General Reynolds. On the twenty-seventh he visited the signal station on Signal Mountain, then went again to the Indian Agency.

Mr. Tatum showed him through the commissary buildings, then proposed that they visit the Indian school. He told his clerk, George Conover, to close the commissary if the Indians arrived, and notify him at once. General Sherman made a short talk to the small Indian pupils, after which he returned to Fort Sill for lunch. About three o'clock the Kiowas arrived, accompanied by their women, children, and dogs, and camped on the flats of Cache Creek east of Quarry Hill. Kicking Bird and his cousin Stumbling Bear, who still were on bad terms with the other chiefs, camped apart from the other bands.[18]

Since it was Saturday, the Indians planned to draw their rations at once. They knew that the following day was the white man's "medicine day," and that Bald Head (Tatum) would not issue anything on that day except "talk." About four o'clock the principal chiefs, including Lone Wolf, Kicking Bird, Satanta, Satank, Big Tree, and others, came to the commissary for their accustomed portions of coffee, sugar, flour, and bacon. Conover told them that the agent wished to see them in the council room. The Indians filed in. They always were glad to be invited to a conference. It increased their self-esteem to argue with the agent. Tatum sat solemnly at his desk. Young Matt Leeper was there to interpret. The other employes were listening through the door. After shaking hands with each chief, Mr. Tatum recounted what he had heard about the killing of Henry Warren's teamsters. He asked if they knew anything about it, thinking that perhaps he might get some hint as to which tribe was guilty. After these questions had been interpreted there was a short silence. Then Satanta rose from the floor, thrust a finger impressively at his own chest and said:

"Yes, I led that raid. I have heard that you have stolen a large portion

[17] Sherman to Reynolds, May 24, 1871.

While Sherman was at Fort Sill he inquired in behalf of Mrs. Elizabeth Clifton concerning her granddaughter, Millie Durgan. The Indians replied to the agent that the girl had been dead for eight years. The Indians had agreed among themselves not to reveal that the girl was still alive. Similar inquiries made to Agent Haworth in later years brought the same response. Mr. Haworth should have made a more complete investigation. (See Archives of Oklahoma Historical Society, File ALS, Captives. See also, same source, Isaiah Clifton to Commissioner of Indian Affairs, May 23, 1871.)

[18] Andrew Stumbling Bear to author, 1935.

of our annuity goods and given them to the Texans; I have repeatedly asked you for arms & ammunition, which you have not furnished, and made many other requests which have not been granted. You do not listen to my talk. The white people are preparing to build a R.R. through our country, which will not be permitted. Some years ago we were taken by the hair and pulled close to the Texans where we have to fight. But we have cut that loos [sic] now and are all going with the Cheyennes to the Antalope Hills. When Gen Custer was here two or three years ago, he arrested me & kept me in confinement several days. But arresting Indians is plaid out now & is never to be repeated. On account of these grievances, I took, a short time ago, about 100 of my warriors, with the chiefs Satank, Eagle Heart, Big Tree, Big Bow, & Fast Bear. . . . ."[19]

Here he was interrupted by Satank, who told him roughly, in Kiowa, not to disclose the names of any more participants.

"We went to Texas," Satanta continued, flattered by the rapt attention with which his speech was being received by the agent, "where we captured a train not far from Fort Richardson, killed 7 of the men, & drove off about 41 mules. Three of my men were killed, but we are willing to call it even. We don't expect to do any raiding around here this summer, but we expect to raid in Texas. If any other Indian comes and claims the honor of leading the party he will be lieing to you for I did it myself!"

At these last words the other Kiowas nodded their heads vigorously in confirmation. Less naïve than the "Orator of the Plains," they were willing that he should have full public credit. It may seem astonishing that Satanta should have made openly such a confession. The word "honor" gives the key to his viewpoint. He saw no disgrace in waging war against the Tehannas, or anyone else. It had been his life profession. On many occasions he and others had entered army posts with white captives for sale. These prisoners were prima facie evidence that murder had been committed. The whites knew this, and Satanta was aware that they knew it. Many times had he bragged to Hazen and others about his exploits. Yet he had received pay, in cash, for these captives—not punishment. Why should he think it would be otherwise on this particular occasion?

The hubbub which arose among the Quaker employes when Satanta's speech was interpreted was thought by him to be a buzz of admiration for his valor and skill. He swelled like a pouter pigeon and reiterated his demand that arms and ammunition be furnished. Tatum, trying to gain time, informed him that the agent had no authority to issue powder and guns, but that there was at Fort Sill a great soldier chief from Washing-

---

[19] Tatum's report to Hoag, a photostatic copy of which is in the Oklahoma Historical Society. The spelling is that of Tatum; the phraseology probably that of his interpreter.

ton. The Indians might go to him, and if he said it was all right the agent would make the issue.

Mr. Tatum then told his clerks to give out the rations. Meantime he went to his office and penned a note which he sent to the fort by George Conover:

> "FORT SILL, IND. TERR.,
> "OFFICE KIOWA AGENCY,
> "5 Mo. 27, 1871

"Col. Grierson,

"Post Commander,

"Satanta, in the presence of Satank, Eagle Heart, Big Tree, and Woman's Heart, has, in a defiant manner, informed me that he led a party of about 100 Indians into Texas and killed 7 men and captured a train of mules. He further states that the chiefs, Satank, Eagle Heart, and Big Bow were associated with him in the raid. Please arrest all three of them.

> "LAWRIE TATUM
> "Ind. Agent."[20]

When Grierson and Sherman read the above letter they called a council of Indians to meet on the front porch of Grierson's quarters. Here they would verify Satanta's confession, and arrest the chiefs as requested by Tatum. The latter was notified to send the Indians to the post. The military had no jurisdiction on the agency premises, and, besides, the Indians would take fright if a large body of soldiers were sent to the camps.

In the meantime Tatum had been talking to Lone Wolf. As a result of this conversation he wrote this note: "Big Tree was also in the raid with Satanta, I am informed by Lone Wolf. Please arrest him also. But release him if found innocent." He decided to deliver this note in person. Before he left he told Lone Wolf to notify the Indians that there was at the post a great army chief who wanted to talk to them.

Meanwhile the cavalry troops at the post made ready quietly in their stables, which were inclosed in stone corrals situated immediately west of the barracks. Behind the high walls and closed gates the troops lined up, mounted and ready for immediate action, yet not visible from the outside. Careful instructions were given to each company commander as to where to go and what to do when the bugle sounded. A squad of armed soldiers was concealed in the front rooms of Grierson's house, and several members of the post guard were outside in the yard.[21]

Kicking Bird and Stumbling Bear were camped in the woods along Sitting Bear Creek, west of where the polo field is today. The two chiefs

[20] From W. T. Sherman Papers, Manuscript Division, Library of Congress.
[21] R. H. Pratt, *op. cit.*, pp. 208-9.

were sitting on the bank getting dressed to attend the conference. Someone from Fort Sill, a friend of Kicking Bird, rode down the dry creek bed, tied his horse to a tree, and came up to the Indians. He warned them not to go to the post, but to decamp at once and ride west toward Signal Mountain.[22]

After the white friend had gone the two Kiowas discussed the matter. Stumbling Bear thought they ought to be present at the council to keep the talk peaceful, even though they ran a risk of being killed. Kicking Bird agreed. They told the women to pack up and be ready to leave at a moment's notice. Then they rode to the post.

It seemed like Sunday. Not a soldier or a wagon was to be seen. The white women and children were all indoors. The windows and doors were all shut. A single grey horse was tied to the fence in front of Colonel Grierson's quarters. A few officers were wandering around with their summer white hats on their heads. Everything seemed peaceful.[23]

When they came to the colonel's house they saw White Bear (Satanta) sitting on the porch. As they drew near they heard him urging them to hurry. He seemed to be excited. On the steps several officers shook hands with them, and slapped Kicking Bird on the back good-naturedly. Satanta came down the steps. Two infantry soldiers who were stationed there with fixed bayonets punched at him and forced him back. Kicking Bird and Stumbling Bear followed him to the porch and sat down. Horace Jones and a number of officers were there. All took seats except General Sherman, who kept pacing up and down the porch. He did all the talking. He wanted Kicking Bird to go to the camps and tell the other Indians to hurry to the meeting.

Satanta spoke up quickly: "Let me go."

But Sherman said, "No, Satanta will not leave."

Kicking Bird went out, untied his horse and prepared to depart.

"Tell everybody to come," Satanta called.

After Kicking Bird had gone Stumbling Bear said to Satanta, "I notice that when you stepped off the porch, the soldiers started to use their guns on you. What's the matter?"

"They aren't treating me right," complained the Orator of the Plains, querulously.

Soon about ten Indians came along on horseback, chatting amiably, accompanied by Kicking Bird. The latter need not have returned. But to him it was his duty to be with his people. He and Stumbling Bear were downhearted, full of growing apprehension. Stumbling Bear, much older and less philosophic than his cousin, kept saying to himself, "We are

[22] Andrew Stumbling Bear to author, 1935.

[23] Indian informants: Stumbling Bear, Hunting Horse, and George Hunt; Pratt, *op. cit.*, pp. 208-9; various letters of General W. T. Sherman, Sherman Papers, Library of Congress.

going to be killed. We are going to be killed." One old Indian, when he saw the two sentries, started to leave. But they pointed their guns at him; he promptly lay down like a whipped puppy. The soldiers tickled him with the points of their bayonets and made him go to the porch.

General Sherman, speaking through Horace Jones, asked the Indians which of them were present at the destruction of Captain Warren's corn train, and which of them threw the burning corn on the bodies of the white men. Satanta, as usual the self-appointed spokesman, took the center of the stage. "He openly admitted the affair," wrote Sherman, "and described the attack exactly as the man did to me at Fort Richardson, only denying that anybody was tied to the wagon wheel and burned; but as Genl Mackenzie found the body, it does not admit of dispute."

As the Indians describe the conference, Kicking Bird privately told the Indians not to say anything more, but Satanta, giving him a scornful glance, thumped his barrel-like chest, and "made a loud talk, saying 'I'm the man.'" General Sherman then told the Indians that three of them—Satanta, Satank, and Big Tree—would have to be sent to Texas to be tried for murder, and that forty-one good mules would have to be given up by the tribe to reimburse the owner of the train. Satanta now commenced to back water. He claimed that although he had been present at the fight he had not killed anybody. He merely had stood back and given directions, and blown his bugle. His young men had wanted to have a little fight and take a few white scalps, and he had been prevailed upon to go with them to show them how to make war. Three of his men had been killed, and he was now ready to cry quits.

In reply to this specious argument General Sherman remarked that it was a very cowardly thing for one hundred warriors to attack twelve poor teamsters who did not even know how to fight, and that if he desired a battle, the troops at the post stood ready to accommodate him at any time.

During this discussion two Kiowa women named Tonk-gooey-ah and Tsain-go-hau-gy were wandering around the yard sight-seeing. Finding a door open in the rear they entered the building. The house was full of armed Negro soldiers. The women tried to rush out, breaking a window in their fright. The soldiers surrounded them, and they stood still.

On the porch Sherman was insisting that the three chiefs would have to go to Texas for trial. On hearing this Satanta flew into a rage. Crying that he would rather be shot on the spot, he flung back his blanket and grasped the hilt of his revolver. As he made this hostile gesture Sherman gave a command. The shutters flew back. There stood several soldiers with their carbines leveled at the Indians.

"Don't shoot! Don't shoot!" yelled Satanta hastily.

Kicking Bird sprang forward. He had seen General Sherman before, on the Arkansas River, he said. As Colonel Grierson and the agent well knew, he had done everything in his power to prevent the young warriors from leaving the reservation and going to Texas. For the sake of the good he had done he now asked Washington to release his friends from arrest, in return for which he would bring back the captured mules.

"Yes," Sherman replied. "We have heard about you, Kicking Bird. The President has heard of you. He knows your name, and has written about you. We all appreciate what you have done. But today is my day, and what I say will have to go; I want those three men.

"I am going to take them with me as prisoners to the place where they killed those boys. There they will be hung, and the crime will be paid for."

Kicking Bird began to lose his calm. "You have asked for those men to kill them," he said. "But they are my people, and I am not going to let you have them. You and I are going to die right here."

Evidently this was not interpreted properly, for Sherman said: "You and Stumbling Bear will not be killed, nor harmed as long as you continue to do well."

During the foregoing conference the people on the porch had heard some horses running below the hospital. Presently a squad of soldiers appeared herding Big Tree, who was minus his blanket. He was out of breath and covered with mud. The Indians gave him a sheet and made a place for him to sit down.

What had happened was this: When the conference started on the porch Big Tree was in the trader's store. The adjutant had instructed Lieutenant Pratt to take a detachment to the store and arrest him. While the soldiers were tying their horses to the hitching rack in front of the store, Big Tree, who was inside dickering with Neal Evans, heard the scuffle of hoofs and the clank of arms. Somewhat startled, he turned from the counter.[24] Adjutant Woodward entered the front door with several troopers. "Seize that Indian, and don't let him escape!" he yelled at Evans. The trader, a small man, took hold of Big Tree somewhat gingerly. The burly Kiowa threw him sprawling on the floor, ran to the rear end of the store, pulled his blanket over his head and dived through a glass window. Big Tree picked himself up from the ground and vaulted over a picket fence which enclosed the back yard. Evans fired at him with a derringer pistol, but missed.

The Indian ran west through a ten-acre vegetable garden. Pratt went around one side with half of the soldiers, Woodward went the other way with the remainder. They called for Big Tree to halt. The Kiowa merely increased his speed. Twenty or more shots were fired at him. Many years afterwards Big Tree used to laugh about this. He said that the bullets were dusting the ground all around him.

[24] Reminiscences of Neal Evans; Pratt, *op. cit.*, pp. 209-10; Big Tree to George Hunt.

A lone gardener standing in the field dropped his hoe, picked up a needle gun, and took a shot at the flying Indian. Big Tree stopped. He said later that the bullet creased his scalp just above the ear. At any rate his tongue was hanging out, and he submitted quietly and allowed the officers to lead him back to the parade ground. He was captured in the edge of the woods about a hundred yards south of the site of the officers' mess building. When Big Tree arrived at the porch the Indians were packed close together, swaying back and forth like drunken men. On all sides soldiers were aiming at them. At a given signal the bugle had sounded.

The gates of the stables were thrown open and the troops—mounted and with their guns loaded—moved quickly to previously designated points. Company D took position across the road east of Colonel Grierson's quarters, facing west. Captain L. H. Carpenter with Company H, formed across the road opposite, facing east. Two squads from another troop came from the rear of the building and stood in the road in front of it. Each troop sent a few men to report to the officer of the day, Lieutenant Orleman, who was stationed at the south side of the parade ground to watch the Indians who were at the foot of the hill.

To-quodle-kaip-tau (Red Tepee), the father of Satanta, Goonsaudl-te, Day-nah-te, Ka-sa-de, and Tine-kau-to rode up the slope past the unfinished guardhouse. Under their blankets were weapons which they were bringing to the Indians on the porch of Grierson's quarters. When they saw Orleman and the guard at the corner of the parade ground they paused a moment. Orleman tried to stop them, thinking that Eagle Heart, one of the men he was ordered to arrest, was in the group. The Indians turned and loped away to the south. One of them let fly an arrow, wounding Private Edward Givins, Company D, in the fleshy part of the leg.[25] The soldiers returned the fire. Tine-kau-to crashed from his horse into a clump of sumacs which stood at the foot of the hill, south of the guardhouse. He was dead. The other Indians rode toward the camps, their hair flying in the wind. This flurry frightened the Quakers at the agency, and stampeded the Indian women and children. In their frenzy to escape, three and four tried to mount each pony. The whole band flushed like quail and hastened west through the mountains.[26]

The Indians on Grierson's porch had seen the Kiowas appear near the guardhouse, and had heard the shooting, but could not tell what had happened because buildings on the south side of the parade ground obscured the view. In a few moments an officer rode up and made a re-

[25] Indian informants: Frank Given and Mo-saip. The latter is a son of Goon-saudl-te. *Army and Navy Journal*, July 1, 1871; Pratt, *op. cit.*, pp. 209-10.

[26] Josiah Butler, *op. cit.*, p. 504.

port. Kicking Bird evidently understood a little English, for he told the other Kiowas that he thought his brother-in-law had been killed.[27]

The soldiers who had been with Orleman came back and made a semi-circle in front of the house, facing it. The Indians were becoming more and more excited. All except old Satank, who sat on the floor calmly smoking his pipe. "If you men want to crawl out of this affair by telling pitiful stories," he remarked, "that is your affair. I am sitting here saying nothing. I am an old man, surrounded by soldiers. But if any soldier lays a hand on me I am going to die, here and now." Kicking Bird was facing toward Medicine Creek. He turned to Stumbling Bear and said, "I see Lone Wolf standing in the edge of the timber, by the top of the bank. I think he is going to leave."

Using the sign language, Kicking Bird motioned to Lone Wolf to come to the porch. He told him that they were surrounded, and that Lone Wolf's proper place was with the other chiefs, even though they all might be killed. Lone Wolf obviously wanted to leave; but he could not do so without incurring disgrace among his own people. Therefore he signaled assent. He rode around to the front of the house, dismounted and laid two Spencer repeating carbines, a bow, and quiver on the ground, tied his horse to the fence, threw his blanket from his shoulder and fastened it around his waist. Then he picked up the weapons and strode deliberately to the porch, calling orders to the Indians in a loud voice.[28] He handed his pistol to Hau-vah-te, saying, "Here. Take this. Make it smoke if anything happens." He distributed the arms among the other Indians, seated himself on the floor, cocked his carbine and held it ready in his lap. The soldiers edged closer, kept their guns pointed directly at the Indians. Sherman continued to walk up and down the porch, talking, as if nothing were out of order, playing the game of bluff and counter-bluff to the very end. The other officers sat in their chairs with nostrils slightly widened. Several of them probably would have preferred to be elsewhere.

Stumbling Bear received a bow and arrows from Lone Wolf. He promptly pulled out a handful of arrows and strung the bow. Kicking Bird and Sherman still were talking.

"Do not say more, Kicking Bird," said Stumbling Bear. "I am not going to talk to the army people, only to my own friends."

"Do you all see Kicking Bird talking to the whites?" he said to the other Indians. "He is a young man, but has good judgment. He has tried hard to keep you out of trouble, but you have paid no attention. See what trouble you have gotten us into. I am going to be the first to die. I can look into your eyes and see that you are whipped. You are acting like

[27] Kicking Bird erroneously thought that Goon-saudl-te had been killed.
[28] Marcy's journal, quoted in Wilbarger, *op. cit.*, pp. 557-59.

women. I don't know what it will be like after death, but I am going to find out."[29]

The officers and soldiers were watching Stumbling Bear, not understanding the words, but realizing from his manner that he was saying something important. He stood up and let his blanket fall. "I only want to kill the big soldier chief." While he was getting ready to shoot, another Indian, a young boy, was muttering to work himself into a proper frenzy and sustain his courage; but the others were beaten and silent. Just then one of the two women gave a whoop to do Stumbling Bear honor.

"That makes me feel better," said the chief. He determined to shoot when Sherman turned from his next walk to the end of the porch. As the general approached, the Indian drew his bow. In his fanatical frenzy the guns of the soldiers were invisible to him. The Indians shouted. One of them grabbed his arm. The arrow flew wildly into the air. Grierson grappled with Lone Wolf, who was aiming his gun at Sherman. They tripped and fell on the floor, knocking over Kicking Bird, who landed sprawling on top.

Sherman's nerve held. He ordered the soldiers to raise their guns. The tension gradually relaxed. Stumbling Bear began to come to his senses. He saw that the soldiers would not shoot unless the Indians forced them to. The Indians sat down again, but gingerly, as if on eggs. It was now almost dark. The Indians on the porch were beginning to get restless and were pushing angrily at the soldiers who were crowding around them.

Sherman told them that he would have to hold the three chiefs, Satanta, Satank, Big Tree; and that forty-one good mules would have to be delivered to him within ten days. Whether through misunderstanding, or poor interpretation, the Indians got the idea that if the mules were delivered within ten days the three chiefs would be released. Kicking Bird began asking the Indians present if they would contribute mules. When the required number had been promised he told Sherman that the Indians agreed to the terms. The Indians then were dismissed—all except the three prisoners. The others jumped off the porch and scattered to their camps, which they found deserted. The next day they overtook some of the women and children near Rainy Mountain. They were still loping along in panic, riding two and three to a horse. Lone Wolf and Kicking Bird continued west in an effort to stop the runaways.

The three chief culprits were led away manacled hand and foot, and were thrown into a cell under the barracks at the southwestern corner of the parade ground. A correspondent from Fort Sill, writing to the *Army and Navy Journal,* says, "The whole garrison was wild with excitement

[29] Andrew Stumbling Bear says that his father told him this story so many times that he "knows it by heart."

during the day, and General Sherman was extolled to the skies for his prompt and decisive action."[30]

"WE KO-EET-SENKO MUST DIE"

The three Kiowa chiefs remained in their cell over the weekend. Sherman, visiting them on Monday, found Satanta in a chastened mood. In reporting his conversation with the Indians, Sherman says: "Satanta claims that many of the captured mules were killed and wounded—that in addition he lost three of his warriors killed, and three badly wounded, and the warrior (Tine-kau-to) here killed makes seven; so, he says, we are now even, and he ought to be let off—but I don't see it."

Sherman did not feel that he could wait longer for Mackenzie to arrive. He left instructions for the prisoners to be turned over to Mackenzie, to be taken to Texas for trial by civil authorities. On May 30 he resumed his journey north toward Fort Gibson, where he was scheduled to address the convention of the Five Civilized Nations at Okmulgee. The night he left Fort Sill another severe rainstorm set in. Cache Creek became unfordable; but the general already was across.

On the following day Ten Bears, Tosawi, Iron Mountain, Horseback, and A-Man-Not-Living, Comanche chiefs, came to the post to find out whether any of their people were liable to arrest with the Kiowas. On their way in they were met by Big Bow, who wanted to send a spy to recover the body of Tine-kau-to. This spy, disguised as a Comanche, found that the soldiers had buried the body. The Comanches told Grierson that they had seen soldiers south of Red River, near the mouth of North Fork. They also had met many of the stampeded Kiowas, moving rapidly toward the western end of the mountains. After them were Kicking Bird and Lone Wolf, very "mad" at Satanta and Satank for causing so much trouble. They said that they would not go to war on this account, and that when they had collected their frightened people they would bring in the forty-one mules. What the Comanches did not report to the authorities was that Kicking Bird had met so much opposition among his people to the proposition of surrendering the mules that he had, in disgust, given up his efforts.

"Two of the Indians," Grierson wrote to Sherman, "wounded in Satanta's fight died after reaching their camp, and two others are not now expected to live, from wounds there incurred. This makes the matter a little nearer even than Satanta supposed when he boasted of his exploit. Yesterday a party of Indians attacked Whaley's Ranch, near Red River Station, and were repulsed—with the loss of three killed, and several wounded. One citizen was killed in the fight."

On June 4 Mackenzie arrived at Fort Sill, reporting that he had lost

[30] *Army and Navy Journal,* July 1, 1871.

the trail of the Indians near Red River. He was greatly surprised to hear that the guilty chiefs were waiting for him in the guardhouse. At eight o'clock on the morning of the eighth, word was passed around that the prisoners were to be transferred to the custody of Colonel Mackenzie, who would take them to Texas for trial. Several army officers, the two post interpreters, and George Washington, chief of the Caddoes, were present to witness the departure. Lieutenant Thompson of the Fourth Cavalry drove up with two wagons, the beds of which were filled with loose shelled corn. A detachment of cavalry followed. This procession halted in front of the cell where the Kiowas were confined. The post officer of the day, Lieutenant R. H. Pratt, brought them out of the building and turned them over to Lieutenant Thurston, who was officer of the day for the Fourth Cavalry.

The three chiefs stood blinking in the bright sunlight. They were handcuffed, and hobbled with iron chains. Suddenly Satank lurched forward as if to shake hands with Colonel Grierson. Actually he had a knife concealed under his blanket. His companions snatched him back, to prevent him from getting them into trouble. Satanta and Big Tree were much subdued. They submitted quietly while the soldiers lifted them into the second wagon. But thin, gray-haired Satank stood aloof and would not budge. Lieutenant Thompson had four men take him by the hands and feet and throw him into the leading wagon.

Satank sat up on the loose grain and complained loudly that he was being treated like a dog. He was a member of the *Ko-eet-senko*, a military order of the Kiowa tribe, something like the Samurai of Japan. Only the ten bravest warriors could be Ko-eet-senko; they were under solemn vow to return from every engagement with honor, or not to return at all. Under the circumstances in which Satank now found himself, he could see no opportunity to return with honor. Furthermore, his son's bones were on the reservation, and he did not care to leave them. Therefore he would die, and join his son in the spirit world.

All this was chanted in a high-pitched, doleful, improvised song, characteristic of the Indians, and much like the wailing heard at a Chinese funeral. Finally he broke into the death song of the Ko-eet-senko:

> "*Iha hyo oya iya o iha yaya yoyo*
> *Aheyo aheyo uaheyo ya eya heyo e heyo*
> *Ko-eet-senko ana obahema haa ipai degi o ba ika*
> *Ko-eet-senko ana oba hemo hadamagagi o ba ika.*"[31]

"O sun you remain forever, but we Ko-eet-senko must die,
O earth you remain forever, but we Ko-eet-senko must die."

Horace Jones realized that Satank was singing his death song. "You

[31] James Mooney, *op. cit.*, p. 329.

had better watch that old Indian," he said to the corporal of the guard. "He means trouble."

The caravan started down the hill, on the road to Jacksboro. Satank's song could be heard all over the garrison. Grierson and Mackenzie walked to his adjutant's office for a final conference before the latter joined the column. In a few moments they heard a number of shots toward the agency commissary. Mackenzie rode to investigate.[32]

As the wagons rumbled down the hill Satank called to Caddo George, who was riding beside the wagons, and, speaking Comanche, which all the Indians understood, said: "Take this message to my people: Tell them I died beside the road. My bones will be found there. Tell my people to gather them up and carry them away."[33] Satanta also had a message to send by Caddo George: "Tell the Kiowas to bring back the mules, and don't raid any more. Do as the agent tells them."

When the wagons reached the place where the Fort Sill railroad station now stands, Satank again intoned his death chant. The soldiers mocked him, trying to imitate the queer sound. "See that tree?" said Satank to the Caddo, indicating a large pecan tree beside the road a few yards ahead. "When I reach that tree I will be dead."

Caddo George dropped back out of the way. Satanta and Big Tree, in the second wagon, sat rigid. Only the soldiers were unalarmed. Not understanding the Indian gesticulations they merely grinned at what they considered savage horseplay. In another moment Satank spoke to a Tonkawa scout who was riding near-by. "You may have my scalp," he said. "The hair is poor. It isn't worth much, but you may have it." The Tonkawa's squaw whooped to honor the brave old Kiowa. Then Satank fell silent, looked up at the sky, and "talked to God." What followed is described graphically by Lieutenant Thurston, who was in charge of the prisoners: "Almost immediately after the song ceased I heard sounds of trouble in the front wagon, it being the one in which Satank was riding; and reining out from the rear of the wagon containing the other two prisoners, where I was riding at the head of my company, I saw Satank seize and attempt to wrench a carbine from one of the guards inside the wagon. The struggle for possession of the weapon was over almost as quick as thought,—ending by the soldier's elevating his heels, and tumbling backwards to the ground over the tail-gate of the wagon, striking on his head. Of course, he left the carbine in the hands of the Indian, who immediately sprang the lever and attempted to throw a cartridge into the chamber; and expecting every instant to see him succeed in the attempt, and knowing if he did, somebody would be hurt, I concluded that the Indian had better die, and die right speedily. I ac-

[32] Pratt, *op. cit.*, pp. 211-12.
[33] Indian informants: George Hunt, Hunting Horse, and Andrew Stumbling Bear.

cordingly gave the order to fire and several pieces were discharged in rapid succession. The Indian fell backwards, and, supposing he was either killed or so badly wounded as to be harmless, I gave the order to stop firing, which was immediately obeyed.

"I was mistaken, however. For, possessing the vitality of a grizzly bear, the Indian was no sooner down than he arose again, and again seized the carbine, and attempted to use it. I immediately gave the order to fire upon him again, and drew my pistol and fired one shot myself. Several shots were fired in rapid succession, and the Indian fell and died in about thirty minutes. He was found to have been shot through the lungs, in the head, in the wrist of his right hand and several other places. I am unable to say who gave the death shot or how many shots were fired.

"There were probably seven or eight. As soon as the firing commenced the two Indians in the other wagon, which was immediately behind and close up to the first, held up their hands. No shots were fired at them.

"I regret to report that the citizen teamster in charge of the wagon containing the prisoner killed was, accidentally, very badly wounded by some person unknown firing at the Indian. This teamster remained mounted on his nigh wheeler during the firing, and, owing to the wagon sheet could not be seen by those firing at the Indian from the rear. He should have dismounted.

"It appears that Satank had secreted a knife so carefully that it was not discovered when he was searched by the officer designated to receive the prisoners from the military authority at Sill. He took this knife with him into the wagon. After being placed in the wagon he succeeded in slipping his handcuffs, severely lacerating his hands in so doing. I cannot imagine where the eyes of the guard could have been while he was doing this. Having gotten rid of the handcuffs, he seized the knife and stabbed one of the guard (Corp. Robinson, Co. D, 4th Cav.) in the leg, which act he followed immediately by seizing the carbine. . . . ."[34]

By the time the commotion had subsided Mackenzie arrived. After a brief investigation he ordered them to leave Satank by the roadside and continue the march. Big Tree says that the last thing he remembers was seeing Satank sitting in the dust, the blood pouring from his mouth, while the cavalry escort was trotting over the high ground south of the little creek which now bears the name "Sitting Bear Creek" in commemoration of old Satank. The Tonkawa scout begged hard for the scalp, but the officers would not permit him to take it. They let him have the bloodstained buffalo robe. The Kiowas were notified that they might

[34] File 1305, AGO. Jim Waldo (Kiowa) says that Satank had concealed the knife in his breechclout.

146

have the body, but none of them ever claimed it. They were still fleeing west, and did not even know what had happened. Satank was buried in the post cemetery. The Kiowas say today that the grave is the one enclosed by iron pipes and a chain.

Satank was a true product of the stone age. Though he was disliked by the whites, and feared, even, by some of his own people, he did not lack courage. He preferred death to what he considered dishonor. In one generation his descendants stepped direct to the modern age. His son Joshua Given became an Episcopal minister. His granddaughter, Ioleta Hunt, was the first Kiowa girl to receive a liberal arts degree, and in 1936 was teaching school among the poor in the eastern part of Oklahoma.

DISPOSITION OF SATANTA AND BIG TREE

Satanta and Big Tree were conveyed to Fort Richardson and lodged in the post guardhouse. They were quickly indicted for murder by a grand jury. Concerning their case, Sherman wrote to Sheridan: "I think it is time to end his (Satanta's) career. The Kiowas accuse him of acting the woman when you held him prisoner, and he has been raiding in Texas to regain his influence as a Great Warrior. Old Satank ought to have been shot long ago, and Big Tree is a young warrior, the successor of Faint Heart, who died last winter. The impudence of Satanta will satisfy you that the Kiowas need pretty much the lesson you gave Black Kettle and Little Raven. . . . . Kicking Bird is about the only Kiowa that seems to understand their situation, but Lone Wolf ought to have been hung when you had him in hand." The two chiefs were brought to trial in the county courthouse at Jacksboro on July 5. The cowboy jury promptly rendered a verdict of guilty, and the judge sentenced the prisoners to be hanged.

At once the sentimentalists in Washington and elsewhere began agitating to have the sentence commuted to life imprisonment. The governor of Texas finally became persuaded to take this step, and Satanta and Big Tree were sent to the state penitentiary at Huntsville, Texas. General Sherman commented on this outcome as follows: "Satanta ought to have been hung and that would have ended the trouble, but his sentence has been commuted to life imprisonment, and I know these Kioways well enough to see that they will be everlastingly pleading for his release. He should never be released, and I hope the War Department will never consent to his return to his tribe. As to Big Tree, I do not deem his imprisonment so essential though he ought to keep Satanta company. . . . . Kicking Bird can keep the Kioways peaceable if Satanta is out of the way, and I don't believe him sincere when he asks for his release, but that he is acting the part to maintain his influence with his own people."

147

Thus far the peace policy had prevented any serious effort on the part of the army to act offensively against the Indians. Colonel Mackenzie thought that the Warren massacre supplied ample cause to organize an expedition to complete the work begun by Sheridan in 1868. Shortly after returning to Fort Richardson he wrote to the department commander, recommending that the garrisons of the frontier posts be concentrated for an immediate campaign against the Indians of the Staked Plains and the Fort Sill Indian reservation. He also wrote to General Sherman:

"Satanta now says that he never came to Texas at all, being a great friend of the whites, and that it was all Satank who was a fool, and very bad.

"The Indians who depredate in Texas west of the Guadalupe River all come from one of two points, the head of the Brazos, or thereabouts, or the Reserve. They are generally Comanches and Kiowas, and those from the Reserve are mixed up with the bands on the edge of the Staked Plains in their depredations.

"To obtain a permanent peace and to give Mr. Tatum, who I regard as an excellent man, an opportunity to elevate these people, the Kiowas and Comanches should be dismounted, disarmed, and made to raise corn. . . . .

"It is very important that the action which has been taken in sending these Indians (Satanta and Big Tree) to this post be sustained. The Kiowas and Comanches are entirely beyond any control and have been for a long time. Mr. Tatum understands the matter. He appears to be very straightforward, resolute, and capable. He is anxious that the Kiowas and Comanches now out of control be brought under. This can be accomplished only by the Army. The matter is now within a very small compass. Either these Indians must be punished or they must be allowed to murder and rob at their own discretion. Mr. Tatum expressed himself so strongly just before I left Fort Sill as to the necessity for action with regard to the Kiowas that I was on the point of bringing my command back and going to look for them, but it was finally concluded that it would be better for me to go back to Texas with the two remaining prisoners, wait a short time, and see what they would do about Mr. Warren's mules, getting in readiness to return with what force I could. . . ."[35]

The plan suggested by Mackenzie was adopted. Ten companies of the Fourth Cavalry were concentrated at Gilbert's Creek. From this point they marched north to Otter Creek. In the meantime Colonel

[35] Mackenzie to Sherman, Fort Richardson, June 15, 1871, W. T. Sherman Papers, Library of Congress.

Grierson moved out from Fort Sill and established a luxurious supply camp on Otter Creek about two miles below the crossing of the old Radziminski trail. Mackenzie arrived at this point about the seventh of August, and after a brief conference between the two commanders the regiments separated and rode northwest along the forks of Red River in search of the runaway Indians.[36]

After their flight from Fort Sill the Kiowas camped west of the present site of Granite. At first they were inclined to start a war of reprisal against the whites. A runner was sent in to warn Caddo George to take his children out of school for safe-keeping. The Caddo gave the Kiowas Satanta's last message, in which the chief had advised the Kiowas to do as the agent told them, and return the mules. This message, and the influence of Kicking Bird, prevented the Kiowas from adopting warlike measures. Kicking Bird was able to collect the forty-one mules required by General Sherman, and on August 11 he brought them in to Fort Sill and turned them over to Mr. Tatum.

Meanwhile Mackenzie and Grierson were searching fruitlessly for the Indians through the rough gypsum belt lying between the North Fork and the Middle Fork of Red River. When Grierson heard that Kicking Bird had delivered the mules he sent Horace Jones to warn the Kiowas to move east of the reservation line, lest they be attacked by Mackenzie. Then he went back to Fort Sill, leaving four of his companies at Otter Creek. Later the Fourth Cavalry straggled in. As soon as Mackenzie was aware that the Indians had returned to their City of Refuge he went back to his base at Fort Richardson.

Colonel Grierson reported by letter to General Sherman: "I have just returned from an expedition to the headwaters of North, Salt or Middle, and Mulberry Forks of Red River. I feel confident that it will have a good effect upon the Indians. I think it would have been better if Mackenzie had moved out west to the headwaters of the Salt Fork and returned south of the main Red River. I think he would have had a better chance to intercept parties of Indians moving southwest or get upon their trail. I have not learned what caused him to change his route. I understand he has crossed Otter Creek and encamped about five miles south on a branch of Cache Creek where he is waiting the arrival of forage from this post before returning to Texas. I left four companies at Otter Creek for the purpose of patrolling along the line of Red River and towards Griffin, and will probably keep a detachment at the mouth of Cache Creek."[37]

Grierson was too sanguine over the effect of the recent demonstration against the Indians. The Quohada Comanches had not been frightened

[36] Ibid.; Mackenzie's journal of the expedition, copy in Fort Sill library.
[37] Grierson to Sherman, Fort Sill, September 5, 1871.

at all, and the Kiowas soon recovered from their fear of Fort Sill. On September 19 a company under Captain Vander Wiele, going out from the camp at Otter Creek to patrol Red River, was attacked at Foster Springs. Foster Larkin, wagoner, Company B, Tenth Cavalry, was killed.[38] On September 22, two civilian cattle-herders were killed near the beef corral on Beef Creek, about three-quarters of a mile northeast of Fort Sill. Both victims were shot in the back, scalped, and one of them had an ear removed. This latter mutilation was the Kiowa trademark. The authorities did not know who committed these murders. Only recently have the Indians revealed that Ko-yan-te, Mo-hain, and Kee-tau-te were the guilty Kiowas.[39]

Lawrie Tatum, not realizing that his superiors disapproved of his policy of calling on the military to punish and discipline the Indians, wrote to Grierson and Mackenzie, asking them to take further steps against the Staked Plains Comanches. He stated that these Indians had in their possession several white child captives whom he wished the two officers would recover. Grierson was not able to participate in this expedition. The Peace Policy prohibited him from taking troops out of the reservation against Fort Sill Indians unless he actually was on the hot trail of raiding parties. It was desired to keep Fort Sill as a place to which the Indians would feel free to go for refuge. If the troops from Fort Sill were constantly acting against the Indians the latter might be frightened permanently away from the agency.

Having seen the success of the authorities at Jacksboro in trying Satanta and Big Tree, the grand jury of Montague County returned an indictment against White Horse for the murder of Mr. Koozer. The clerk of the court wrote Colonel Grierson asking if he could send a deputy to arrest this Indian. Grierson and Tatum were not able to accede to this request. The Indian Bureau had not approved the action taken against Satanta and Big Tree, and besides, White Horse was very much at large.[40]

Colonel Mackenzie was under no such restrictions as the commander at Fort Sill. Shortly after his return from the first expedition he commenced organizing a second one, this time against the Indians around the head of the Brazos River. He concentrated his force at a supply camp at the site of old Camp Cooper, five miles north of Fort Griffin, and

[38] Post Returns, Fort Sill. A subpost, known as Camp Augur, grew out of these patrol camps established on Red River. Camp Augur, named for General C. C. Augur, later commanding Department of Texas, was a temporary outpost of Fort Sill located about five miles southwest of site of Grandfield, Oklahoma.

[39] Post Returns, Fort Sill, September, 1871; Old Files, AGO; Reports of Battles and Engagements in the Department of the Missouri, Old Files, AGO; Josiah Butler, *op. cit.*, p. 510; George Conover, *op. cit.*, pp. 107-8; Frank Given to author, 1935.

[40] Old Files, Fort Sill.

moved up the Freshwater Fork of the Brazos (White River). On the night of October 9 he camped near the junction of Canyon Blanco and White River, at the foot of a butte called Mount Blanco.

Shortly after midnight a band of Quohadas under Quanah rode through his camp, shooting, yelling, ringing bells, and dragging buffalo hides on the ends of their lariats. Mackenzie's animals were stampeded. The Comanches made off with about seventy of them. The next morning, about daylight, Lieutenant R. G. Carter, Captain E. M. Heyl, and several soldiers rode in pursuit of a group of Indians who were still in the vicinity. When they had gone about two miles from the main body they suddenly saw the whole Comanche party of several hundred warriors in their immediate front, preparing to charge. The cavalry horses were too tired to permit the men to escape. Carter held the men together with such skill and gallantry that he was later awarded the Congressional Medal of Honor. One soldier was overtaken and killed by the Indians before Lieutenant Boehm's scouts came to the rescue.[41]

This affair is described by an old Comanche participant as follows: "When I was a young man on the prairie we had fights. Once we were camped on White River near Quitaque, when our scouts reported that the soldiers were coming. At night we ran off their horses; we got a lot of them. In the morning the soldiers came after us. Parra-o-coom began to talk loud, saying, 'Get all your good horses up.' Parra-o-coom was our chief. He was a great big man with curly hair. He was a bad fellow, always wanted to kill people. Wild Horse was our second chief. He and Parra-o-coom always wanted to have hand-to-hand fights with the whites. Parra-o-coom made a talk: 'When I was a young man I met things straight ahead. I fight. I want you men to do the same. Be brave.'

"We got out our war shields, tied up our horses' tails, and tied our sheets around our waists. Then we had a parade. No one would listen to commands until Parra-o-coom gave the word. When we made a charge the soldiers commenced to fire. The bullets came toward us like the roar of a sling whirling through the air. Some of the soldiers were dismounted, some mounted. They were about 250 yards away. None of us got hit. Our medicine man must have been very powerful. We had great faith in him.

"One of the soldiers got behind. We killed and scalped him. The scalp was no good, but we had a big celebration over it anyway.

"The soldiers had some Tonkawas with them. The Tonkawas are bad. They eat people. They think human game tastes better than deer or buffalo."[42]

[41] R. G. Carter, *On the Border with Mackenzie,* pp. 165-78; (Washington: Eynon Printing Co., 1935); William Grantham to author, 1933. Mr. Grantham was brought up by Quanah Parker, from whom he learned the story.

[42] Cohaya to author.

The Comanches escaped into the Staked Plains. Mackenzie followed them until forced by a blizzard to turn back. When the storm came, the Comanche village, packed on travois, was visible through the sleet, but was moving rapidly away. Mackenzie might have overtaken and destroyed it, but he considered the health and safety of his command. This was contrary to his usual hard-driving policy, but the troops were far from their supply train, and were not prepared for campaigning in a blizzard. So the Quohadas escaped unpunished.

THE RAIDS OF 1872

During the winter of 1871-72 the Kiowas remained quiet, waiting to see what the authorities were going to do with Satanta and Big Tree. As Hunting Horse remarks, "They slowed down on the raids, but their minds were on it." The Comanches did not slow down at all. The northern and western counties of Texas were favored by their presence to such an extent that Colonel Mackenzie reported that ". . . . the outrages committed by Indians have been more frequent than I have ever known them here or at any other point. . . ."[43] Satanta or no Satanta, the Kiowas could not stand much inactivity. The Comanches were getting too far ahead of them in the pursuit of their common occupation. About the first of April Big Bow led a large party south toward the Rio Grande. White Horse was second in command.

Across what is now Crockett County ran the wagon road from San Antonio to El Paso. A principal stopping place on this road was Howard Wells, uninhabited and lonely. On April 20 Big Bow's party attacked at this point a wagon train loaded with small arms and ammunition belonging to the government. There was no military escort present. Seventeen Mexican teamsters were killed, and the contents of the wagons were carried away by the Indians. Toward evening of the same day two troops of the Ninth Cavalry from Fort Concho, while on patrol, stopped at the Wells to camp for the night. Captain Cooney found the remains of the wagon train with seventeen charred bodies in the smoking ashes.

He led his men along the trail of the Indians, who were discovered camped on the side of a mountain near-by, within sight of the scene of the massacre. Tired and thirsty though the soldiers were, they assaulted the position at once. The Indians were full of fight. They had plenty of firearms, and excellent cover. An officer and an enlisted man were killed.[44] It was a victory for the Kiowas, but during the night they withdrew,

[43] File 1582, AGO 1872.

[44] Reports of Battles and Engagements in the Department of the Missouri, AGO, Old Records Section. Major G. W. Schofield, post commander at Fort Sill, states that the Indians freely and fully described the Howard Wells affair (Schofield to AAG, Department of Texas, July 6 and July 20, 1872; *ibid*, August 5, 1872).

leaving behind them the stock which they had stolen from the wagon train. In the engagement White Horse was shot in the arm, and Tau-ankia, son of Lone Wolf, was shot in the knee.

Kom-pai-te, brother of White Horse, and another boy had started on this raid. But when the Indians made their "headquarters," south of Red River, the chiefs told them that they would have to stay and look after the spare horses. They were too young to go on the expedition. The main band continued south without them. A few days later a party of Comanches came along and permitted the boys to join them. During the Comanche raid these young Kiowas were successful in stealing some fine horses. On May 19, during the return trip, the Indians attacked L. H. Luckett's party of surveyors seven miles east of Round Timbers, 25 miles from Fort Belknap. The two young Kiowas were killed, and Pohoc-sucut, the brother of Tabananica, was wounded in the foot. Long Horn brought the story of the disaster back to the Kiowa village.[45]

When White Horse returned from the Howard Wells massacre and learned that his brother had been killed in Texas he at once organized a revenge-raid. Five other men and one squaw made up the party. White Horse said that he was not going to return from Texas until he had killed a white man or been killed himself. He left the reservation early in June and went to the Brazos River, near the site of old Camp Cooper, where settlers were beginning to reoccupy some of the deserted farms.

At 5:30 on the afternoon of Sunday, June 9, Mr. Abel Lee was seated in a rocking chair under the roof of the porch joining the sections of his double picket-house. He was reading a newspaper recently received by mail. Mrs. Lee, her three daughters, and a son were inside the dwelling. The Clear Fork of the Brazos trickled peacefully past the house, only a few yards away. Indian danger seemed remote; Fort Griffin was only sixteen miles up the river.

But White Horse and his raiders were creeping down the stream bed, now almost dry. White Horse took aim at the old man through the leaves of a tree, and fired. In a moment a crying sound came from the house. The Indians rushed in the open door. Mrs. Lee, startled by the shot, had seen her husband slump out of his chair and fall half inside the door. A great red stain was spreading on the front of his white Sunday shirt. The woman and her children were cowering in terror over the body when the savages bounded in the door. They attempted to escape by a rear exit. Mrs. Lee fell wounded with an arrow between her shoulder blades. Two of the shrilling Indians pounced on her. One of them skinned all the hair from her head, then cut off both her ears. The other slashed off one of her arms.

The children ran through a vegetable garden in the rear of the house.

[45] File 1582, AGO; Stumbling Bear to author.

Frances, aged 14, was slain with a single arrow. Millie, aged 9, stopped to help her sister, and was captured. Susanna, 17, and John, 6, were hunted down in the shrubbery and made prisoners. Then the Indians shot a few more arrows into Mr. Lee and removed all the skin from the top of his head. Susanna, Millie, and John were yanked inside the house, past their mother, who was still breathing, and were forced to watch the Indians plunder the house. Then they were put on horses and taken north to the Indian reservation.[46]

Neighbors discovered the tragedy the next day and reported it to Fort Griffin. Lieutenant E. C. Gilbreath went out with ten men and two Tonkawa scouts to investigate. A storm had filled the river during the night so that he was unable to cross. He learned the details by shouting across to citizens who were at the Lee house burying the bodies. Nothing more was heard of the Lee children until the council at Fort Cobb in July.

White Horse and his companions were as cruel as the gangsters and other public enemies of the present day. But they lived among a people who thought it proper to kill and torture their enemies. Their triumphant return to the Kiowa camp was greeted with vociferous applause. The scalp dance lasted all night, and was repeated for several successive nights. White Horse's mother forced Susanna Lee to carry water for the dancers. She made the girl take part in the dance. After the celebration was finished the Lees were distributed as slaves among the warriors who had participated in the raid.

Other Kiowas were making revenge-raids at this time. An-pay-kau-te, the oldest son of Satank, was engaged in "wiping out" his father's death. It was he who had killed Wagoner Foster Larkin the previous fall. On June 4 An-pay-kau-te, with Ko-ta, Tan-kone-kia, and Kone-bo-hone went to Craig Hill, two or three miles north of Fort Sill, where the present highway to Medicine Park passes over the first hill, going west. They saw Frank Lee, a young man from New York who had come to the wild west to learn to be a cowboy, driving cattle south toward the post. Frank was unarmed. When he saw the Indians advancing with smiles on their dark faces he went up to shake hands with them. They shot him several times, stuck a knife in his side, and cut off his scalp and one ear.[47] Corpio, a Mexican Indian, reported that they passed his camp soon afterward, firing their guns in the air and shouting.

Agent Lawrie Tatum was greatly upset when he learned of these revolting episodes. He wrote a letter to Major Schofield, commanding Fort Sill, stating that the Indians were uncontrollable by him, and desired that the military authorities arrest the guilty parties. This request

---

[46] "WLF" in *Army and Navy Journal*, September 7, 1872; File 1582, AGO; Indian informants: Stumbling Bear and George Hunt.

[47] Frank Given to author. *See also* File 1582, AGO.

was disapproved by Enoch Hoag, superintendent of the Indians, and by the head of the Bureau of Indian Affairs. These benevolent pollyannas considered that the reports from Fort Sill were greatly exaggerated. They felt that only a little more time was needed to reform the Indians by kindness and by conference. As a matter of fact, another conference was at that time in the making, and they did not want to spoil it by annoying the Indians. The Five Civilized Nations, in their annual convention at Okmulgee, had voted to hold a meeting with the Plains tribes, in which efforts would be made to persuade the wild brethren that the savage life did not pay. Enoch Hoag could not be present himself, but he intended to send his chief clerk to sit in on the proceedings.

Meantime the Comanches had been stimulated by the Kiowa successes. On the night of June 15 a young warrior named Tenawerka, with five other Quohadas and Kotchatekas, came down to Fort Sill to make a raid on the new stone quartermaster corral. It was a bright moonlight night. They approached the post from the northwest. About two o'clock on the morning of the sixteenth, as they came near the corral, a severe thunderstorm rushed in from the mountains, obscuring the moon. Under cover of the rumble of thunder and hiss of driving rain the Indians rode up to the gate of the corral. The watchman on duty had taken shelter in the corral boss's quarters nearby. Tenawerka dismounted and opened the gate, which was secured only by a chain and harness snap. All the mules and horses, fifty-four in number, were successfully stolen and driven to the Comanche camps near the site of Hobart. Fear of being arrested for this impudent feat prevented Tenawerka from again visiting Fort Sill until 1933, although he had lived within twenty miles of the post for sixty years. His beady little eyes twinkle today as he tells the story.[48]

G. W. Schofield and Tatum did not twinkle when they learned about it. They were sorely irked. But Tatum knew that it would do no good to write to Enoch Hoag about the matter, and Schofield took so little pride in it that he did not care to advertise it too much by making any lengthy report to his superiors.

THE COUNCILS OF 1872

The Indian conference convened at old Fort Cobb (then an abandoned post) on July 25. Representatives of the Five Nations were there. John D. Miles came from Darlington with some of his Cheyennes and Arapahoes. Jonathan Richards was present with a company of Caddoes, Wichitas, and Delawares. Lawrie Tatum and Horace Jones arrived from Fort Sill. Cyrus Beede came from Kansas to represent Enoch Hoag. But no Kiowas or Comanches put in an appearance. Since the powwow was

[48] Tenawerka to author; Schofield to AAG, Department of Texas, June 21, 1872.

principally for the benefit of these erring people it seemed useless to proceed until they arrived.[49]

For eight days the eager conferees marked time. The Cheyennes grew weary and went back to their own agency. Lawrie Tatum announced that he had a message from Fort Sill that his wife was sick. He also left. Cyrus Beede's lip curled. He insinuated that Tatum was afraid of the Kiowas, and had departed because the Cheyennes were no longer there to protect him. Finally, on Saturday, August 3, all the Kiowas except Big Bow came in. Two bands of Comanches were not represented; namely, the bands of Mow-way and Parra-o-coom, both of whom had refused to participate in the council.

White Horse swaggered up to Horace Jones and inquired loudly, "Where is Bald-Head (Tatum)?"

"Gone to Sill," Jones replied.

"Well," grunted White Horse. "I was looking for him to kill him. And you too. But he is gone, and you are of little value, not worth bothering about."

The Kiowas were feeling superior. One of them boasted to Horace Jones that White Horse had personally killed three men at the Howard Wells affair. They said that Big Bow and White Horse were the leaders there. They acknowledged the killing of Frank Lee near Fort Sill, and lauded themselves for several successful raids in Texas and around Fort Sill. They stated that White Horse and Big Bow had engineered the Lee massacre on the Brazos River, and smilingly admitted that they had the three Lee children in their possession.

A spokesman for the Five Nations opened the oratory by admonishing the Kiowas and Comanches for their savage ways. He urged them to take up the white man's road. To this the wild men replied that they would give up their bows and arrows when the white man gave up his papers and his books. The civilized Indians then informed their nomadic brethren that in a few years the buffalo would be gone. They should settle down and raise crops lest they starve. The Kiowas and Comanches responded that it did not seem possible that so awful a calamity could happen as the total disappearance of the buffalo; but, if such a danger was impending, they would abstain from killing the buffalo for a year or two in order to allow them to multiply. In the meantime they could get along very nicely on cattle stolen in Texas.

Lone Wolf was chief speaker for the Kiowas. In reply to a demand made by Cyrus Beede for the return of the captives and of the government mules stolen at Fort Sill, he replied, in substance: "The government must move Fort Sill and all the troops out of the Indian country.

[49] Complete report of council at Fort Cobb is found in File 1582, AGO. *See also* George Conover, *op. cit.*, pp. 37-39.

156

The reservation must be extended to the Rio Grande on the south and the Missouri or the Sioux line on the north. Satanta must be brought to us so that we can see his face and know he is alive, and he must be given up to us. Then we will be ready to comply with the demands made upon us and make peace."[50]

In a talk outside the council Lone Wolf said that the Kiowas would make no promises about raiding in Texas. All the other chiefs agreed with him that the plundering of Texas was their legitimate occupation. Incidentally it was noted that Tau-ankia, the son of Lone Wolf, was limping from a severe wound in the knee received at the Howard Wells fight, and that White Horse had a wound in the arm.

Cyrus Beede appears to have lost some of his forbearance when he heard the insolent demands of the Indians, and their refusal to deliver up captives and stolen property. As the council broke up he hinted that if the Indians persisted in their unrighteous course the military would be used against them.

Kicking Bird, who had taken no part in the proceedings, now came to Beede and told him that he was sorry that his friends had talked so foolishly. He promised to use his influence in obtaining the release of the Lee children. Lone Wolf also showed a better spirit. This persuaded Beede that the Peace Policy was succeeding after all. In a letter to Enoch Hoag he indicated that the Indians were showing a friendly attitude. Then he went on to sneer at the military for losing the stock from the corral at Fort Sill, and for losing a wagon train at Howard Wells. The latter affair, he said, "furnished the Indians with an ample supply of the latest and most approved style of arms, and plenty of ammunition, to enable the most warlike tribe to continue their raiding and successfully cope with any military force sent among them."

Then in the next paragraph, with airy inconsistency, he recommended "considerable moderation of the ruling heretofore made by the Department in regard to the purchase of arms and ammunition by the Indians of this agency (be made) of the traders. Let the traders sell at the discretion of the agent. Everything indicates the best feeling toward the government on the part of the Indians."[51] An indorsement on this letter by General Sheridan remarks, "The writer of the within communication is a little too simple for this earth."

The gentlemen in charge of the Indian department now thought it high time to hold an official council with the Indians. The principal purpose therefor was to induce the Indians to send delegates on an excursion to Washington. The commissioner wrote several pages justifying this course. His concluding paragraph sums up admirably the arguments

[50] File 1582, AGO.
[51] Beede to Hoag, June 21, 1872.

157

presented: "As it is at once cheaper and more humane to bring the savages to a realizing sense of their weakness and the impossibility of long contending with the government, by giving a few chiefs and braves free rides on railways and Broadway omnibuses, than by surprising their camps on winter nights and shooting down men, women, and children together in the snow, it will be well to continue this system, in moderation as to the amount of expenditures, and with discretion as to the subjects of it, until the occasion for thus impressing the minds of the Indians shall have passed away."[52]

All very sound reasoning. But it did not work out the way it should. The Indians who did not make these trips would not believe the stories of those who had. They thought that the latter were only spoofing them. Lone Wolf went twice. So did several others. Yet they remained as wild as ever. Only the aged chiefs adopted the white man's road. They were too old to do any more fighting.

Henry Alvord of Virginia, late captain of the Tenth Cavalry, and Professor Edward Parrish of Philadelphia were appointed special commissioners to visit the Indians and bring some of them on the proposed tour of the national capital. They traveled west by way of the central superintendency at Lawrence, Kansas, where they read Beede's report of the recent council at Fort Cobb. From this they learned that in order to induce any Kiowas to go to Washington it would be necessary to have Satanta and Big Tree brought from Texas, at least temporarily. It was rather a staggering task to persuade the governor of Texas to release, even temporarily, these notorious prisoners, but Captain Alvord succeeded. Satanta and Big Tree were turned over to a troop of the Fourth Cavalry from Fort Richardson, and were started toward Fort Sill. It was planned that the Indians would be permitted to see their chiefs at that point, after which they would go to Washington. Colonel Grierson went north to meet the commissioners, leaving the post under command of Major G. W. Schofield. Schofield considered the attitude of the Indians around Fort Sill so alarming that it would be unsafe to permit them to meet Satanta and Big Tree at the post. He knew that when they found out that the chiefs were not to be released they would make an effort to take them by force.

Fort Sill was a small place, with a small garrison. It was set alone in the vast expanse of prairie, far from any possible source of help, and surrounded only by wild animals and wilder Indians. Therefore Schofield sent scout Jack Stilwell with a plea to the commander of the troops of the Fourth Cavalry to take his prisoners elsewhere—any place except Fort Sill.

Stilwell found the escort many miles south of Red River, but moving

[52] *Report of Commissioner of Indian Affairs, 1872,* p. 99.

steadily north. Lieutenant R. G. Carter was in command. After reading Major Schofield's message, and consulting with Stilwell as to the conditions at Fort Sill, Carter decided to convey his prisoners to Atoka, the point on the Missouri, Kansas and Texas railroad from which the delegation would go to Washington. This was far enough from the Kiowa country to reduce the danger of uprising. Carter stopped en route at Gainesville, Texas, where he obtained telegraphic confirmation from San Antonio of the change in plans.[53] The commissioners arrived at Fort Sill to assemble the Indians for the council. Professor Parrish became ill and died. He was buried at Fort Sill. Alvord went on alone and collected the Indians at Leeper's Creek, six miles west of the site of Anadarko.

The conference was similar to all preceding meetings between representatives of the government and the Indians, and was, in its eventual effects, equally futile. As usual the remarks of the Indians are most instructive and entertaining. Captain Alvord's report says: "The chiefs of the Koatcha-tekas and the Quahadas claimed to be at peace with the government, but frankly stated that they preferred and proposed to continue their prairie life, seeing yet no sufficient inducement to change, and that they could not control their young men in raiding more or less. . . . . Attention is invited to the appended speech of Tabby-nanny-ker (Tabananica), Comanche, a chief of fine physique, unmistakable talents, and great power. After disclaiming all sympathy with raiding and atrocities in the settlements, and his desire to avoid and prevent conflict, he frankly stated his desire to roam the plains for the present. . . ."

One of Tabananica's outstanding characteristics was his bull-like voice; and when he told Alvord that he would rather stay out on the prairie and eat dung than come in and be penned up in a reservation, the commissioner, and every one else within a radius of a quarter of a mile, knew that he meant what he said.

Mow-way (Shaking Hand), the Kotchateka chief, was another Comanche of impressive appearance. His typically Indian features would have attracted a sculptor. In his scalp-lock he wore as sole ornament a huge bear claw which he had taken in a hand-to-hand fight with a grizzly. Mow-way favored peaceful relations with the whites; his natural inclination was one of kindliness and friendship. But he was not ready to become a government pensioner. "When the Indians in here are treated better than we are outside, it will be time enough to come in," he said.

After considerable difficulty Alvord succeeded in securing delegates for the junket to Washington. Ten Bears and several minor Comanche chiefs agreed to go; the Kiowas sent Lone Wolf, Stumbling Bear, Sun

[53] R. G. Carter, *op. cit.*, pp. 335-68.

Boy, Fast Bear, Woman's Heart, Red Otter, Wolf-lying-down, and young To-hauson—all famous warriors. Major Schofield furnished wagons from Fort Sill. In these the strangely assorted sightseers started for the railroad station at Atoka, 165 miles to the east. Soon after the party reached Atoka, Lieutenant Carter arrived with his two prisoners, Satanta and Big Tree. Alvord was not willing to risk a meeting between the prisoners and the other Indians at this point, so far from civilization. He still feared, as had Major Schofield, that the Indians might attempt to take the prisoners by force, or at least that there would be an unruly demonstration. So Carter and his prisoners spent the night in the brush, while the main delegation of Indians was sent on to St. Louis. Then he followed by a later train. The meeting between the Indians and the prisoners at St. Louis, according to Alvord, was impressive and affecting.

Then the prisoners were conducted back to Texas, and the delegation went on to Washington. Here they met the Commissioner of Indian Affairs, were presented with large silver medals, and were shown the sights of the city. The commissioner, in his effort to please the Indians, and get them to agree to stop raiding, made one serious blunder. He promised that Satanta and Big Tree would be released on March 1 of the following year, dependent on the good behavior of the tribe in the meantime. The commissioner had no right to make this promise. The two chiefs were prisoners of the sovereign state of Texas, not of the Federal government.

Most of the Indians were unharmed by the trip to Washington. But it was too much for Ten Bears. When the party arrived at Fort Sill the old chief was sick. His people had deserted him, so the agent gave him a bed in the agency office. Here Ten Bears died, a pathetic figure, alone in the midst of an alien people, in an age he did not understand. Once he had been a mighty warrior, respected of his people. But in his old age he had taken the white man's road. His people cast him off. The white man's road did not bring him happiness.

MACKENZIE STRIKES THE QUOHADI

The army authorities had little confidence that the councils and trips to Washington arranged for the Indians by the Indian bureau would induce the savages to give up their white captives or stolen stock. General Sherman knew a better method of bringing the Indians to a proper realization of their impotence to resist the United States. The troops at Fort Sill could not be used against the Indians on account of the Peace Policy. This policy, however, did not apply to Indians off the reservation, nor to troops stationed in Texas operating outside the limits of the reservation.

In September Colonel R. S. Mackenzie was sent against the Quohada Comanches who roamed the wastes west of the Fort Sill Indian reservation, and who had, up to this time, defied the government. Mackenzie marched from a supply camp at the site of old Camp Cooper (near Fort Griffin) into the Staked Plains. Parra-o-coom, great war-chief of the Quohada, and Mow-way, head man of the Kotchateka band, were closely associated. In the fall of 1872 several of their villages were scattered along McClellan Creek and the North Fork of Red River. On September 29, Colonel Mackenzie surprised and destroyed the largest of these villages.[54]

Mackenzie's description of this fight is as follows:[55] "On the 29th, with the five cavalry companies, in all 7 officers and 215 enlisted men, and Tonkawa scouts, the march was taken upon McClellan Creek which was reached at a point about four miles above the forks of the stream. After marching two miles, two fresh trails were found by the Tonkawas —one of two horses, and another of one mule. Judging that the trail of the mule led in the direction of the camp of the Indians, it was followed at a rapid gait, from about 1 o'clock P.M.—by the Tonks, urged and assisted by Captain Davis. After a quick march of about twelve miles the village was discovered nearly four miles distant. The command moved out at a gallop and reached the village about 4 P.M.

"After a brisk fight of about half an hour, the village was entirely carried, resistance to any extent being made at only one point, where three companies were engaged from time to time. F Company being engaged from the commencement to the close more continuously than any other—D being sent after the horses, and I Company having attacked handsomely the right, charged dismounted through a small village somewhat detached, and pursuing retreating Indians, did not rejoin the command until nearly dark. A Company was also sent after the horses. . . . .

"The village consisted of about 175 large lodges, and a number of smaller ones—in all 262, and was situated on the North Fork of Red River, about seven miles above the mouth of McClellan's Creek.

"In the fight twenty-three Indians were killed, whose bodies fell into our hands, and one mortally wounded has since died, and many are said to have fallen or have been thrown into a deep pool of water which was immediately under the bank where the main resistance was made—and it is my opinion that a number were killed that were not reported.

"Between 120 and 130 women and children were captured. Some of them were very old, and some, being mixed with the men, were too badly wounded to be moved. We left their camp after dark with 124, of whom

[54] *Army and Navy Journal,* November 16, 1872.
[55] Mackenzie to AAG, Department of Texas, October 12, 1872.

161

one man and seven women and children have died on the march, some of them from injuries received during the fight. All such were accidental, and they have had the best possible care, but the surgeon cannot make them follow his instructions. . . . .

"Their lodges generally were burned, and a large amount of property was destroyed. The command was moved some two miles from the village shortly after dark and on the following day we moved near 18 miles. We captured a large number of horses and mules (about 3000), but the Indians succeeded the night after the fight in stampeding them by riding a little distance from camp yelling and firing pistols. . . . ."

Mackenzie lost four men killed, and several wounded. He recaptured two Mexican boys, taken by the Indians in Texas. Forty-two mules found in the Indian herd were recognized as some which had been taken by the Indians at the Howard Wells massacre in the spring.

Comanche informants give an account of the fight which agrees well with that of Mackenzie: "Mow-way not there," they say. "He with the Peace People. Chief in charge of camp was Kai-wotche. Second chief, Patch-o-ko-naiky (Beaver). There were lots of grapes near our camp. Kai-wotche went out to look around. He was riding a mule. It was a little after noon. The soldiers and Tonkawas charged in and saw him, but he got away to warn the village. The soldiers arrived almost at once. They were on horseback. Quite a few Comanches were killed and more were wounded. Three of them were good warriors.

"The soldiers were hard to kill with arrows because they got in gulches. Kai-wotche was killed. Also his wife. The fight lasted until about sunset. Our women came out of the brush with their hands in the air, and surrendered. Their husbands had run off and left them.

"One of the chiefs came down to the lower village and said, 'The soldiers got all our horses.' So we tied up the tails of our ponies and came on them at night. We got all our own horses back and some of the soldiers' too. The women and children were under close guard. The soldiers took them down into Texas and fed them good.

"Those were dangerous days. We Comanches had to get up early, eat our breakfast quick, and be ready to fight. Now we have houses and can lie in bed. No danger. Have peace."[56]

Although Mackenzie had not succeeded in holding the captured herd, he had taught the Indians a lesson. He showed them that the Great White Father had a long arm and a heavy hand which he could use if he chose. Shortly after the battle Parra-o-coom brought his people to the vicinity of Fort Sill. They had with them a number of captives, mostly Mexican children, whom they wished to trade for their own women and children

[56] Indian informants: Cohaya and Mumsukawa—both participants in the fight with Mackenzie. Cohaya is crippled with gunshot wounds.

who were in the hands of Mackenzie. They told Tatum that they had had their fight with the soldiers, had been whipped, and now were ready to remain on the reservation and send their children to school. They even promised to try a hand at farming. But before they would do any of these things Tatum must restore their women and children.

Mr. Tatum saw he had the Quohadi at a disadvantage. He told them he would ask Mackenzie to return four of their women if they would give up four captives which he knew were with them. By bargaining in this fashion the agent managed to procure the release of several young Mexicans. One of these was a boy named Presleano, who was a slave of Parra-o-coom. This was the first time Tatum had met the famous war chief face to face. Parra-o-coom (Bull Bear) was a true savage, and a formidable one at that. But he was so overcome at having to give up his little Mexican pet that he shed tears. The western Indians, contrary to popular conception, were and are an emotional people, considerably less stoical than many of their Nordic neighbors. The Indians having released several captives, Mr. Tatum wrote to Mackenzie, who in turn sent to Fort Sill four Comanche women. One died on the way, but the others arrived in good health, much to the joy of their kin.

The beneficial effects of Mackenzie's campaign endured for several months. During December the Comanches brought in and surrendered most of the stock which had been stolen from the quartermaster corral by Tenawerka. Kicking Bird delivered up seventeen mules, which were a part of a herd captured by the Kiowas near Camp Supply earlier in the year.

CHAPTER EIGHT

THE PAROLE

RELEASE OF THE COMANCHE WOMEN—PAROLE OF SATANTA AND
BIG TREE—THE ULTIMATUM—SEARCH FOR COMANCHE
RENEGADES—DEATH OF TAU-ANKIA AND GUI-TAIN

DURING the winter of 1872-73 most of the Comanches camped close to the agency. This was the first time they had all done so, and the Texas border enjoyed unprecedented quiet. The Indians were waiting to see what would happen to the prisoners in the hands of the authorities. These were the prisoners taken by Mackenzie, mostly women and children, who were held in a stockade or corral at Fort Concho. The prisoners were well treated, receiving so much food that most of them got fat. It was a favorite amusement of the army wives at Fort Concho to stroll down to the corral to see the prisoners. The Indian women always wanted to trade children temporarily, so that they could enjoy the novelty of fondling white papooses. The white women did this once—then they discovered that they and their infants were covered with lice.

At Fort Sill, the Comanches were on Cache Creek, the Quohadi being south of the agency, in the area now occupied by the town of Lawton, while the more friendly Comanches under chiefs Horseback, Howea, and Cheevers, were north of the post, near Chandler Creek. The Kiowas were divided into two elements. Kicking Bird, with about a dozen chiefs who followed his lead, was camped on Two Hatchet Creek, two miles south of Fort Cobb. Lone Wolf and the more hostile elements camped north of Mount Scott.

A Quaker named Thomas Battey went to Kicking Bird's camp about this time for the purpose of establishing a school for children. The Indians thought he had come to take census and, as they were superstitious about being counted, most of them resented his presence. The school never prospered, but Battey was able to keep Kicking Bird friendly. The latter was under a great deal of pressure from his own people to turn against the whites.[1]

---

[1] Thomas C. Battey, *A Quaker Among the Indians*, pp. 93-103 (Boston: Lee and Shepard, 1891).

Lawrie Tatum, seeing that his superiors disapproved his policy of asking the army to punish the Indians, and feeling that, if Satanta and Big Tree were released, his position would be untenable, submitted his resignation. He was succeeded, on March 31, 1873, by James Haworth. Mr. Haworth was a thoroughgoing Quaker, and a firm adherent of the Peace Policy. His first official act was to dispense with the military guard at the agency. That the Indians did not immediately cause disorder was taken by him as a sign that they appreciated his show of confidence in them. As a matter of fact it indicated nothing of the sort. The Indians were on pins and needles lest an irresponsible young brave commit some overt act which would jeopardize the chances for release of the Comanche women and Satanta and Big Tree.

When the first of March arrived the government, instead of setting Satanta and Big Tree free, sent Cyrus Beede to tell the Kiowas that Washington had not forgotten its promise, but that unforseen difficulties had arisen, and the prisoners would be released in June. The unexpected difficulties were that Texas did not want to release the Kiowa convicts, and there was no legal way whereby she could be forced to do it. Agent Haworth was informed that the governor of Texas was expected to visit Washington in the near future, at which time the commissioner of Indian affairs would get President Grant to persuade Governor Davis to save the face of the Federal government by freeing Satanta and Big Tree.

As spring came on, it became increasingly difficult for the chiefs to keep their young men from the warpath. Kicking Bird and Lone Wolf succeeded in holding the Kiowas quiet, though Kicking Bird's influence was diminishing rapidly. The Comanches were not so conscientious. On March 15 several young men from the bands of Tabananica and Esa Rosa (White Wolf) passed Kicking Bird's camp on their way to Texas. The Kiowa chief, by threatening to kill their horses, was able to prevent some of the Comanches from going, but a few slipped by him and continued south. There were other incentives for restlessness among the Indians at this time. The government was engaged in surveying the Indian reservation. The Indians did not understand what it meant to have parties of white men in their range, setting up stakes and running lines. They felt a superstitious fear about it, and also were fearful that the whites were planning to divide up the land for settlement. The Cheyennes and Osages were especially uneasy. They made several overtures to the Kiowas and Comanches to join with them against white aggression, but the proposals bore no fruit.[2]

The first of June came and passed. The Indians still waited anxiously for the release of the prisoners. The recent treacherous murder of General Canby and Dr. Thomas in the West (by Modocs) caused such hard

[2] *Ibid.,* pp. 156-60.

feeling throughout the United States against Indians that the governor of Texas changed his mind about releasing Satanta and Big Tree. The Comanche women and children, however, were still in the custody of the army, so it was possible for the Federal government to order their release. One warm day, the tenth of June, a large group of Comanches were lying around the Fort Sill agency, dispirited and complaining over the continued non-arrival of their relatives, when a cloud of dust was observed in the south. An advance runner brought in word that the Fort Concho prisoners were approaching. The Indians began shouting joyously. They jumped on their ponies and rode at full speed to meet the caravan.

The women and children were under charge of Captain Robert McClermont. He had brought his convoy safely through the Texas settlements, though he had been forced to resort to a ruse to pass Jacksboro without having his hostages attacked by the citizenry. The reunion of the Comanches was a demonstrative one. The women testified to the good treatment they had received at the hands of their captors. The delighted husbands and fathers embraced Captain McClermont. Many of them said that never again would they raise their hands against the army.

The happy occasion was marred for the Quakers by the realization that the government was going to welsh on its agreement with respect to Satanta and Big Tree. Thomas Battey was given the thankless mission of informing the Kiowas. Before he departed for the Indian camps he wrote a letter to the commissioner, setting forth the fact that the Kiowas had faithfully lived up to their part of the agreement, and urged that reconsideration be given to the release of the chiefs. Battey found the Kiowas on Sweetwater Creek, preparing for their annual Sun Dance. Most of the Comanches, as well as a large number of Cheyennes and Arapahoes, were with them. Battey noted that each chief accepted the pipe which passed from hand to hand. This meant that all were committed to any warlike policy which might be adopted. The question under discussion was whether the tribes should go to war if Satanta and Big Tree were not released.

First they asked Battey what news he brought. Battey was in a dangerous spot. He hardly knew how to word his reply. "Bad news," he blurted. An ominous silence settled over the assemblage. To-haint, the Tai-me Keeper, or Great Medicine Man, who was in charge, solemnly filled and passed the pipe. When it had been smoked out he asked Battey to explain. The Quaker missionary told of the Modoc tragedy and gave it as the reason "Washington" had changed his mind with regard to Satanta and Big Tree. The Indians were genuinely surprised. They had never heard of the Modocs. They could not understand how so remote an event could affect them. The majority of the chiefs favored going to war at once. First they would kill Battey. Then they would hide their women in the middle of the Staked Plains, divide into two small parties and simultaneously attack the border settlements of Texas, New Mexico, and Kansas. The available strength of the combined tribes was over a thousand warriors. Battey begged for time. He urged the Indians to wait until he had received a reply from the letter which he had written to the commissioner. Perhaps Washington's heart would soften when he heard that the Kiowas had been well behaved all winter.

Kicking Bird, up to this time, had not joined in the talk. Satanta's father taunted him, asking him why he, who had forced them to keep peaceful, now remained silent like an old woman. Kicking Bird was confused. He saw that his efforts to maintain peace were about to go for naught. But Battey's last remark encouraged him. He too asked that the Indians wait a little longer, until the letter had been answered. Curiously enough, the Indians agreed to wait. For the next three weeks Battey was held as a hostage in the Kiowa camps. The mental and nervous strain was so great that he became an invalid. Finally there came the good news that the governor of Texas had agreed to restore the prisoners to their people. It was learned that he would bring them to Fort Sill in October. In the meantime the Indians were enjoined to abstain from raiding, lest the governor change his mind.

The Comanches had received their women and children. True, the chiefs had promised to stop raiding. But what was a promise to the young men, when summer had arrived, and war ponies were fattening on the green grass? The opening of the annual raiding season was overdue. A few members of Isa-habeet's band went to the vicinity of San Antonio to steal horses. Other small parties prowled along Red River and killed a surveyor. Colonel Davidson reported in July that he was satisfied in his own mind that the Indians had settled upon a definite time to commence raiding.

A new commander had come to the post of Fort Sill, and the Indian agency also was under a new management. Lieutenant Colonel John W. Davidson, Tenth Cavalry, became post commander about the same time that James Haworth became agent. Davidson and Haworth did not get on well together. Davidson was not as firm an advocate of the Peace Policy as Grierson had been, and Haworth was not as cordial to the military as his predecessor, Tatum. The colonel did not agree that the Indians were friendly. It seemed to him that war was sure to break out in the not distant future. Being new to the country, he decided to make a scout over the terrain in which he might expect to operate in case of hostilities.

Colonel Davidson left Fort Sill on August 19 with most of the troops

167

comprising the garrison. It was his intention to punish such Indians as might be found off the reservation, engaged in marauding on the border of Texas. The march was down Cache Creek, west along Red River to Buck Creek, then north to the Elm Fork of Red River, thence back to Sill. During the march Davidson found the fresh grave of Hank Medley, the surveyor recently killed by the Indians. The closing paragraph of Davidson's report verifies the contentions of Sherman and Sheridan: "Evidence was found to spare that the Indians are constantly marauding upon the borders of Texas, that the reservation is a "City of Refuge" for them, that it is almost impossible for our troops to catch an enemy with the eye of a hawk and the stealth of a wolf, who knows every foot of the country, and that an effective method of stopping this state of affairs, while the government feeds and clothes the reservation Indians, is to dismount them and make them account for themselves daily."[3]

While Davidson was absent from the post a wild rumor got into the newspapers in the East to the effect that the Indians had attacked and sacked Fort Sill, wiping out the entire personnel of the fort. Around Fort Sill, however, the Indians were unusually quiet, waiting for the arrival of Satanta and Big Tree.

PAROLE OF SATANTA AND BIG TREE

On August 19, 1873, Satanta and Big Tree were turned over to Lieutenant Hoffman and left the Huntsville prison (Texas) for Fort Sill. The people of Texas, especially those on the frontier, learned of their release with great regret. This feeling militated heavily against Governor Davis, who was seeking the nomination for reëlection. The two Kiowa prisoners arrived at Fort Sill on September 4, and were lodged in the newly completed guardhouse. Governor Davis, accompanied by several of his staff, arrived on October 3. The commissioner of Indian affairs, Mr. E. P. Smith, came from Washington, and Enoch Hoag, superintendent of the Plains tribes also was present.

The importance of the occasion attracted to Fort Sill several correspondents from the big eastern periodicals. A correspondent of *The Nation*, writing from Fort Sill on October 5, said: "This is the best-arranged and most complete military post I have yet seen. The barracks, officers' quarters, and quartermaster building are built of limestone around a square parade ground. . . . Hard by are a fine hospital and guardhouse. . . . My conviction is that the Quakers and their policy are a bloody nuisance. Under their management this reservation has become a city of refuge for the Indians that maraud and murder in Texas. The Quakers can't keep them in the reservation. Bands of them go away from the proximity to this post that affords them protection,

[3] Davidson to AAG, Department of Texas, September 16, 1873.

168

under the pretext of taking a buffalo hunt on the plains, and turn up in Texas, where they help themselves to scalps and horses, that can easily be identified by their brand when they get here. The Quakers will not let the military force them to give them up. . . ."

On the day following the arrival of Governor Davis a meeting was held to determine the place for the main council. The Indians objected strenuously to having it in the post. They had not been there since the three chiefs were taken prisoner on Grierson's porch, and they claimed it was a bad place. Governor Davis and his friends were reluctant to confer with the savages away from the shelter of Fort Sill, and, as they held the whip hand, the post was selected as the place for the council.

The council was held October 6, in front of Colonel Davidson's headquarters, on the south side of the parade ground. Here was stretched a tent fly, with chairs and a table placed for the governor and other notables. The two prisoners were brought from the guardhouse, and sat on a bench, under guard of a few colored cavalrymen. During the session the garrison was held in quarters—officers on hand, one troop in stables with horses saddled, and every other precaution was taken against disturbance on the part of the Indians.[4]

The Indians came into the post dressed in all their finery, and seated themselves on the grass around the council tent. Tsa'l-au-te, son of Satanta, arrived on a fine horse which one of Governor Davis' aides recognized as his property. But the aide was forced to swallow his indignation. Commissioner Smith opened the proceedings with a brief address of welcome, then introduced the governor of Texas. Governor Davis cleared his throat, smoothed out his handsome forked beard, and said: "I have brought back Satanta and Big Tree. You see them. They were prisoners of Texas and their lives were forfeited to the Texans, but they have spared them. . . . we want to be at peace with the Kiowas and Comanches. Satanta and Big Tree can tell you how they were treated while prisoners in Texas. . . ."[5]

A touching incident interrupted the speech-making at this point. An aged and frail-looking, but wiry Indian, the father of Satanta, stepped forth and, with earnest gesticulation, made in the Kiowa tongue a strong appeal to Governor Davis for the release of his son. The action of the old savage was so expressive that the aid of an interpreter was scarcely necessary, and, as his speech was unexpected, no one interpreted any of it until he had finished and stepped back among the spectators. During his appeal the old man laid his hands on the governor's head and said, "I am a poor old man. I want you to pity me and give up my son. The Indians love their children as much as the white people do theirs.

[4] File 4447, AGO, 1873.

[5] File 4447 gives a verbatim account of all that happened at the council.

You have your wife and children. Take pity on me; gladden my heart by the immediate release of my son. Never again will we raid upon Texas." Nothing could have been done or said under the circumstances that would have been more eloquent. Satanta then spoke as follows: "I want all the chiefs present here today to make a new road, and particularly the Quohada Comanches. I want them to quit raiding into Texas, to listen to whatever Commissioner Smith brings them from Washington, and to do whatever he says. We have been kindly treated in Texas. I heard that the Kiowas were told that we were dead, but the Texans treated us well. My heart feels big today and I will take my Texas father to my breast and hold him there. I am half Kiowa and half Arapaho. Whatever the white man thinks best I want my people to do. Strip off these prison clothes, turn me over to my people, and they will keep their promise. . . ."

Governor Davis enumerated the conditions which must be fulfilled before he would release the two prisoners: The Indians must settle down on farms near the agency, with a government official in each camp to check on their behavior. Rations must be drawn by each Indian in person, rather than by the head men; they must be drawn every third day instead of at fortnightly intervals. Every Indian capable of bearing arms must answer roll call on ration days. The Indians must give up their arms and horses, and become farmers like the civilized Indians.

"In the meantime," he said, "Satanta and Big Tree are to remain in the Guardhouse until the Commanding Officer at Fort Sill is satisfied that these conditions have been carried out. When released, they must further understand that Satanta and Big Tree are liable to rearrest and punishment for their old crimes if they break these conditions, that they are not pardoned. I have consulted with Commissioner Smith and General Davidson and am satisfied if you really desire peace you can carry out these terms. . . . If these conditions are not complied with, it will be better for the people of Texas to resort to open war and settle this matter at once."

Agent Haworth here hastened to disclaim any responsibility for the terms of the governor. He wanted to be sure that the Indians knew that they did not come from him. Lone Wolf, as principal chief of the Kiowas, made a reply to the governor. "This is a good day. I have heard the speech of the Governor of Texas and I and my young men have taken it all up. I looked through it for something bad. It is the very talk I would make to these people myself. My friends, you have come a long way to make a good road. You have already made our hearts good by bringing back these prisoners. Make them still better by releasing them today. I try to do what the agent requires of me. Though the tribes have different names, we are all one people, of one mind just as the whites from different parts are alike. I call on the Sun, our father, and the Earth, our mother, to witness the truth of what I say."

Kicking Bird attempted to make a speech at this point, but the other chiefs did not want him to steal their show. Satanta growled something at him and he sat down. Lone Wolf continued: "This country has been given by Washington to the Kiowas and Comanches, and we love it. We will do all you want if the chiefs are turned over to us. But if not, we will go away feeling bad. . . ."

Horseback, the Comanche, said: ". . . It makes my heart feel sad to see my two old friends prisoners here today. I was sick and bleeding from the lungs, but I tried to come here. I do not know what the other Indians here may think, but I am willing to comply with all I have heard. To make a white man of me, build me a house and give me a patch of land. But above all, release Set-tainte and Big Tree. It is true some of the young men go to Texas, but Washington has not built houses for them. I look like a humble chief, but I have done a good deal towards getting back captives and stock, and I think for that reason the Texans and I ought to be good friends. If my talk now falls to the ground I will leave here today with a crying heart."

Pacer, the chief of the Kiowa-Apaches, spoke next: "Tell the Governor of Texas we are about to take a new road, and throw the old one away. . . . I have worked hard to keep the peace and will work still harder. My people know nothing of all this killing and stealing. They do not raid in Texas. I am glad you will give us men to watch our camps, and I want you to give them to us right away. I can't say if the other tribes go to Texas, but I think if houses were built for them they would not go. We are [Indian] men, but our children will be white men. Build us houses and teach our children to read and write, but above all release Satanta and Big Tree. This is my talk, and the talk of the Apaches." Then he continued in a wistful tone, "I wish we could all live together as we did in Mexico. When I come into the post [Fort Sill] a soldier will hollow [sic] out, 'Stop there. Go to the other side of the creek,' or something of that sort. That is not the way to live like friends. When I come to buy bread a soldier stops me, with a bayonet at my breast."

Asa-toyeh, the Penateka Comanche who had guided Grierson's expedition to Fort Sill in December, 1868, said: "My heart feels good to meet my Texas father. I have not much to say. I tried to do what I have promised my father in Washington, and want him to do what he promised. Your talk today is my talk to my young men. My heart cries to see my friends prisoners. I do not like to see this soldier post on my land. For some time whenever I come into the post to see my friends among the officers I am stopped. I saw much prettier houses in Washington and could go into all of them. I can't understand why I can't do the same here. You must have something bad in your houses here that you do not want me to see. This is a good day and when the sun goes down I would like to see the prisoners given to their people."

Commissioner Smith thought he ought to rebut the implication of Asa-toyeh that the promises made by the Indian department had not been fulfilled. Turning to the interpreter he said:

"Ask him if he had not a house built for him and all the help promised him at Washington given to him this summer."

Asa-toyeh replied: "Yes. I had. And I began to work on my farm, when a white man came out to help me, and spoiled it all."

Quirts Quip (Chewing Elk), a Yapparika Comanche chief, enlarged on the theme that the government ought to give the Indians houses, money, and other good things: "I have only one heart and therefore not much to say. I was told by the great father at Washington that we were all his children and that I must advise the Kiowas and Comanches. I was told that the agent would build me a house and give me some stock. This was last fall. The spring and summer have come and these promises have not been fulfilled." Quirts Quip also recalled that he had visited the place where the great white father made his money: "I saw big piles of money in Washington. Washington could give me some if he wanted to. I don't know what becomes of so much money, whether it goes down into the ground, or where it goes. Satanta and Big Tree were promised to us and I do not think it right to hold them any longer. It is true some of my young men slip off to Texas, but then Washington has not kept *his* promises. We have friends in the post, but are not allowed to see them. You must have a big bug or a snake hid in there. When I went to Washington I saw much prettier houses and big looking-glasses, and was allowed to go where I pleased. Mr. Tatum gave me a piece of land, but the first night I stopped there a big thunderstorm came right over the house. I thought this was bad medicine and lit out and have never been there since."

Buffalo Good, a Wichita (Waco band) chief, said: "I am a Texan too. Sam Houston told me a long time ago that the Wacoes and Texans were brothers though we are of different color. . . ." Here Mr. Buffalo Good slipped into the favorite Indian style of flattery: "Sam Houston was the greatest father we ever had, and I think that Governor Davis resembles him. The best agents we had were Texans." Having smoothed the way by this bit of soft soap the Waco came to the point of his address: "Give us the land and plow it for us, and don't fool any longer about it. Since I came from Texas I have been living on the Washita for a number of years and am still a poor man. The prisoners ought to be given up today. They have learned their lesson. Let them go. That is what you do with your own white men. . . ."

172

Commissioner Smith could not let pass the slurs made on the department. He asked: "Did not the agent send a man to show you how to farm?"

Buffalo Good: "After a great deal of arguing and nearly fighting with the agent he gave me a man."

Mr. Smith: "Did you make any use of this man?"

Mr. Good: "I wanted him to break up the land first."

Mr. Smith: "Exactly. You wanted him to do all the work."

Guadalupe, chief of the Caddoes, made the final speech for the Indians: "I do not belong to this agency but come to see and hear what occurs at this council. I have time and again advised these Indians for the sake of the Caddoes to cease going on the warpath, but I am sorry to say that it has not stopped. I used to live out on the Brazos, and I defy any man to say that I or my people have ever raided on any one. These very Kiowas and Comanches that are here today were the cause of my tribe being removed from Texas. I too am tired of trifling with these raiding Indians. If they won't quit let them say so. My tribe has been raising cattle and hogs and farming on the Washita, and these raiders interfere with us as much as they do with the whites. I am dressed in the hat, pants, and boots of a white man. I did not steal them, but bought them with money from my farm. I talk this way to my red brothers, for I feel it is for their own good. I have the white man by the hand and am bound to be his friend. I would like to see settled this trouble between the state of Texas and these Indians. I think that Satanta and Big Tree have been sufficiently punished, but that is not my affair. It is between the Texans and the Kiowas and Comanches."

Governor Davis listened attentively to the arguments of the Indians, but did not recede from the position which he had taken. "I will not change my conditions," he said. "If they love Satanta and Big Tree, the sooner they comply, the sooner these prisoners will go to their camps. They all understand me, so there is nothing further for me to say."

Pollyanna Hoag sparred for time. "Tell the Indians," he said to the interpreter, "that the Governor says he made no promise until now, that about a year ago the great father promised that if they kept out of Texas these men would be pardoned. . . ." And he went on trying to explain to the Indians how Washington was unable to make Texas fulfill the promise which Washington had given. But as the principle of states rights was never fully understood by the whites themselves, it was futile of Hoag to expect the Indians to comprehend it.

Then, turning to Mr. Davis, Hoag said, "Now as the Superintendent of these Indians, I appeal to your excellency, as this has been promised by the President and by the Secretary of the Interior, is it not unwise not to release them?"

173

Governor Davis did not relent. Hoag switched to a new line of attack: "I would like to ask of the Governor," he sneered, "Does he mean to leave it discretionally with the commanding officer of the post when to release these prisoners?"

"I will give it to you in writing, sir," Davis shot back. "I have implicit confidence in General Davidson. I have known him for years, and believe that when he sees the conditions fulfilled he will release them. They can comply with them in thirty days if they wish to."

Hoag thought of another objection to the governor's plan: "We cannot place men within their camps except you first release Satanta and Big Tree."

"Then, sir," replied Davis, his eyes flashing, "if they are as warlike as all that, if they are that unreasonable, we had better settle it right now. That is the shortest way to answering that!"

Commissioner Smith sided with the governor. "What the governor has asked from them today," he said, "I am here to demand for Washington right now. They had no reason to raid in Texas, except for mischief alone. The governor told them to stop, and I tell them the same. When your captive women and children were given back to you last spring you gave your solemn pledges not to raid in Texas again, but scarcely had these women and children got here when your young men were again down in Texas. Now before the sun is this high, have those Comanche murderers (Smith here referred to five supposed outlaws) right on this spot, and I and the governor will no longer disagree, and you will get your captives. Now go home and talk about this and talk about nothing else." On this sour note the council ended. The Indians went back to their camps, grumbling among themselves.

Commissioner Smith and Agent Haworth spent the following day striving to get the governor to change his conditions. Finally he consented to another meeting, in which he intimated that the prisoners would be freed. In the meantime the Indians brooded in their camps. They were sure that the chiefs would not be released voluntarily. Even Kicking Bird was discouraged. He said, "My heart is a stone. There is no soft place in it. I have taken the white man by the hand, thinking him to be a friend, but he is not a friend. Washington has deceived us. Washington is rotten."[6]

Lone Wolf said, "I want peace—have worked hard for it—kept my young men from raiding—followed the instructions Washington gave me to the best of my knowledge and ability. Washington has deceived me—has failed to keep faith with me and my people—has broken his promises. And now there is nothing left us but war. I know that war

<hr>

[6] Battey, *op. cit.*, pp. 202-3.

with Washington means the extinction of my people, but we are driven to it. We had rather die than live."

The Indians held a secret meeting that night at which they plotted to take the prisoners by force if necessary. Next morning, while waiting for the high officials to arrive for the second council, several agency employes and clerks from Evans' trading store were standing in the hall of post headquarters. Pe-ah-rite (Big Buttocks), son of the friendly Comanche chief Horseback, came up to George Fox and C. E. Campbell and asked Fox if Campbell was a particular friend. On being assured that they were like brothers, the young Indian remarked, vaguely, "This is a nice day on which to die, and you and he and I will remain here and die together."[7]

Fox and Campbell were somewhat surprised by this statement. But they thought that the Comanche was merely using some peculiar Indian expression of greeting. They did not find out until later that he was, in an indirect way, trying to warn them of the extreme danger of attending the council. Before the conference began the Kiowas had stationed their warriors around in front of the building, with arms concealed under their blankets. If their two chiefs were not released, they were going to shoot down the small guard of soldiers, the governor of Texas, the commissioner, the agent, and all the other white men. Fleet horses were ready for Satanta and Big Tree. Two or three women loitered on the outskirts of the crowd to give an appearance of a casual and ordinary state of affairs. But they were mounted, and ready to flee when the shooting started.

Governor Davis was probably unaware that the Kiowas were prepared to take such a desperate step. Everything was set for a big blow-off; then the door of the lion's den was opened and out walked a mouse. Without preliminaries the governor made a short speech in which he alluded to the faithful performance by the Kiowas of their part of the obligation imposed by the Federal government, and then turned the chiefs over to their people, without a pardon. This left Satanta and Big Tree occupying the status of parole. The liberated chiefs solemnly embraced the governor and the principal chiefs present. Then they departed in company with the agent, and after a brief visit at the agency office went to their camps on the prairie.

THE ULTIMATUM

After the governor of Texas left Fort Sill some of the excitement incidental to the release of Satanta and Big Tree died down. Governor Davis had had his council. Commissioner Smith thought that he would have one too; so he called a meeting at the agency commissary. He had

[7] Charles E. Campbell, "Down Among the Indians," *Kansas Historical Collections*, Vol. XVII.

promised Mr. Davis that he would inform the Kiowas and Comanches that any raiding on their part would abrogate the parole of Satanta and Big Tree; and it was necessary to tell the Comanches that since they had violated their agreement by allowing several of their people to raid during the summer, after the women and children were restored to them, they must surrender five of their warriors to be held as pledges that they deliver up the five guilty raiders. This also had been a part of the agreement he had made with Davis.

Commissioner Smith's council convened on the afternoon of October 8, 1873, in the big room of one of the agency commissaries near Quarry Hill. The government was represented by Superintendent Enoch Hoag, Commissioner of Indian Affairs E. P. Smith, Agent James Haworth, Post Interpreter Phillip McCusker, and a number of clerks and recorders. Nearly all the chiefs of the Kiowas and Comanches were there. Only the principal ones could get into the room. The rest congregated on the outside, peering through the windows.

Commissioner Smith reminded the Comanches that they had violated their promises by permitting several of their young men to go on raids after the women and children had been restored to them. They must deliver to him the five guilty men who had perpetrated the outrages, or five others to be hostages until the others were brought in. Then he turned to the Kiowas and demanded that they too give him five of their warriors as a guarantee that the tribe comply with the conditions imposed by Governor Davis for the release of Satanta and Big Tree.

The Indians thought that surrendering their young men to the whites meant that they were to be given up to torture or death. That would have been the Indian custom. When the commissioner's speech was interpreted they all placed their hands over their mouths in the native sign of surprise and consternation. The peculiar Indian "T-t-t-t-t" was heard all over the room. Then, as the full import of the commissioner's ultimatum was understood, the assemblage was thrown into a chaos of angry shouts and indignant protests. Cartridges clicked as they were shoved hastily into rifle magazines. Bowstrings twanged as warriors tested their weapons.

Lone Wolf, in a voice choked with emotion, demanded to be heard. This quieted the Indians for a moment. During the lull Lone Wolf told the commissioner that the road he prescribed was too hard. The Indians could not follow it. The commissioner, frightened and angered by the noisy conduct of the Indians, vented his feelings indiscreetly by accusing Lone Wolf of crying and acting like a baby. This set the Indians off into another outburst of rage. The young men who were crowded outside now rushed in and demanded of the chiefs that they be allowed to kill the old fool who wanted to kill their young men. The chiefs, still in control of the situation, told the young men to be quiet; it was not yet their turn to say anything.

Cheevers arose and turning to the interpreter said, "Tell that Washington chief that I am a Comanche and that my people have been doing no wrong (his particular band had been quiet for two years), and should not be asked to pay for any wrong done by the young men of other tribes. But I know that there are bad men among all people, among white men as well as among Indians. Those among us who have persisted in bad actions, contrary to the wishes and orders of the chiefs, are renegades, and we have cast them out. They are the ones who are bringing all this trouble on the Indians. You will find them west of Antelope Hills. You ought to round them up; and when you do, you may keep them as long as you choose, but do not ask these good young men of either tribe to sacrifice themselves for the evil done by others."

Black Horse, second chief of the Quohadas, thrust himself into the arena, clutching in one hand a rifle, and beating his chest with the other, and said, "Tell that old man I am Black Horse, a soldier chief. He may take me if he can, but he may have a little trouble in doing it!" McCusker thought it unwise to interpret this speech, as the commissioner was beginning to puff up and grow red. A violent discussion followed among the Indians, resulting in the withdrawal of Black Horse.

The calmer and more judicial element among the Indians still predominated. Kicking Bird, Woman's Heart, and others made speeches, generally confirming Cheevers' remarks. Kicking Bird, as usual, was the most eloquent and pleasing. But the statements of Cheevers made a good impression on the commissioner. The latter promised the commissioner that he and a number of his men would go with troops to catch the outlaws. This proposition was of necessity agreed to. Mr. Smith could not point out the five guilty Comanches, nor even name them. Cheevers claimed they were out on the plains, still depredating. The Indians were given thirty days in which to capture the renegades. At the end of that time, unless satisfactory reports were made, rations would be withheld.

The council, which had threatened to end in a general massacre, dispersed quietly.

THE SEARCH FOR THE COMANCHE RENEGADES

Cheevers selected five Comanches, and the Kiowas furnished five of their men, to accompany the troops in search of the supposed outlaws. They were regularly enrolled as military scouts and were given arms and uniforms by the quartermaster at Fort Sill. A troop of cavalry was detailed to go with them.[8] During the month prescribed for the search

[8] The officers with the troop were Captain Phillip L. Lee, Lieutenant Silas Pepoon, and Lieutenant J. Will Meyers (File 4447).

177

the redoubtable Cheevers led the troops toward Double Mountain, Texas, where the renegades were supposed to be. As they arrived at each site suggested by Cheevers as being the hiding place of the outlaws, the latter claimed that the quarry had just gone to some other place. Finally, he announced that they must have fled to Mexico.

A humorous incident is related by the Kiowas which shows the manner in which the whole farcical affair was conducted by the Indians: The expedition was riding along the trail southwest of Fort Sill, when one of the officers at the head of the column lost his watch. Straggling along in rear of the troops, basking in the warm October sunshine, was Gotebo, brother-in-law and late bosom companion of Big Tree. Shortly after crossing a little stream Gotebo saw something bright in the sand. He dismounted and found a gold watch, which he concealed in his clothing. A little later the party halted to rest in the shade of a clump of mesquite. The lieutenant commenced fumbling in his pocket for something. Gotebo, some distance away, noting this, hastily buried the watch in the earth.

"Everyone assemble here," called the officer. "I have lost my watch. Has anyone seen it?"

Gotebo and the other Indians stood silent.

"The watch has my name on the case. I had it in my pocket only a few minutes ago. It cannot be far away. Scatter and see if you can find it."

"Too hot," grunted the Indians. "We don't want to look."

"The watch was a graduation present. I value it highly," urged the officer. "I will give five dollars to the Indian scout who will bring it to me."

Gotebo pricked up his ears. Five dollars was the price of a pony.

"My medicine is very strong," he announced. "Maybe can catchum watch."

"Fine. Go ahead."

"No can make medicine for five dollars," Gotebo suggested, blandly, "Make him for ten dollars."

"Oh, all right," groaned the officer. "Anything to recover the watch."

Gotebo arose deliberately, struck a meditative pose. He rolled his eyes heavenward, and commenced making mystic passes, bending over, straightening up, advancing and retreating with mincing steps. All the while he was drawing nearer the place where he had concealed the watch. When he arrived at the supposed hiding place he increased the tempo of his gyrations, and commenced a falsetto chant, working up to a grand climax at the point where he expected to produce the lost article. At this crucial moment, to his great and secret embarrassment, he discovered that he had forgotten where the watch was buried. The whole performance had to be repeated, while the audience of soldiers and Indians looked on with skeptical grins. Eventually Gotebo uncovered the watch with the toe of his moccasin, and held it up with a dramatic flourish. He accepted the promised reward with a virtuous expression. Then he was disconcerted to notice the officer staring at him hard.

"You are a clever fellow," remarked the latter dryly. "Now we'll try another bit of magic. I'll hide the watch myself, so that you have no idea where it is. If you can go through the same monkey business and find it, I'll give you fifty dollars. Otherwise you give me back the ten."

"No, no!" protested Gotebo, hastily. "My medicine no good that way. Can only find things which been lost."

The officer continued to stare at him, while the other Indians held their sides in merriment.

When the expedition returned to Fort Sill, the Indians reported that the search for the renegades had been unsuccessful. For a few days nothing happened, and the Comanches congratulated themselves that they had put one over on the commissioner. But ten days later a letter arrived from Washington directing the agent at Fort Sill to stop issuing rations to the Indians until further orders. The Indians were informed that if five young men were not delivered within ten days, the whole business would be turned over to the army to take such action as it saw fit.

The Comanches seemed to think that Washington was bluffing again. Most of them promptly moved out on the plains. A number of raiding parties departed for Texas and Mexico. The position of the friendly chiefs like Horseback was difficult. The old man told the agent that if he stayed close to the post, where there was no game, he would starve. If he moved out on the prairie he probably would be attacked by the troops. What could he do? He was too sick (tuberculosis) to run or fight. His tribesmen had thrown him away, and the white man would not feed him. The unfortunate chief remained in his camp a few miles north of Fort Sill and eked out a miserable existence on the food given him from time to time by officers at the post.

Agent Haworth wrote to Washington, trying to get the department to modify the terms imposed on the Indians. In the meantime the allotted ten days elapsed, and it looked as though there would be war. But the commissioner *was* only bluffing. He had no idea of using military force on the Indians. Haworth did not know this, and, fearing that the Kiowas might be drawn into what appeared an inevitable conflict with the Comanches, sent Thomas Battey to persuade the Kiowas to move in close to the agency where they would be safe. Lone Wolf's villages were north of Mount Scott; Kicking Bird was near Murder Mountain, about three miles south of the site of Fort Cobb.

Mr. Battey first visited Lone Wolf. He read a letter sent by the agent, and explained the cause of the incipient trouble with the Comanches. He urged Lone Wolf to bring the Kiowas in to the agency, and to remain neutral or friendly if war broke out with the Comanches. Lone Wolf requested time to consider his answer. That night, before he retired, he built a little fire of cedar twigs in the center of his lodge. Then he stood before it naked, and taking smoke in his hands, rubbed it over his body. Thus he devoutly made medicine, requesting guidance and wisdom from the Great Spirit.

In the morning he dictated the following reply to the agent: "If any young men of the Comanches or Kiowas go over into Texas and get killed, I think that is all right. If they kill any white people there I do not want the whites to come upon us here, for this is a country of peace. Catch them there. Kill them there. My friend, I want you to tell my father at Washington that I do not want any war here in this country of peace that he gave to us. I do not want the soldiers to molest us in it. ... I wish Washington would let it pass [the trouble with the Comanches]. If those foolish young men have killed any of the people of Texas, they are dead. Some of those young men have been killed; they are dead. Let it all pass; do not let it make trouble among the living. I never hear of any bad news from any other direction; but from Texas I hear often that somebody is killed. I know nothing about it—only what I hear. I want you to sit still, and by and by I will come and see you. We have killed a great many buffalo, have many hides and much meat, are loaded heavy, and must come in slowly. My friend, I do not want you to get excited and act in a hurry. If you hear bad news, do not be excited, but sit still. You must not believe the Comanches when they say the Kiowas have been raiding in Texas, for it is not true; they have not been there."[9]

It was easy for Lone Wolf to be calm and philosophic when talking about the Comanches killed in Texas. But when his own son was killed there, as he was a few days after Lone Wolf made this speech, the chief was unable to say "It is all right; he took his chance."

Battey next visited Kicking Bird. The latter was angry when he heard of the commissioner's action. "This country," he said, "was given by Washington to his red children. I now see white men in it, making lines, setting up sticks and stones with marks on them. We do not know what it means, but we are afraid it is not for our good. The commissioner, by making one bad talk has set all this country on fire. He has required a very hard thing, which was not in the road our fathers traveled. It is a new road for us, and the Comanches cannot travel it. They cannot bring in the five men. If they attempt it, many women and children will be killed, and many men must die. . . .

"I have taken the white men by the hand; they are my friends. But the Comanches are my brothers. By and by, when I am riding on the prairies, and see the bones of the Comanches or the skull of a white man,

[9] Battey, *op. cit.*, pp. 216-29.

my heart will feel sad, and I shall say, Why is this? It is because the commissioner made a road the Indians cannot travel. If Washington would put all his soldiers along the frontier, and kill every young man who goes across the line we would cry for them. But it would be all right. When they cross the line they take the chance of war. I do not want to see trouble in this land of peace. But I fear that blood must flow, and my heart is sad.

"The white man is strong, but he cannot destroy us all in one year. It will take him two or three, maybe four years. And then the world will turn to water, or burn up. It is our mother, and cannot live when the Indians all are dead."

The Quaker emissary told Kicking Bird that there was no reason why the Kiowas should involve themselves in trouble with the government on account of the Comanches. "If you love the Comanches," he said, "who by getting on the bad road after Washington gave them back their women and children, made such very hard work for you and your friends to get back Satanta and Big Tree—if you love them better than your wives and children, and thus stay out and miss your rations and annuities, then the loss will be yours, and you cannot blame the agent for it." Gradually, under Battey's persuasive arguments, Kicking Bird's attitude changed. He agreed to lead his band back to the agency. But the raiding in Texas broke out afresh.

Governor Davis thought that Commissioner Smith and Superintendent Hoag had sold him out. On October 31 he telegraphed to Mr. Smith that large numbers of Indians were seen prowling recently, and since the conference, in Denton, Wise, Jack, and Wichita counties. He suggested to the Secretary of War that he be allowed to raise a regiment of Texans for the defense of his borders. General Sheridan remarked that the proposal of Mr. Davis was not a good one, that no amount of troops acting defensively could protect the border. He recommended offensive action, with a winter campaign based on Fort Sill. The general offered to conduct the campaign personally, and promised to settle the whole affair speedily, and finally. His only stipulation was that the Indian Bureau give the army authority to go ahead untrammelled. With this General Sherman was in complete accord. He said, "If the Indian Bureau will confess their inability to restrain these Indians and turn them over to the military we will find troops enough without asking any from Texas."[10]

But the Indian Bureau would not agree. Things were allowed to slide until, on December 9, a correspondent writing from Fort Sill remarked, "Indian matters are in status quo. The five Comanches demanded as hostages for Satanta and Big Tree, and for the good behavior of the

[10] File 4447, AGO.

181

Comanches, have not been delivered up. . . . I presume the Kiowas are laughing in their sleeves (or would if they had any sleeves) at our discomfiture. Of course Satanta and Big Tree will at once deliver themselves up to be returned to the Texas State prison, upon the Comanches failing to produce the required hostages; but some folks are so obtuse as not to see it."

DEATH OF TAU-ANKIA AND GUI-TAIN

Shortly after the Fort Sill conference of October, 1873, at which the Indians promised to take up the white man's road and cease raiding, in return for the release of Satanta and Big Tree, a number of Comanches and Kiowas went south after horses and scalps. There were nine Kiowas and twenty-one Comanches in the party. The Kiowas were under Pago-to-goodle (One Young Man), a noted warrior. The others were Ma-may-day-te, Tau-ankia (Sitting-in-the-Saddle), Eonah-pah, Komal-ty (Friendship Tree), Sau-on-de-tone (Working Bird's Tail-Feathers), Tape-day-ah (Standing Sweat-House), Ye-ah-hau-tone (Two Hatchets), and Gui-tain (Heart-of-a-young-Wolf). All of these young men were of the *on-de*—the aristocracy of the Kiowa tribe. Tau-ankia was Lone Wolf's favorite son, and Gui-tain, a lad of fifteen, was the son of Red Otter (brother of Lone Wolf). The identity of only two of the Comanches is known. One was Long Horn, a Yaqui by birth, captured when a boy in Mexico; the other was the uncle of Isa-tai, a prominent Comanche (Quohada) war chief and medicine man.[11]

During November the Indians rode swiftly south through Texas, making from sixty to eighty miles a day. Toward the end of the month they arrived in Edwards County, near South Kickapoo Springs, on the West Fork of the Nueces River. They made their "headquarters" a few miles from the springs, leaving their spare animals, thirty-one in number, hobbled and unguarded in a little valley. Then they continued into Mexico, crossing the Rio Grande between Eagle Pass and Laredo. They killed fourteen peons on the Olmos and captured one hundred and fifty horses and mules. Two Mexican boys were taken as prisoners.[12]

On December 2 they turned back toward Guerrero; at Laguna del Gato they captured a youth named Rodrigues. During the next few days they retreated north, driving their captured animals before them. On the sixth, at the crossing of the Laredo and San Antonio road, they killed two Americans. One of the Mexican captives, Perez, escaped that night. Rodrigues got away the following night. The fugitives alerted United States troops which were camped in the vicinity.

[11] Indian informants: Tonemah (brother of Gui-tain), Hunting Horse, and Stumbling Bear.

[12] Report of Colonel John Hatch, Fort Clark, and affidavits of Mexicans (File 4447).

Lieutenant Charles L. Hudson was on a scout north of Fort Clark with forty-one men of the Fourth Cavalry. On December 7 he found the Indian ponies near South Kickapoo Springs, which he took in charge, and waited in ambush for the Indians to return. On the ninth, on receiving word from Fort Clark concerning the movements of the savages, he hastened to intercept them. After marching east eight miles Hudson saw the Indians on the side of a high ridge, two or three miles distant. They were resting their horses.[13]

As the soldiers approached the Indians dismounted and took position on the crest of the ridge, tying their horses behind the line. They opened fire on the troops with carbines at a range of four hundred yards. It had been raining, and the sky still was overcast. Hudson's men toiled up the steep slope, the horses sliding and stumbling on the wet slippery rocks. Hudson continued his painful climb without replying to the fire of the Indians until he had placed his troop on the same level of the ridge with them. Then he dismounted his men, took cover, and opened a hot fire at seventy-five yards. The Indians stood about ten minutes of this, when Hudson saw some of them break and commence to run. At once he mounted his men and charged. The pursuit quickly became a rout. The soldiers kept at it as long as a single Indian could be found. At least nine were killed. One trooper was slightly wounded. Fifty animals were captured.

When the Indians began to run Tau-ankia was left behind. He was limping badly from the effects of his old wound received the preceding year at Howard Wells. His comrades failed to pick him up. Young Guitain saw his cousin about to be overtaken by the soldiers. Bravely he turned back to help him. Hudson, riding at the head of his men, killed Tau-ankia with a pistol. A trooper shot down Gui-tain. The other Indians did not pause in their flight. Isa tai's uncle also was slain by the troops.

One of the dead Indians was described by the soldiers as being a tall, well-built Indian, about thirty years old. He was light-colored, and had fine, dark brown hair. On his head was a headdress of crow feathers, with black cow horns and a brow band of blue and white beads. He had a ring of silver on one finger, with an oval plate nearly two inches long, shaped like a scoop. One of the other Indians wore a headdress of owl feathers, colored yellow, with heifer horns, also stained yellow.

News of the disaster reached the Kiowa camps on January 13, 1874. The whole tribe wailed dolefully, for both Tau-ankia and Gui-tain were exceedingly popular. Lone Wolf went into deepest mourning. He cut off his hair, killed his horses, burned his wagon, buffalo robes, and lodges. From that time on he was definitely hostile to the whites, and thought

---

[13] Report of Lieutenant Charles L. Hudson (File 4447).

only of revenge. Though he did not know it, the slayer of his son was also dead. On January 4 Lieutenant Hudson was accidentally shot and killed in his quarters at Fort Clark by his room-mate, who had just finished cleaning a gun.[14]

[14] Dispatch from Fort Clark in *Army and Navy Journal,* January 24, 1874.

PART III

THE LAST WAR

CHAPTER NINE

THE OUTBREAK

CAUSES OF THE OUTBREAK—THE COMANCHE PROPHET—LONE WOLF'S
REVENGE—END OF THE PEACE POLICY—THE ANADARKO AFFAIR

I T WAS obvious at Fort Sill, even as early as January, 1874, that the
year would be marked by increased raiding on the part of the Indians. On January 28 a small detachment of troops (under Corporal
J. W. Wright, Company C, Twenty-fifth Infantry) returning from Camp
Augur was fired at on Deep Red Creek by a party thought to be Comanches. Inhabitants of the Texas border began to lose stock. Indian trails
were seen here and there. Lieutenant Colonel Buell in a fight at Double
Mountain killed ten Comanches. Various other skirmishes occurred in
Texas. Altogether, counting the Indians killed by Lieutenant Hudson,
thirty Kiowas and Comanches were slain during the winter.[1]

On account of these losses the Indians burned for revenge. In those
days two principal motives led the Indian to war. One was the urge
toward personal glorification and prestige. The other was desire to
obtain revenge for relatives killed by the enemy. These were the main
causes of the Kiowa-Comanche outbreak of 1874. There were other
elements which entered into it, but to a lesser degree. One of these was
the slaughter of buffalo by white hunters. The killing of buffalo for their
hides had been going on for some years; but the industry was given fresh
impetus by the development of high-power repeating rifles, the penetra-
tion of railroads into the prairie, and the discovery that buffalo leather
could be used in the manufacture of harness.

The Indians regarded the bison as a gift of God. "They are our cattle,
our money," they used to protest to the white men. "Why do you wish to
destroy them? They are all we possess." Not only were the buffalo
essential to the Indian's well being but also they were a part of his spiritual life. In part his religion was associated with the existence of the vast
herds that roamed his sun-swept prairie. A full appreciation of the In-

---

[1] Various official reports, telegrams, and letters filed in Old Records Section, AGO, for
1874; C. E. Campbell, *op. cit.*, pp. 643–44.

dian's feelings and sentiments in this regard can be gained only by association with the few remaining oldsters of the tribes. From them alone can be learned the full significance of what the extermination of the buffalo meant. It was death—physical and spiritual.

Another cause for the outbreak was the general resentment at being forced to live on a reservation, far from where the game abounded, dependent mostly on the scanty ration supplied by the Indian Department —a ration so meager that in the winter of 1873-74 the Indians who remained close to the agency were forced to kill their horses and mules for food.

Resentment was not confined to the Kiowas and Comanches. It extended also to the Cheyennes and Arapahoes. The latter reported to their agent that the Kiowas were trying to involve them in a general war against the whites. The Kiowas, in turn, maintained that the Cheyennes were trying to involve them. The Comanches said nothing. All were equally hostile. As spring approached the Indians became more restless. On February 12 one of the surveyors of Mr. Hackbush's party was killed northwest of the Anadarko agency by Indians supposed to be either Kiowas or Cheyennes. On March 27 Indians fired into a company of soldiers near Fort Sill. The troops returned the fire, and from the bloody trail and war bonnet found the next day it was believed that several were wounded. On the night of April 9 Indians fired into Camp Augur from a range of eighty-five paces.

During March there was great activity at Fort Sill. The companies of the Tenth Cavalry there at the time—B, C, and M—were preparing to move out for their summer's work in protecting the northern frontier of Texas. Company H was at Camp Augur on Red River; Company K marched to relieve it. During the winter the Tenth Cavalry had been recruited up to strength, remounted, and rearmed. The new arms were the Springfield carbine (which replaced that old favorite, the Spencer), and the Colt's breech-loading revolver.[2] On the twenty-eighth Colonel Davidson learned that Lone Wolf was organizing a party to go to Texas to recover the bodies of Tau-ankia and Gui-tain. The commanders of the posts in Texas were cautioned to be on the watch.

Lone Wolf went with this party but, on account of a peculiar custom, he placed Mamay-day-te in active charge of the expedition. The latter was selected because he had been Tau-ankia's boyhood friend, and, besides, was considered partly responsible for the loss, he having been one of the co-leaders in the fight with Lieutenant Hudson. Long Horn acted as guide, for he claimed to know exactly where the bodies lay.

Cavalry scouting parties were sent out from various posts to intercept Lone Wolf. Captain E. B. Beaumont, Fourth Cavalry, with seventy

[2] *Army and Navy Journal*, March 2, 1874.

men, went south and west from Fort McKavett. He divided his command into two parties, but found no Indian trail. Major Bankhead with two companies went from Fort Clark. On visiting Hudson's battlefield he found a large trail, which he followed immediately. The Indians had been there just before he arrived, had picked up the bodies and departed. At one time during the pursuit Major Bankhead came so close to the Indians that the latter again were forced to abandon the two bodies which they had come so far to reclaim. In haste the bodies were buried in a cleft high up on the mountainside, where they remain to this day, as far as the Kiowas know, for they never went back.

The troops followed Lone Wolf's trail, which led north, across the country west of old Fort Terrett. This region was almost entirely devoid of water, being for some distance a portion of the Staked Plains. The command found water but twice in ten days, the extreme drouth and dust making traveling doubly difficult. Major Bankhead, after following the trail for two hundred and forty miles, came out near Johnston's Station, on the main El Paso road, twenty-eight miles above Fort Concho (San Angelo). Here he found that the Indians had attacked the herd of a company of the Ninth Cavalry, had killed a trooper, captured some twenty-two animals, and succeeded in escaping north. Major Bankhead saw that the Indians had thus obtained a remount of fresh horses, and as his own animals were exhausted after the long and rapid march, he did not pursue farther.

The Indians returned to the reservation, and camped again at the western end of the Wichita mountains, where they planned to hold the annual Sun Dance. A number of Cheyennes and Comanches were loitering near to watch the celebration.

THE COMANCHE PROPHET

Colonel Davidson had a talk with Asa-Havey and Asa-Toyeh, in which he inquired as to the cause of the evident unrest among the Comanches. What was their complaint? The Indians replied that the Comanches had nothing to complain of on the part of the government, the agent, the troops, or the whites in general. During the spring, however, there had arisen among them a "prophet," who told them that he had had an interview with the Great Spirit.[3]

The Great Spirit had informed the prophet that the Caddoes, Wichitas, and other Indians who were adopting the mode of life of the whites were going downhill fast, in means and in population, and that the Comanches would suffer likewise if they followed the same road. The way for them to be again the powerful nation they once had been, was to go to war and kill off all the white people they could.

[3] Report of Colonel Davidson, File 3144, Old Files, AGO, July 30, 1874.

This Comanche prophet was Isa-tai (Rear-End-of-a-Wolf), a Quohada war chief whose uncle had been killed in the fight with Lieutenant Hudson. Isa-tai had been brooding over this sad event, and had determined to stir up the whole tribe in a grand war of revenge against the whites. In order to do this he pretended to have supernatural powers. This gave him an immediate and respectful audience, or at least a curious one. Stories went the rounds that Isa-tai could belch up whole wagonloads of cartridges, then swallow them again. He could foretell heavenly phenomena. He could make the Indian warriors impervious to the bullets of the white men. Isa-tai planned to gather all the Comanches at one place to inflame them against the whites. In order to do this he announced a great sun dance or medicine dance. The Comanches, unlike the Kiowas, had never held a Sun Dance. But they were greatly interested. The place announced for the assembly was at the junction of Elk Creek and North Fork of Red River.

All Comanches were invited—nay ordered—to attend. Kiowas, Cheyennes, and Arapahoes also came in large numbers. Mexican purveyors of contraband from Santa Fe were there. The whisky bottle was much in evidence. Friendly Indians, like Horseback, and others who had come largely out of idle curiosity, saw that war was in the making. They tried to go home. But the others would not permit them to do so.

The topic of conversation at the great smoker which was held simultaneously with the dance was, "When and where do we attack the Tai-bos (whites)?"[4] Some were in favor of exterminating the Tonkawa Indians first, for it had been reported that these cannibals had been found eating dead Comanches, after one of the recent skirmishes with the troops in Texas.[5] But there seemed to be a suspicion that the troops in Texas were on the lookout for this very thing. The idea was given up. Next it was suggested by Quanah that everyone ride to Adobe Walls, a former trading post in the Texas Panhandle, to clean out a party of white buffalo hunters who were known to be located there. This suggestion met with instant and universal enthusiasm. Parra-o-coom (Bull Bear), mighty leader of the Quohadi, should have organized the war party. But Bull Bear was on his deathbed; he had contracted pneumonia. He died while the Battle of Adobe Walls was being fought, and was buried on Elk Creek.[6]

Isa-tai and Quanah, the son of Cynthia Ann Parker, took charge. Quanah was then only a young man, scarcely recognized as a chief. But

---

[4] Report of Kicking Bird, interpreted by George Fox, in File 2547, AGO, 1874; Thomas C. Battey, *op. cit.*, pp. 302-4; James Mooney, *op. cit.*, p. 201; Lawrie Tatum, *op. cit.*, pp. 189-90.

[5] James Mooney, *op. cit.*, p. 201.

[6] Comanche informants: Timbo, son of Parra-o-coom; Yellow Fish, old Quohada Comanche; Poafebitty.

190

in the attack on Adobe Walls, which took place June 27, 1874, he towered above the other war leaders—Isa-tai, Mow-way, Tai-hai-ya-tai, Wild Horse, Isa-habeet, and others—so that his name is remembered principally as the Indian leader in that much-publicized fight. Quanah also had been influential in inducing a number of Kiowas and Cheyennes to participate. Among those who smoked the pipe with him and fought in the battle were Satanta, Bird Bow, Lone Wolf, White Shield, White Horse, and Howling Wolf.[7]

Co-hay-yah, a gnarled old Comanche warrior, describes the battle succinctly as follows: "We lost the fight. The buffalo hunters were too much for us. They stood behind adobe walls. They had telescopes on their guns. Sometimes we would be standing 'way off, resting and hardly thinking of the fight, and they would kill our horses. One of our men was knocked off his horse by a spent bullet fired at a range of about a mile. It stunned, but did not kill him." The Indians lost about fifteen killed; and a larger number were wounded. Among the Comanches killed were Tsa-yat-see, the father of Howard White-Wolf (and a brother of Esa Rosa), Co-bay, Esa-que, Tasa-va-te, and a Mexican named Sai-yan. As a result of the dismal failure at Adobe Walls, Isa-tai lost face. Many of the Indians were in favor of giving him a sound whipping with their quirts. But he had a plausible alibi, claiming that someone had spoiled the medicine by violating a taboo. Today the Comanches have forgotten and forgiven. They refer to Isa-tai simply as "that comical fellow."

The unrest was not confined to the Kiowas and Comanches. The Cheyennes and Arapahoes also went on the warpath. On July 3 a wagon train under charge of Patrick Hennessey was destroyed at the site of the town of Hennessey, and several white men burned to death. Word of this outrage reached Darlington on the same day that news of the Adobe Walls fight was received. John D. Miles and his Quaker associates were thrown into an intense state of excitement and alarm. The number of men available for the defense of the Cheyenne agency was negligible. The nearest military post from which help might be obtained was Fort Sill, seventy-five miles to the south. Mr. Miles abandoned the traditional Quaker policy of nonresistance when confronted with active danger to his women and children. He sent for troops.[8]

John Murphy was asked to ride to Fort Sill for help. The young Irishman started at sundown. He reached the post at reveille the next morning. It was a heroic ride—but useless. Although the commander at

[7] Hunting Horse to author.

[8] Report of Scout Jack Stilwell, File 2928, AGO, 1874; Pope to Sherman, July 7, 1874, Old Records Section, AGO; General File 2815, Old Files, AGO, 1874; C. E. Campbell, *op. cit.*, p. 645.

191

Fort Sill promptly dispatched a troop of cavalry to Miles's assistance, they never reached Darlington. When they arrived at Anadarko, on their way north, the agent at the Wichita agency, after obtaining approval from Sill, held them there. He also was frightened. And there the troops had to stay, for Darlington was not in the same military department as Fort Sill, and the commander at the latter place was duty bound to take care of his own people first.

This left Mr. Miles high and dry. He telegraphed to Washington. Troops from Kansas were sent to Darlington. An advance detachment under Lieutenant Frank D. Baldwin went out into the Staked Plains and rescued the white men at Adobe Walls.

LONE WOLF'S REVENGE

After the Adobe Walls fight the Kiowas went ahead with preparations for the Sun Dance. The gathering was held on the North Fork of Red River at the "End of the Mountains." The dance commenced on July 3 and ended on the seventh. During the ceremony Satanta, in thanksgiving for his release from prison, presented his red medicine arrow to Ah-to-tainte (White Cow-bird), thus resigning his chieftainship. The customary gaiety of the occasion was marred by the fact that the people were still sorrowing over the death of Tau-ankia and Gui-tain.[9]

On the evening of the day the great festival came to an end, three-fourths of the tribe, under the leadership of Kicking Bird, packed up and departed for Fort Sill, in order to keep clear of the coming war. This was a triumph for Kicking Bird, for great pressure had been placed on the Kiowas, not only by the Comanches, but by the Cheyennes and Arapahoes, to join in the general outbreak.[10]

Lone Wolf remained in camp with a group of the more hostile and adventurous. He was making a strenuous effort to recruit a party to go to Texas to avenge Tau-ankia and Gui-tain. But in his zeal to win converts he made the mistake of resorting to ridicule. He criticized those who had been with his son when the latter was killed, and intimated that if they had done their duty the tragedy would not have occurred. As a result of his remarks most of the young men sullenly refused to go. Finally, on the afternoon of July 10, the popular medicine man and war chief Maman-ti said he would lead the raid. At once the whole tone of the meeting changed. Distrust and doubt gave way to enthusiasm. The Kiowas, shouting and dancing, held a parade around the big encampment. Old men vigorously thumped sheets of rawhide; women and young girls circled the medicine lodge in the stately rhythm of the tribal dance.

[9] James Mooney, *op. cit.,* p. 338.

[10] Kiowa informants: Aytah, widow of Set-maunte, and Hunting Horse. Old Man Horse, as he is known at Fort Sill, was an enthusiastic participant in this raid.

With prolonged whoops they strengthened the warlike ardor of the men. The warm evening air carried to the near-by hills the weird sounds of the favorite battle songs. A camp crier cantered around the village calling, "After dark everybody come to the tepee of Do-ha-te!"

The lodge of Maman-ti, the Do-ha-te, stood on top of the hill, overlooking the village. After the last rays of the sun had painted scarlet and gold stripes across the sky, and purple shadows were blackening in the canyon, the people climbed the slope to the lodge of the medicine man. They seated themselves respectfully before it. Soon the rustle of wings was heard, followed by the eerie cry of the hoot owl.

Maman-ti emerged from the darkened tepee.

"The revenge raid will be a success," he announced solemnly. "At least one enemy will be killed. None of us will die."

A shout went up from the men: "Everybody saddle up now. Don't wait until morning! Everybody must go!" The warriors rushed to their tepees to make ready. War paint, shields, medicine must be packed in rawhide saddle bags. Weapons must be examined and selected. The women ran to catch and saddle their braves' favorite war ponies.

Tahbone-mah (later known as I-see-o) and Tsain-tonkee (Hunting Horse) were carried away in the general enthusiasm. It was the latter's first raid. Among the experienced warriors were Lone Wolf, Red Otter, Pago-to-goodle, Mama-day-te, Komal-ty, To-hauson, Tape-day-ah, Eo-nah-pah, Ye-ah-hau-tone, Ah-tape-ty, Quo-to-tai, Pauddle-tah, Talia-koi, Que-an-on-te, Sait-kop-te, Little Chief, Singing Tree, Mut-sat-se, Qui-tan, Tay-bodal, Sait-keen-te, Kia-hia-ko-ke, and Sankey-dotey (Medicine Feather). Most of these were well known in later years around Fort Sill as scouts and Indian police. Altogether there were about fifty warriors in the party.

Everyone was ready by midnight. Morning of the eleventh found them below the site of Mangum. They did not pause, but pushed south at a steady gait. At noon they were near the Red River, where they encountered a big herd of buffalo. They stopped to kill a few and have a grand feast. Then they forded the stream and made headquarters where there is a little hill covered with prairie dog towns, just north of the present site of Quanah, Texas. They changed from tired horses to fresh ones. Saddle girths were examined, extra equipment cached, and spare mounts hobbled. No one was left on guard at the headquarters. All went on the raid.

Soon after they crossed the Big Wichita River a herd of Texas cattle was found. The Indians shot several steers, built a hot fire of mesquite wood, and threw the whole carcasses on the fire. When the meat was barbecued to their taste—half raw and half charred—they gorged themselves. The left-over cooked meat was cut into chunks and taken along as "lunch." Late in the afternoon they resumed the march. After traversing twenty or thirty miles of flat prairie, sparsely covered with mesquite, they came to a rough, rock-strewn country broken by low buttes and patches of scrub oak. They camped for the night on the side of a hill somewhere east of the site of Seymour. Here Maman-ti again consulted his owl. He stated that in the morning one or two whites would be killed, that men mounted on grey horses would do the work, and that the youngest member of the party (Hunting Horse) would receive as his prize a fine bay horse. The prophet-leader concluded by shouting, "That's all. Each man get himself painted and ready before sunrise."

The painting of a Kiowa warrior was a carefully observed ritual, and conformed to the color and designs on his war shield. The tribe had a well-defined system of heraldry, which in many cases was hereditary. To-hauson, for example, who came from a famous line of chiefs, carried a yellow shield decorated with blue dots. His body above the waist was painted to match the shield. Black stripes were painted on his face, running diagonally from his eyes outward, which made him look like a huge raccoon. Tahbone-mah was striking in sky-blue with dark blue dots. Hunting Horse was clay-white with scarlet streaks. Maman-ti and his three apprentices—Sankey-dotey, Ho-an-t'agia, and Do-ha-san—were colored pure white with the figure of an owl in blue on their chests and backs. Lone Wolf, Mama-day-te, and Red Otter, being in mourning, were not painted. They wore their hair undone, and, like the others, were stripped to the waist. All of the Indians decorated their ponies' manes and tails with strips of red flannel and gay calico. Warriors who were entitled to wear war bonnets had them on. The whole crowd made an exciting and barbaric display of color. They dressed like this only when they were on a war raid.

At daylight on July 12 the Kiowas mounted their horses and rode past Flat Top Mountain toward Cox Mountain. The heat of the July sun shimmered from the rocks. Now and then a brave jumped from his horse at a water hole, drank from the saline stream, and filled his water-skin suspended from the saddle. Several young men galloped ahead to scout the country to the south. A single shot was heard far down in the timbered country. The sun mounted higher in the yellow sky. But still no enemy appeared. At length they came to the broad plain lying west of Cox Mountain, where the wagon road ran between Jacksboro and Griffin.

"This is the place where we killed the wagon teamsters!" someone shouted. "Let's go and see the place where we buried the Comanche." So they rode to the top of the little sandstone hill and looked curiously at the heap of bones weathering under a pile of rocks. Then they descended the slope to the east and cantered across the prairie toward Cox

Mountain. They climbed up through the timber and paused to rest on the summit. It was nearly noon. The Kiowas ate the remainder of their cooked beef, drank sparingly from the water-skins. For a little while they rested there, listening to the wind sighing and moaning in the trees. The sound made them uneasy. Prairie folk that they were, the combination of the ghostly whispering of the breeze, the sense of loneliness, the weird silences—all stirred up a fear of the unknown.

Suddenly one of the Indians spoke sharply: "Look! Look! Four cowboys coming on the southwest side. Everybody mount up!"

By the time the Indians had picked their way down the mountainside the cowboys were nearly a mile away, riding leisurely east toward Loving Ranch. The Indians charged after them in a noisy cloud of dust. But the whites put spurs to their mounts and vanished into the timber bordering the southwest end of Lost Valley.[11] The Indian pursuit went to pieces at the place where there is an outcrop of sharp rocks, near the head of Cameron Creek.

"Our horses are too hot! We've hurt them already," cried Maman-ti. "See—their feet are bleeding." He looked around. "Hurry up! Hurry up!" he shouted at the slower braves straggling in. "Here are some cattle in the valley. Let's kill some and fix shoes for our horses." They shot several calves, and tied wet pieces of the green warm hides to the hoofs of their ponies. Then they rode east to a place where a little stream emerges from a gap between two sharp peaks. They climbed to the top of these hills to scan the surrounding country for some trace of the escaping whites. Once more they heard the wind howling through the trees and crags. Again a feeling of superstitious fear came over the young men. Lone Wolf perceived this. He began haranguing them: "Don't be scared. If any Texans come, and chase us, don't be afraid. Be brave. Let's try to kill some of them. That's what we came here for." While the chief was talking one of the Indians caught the glint of sunlight on a gun barrel in the valley below.

"Look! Look!" he cried. "At the place where we killed the calves—white men coming!"

The Kiowas mounted their jaded ponies. Led by Maman-ti they rode northwest along the ridge, until they could see the enemy better, through an opening in the mesquite. There were only a few of them, all wearing tall white hats. They appeared to be exceedingly well armed. They were approaching the Indians, and seemed to be following the fresh trail, for their eyes were on the ground.

Maman-ti made a quick plan. "The enemy probably see us already,"

[11] Hunting Horse and Mr. Oliver Loving (Jermyn, Texas) to author. These two informants pointed out on the ground the events described. Mr. Loving's father was one of the cattlemen pursued by the Indian war party, of which Hunting Horse was a member.

he said. "All of you men hide here on the hillside, and be ready to charge them from the side and rear. Ad-la-te (Loud Talker) and I will ride down in front of them and act as bait." So the two Indians rode into the valley below, then dismounted, came out in plain sight of the Tehannas, and commenced to lead their horses north, as if they were worn out and could not be ridden. At once the white men galloped in pursuit. Then the main body of Indians came tearing into them from the east.

The white men were Texas Rangers, part of the personal escort of Major John B. Jones, commanding the Texas Frontier Battalion. Unknown to the Kiowas, a party of Comanches were raiding in the same area. The previous day they had killed a cowboy named Heath at Oliver Loving's corral. They had left tracks all over the countryside. The rangers were gathering to drive them out of the country. Major Jones with about twenty-five men, parts of detachments from several companies, was on an inspection tour.[12] Jones and his men had struck the trail of the Indians on Salt Creek, and had followed it for several hours. It was a broad, plain track; they could see where the Indians had dismounted at water holes, and now and then they found chunks of charred beef which the Indians had dropped. As they approached Lost Valley from the west, the trail seemed so fresh that the dust had scarcely settled. Several of the rangers, nearly all young and inexperienced men, galloped ahead to find the trail, which by now had broken up where the Kiowas had chased the cowboys.

Suddenly they ran into the ambush which Maman-ti had prepared for them. In the first rush the rangers were forced north toward Cameron Creek. Here they rallied around Major Jones, and began firing at the circling Kiowas. Ranger Lee Corn was shot in the arm, but managed to crawl unseen into the brush along the creek. A man named Wheeler stayed with him and helped bandage his wound.

Major Jones, a small fellow, but possessed of an iron nerve, kept his men together by giving instructions in a cool voice, as if it were all in the day's work. The Indians were riding entirely around them in a huge circle, yet some distance away. It must be remembered that the Kiowas were on a revenge raid, which demanded that they get two scalps or make two coups and return to their homes without losing a man. So they took no unnecessary chances.

Captain Stephens said, "Major, we will have to get to cover soon, or we all will be killed." Jones agreed. He ordered the rangers to charge south through a place where the Indian circle was the thinnest, and en-

12 *Frontier Times*, ed. by J. Marvin Hunter (Bandera, Texas): Ed Carnal, "Reminiscences of a Texas Ranger," Vol. I, No. 3, pp. 20-24; "The Loss [sic] Valley Fight, Reminiscences of Walter Robertson," Vol. VII, No. 3, pp. 100-104; Thomas F. Horton, *History of Jack County* (Jacksboro: *Gazette Print*, 1933), pp. 52-53.

deavor to gain the shelter of the woods which bordered a dry gully at the head of the valley. The sortie was successful. In their enthusiasm the young Texans followed the Indians to the foot of two low, rock-capped hills on the west side of the valley. Some of the men rode too close. The Indians turned like treed cougars. George Moore, riding a big black horse, was wounded, but got away. William A. Glass was less fortunate. He was seriously hurt, and fell helpless between the opposing forces. His companions thought he was dead. Nobody stopped to bring him in.

Major Jones ordered his men to take position in a shallow depression which lay about three hundred yards east of the ridge on which the Indians were. The men dismounted, tied their horses in the scrub, and commenced sniping at the Indians. Major Jones remained on the level ground behind the gully, in order to observe the movements of the enemy, and to set an example of coolness to his men. There was a danger that some of them might break and try to make a run for it. This would have been fatal.

Presently Billy Glass began crying piteously for assistance. Two Indians could be seen sneaking toward him, bobbing and ducking between two large trees which stood apart on a low ridge to the left front. "My God!" Glass screamed. "Don't let them get me. Won't some of you fellows help?" Under cover of a heavy fire, three men ran out and carried him in. They were in as much danger from the bullets of their friends as from those of Indians. A hot fire was directed at one of the trees behind which the Indians had taken refuge. Soon the Indians disappeared. Major Jones posted William Lewis and Walter Robertson on the ridge, behind one of the trees vacated by the savages, in order to protect the flank and rear of the rangers' position. But the Kiowas made no further charges. The fight settled down to a siege. The rangers suffered from thirst. The wounded kept calling for water. Jones forbade any of the men to leave, though several volunteered to take canteens to the water hole in Cameron Creek, a mile or so to the north.

Toward evening the firing died down. One or two Indians could be seen riding over the hills to the north. It looked as if they were withdrawing. Mel Porter and David Bailey could stand the cries of the wounded no longer.

"I'm going for water, if I get killed," said Porter.

"And I'm with you," muttered Dave Bailey.

It was foolhardy. Major Jones had forbidden it. But go they would. The others watched anxiously while they galloped through the mesquite and disappeared over the bank at the water hole. In a moment Bailey reappeared and sat on his horse on the near bank, watching for Indians, while Porter filled the canteens. No Indians appeared. It looked as if they would be successful. Suddenly the men in the gully saw about

197

twenty-five Indians riding headlong from the west toward the men at the water hole. They fired their guns frantically to warn them. Bailey waved and shouted at Porter, then commenced to gallop straight back toward his companions. Porter emerged from the creek and rode northeast, with two Indians gaining on him at every jump. If poor Bailey had detoured to the east instead of trying to go straight back, he might have made it. But the Indians were coming from the west, and were between him and safety. Suddenly his horse shuddered and stopped. The Indians crowded around him immediately, and the watchers realized that it was all over.

After dark Major Jones had the men tie Billy Glass, who had died, on a loose horse abandoned by the Indians. Then the rangers started toward Loving Ranch, circling far out to the east to avoid lurking savages. Nearly all of their horses had been killed. Mounts were available only for the wounded. Late that night the bedraggled force arrived at the ranch, where a messenger was dispatched to Fort Richardson for assistance.

Hunting Horse describes the fight from the point of view of the Kiowas: "When we made our first charge the white men stopped and began firing at us. The bullets went Chu! Chu! Soon the enemy charged at us. We rode south in great haste. Red Otter's horse was hit, and sat down suddenly and began to scream with pain. Red Otter slid off neatly, and with his red cape streaming from his hand commenced dodging around to escape the bullets. I thought the whites had him, but Set-kop-te (Paul Saitkopte) galloped up to him, reached down a hand, and pulled him up behind. They got away safely.

"We all rode south through the valley. I was on an old grey plug, which lagged far behind. I thought they would catch me sure. One white man, riding a fine big black horse, was following us close, making it hot for us. He was way out by himself. Maybe he didn't know his friends were so far behind. Or maybe his horse was running away. Presently we reached the shelter of the wooded ridge, where we stopped and commenced firing back at the enemy. Tsen-au-sain dismounted, took a careful aim at the man on the black horse, and shot him off. The man went limping into the brush to the east.

"We could see the leader of the whites motioning his men to fall back. One of them was slow. Tsen-au-sain shot him down. 'I got one,' shouted Tsen-au-sain, 'Everybody back now!'

"But nobody was able to touch the fallen enemy to make coup. We had to make coup or the revenge would not be complete. We could see the man lying there in plain sight. The heads of the other rangers could be seen sticking up from a dry stream bed. Nobody dared go close enough to make coup.

198

"Red Otter got desperate. He called for volunteers. Not a warrior spoke up. I remembered the prophecy of the medicine man. It was my chance. I said I would go with Red Otter. Red Otter ran forward and took position behind a large tree. He signaled for me to join him. I ran forward and crouched behind the tree. The bullets were throwing the bark in our faces. Then we ran to another tree. But the bullets came thicker. Red Otter said it was too dangerous. We ran back behind the hill.

"The trench where the rangers were hidden was so far away that I couldn't reach it with arrows. Only the men who had guns stayed out in front and kept firing at the enemy. They could see the rangers' horses tied in the mesquite. They killed most of these.

"As the day grew shorter it looked as though we were not going to be able to get any of the whites. Finally Maman-ti made a new plan. 'We've got to cheat those fellows,' he said. 'We know they will have to go for water soon. So we will pretend to go away, but will leave some men, with the fastest horses, near the water hole. They can charge the whites when they come for water.'

"So we rode slowly north, keeping out of sight behind the ridge, until we crossed the dry creek bed above the water hole. A big bunch remained here, hidden in the timber to watch for the enemy. The rest rode toward the hills which lie north of the creek. Some of us felt thirsty. Tahbone-mah and Quo-to-tai started back to get a drink. I was just going to join them, when somebody called, 'Come back quick! Two of them are going for water now!' Tahbone-mah and Quo-to-tai hid in the trees along the stream.[13]

"In a few moments two white men came riding swiftly to the water hole. One was about fifty yards ahead of the other. The first one, who was carrying several canteens, rode down into the creek, out of our sight. The other remained up on the bank to watch. Soon the Kiowas who had been ordered to charge them rushed in from the west. The Texan on the bank rode south. The man in the creek came out on the north side and started galloping in the opposite direction, with Tahbone-mah and Quo-to-tai after him.

"At first Quo-to-tai was in the lead, but in a moment Tahbone-mah, who was riding a big grey—a famous racer—passed him. The white man turned in his saddle and kept shooting at the two Indians. He fired the last shot almost in Tahbone-mah's face, then threw his empty pistol at Tahbone-mah. The Kiowa man dumped his enemy off with a lance, and herded the riderless horse off on a circle to the left. It was a fine bay, and he later gave it to me. Tahbone-mah couldn't go back to make coup

[13] Tahbone-mah later became famous as the army scout I-see-o. He adopted the name I-see-o in 1892, when he enlisted. He is an uncle of George Hunt.

199

on the man he had knocked down, because there was heavy firing coming out of the woods along the stream.[14]

"When I got to the place where they had killed the other ranger, I learned that Dohauson had thrust him off his horse with a spear, but that Mamaday-te had made first coup by touching him with his hand. Lone Wolf and Maman-ti and everybody was there. Lone Wolf got off his horse and chopped the man's head to pieces with his brass hatchet-pipe. Then he took out his butcher knife and cut open the man's bowels. Everyone who wanted to shot arrows into it or poked at it with their lances.

"Presently Lone Wolf stood back to make a speech. He said, 'Thank you, Oh thank you, for what has been done today. My poor son has been paid back. His spirit is satisfied. Now listen! It was Mamaday-te who made the first coup. Because of this, and because he loved my son, I am going to honor him today. I am going to give him my name. Everybody listen! Let the name of Mamaday-te stay here on this battleground. Let the name of Mamaday-te be forgotten. From now on call him *Lone Wolf!*'

"After Lone Wolf had finished his talk we all sang a few verses of the Victory Song, then got on our horses and started home."

Mel Porter, after he had jumped or been thrown (by Tahbone-mah) from his horse near the water hole, dived into the creek and swam under water. When he came up he was nearly shot by Lee Corn and Wheeler, who thought he was an Indian. It was the fire of these two men which had caused Tahbone-mah and Quo-to-tai to sheer off at the last moment. The three rangers stayed in the brush until after dark, when they made their way to Loving's Ranch. The next day Major Jones's men came back to look for Bailey's body. The young Texans caught their breath when they saw the condition it was in. They scooped out a shallow trench in the sand.

William Glass was buried at Loving's Ranch.

END OF THE PEACE POLICY

When Lone Wolf's party returned to the "headquarters" on Red River they found that soldiers had been there looking for them. This caused them no little worry—an anxiety made more acute by the arrival of a messenger from Kicking Bird with orders sent by the agent for them to report back to the agency at once. They wondered if the soldiers had discovered that they had been absent on a raid into Texas. But the message was in consequence of secret instructions sent by Enoch Hoag to Agent Haworth, warning him to get all his Indians into the near vicinity

[14] I-see-o named one of his daughters, "Threw-a-Pistol-in-his-Face," in honor of this event.

200

of the agency before the military separated the sheep from the goats and attacked the latter.[15]

It is difficult to realize that the Quakers, in spite of their experiences of the previous four years, and the obvious failure of the Peace Policy, should have been so indifferent to the immediate needs and safety of people of their own race as to attempt to prevent the army from bringing much-needed discipline to the Indians. They were not even fair to those Indians who had been steadfast in their friendliness to the government. Haworth's reprehensible action in sneaking Lone Wolf and his band, whose weapons still reeked with blood, into the City of Refuge had the effect of placing guilty Indians under the same protection and patronage as the innocent. It was a rank injustice to the latter.

Steeped in misguided idealism Hoag and Haworth sat in their respective snuggeries at Lawrence, Kansas, and Fort Sill pondering on ways and means to thwart the army in its plan to bring the savages under control. The crackle of gunfire, the vicious war whoop, the anguished cries of victims along the border, waxed unheeded by Messrs. Hoag and Haworth. Apparently their sympathies were all with the Indians—in this instance misplaced sympathy since the Indian reservation was not being invaded by the Texans. The red warriors went to Texas voluntarily, actuated solely by a desire for blood, lust, and plunder. Even when, on May 18, the Indians stole all of Mr. Haworth's stock from the corral, his love for his red brethren did not falter. As one old Comanche says, "He used to pray for us all the time." Lone Wolf among others, was unaffected by these prayers. But he was afraid of being punished by the soldiers for the Lost Valley raid, so he camped several miles east of the post, at the foot of Bald Ridge. For a few days he was unmolested, as the military officials did not know he was there, and authority had not been received from Washington to take the field against the hostiles.

Military action not being immediately forthcoming, the Indians again became cocky. The Cheyennes, for example, sent word through Phil McCusker that they were coming down to clean out Fort Sill and all its inhabitants. The local Indians, not to be outdone, commenced to depredate near the post. Teamsters bringing in supplies, men cutting wood for the contractors, herders taking care of cattle, and even white men living with friendly Indians were murdered. On the evening of July 13 Indians attacked J. S. Evans' wood camp, eleven miles from Fort Sill. Colonel Davidson dispatched Lieutenant Smithers with a detail of troops. This officer arrived in time to recover fifty-two head of cattle which the Indians had run off; he found the body of one of the herders, scalped and filled with arrows.

[15] General File 3300, AGO, 1874.

The condition became so serious that Colonel Davidson issued the following order:

"Fort Sill, July 17, 1874.—The hostile bands of Comanches, Cheyennes, and Kiowas having committed depredations and murders upon Government employes within the Reservation, and within a few miles of this post, some marked line must be drawn between the hostile and friendly portions of those tribes. In order that troops and others may be able to distinguish those who are friendly—all such Indians must form their camps on the east of Cache Creek at points selected by the agent."[16]

Under the circumstances this order does not seem unreasonable. But it angered the agent, Mr. Haworth, who considered that the military had no right to issue orders affecting the Indians. He would not admit that the Peace Policy was through, and that the safety of the whites was now paramount. He protested Davidson's order, saying that there was no grazing for the Indians on the east bank of Cache Creek. In this the agent was correct. Much of the grass had been burned. This had occurred when Lone Wolf and his band stampeded to Keechi Hills. As a ruse they had left their camp fires burning, which resulted in a prairie fire.[17]

Colonel Davidson paid scant attention to Haworth's fulminations. He issued another order which concluded with the provision that "no Indian will enter the post unless accompanied by the Interpreter, Mr. Jones." There was a ludicrous aftermath to this order. The evening of the day it was promulgated Horace Jones went to the trader's store for his customary conviviality with a number of cronies from the officers' line. The party broke up about twelve o'clock, and "Colonel" Jones, as he was called—he was a "midnight" colonel—set a course for home. As he weaved up the diagonal path leading to the post he was stopped by a recruit sentry.

"Halt. Who is there?"

"Mr. Jonesh, Posht Interpreter," was the somewhat thick reply.

"What do you want?"

"Why confound it, I want to go home."

"You cannot pass, Mr. Jones," the sentry informed him, firmly.

"And why not?"

"I am sorry, but the new post order says you cannot enter the post *unless accompanied by an Indian!*"

And the fuming "Colonel" was forced to go to the guard house to straighten out matters, before he could go to his quarters.[18]

[16] Old Files, Fort Sill.

[17] During July, according to the Post Returns, most of the garrison of the post was absent on patrol duty along Red River. No doubt this accounts in part for the boldness of the Indians near the post.

[18] Reminiscences of W. H. Quinette (MS).

202

News of the recent atrocities near Fort Sill quickly reached the ears of General Sherman. He telegraphed to General Sheridan: "Don't you think it would be well to order the 6th and the 10th Cavalry to converge on Fort Sill and settle this matter at once? Word could be sent the friendly Indians in advance to collect for safety at Fort Sill. The hostiles should be stripped of all horses, mules, etc. Unless something is done now, the rascals will merely rest awhile and start afresh."[19]

General Sheridan wired an answer the following day: "I coincide with you fully that General Pope should make some use of the 6th Cavalry to take the offensive. I wanted him to do so a week ago, but he asked for further time. He is so taken with the idea of a defense that he does not see the absurdity of using cavalry that way. I will make him use his cavalry on the offensive, and will stir up the 10th also. See Delano and get as much cover as you can and let me know the result."

Sherman lost no time in obtaining the "coverage." The following plan was submitted to the President: A date was to be fixed, by which time all Indians who wanted to be friendly with the government should report at their agencies, be enrolled by name, and answer periodic roll calls held by army officers. Those who did not do this were to be considered hostile; troops were to be sent after them and to punish them severely, until they surrendered and came into their agencies, where they were to be dismounted and disarmed. The men were to be held as prisoners of war; the bad leaders and criminals were to be selected for special punishment. Where satisfactory proof could be established of their guilt in murder and kidnapping, they were to be tried by a military commission and punished or executed, if necessary, at their agencies. Those who were notoriously disaffected, but against whom no definite proof existed, were to be deported to some seacoast fort and held indefinitely as prisoners. The President told General Sherman to go ahead. This order was communicated to the Secretary of the Interior. On July 26 orders were received simultaneously by the post commander and the agent at Fort Sill turning the management of the hostile Indians over to the army. The next day Colonel Davidson published an order requiring friendly Indians to enrol. He gave them until August 3 to complete the registration. Haworth was furious. He protested that the time given the Indians was too brief. But Davidson had made the time brief to prevent an influx of the entire group of hostile Comanches. Haworth's act of notifying the Indians on July 6 already had had the effect of bringing in nearly all of the Kiowas to mingle with the friendly Indians. The purpose of the enrolment was to separate the friendly from the hostile, yet Davidson could hardly order the Kiowas to leave, even though he was morally sure that some

[19] File of telegrams, Hq. Army, Old Records Section, 1874.

of them had just come in from raids, and that many of them were not friendly at all.

Haworth tried to delay the enrolment by saying that it would take him at least a month to complete it. When Colonel Davidson differed with him, saying that it could be made in two days, the agent lapsed into surly silence, and would not make the enrolment. Colonel Davidson paid no further attention to him, but ordered Captain Sanderson, Eleventh Infantry, to perform the duty.[20] Certain chiefs were declared outlaws, and notified that they could not come in except as prisoners of war. Included in this category were the Comanche chiefs Red Food (Pe-arua-akup-akup — literally, Big Red Meat), Isa-nanica (Hears-a-Wolf), Black Duck, and Little Crow (son of old Ten Bears); it was fairly well known that they had participated in the attack on Adobe Walls. Lone Wolf of the Kiowas also was outlawed; the authorities were not sure what he had been doing, but they were quite certain that he had been up to some devilment.

Colonel Davidson left Fort Sill on July 30 with three companies of cavalry; he went to the Indian camps to make the enrolment. On July 31, Captain Sanderson visited the Comanche village, ten miles north of Fort Sill, where he had no difficulty in enrolling the Indians belonging to the bands of Horseback, Cheevers, and Quirts-Quip. There were only thirty men in this group. The following day he went to the Kiowa camp, near-by. The agent did not show up, Horseback having warned him that it was dangerous there. Captain Sanderson found that the Indians had all their horses tied up, which was a bad sign. A war party had just come in with a scalp (yet the Kiowas were supposed to be friendly). Some of the chiefs were at breakfast, others were horse-racing, on picket watching the soldiers, smoking in their tepees, and so forth. There was no commotion, but Kicking Bird was not able to assemble enough of the men to make it worth while to go on with the proceedings. Sanderson thereupon told Kicking Bird to appear at the agency with his men the following day to receive their certificates of enrolment. On his return from the Kiowa camp he completed the enrolment of the Kiowa-Apaches. On August 3 the Kiowa chiefs came in as ordered, but showed a very bad disposition. Woman's Heart was particularly overbearing and insulting. Sanderson wanted to arrest him, but the agent was afraid of trouble. The time for registration was extended until the eighth in order to enrol the Yapparikas under Iron Mountain, Yellow Moon, Howea and Prairie Fire—thirty-two warriors all told.

The enrolment of the so-called friendly Indians now was complete. But it was quite evident that hostilities soon would commence against the hostile Indians. On August 13 two troops of cavalry went from Fort

[20] File 3300, AGO, 1874.

Sill to construct a supply camp, protected by a redoubt, on Otter Creek. This place was to be used as a relay point in forwarding of supplies to the Fort Sill column when it took the field.[21]

The Indians also were busy. On August 19 they killed an unknown white man at Signal Mountain. Two or more civilians were camped in the unused stone blockhouse on top of the mountain. On the morning of the nineteenth one of them came down the hill on the north side, where the road now runs over the saddle to West Lake, to draw a bucket of water at a little spring. Six or eight Indians were waiting for him in the bushes. They killed and scalped him. The Kiowas in this party were Sait-ap-ay-toi (Afraid-of-a-Bear), Ko-koi-dain (Elk-Tongue), and Pone-audle-tone (Snake Head), alias Paul Zontam. The other members of the band were Cheyennes.[22] Troops came out from Fort Sill and buried the body on the side of Signal Mountain. The following day, August 20, was ration day. Immediately after receiving their rations, Kah-tia-son and several members of Satanta's band—all recent enrollees—went three miles from their camps on Cache Creek to about where Geronimo's grave is today, and killed two white men. They later boasted to Phil McCusker that they threw one of the bodies into the creek. It was not recovered. That same afternoon the Indians killed Steve McKibbon and John Collier, cowboy employes of Christopher C. Mill, a cattleman from Texas, on the road eight miles south of Fort Sill. Troops from the post went out to bury the bodies and attempt to catch the Indians. But the culprits had disappeared. After committing these murders all of the enrolled Kiowas except Kicking Bird's band went north to the Wichita agency at the site of Anadarko. Included in this group were Woman's Heart, Poor Buffalo, and Satanta, all of whom had enrolment papers in their pockets. They joined their outlawed principal chief, Lone Wolf. Many prominent Comanches with their bands also were there, including Tabananica, White Wolf, Wild Horse, Mow-way, Isa-tai, Red Food, Black Duck, and Little Crow. They all squatted at or near the Wichita agency, in defiance of orders. They tried to force the agent to issue rations to them, and they annoyed the tame Indians (Caddoes and Wichitas) by plundering their melon patches and corn cribs. Agent Jonathan Richards was absent, the agency being in the charge of a clerk named Cornell. Mr. Cornell sent a message to James Haworth at Fort Sill, telling him that some of his bad Indians were there, and would he please come and get them. Haworth

[21] This redoubt, the remains of which are near Tipton, has been called Fort Beach, for Captain W. C. Beach, Eleventh Infantry, who was in charge of its construction. In recent years it has also been called Fort Otter, and has been confused with Camp Radziminski. It may have been built on or near one of the first sites of Radziminski.

[22] Report of Persons Killed by Hostile Indians near Fort Sill in 1874, Old Files, AGO; Kiowa informants: Frank Given and Hunting Horse.

sent Frank Maltby to tell the "friendly" enrollees to come home. Maltby soon returned with the information that the Indians ignored him.

At 6 o'clock in the evening of August 21, 1874, Colonel John (Black Jack) Davidson was sitting on his veranda in his shirt sleeves sipping a long cool drink. The evening breeze eddying across the parched parade ground brought small relief from the heat which had been scorching the prairie for over a month. An orderly rode up on a dripping horse, dismounted, and handed the colonel a message. It was an urgent dispatch from Captain Gaines Lawson, commanding a company of the Twenty-fifth Infantry which was on guard duty at the Wichita agency. Lawson stated that a band of Noconee Comanches, consisting of sixty lodges, under Red Food, was camped at the agency. In his opinion there was going to be trouble. Colonel Davidson sent for Adjutant Sam Woodward. At ten o'clock that night four troops of the Tenth Cavalry, mounted and fully armed, formed on the parade. Colonel Davidson climbed into the saddle and led them toward Anadarko, thirty-seven miles to the south.[23]

The following day, Saturday, August 22, was ration day at the Wichita agency. The Penatekas, the Wichitas, Caddoes, and Delawares were all present to draw their rations. Beef was issued in the morning, and the Indians were scattered through the field south of the agency, about where the city dump now is, butchering their steers. Red Food's Comanches and Lone Wolf's Kiowas were on hand to help themselves to meat which did not belong to them. The Washita River at Anadarko makes a bow to the south, with a bluff stretching across the chord of the bow. The agency was at the foot of the hill, while above to the northeast, on a spur of the hill, were Shirley's store and residence. West of the site of Riverside School was the agency sawmill. Red Food's camp was southeast of the site of the school. The agency commissary and corrals stood about two hundred yards east of Red Food's camp.

About ten o'clock in the morning Indians living south of the Washita brought in word that Colonel Davidson's column was approaching on the Fort Sill trail. Findley Ross, a young white man in charge of the sawmill, noticed the Indian women and children begin to hasten north over the hills. A little later one of the soldiers detailed to guard the mill told him to close up the place and take the employes to the agency.[24] For the next two hours nothing happened. The agency personnel had just finished their noon meal when the head of the Fort Sill column appeared on the high ground south of the site of Anadarko. The disaffected Indians

[23] Colonel Davidson's report of engagement, File 3624, AGO, 1874.
[24] Old letter from Findley Ross to George Conover.

began to stir about in their camps. The chiefs shouted, "Get on your horses! Maybe they are going to fight us."[25]

Up on the hill at Shirley's house the women and children of the trader's household, realizing that something interesting was about to happen, were watching through field glasses from an upstairs window.[26]

Colonel Davidson rode to the agency and told Cornell to send for Red Food. When that chief arrived he was informed shortly that he and his people must give themselves up as prisoners of war. He must also surrender his weapons. Red Food objected at first, but Tosawi and Asa-toyeh persuaded him that it would be safer to submit. Colonel Davidson sent Lieutenant Woodward and forty men with Red Food to the camp to collect the arms and receive the surrender of the warriors. When they reached the tepees Red Food refused to give up the bows and arrows. These had never, in previous agreements, been classed as weapons. A messenger was sent to Colonel Davidson for his decision. While waiting for an answer a number of soldiers were standing in the camp holding Red Food's horse by the bridle to prevent the chief from making a dash for liberty. Kiowas loitering in the brush in rear of the camp commenced taunting the Comanches. "If you give the soldiers your bows and arrows, you are women," they sneered. "Act like men. If you have trouble with the soldiers, we'll help you." Red Food could not endure much of this. Suddenly he gave a defiant whoop, and as one of the Indians says, "he made a somersault leap from his horse," waved his blanket to frighten the soldiers' horses, and ran into the brush along the creek.

The soldiers fired several shots at him without effect. The Kiowas returned the fire from the bushes. The fight was on. Davidson previously had sent Lawson's company of infantry to the sawmill, with orders to cut off the Indian retreat if hostilities commenced. When the firing started in Red Food's camp Lawson advanced through the timber, firing at the Indians, who were taking to the hills.[27] But in a few moments the Indians rallied and came back at Lawson, circling, yelling, and shooting in their customary fashion. The noise was tremendous. Great clouds of white smoke rolled across the field, obscuring the view of the opposing sides. Thousands and thousands of lead slugs hurtled through the air, mostly too high to do any damage. The fracas lasted about ten minutes. It was an exciting spectacle, but the only damage suffered by either side

[25] Indian informants (all participants or witnesses): Hunting Horse, Timbo, Poafebitty, Silverhorn.

[26] Mrs. John Coyle to author. Mrs. Coyle, in 1874 a young school teacher, was visiting at the Shirley home, and saw the entire affair from the house on the hill.

[27] An excellent eyewitness' description of the fight is given in the *Army and Navy Journal*, September 5, 1874.

occurred when an Indian was bruised by falling from his horse in the confusion and smoke.

The audience of non-combatants in Shirley's house was enjoying the drama immensely until Mr. Shirley decided that he ought to go to the agency for help. He ordered a negro servant to go to the corral and saddle his horse. As this boy ran across the yard, a group of Indians, rushing up the hill to get away, shot him. The unfortunate darky was badly wounded. He lay in the edge of the brush all afternoon, crying for help. But no one dared go out to bring him in, and about sunset he died. Tally one for the Indians.

After it was evident that Lawson had cleared the area of hostiles, Colonel Davidson ordered the rest of the command to advance to the deserted camp. The four cavalry troops were lined up with their backs to the commissary. As they moved forward they were fired into from the rear by Indians lurking around the buildings and corrals. These were Kiowas from the bands of Woman's Heart and Poor Buffalo. Those eminent parolees, Satanta and Big Tree, were in the group. Two of Davidson's men and several horses were wounded. It was a moment of great uncertainty for Colonel Davidson. A large number of friendly Indians were all around. The commander had no wish to hurt them. His men could not, in the confusion, distinguish a friendly from a hostile. But something had to be done at once. The soldiers could not stand idle while the Indians shot at them. They were about to pour a volley into the Indians who were running around the Penateka camp, when old Tosawi rode out, at great risk to his own wrinkled hide, calling, "No shoot there! Him Penateka house. Him mighty good friend!" The tops of the Penateka tepees already were like colanders from the wild shooting of Lawson's men.[28] Davidson diverted his fire to a number of Indians who were skulking along the timber at the edge of the river, and who were evidently bent on circling the soldiers from the east. The cavalry, still mounted, rushed to the timber, then dismounted to fight on foot. But the Indians had faded away. For a few moments there was a lull while the officers stared about through the trees trying to locate something to shoot at.

The colonel did not know from which direction the next attack would come. He sent Captain Little's company to flush the remaining Indians from among the buildings and corrals. These were Kiowas. They moved down the river about four hundred yards, crossed to the south side, and commenced to pillage the farm house of a Delaware. The Indians were beginning to have an excellent time, and it looked as though the Wichitas and Caddoes would join in the fun. Davidson nervously threw his entire force across the river and ordered Captain Carpenter to drive the Indians

[28] C. E. Campbell, *op. cit.*, p. 648.

away from the farm of the Delaware. Carpenter mounted his company and made a gallant charge. The Indians fled, but one sergeant was wounded. While the soldiers were in the timber shouting hoarsely at one another and trying to decide what to do next, some of the Indians went several miles downstream and killed four civilians. These men were in the fields cutting hay, and did not hear the shooting at the agency. The Kiowas say that the Caddoes and Wichitas were mixed up in this.[29] Tally five for the Indians.

The remainder of the wild men went up the hill, passing east of the agency. They stopped to loot Shirley's store. When they were finished here the building was knee-deep in broken chinaware, canned goods, and knick-knacks. They found a roll of paper currency of the five-, ten-, twenty-five-cent denomination known as shinplasters. Not knowing the value of this money they used it as cigaret papers. They tied yards of gaily-colored silk ribbons to the manes and tails of their ponies. One brave fastened the end of a bolt of ribbon to his horse and went galloping away, spreading the ribbon over the hill. Another seized the loose end of a roll of calico and similarly strewed it over the landscape. Davidson sent Captain Viele's company to break this up. As it was growing dark, the Indians retreated west. Some of the Kiowas went to Cobb Creek. Here they met another band under Ayan-te and Co-yan-te, who wanted to participate in some of the good times. So they all went back at daylight to renew the excitement.

When the evening of the first day arrived, and the shooting died down, Davidson organized the agency for defense. The civilians were impressed into service as guards. During the night several of them shot at stumps which they thought they saw moving upon them. Six troopers were detailed to burn Red Food's camp. Several tons of dried buffalo meat, buffalo robes, lead, powder, and many potential museum pieces such as lances, bows, painted doeskin, and the like, went up in smoke. While this was going on a number of Indians returned to the south side of the river and began shooting. A company which had gone there to forage was driven back and had to be reinforced. The troops dug a series of trenches on the south side of the stream. There were no casualties.

At daylight on Sunday some of the Kiowas and Comanches came to the top of the hill and looked down at the store. They saw bright things scattered around in the grass, and realized that there still was much plunder which they had not secured. Far below, in the bend of the river, they could see many soldiers in their trenches. A crowd soon collected

[29] A few months after the fight Lieutenant Pratt went to Anadarko to obtain evidence against the Indians who killed the civilian hay workers. His report implicates Caddoes, Wichitas, and a Pawnee, as well as Kiowas and Comanches. On the same day that the fight occurred at Anadarko, Indians near Fort Sill killed two Mexicans on Beaver Creek eight miles east of the post.

on the hill. There were Quohadas, Kiowas, Delawares, Caddoes, and Wichitas, all excitedly telling the newcomers what had happened the day before, and how they had killed several white men and a negro. An-zai-te mounted his horse and rode down to the store. He brought back an armload of blue blankets, which he distributed among his friends. Buffalo Tom also went down. But they had to be careful. A crowd of soldiers was at the foot of the hill. Some of them were coming up. (It was Captain Carpenter with three companies.) A squad of soldiers got nearly to the top of the hill and hid behind some rocks. The Indians began to dismount. But Chee-na-boney, a big fat Comanche riding a grey horse said, "Don't bother. Stay on your horses." Just then he saw some more soldiers and started to run. The soldiers fired, and hit Chee-na-boney in the back of the head. Tally one for the troops. Now the Indians could see some skirmishing going on across the river, where the trenches were. The Kiowas wanted to go over and attack. But the Wichita chief, Buffalo Good, said, "No. Let's not have any more trouble. There may be more soldiers coming from the fort. The Wichitas will all go down the river, and the Kiowas go upstream." So they agreed. But before they went they fired the prairie grass, and tried to burn the agency. The troops set backfires. But these got out of control and did more harm than good. Nevertheless, by laboring manfully the soldiers saved the agency. Thus ended the "Battle" of Anadarko.

The Anadarko affair produced an effect which was highly satisfactory to the military authorities. The hostile Noconees were scattered with a loss of all their property. Lone Wolf's Kiowas, most of whom had been friendly in name only, were shown in their true colors. The line demarking the friendly from the hostile was clearly and completely defined. Furthermore the Indians saw at Anadarko, some of them for the first time, that the government was in earnest and in a condition to enforce its will. The affiliated bands at the Wichita agency were firmly settled in their allegiance to the United States—so much so that they immediately offered a number of their young men as scouts to accompany military expeditions during the coming campaign. Thirty or more of them were enlisted under the command of Lieutenant R. H. Pratt. While the first effect of the Anadarko demonstration was to scatter the Indians and frighten a number of enrollees away from the agency, within a short time those who feared the heavy hand of the military returned in complete submission, so that by the end of September there were collected at Fort Sill 479 Comanches, 585 Kiowas, and 306 Kiowa-Apaches. These comprised nearly half of the total population of the three tribes. The remainder were believed to have fled to their favorite haunts west of the mountains. This was a region bound, roughly, by Otter Creek on the east, the Canadian River on the north, the center of the Llano Estacado on the west, and the upper reaches of the Clear Fork of the Brazos on the south. It was a rough, broken country, in which potable water was scarce, grass poor and thin, and roads nonexistent. Here lived the Quohada Comanches, never a party to any treaty, and rarely visitors at the agency—one of the last untouched bodies of wild men in that part of the continent. Here also was the hideout in which raiding bands were wont to seek refuge when the troops pressed them too closely. Custer and Evans had penetrated it in '68, Mackenzie in '71 and '72; but it was only partially explored, poorly mapped, forbidding in aspect.

General Sheridan's plan of campaign contemplated a convergence on this area from four different directions: Colonel Nelson A. Miles was to move south from Camp Supply; Major William Price east from Fort Union, New Mexico; Colonel Mackenzie north from Fort Concho, Texas; and Colonel Davidson west from Fort Sill. In addition to this a fifth column under Lieutenant Colonel Buell was to operate between Davidson and Mackenzie. The old style of chase and charge was to be discarded. The new method was to keep the Indians everlastingly on the move, giving them no time to rest or graze their ponies, or to hunt game for their own subsistence. The idea was to wear the Indians down and force them to surrender. It was to be humane, thorough, final.

The summer of 1874 was the driest and hottest for many years. Like that of 1868, it was distinguished by a plague of grasshoppers. These pests, increased immeasurably in their peculiar cycle of life, flew in sky-darkening clouds, eating all the vegetation in their path, leaving the prairie bleak, brown, and desolate. The streams which in ordinary years were abundant throughout the year now were barren, except for an occasional water hole. These conditions were a detriment to troops and Indians alike, but the latter knew the country better, were aware of the location of every water hole, and had many spare horses, while the soldiers were restricted to one apiece. Forage contractors, impeded by the drouth, were tardy in making deliveries of corn. For these reasons pursuit was delayed until the fall rains set in.

During the first week of September preparations at Fort Sill were carried to completion. Officers could be seen hurrying from their quarters to the adjutant's office, thence to barracks and stables. First sergeants, supply sergeants, stable sergeants, all were burdened with detailed lists and reminders until they tore their hair in distraction. Ammunition was drawn from the magazine, dry rations were packed in boxes, stores of grain collected. Saddles were cleaned and oiled, guns inspected, wagon wheels greased. At the stables shoeing and condition of animals' backs received minute attention. To veterans of "The War" it was reminiscent of the beginning of Sheridan's Shenandoah campaign. That commander never left things to chance. He did not permit his subordinates to do so. But they knew that if his preliminaries were careful and deliberate, his blows, when they came, were swift, hard, unrelenting.

In the evenings the customary lawn croquet and small talk languished. Fireflies winked knee-deep on the parade ground, cicadas throbbed in the trees. Officers gathered in groups on the verandas of their quarters to discuss plans for the coming campaign, while for once the chatter of the ladies was hushed. Members of the regiment who were on leave cut short their hard-earned vacations to rejoin their commands. Though pay day had come and gone, not a soldier was drunk. Not a man cared to be left in the post when Davidson set out.

Word came in that Colonel Miles, moving out from Camp Supply while Davidson was busy at Anadarko, had skirmished with the Cheyennes near the head of the Washita, driving them south to the Staked Plains. Excitement rose. Finally, on September 10, the Fort Sill column took the field. In Davidson's force were six companies of the Tenth Cavalry, three of the Eleventh Infantry, a section of mountain howitzers under Lieutenant Keliher, Pratt's Indian scouts, the white guides and scouts—Jack Stilwell and Jack Kilmartin—interpreter Phil McCusker, and a party of ten volunteer civilian guides, including J. J. Sturms, the Harper brothers, and others. The protection of the post was not overlooked; two companies each of cavalry and infantry remained there. The Wichita agency also was guarded by three companies of infantry under Captain Lawson. Davidson headed north to the Washita, then turned upstream in search of the hostiles. But he was too late. They had fled westward.

CHAPTER TEN

THE WRINKLED-HAND CHASE

FLIGHT OF THE INDIANS—ATTACK ON CAPTAIN LYMAN'S WAGON
TRAIN—PALO DURO CANYON—MOPPING UP

A FTER the Anadarko fight the Kiowas and Comanches rendez-
voused at Swan Lake, near Fort Cobb. Here they were met by
messengers from Kicking Bird, who persuaded some of them to
return to Fort Sill and be forgiven by the government. The majority,
however, voted to continue their flight to Elk Creek, and not to stop a
single "sleep" until they arrived there. But when they came to Elk Creek
it did not seem sufficiently remote from Fort Sill to be safe. After stopping for a little rest, the Indians went northwest to the head of the creek.
They soon became miserable. Tremendous thunderstorms beat down the
prairie grass. The plains were flooded. The lightning played from cloud
to cloud, frightening the Indians, who never relished a storm. The Fort
Sill column had not yet started in pursuit, but the Indians did not know
this. They thought that the soldiers must be close behind; so they continued their flight toward the Staked Plains, stopping only to chase
buffalo for food, or to graze their horses.[1]

Maman-ti and Lone Wolf decided that they should hide in Palo Duro
Canyon. Mow-way, Tabananica, and many others already were in that
area. But when they reached the head of the Washita, Big Bow wanted
them to change the plan. He thought they ought to turn east to avoid
the troops under Miles and Price, who were known to be operating along
the edge of the Staked Plains. Consequently the Indians wandered about
between the Washita and the Canadian for several days, undecided as
to what course they should pursue. Finally they headed southwest toward
Palo Duro Canyon. On the night of September 7 they camped in the sand

[1] The flight of the Indians from Fort Sill in 1874, and the subsequent campaign, is
remembered better by the old Kiowas and Comanches than any other phase of this early
history. The best account obtained by the author was that of Botalye. Other informants
were Hoodle-tau-goodle (foster sister of Tehan), Silverhorn, Yellow Wolf, George Hunt,
Sam Ahetone, Poo-lau, Yee-goo, Mo-saip, Ay-tah, and Tsain-tonkee.

hills near the head of the Washita. Fifteen miles to the west could be seen the cap rocks marking the edge of the Llano Estacado. Maman-ti announced that they would move west into the breaks of the plateau on the following day.

But several days were to elapse before the Indians resumed their westward flight. Early in the morning a young man named Tehan rode back along the trail to look for some horses which he thought had strayed away from a previous camp-site. Tehan was a white boy about eighteen years old; his name had been given him from the fact that he had been captured in Texas. He was a giant of a fellow, with red hair and a red, bull-like neck.[2] He was an apprentice warrior, having been on a raid with Big Bow that same summer, in which he had depredated in his native land. When the Indians advised Tehan that it was unsafe to go back along the way over which they had fled, he laughed scornfully. "I'm a white man. I still understand their language. I am not afraid." His foster father gave him an old muzzle-loader and let him go.

Lieutenant Frank D. Baldwin, Fifth Infantry, riding with three soldiers from Colonel Miles' camp on the Sweetwater to Camp Supply, saw Tehan. He thought he was an Indian, and, believing him to be a sentry from a near-by village, decided to capture him lest he arouse the other Indians. Tehan was riding along on a dun mule, his eyes on the ground, absorbed in following the trail of a wounded deer. He did not see the soldiers approach until suddenly he heard a noise and looked up. Four soldiers were staring at him, not ten yards away. He raised his gun to shoot, but the soldiers did not even draw their weapons. They saw that he was a white boy dressed as an Indian.[3]

"What are you doing here?" Baldwin asked in surprise. "Are you living with the Indians?"

"Yes," Tehan replied shortly, searching for the unfamiliar words. "They treat me good."

Baldwin then offered to take the white captive back to his own people. Tehan pretended to be delighted. He was afraid the soldiers would shoot him if he ran. So he went with them. They kept a sharp eye on him all day long; he saw no chance to escape. All night they rode. At dawn they met a train of wagons hauling rations from Camp Supply to Colonel Miles. Captain Wyllys Lyman was in charge. Baldwin turned Tehan over to him.

During the day the Indians had waited for Tehan to return. Toward

[2] Joseph Griffis, a resident of New England, claims that he is Tehan. He does not answer to the Indian description of that person, who the Indians insist was a large, muscular blonde. "He looked like an Irishman," they say. As "Tehan" was the word meaning Texan (*Tejan*), there may have been more than one Tehan.

[3] Captain Lyman's official report, Lyman to Baird, September 25, 1874, File 2815, AGO, 1874.

214

evening they became worried and sent out searching parties. Signs on the ground showed what had happened. All through the night the Kiowas scoured the country for Tehan and his captors, intending to rescue him. Early in the morning a few of their advance scouts saw a wagon train approaching from the north. On each side of it was a column of "walk soldiers." Some of the scouts rode forward to delay the advance of the train, while two selected men galloped south to notify the main village. The Indian camp had been packed, and was on the move. The chiefs saw the two messengers approaching—riding in small circles, drawing ever nearer. This meant that the enemy had been sighted. To receive this important news required a special ceremony, no matter how pressing the intelligence might be. War could not be fought properly unless all the proprieties were observed. Maman-ti prepared a small altar of buffalo chips. He and the other leaders stood behind this, chanting, while the messengers came near and dismounted. The medicine man then plucked a wisp of sage straw, which he placed in the hair of the senior messenger. The latter sang a verse of a special song, then stated his intelligence. At once Maman-ti set up in business as a prophet. The people brought him presents to make the proper incantations for victory. Then the warriors commenced to daub themselves with bright paint. They uncased their shields and war bonnets, tied red flannel strips in the manes and tails of their horses, turned their spare clothing over to their women. One or two of the young girls, thrilled by the warlike preparations, commenced uttering tremolo whoops. "Be quiet!" growled Poor Buffalo. "You women will be the cause of some of these young men getting killed today."

ATTACK ON CAPTAIN LYMAN'S WAGON TRAIN

Captain Lyman first sighted the Indians at eight o'clock on the morning of September 9. His thirty-six wagons were moving south toward the Washita in double column, twenty yards apart, ready to be corralled instantly should danger appear. Company I, Fifth Infantry, about fifty men, marched on either side in single file, as guards. Lieutenant Frank West with thirteen troopers of the Sixth Cavalry rode ahead as skirmishers.[4]

The Kiowa scouts opened fire at long range, but Lieutenant West drove them from each succeeding crest, thus permitting Lyman to move steadily south. By two o'clock in the afternoon he had covered twelve miles, and was within a mile of the Washita, near the mouth of Gageby Creek. He had just negotiated the passage of a deep ravine when the

[4] Description of battle taken from the following: Captain Lyman's report; File 2815, AGO, 1874 (various dispatches and reports); Nelson A. Miles, *Personal Recollections* (Chicago: Werner Co., 1896), p. 172; Report of Colonel Miles, File 2815; Report of Major W. E. Price, File 2815; Andres Martinez (Andele) to author, 1935; Indian informants cited previously.

main body of Indians, whose presence he had not suspected, suddenly appeared in rapidly moving masses on his front and both flanks. Lyman shouted orders to form the corral. The infantrymen quickly wheeled to the right and left oblique, forming two lines, like the head of a spear, covering the front of the train. Lieutenant Granville Lewis hastily organized a few men for defense of the rear of the train. All this occupied only a few seconds, but the Indians were upon them, charging with reckless fury from all sides. Sergeant De Armond, a gallant and experienced soldier, fell dead. Almost immediately after, Lieutenant Lewis was down with a severe wound in the knee. For a tense moment it seemed that the whole command would be overrun. But the men, all regulars, held firm. Presently the Indians were cantering back out of range.

No more rushes were made by the Indians that day. They took positions on the surrounding knolls and kept up a lively fire with all manner of weapons. Toward evening they mounted again and commenced circling the wagon train. The number of warriors in the revolving mass increased until it became an awesome display of barbaric horsemanship. Some of the braves sat erect on their ponies, brandishing decorated lances and shields. Many indulged in gymnastics, throwing themselves out of sight on the far sides of their mounts; or stood erect on their horses' backs, with lofty red-and-white headgear flowing in the wind. A few galloped at full speed faced to the rear. All maintained a constant yammer of insulting and defiant yells and gestures. As the blood-dipped sun sank behind the dunes they continued to rush past, swiftly appearing and disappearing, showing wild and portentous against the purple-and-rose sky.

When darkness fell the soldiers commenced feverishly to throw up breastworks, digging in the sand with their hands or mess cups, carrying grain bags and cases of food from the wagons to form protection. As the stars came out, the ridge grew quiet. But when the first coyote howled in the distance the fire was resumed, continuing off and on throughout the night. The soldiers spent the time deepening their rifle pits. When daylight came it was seen that the Indians too had dug pits. The muddy buffalo wallow where the white men at first had obtained water was now under fire.

Through the second day the fire continued spasmodically from both sides. The bullets could be seen sparsely flecking the yellow grass, conspicuous in the slanting sunlight, raising little spurts of sand in the faces of the blue-clad men. As the day wore on the soldiers began to suffer from thirst. Canteens were empty now. Water in the kegs was low. When darkness came there was considerable clamor for water, but Captain Lyman forbade any man to risk his life by going to the water hole.

Toward midnight the commander conferred with Scout William Schmalsle. The brave little German volunteered to ride to Camp Supply for help. He was sure he could steal through the Indian lines. While Lyman was watching him go, a small party of soldiers and teamsters on the other side of the stockade made a dash for the water hole. With them was Tehan, who had convinced the white men that he was friendly. A volley came from the Indian rifle positions. The soldiers ran back to the wagon train—but not Tehan. He had rejoined his adopted people.

The Indians describe the return of Tehan: "When Tehan came back that night, he had on a uniform, with a new pair of pants. He told us that the soldiers were starving for water, and that he was going to help us fight them. We told him that they were his own people, and asked him what was the matter. Tehan replied that he liked to eat raw liver so well that he was going to stay with the Indians."

On the third day of the siege Botalye performed a feat of heroism which has become famous in the Kiowa tribe. Yellow Wolf, Set-maunte, and a number of other experienced warriors were behind a hill preparing to make a dash into the soldiers' lines. "Watch us!" they cried to the other Indians. "See those trenches at both ends of the corral wagons? You watch. We are going to ride right through between those trenches." Set-maunte mounted first. His brother rushed up, snatched off his war bonnet, and ordered him not to go. "Don't be foolish. It's too dangerous." Then Yellow Wolf put on his bonnet. A relative yanked it off and told him to "cut it out."

But no one had paid any attention to Botalye. He was very young, scarcely a man. Besides, he was half Mexican, not recognized as of first rank in the caste of the tribe. Only the medicine man observed his preparations, and that dignitary did not deign to interfere. Botalye tied his white sheet around his waist, threw down his scarlet blanket, leaped on his pony. "Friend, they stopped you," he cried to the famous Yellow Wolf. "But I'm going. I'm going to see how much power they have." His heart was galloping faster than his horse. His chum Pai-kee-te was right behind him. But as he swept out into the open and down the slope, his partner turned back. Botalye went on alone. Bullets twanged on all sides. Friend and foe were firing as fast as they were able. Botalye dashed through the enemy line. He could see the startled faces of the soldiers. They could not hit him. He returned to the shelter of the hill. As he came over the crest he tried to make a triumphal cry like the call of the wild goose. But it sounded only like the yelp of a frightened puppy. He had had no experience.

He turned to plunge through the soldiers' trenches again. The Indians called to him to come back. He would not listen to them. This time he was sure he would be killed. The bullets cut off two feathers which were bobbing bravely in his scalp lock. He flung himself over the side of his horse in the manner which he had practiced so many times as a boy.

217

A leaden slug seared the saddle horn beside his fingers. Another cut the knot of the sheet at his back. The Kiowas saw the cloth fly. As he circled back they snatched at his bridle, called furiously on him to stop. But he wouldn't listen to them. He was going to make four charges. No one had ever done this before.

When young Botalye returned safely from his fourth passage of the wagon train the Indians crowded around him. He vaulted from his pony, his face glowing with triumph. Satanta threw his arms around him. "I could not have done it myself," cried the noted chief. "No one ever came back from four charges. Usually once or twice is enough. I'm glad you came out alive." Other famous chiefs, including Lone Wolf, Big Tree, and To-hauson, congratulated him. Poor Buffalo, the chief of his band, said, "I'm going to give this young man a new name. If any danger comes we may depend on him. I name him Eadle-tau-hain (He-wouldn't-listen-to-them)!"

Later in the day two "friendlies" from Fort Sill—Quitan and Smokey—arrived with messages from Kicking Bird directing the Indians to come in and give themselves up. The excitement was too much for Quitan and Smokey. They recompensed themselves for their hard trip from the post by joining the other Indians in the attack on the wagon train.

The next thirty-six hours were a nightmare of suffering and uncertainty for Lyman and his men. Had Schmalsle succeeded in winning through to Camp Supply? How much longer could Lieutenant Lewis and the other wounded men live without medical treatment? How much longer could any of them survive without water? Desperate with thirst, the soldiers broke into the stores in the wagons, hacked open cans of fruit, and drank the juice. Nothing had ever tasted so good.

On September 12 a heavy rain set in. The men became as uncomfortable with cold as they had been with heat. But they were able to collect drinking water. They lay shivering in puddles, anxiously scanning the bleak horizon for signs of approaching reinforcements. By the thirteenth the savages apparently had withdrawn. But for fear some of them might be lying in ambush nearby, the men did not dare leave their trenches. Finally, moving objects were seen shimmering through the mist far to the west. Captain Lyman ordered the men to fire several volleys to attract attention. The column looked like soldiers. He sent several men out on a hill to see if they could determine who the strangers were. They came back and reported that it was Indians moving north. As a matter of fact the column seen by Lyman was a force under Major William E. Price, commanding the troops from New Mexico. Price heard faintly in the distance the volleys fired by Lyman. He sent out flankers. They reported that they saw nothing except a few Indians on a hill. Price was not anxious for more trouble with the Indians. He shied away. For Major

Price had just come from a fight with the Indians. His force of less than two hundred men impressed him as being too small to handle the many hundreds of hostiles who had circled and shouted at him for some two hours. Had he but known it, these were the Indians who had besieged Lyman, and who were beginning to move their villages away from the area where so many troops were appearing.

About a hundred of these Indians, mostly Kiowas and Comanches, had gone south of the Washita on the twelfth, where they ran into four soldiers and two civilian scouts who were riding with dispatches from Colonel Miles to the wagon train. Four of the whites were wounded almost immediately, one mortally. But they managed to dig a little depression in the sand, from the shelter of which they stood off the circling Indians for the rest of the day. All through the night they remained there. In the morning the Indians were frightened away by the approach of Major Price's command. One of the scouts, William Dixon, who had volunteered to go for help, made contact with Price. "The suffering of these men was extreme," says Price, "and their condition fearful. In a hole six feet square and a foot and a half deep were one corpse and three badly wounded men, the hole half full of water and blood, and they had to keep bailing it out to keep from being drowned, yet these men had kept up their courage and defended themselves until the Indians left upon the approach of my command." On the morning of the fourteenth, while Price was still wandering around the prairie, supposedly looking for the wagon train, help came to Lyman from Camp Supply, as a result of the message carried by Schmalsle. The wagons moved out painfully to join Colonel Miles' main column, which was badly in need of rations.

It now seemed to the Indians that their country was absolutely swarming with soldiers. Their martial ardor cooled rapidly. They commenced to argue amongst themselves. The women and children were complaining of hunger. The horses were weak from too much work and too little food. Nevertheless Maman-ti, Lone Wolf, and the irreconcilables voted to continue west into the Staked Plains. Woman's Heart dissented. He was ready to throw himself on the mercy of the government. Satanta and Big Tree, their consciences not altogether easy, decided to go with him. Others joined the group. They turned back near Antelope Hills, missing by a day or two Colonel Davidson's column from Fort Sill, which was searching for them. They went to the Cheyenne agency at Darlington, where they expected to receive more consideration than would be extended to them by the authorities at Fort Sill. In this, however, they erred. Satanta and Big Tree were placed in chains, the others under guard, and the whole gang was sent without delay to Fort Sill, where the warriors were placed in confinement.

Satanta surrendered to Colonel Neill on October 4. The same day

General Sheridan telegraphed to the War Department recommending that Satanta be returned to the Texas authorities in accordance with the agreement made with Governor Davis a year before; and that the other guilty Indians should be tried and their horses sold or shot. On October 6 the President gave his approval. Within twenty-four hours Satanta was on his way to Texas.[5] It was not a moment too soon. Just as Sheridan had suspected, when Hoag and Haworth discovered that Satanta was in the clutches of the military they commenced pulling wires to save him. Haworth wrote a silly letter to the commissioner of Indian affairs, saying that the Indians were at last in a proper frame of mind for kind handling. He recommended that instead of being disciplined by the military at Fort Sill, they be sent to some other agency, where a change of atmosphere would make good men of them. Mr. Hoag also strove hard to keep Satanta from going back to prison. But he was too late. Sheridan and Davidson saw to that.

In the meantime the Wrinkled-Hand chase went on apace. Colonel Davidson's column marched north of the mountains and headed for the North Fork of Red River. On September 17, when near those sulphur springs south of the site of Carnegie, which the Kiowas call Zodal-tone Springs, the advance elements of the command surprised a lone Kiowa named Little Chief. Little Chief had lost contact with his family during the confusion following the attack on Lyman's wagon train, and was searching for them. The soldiers tried to disarm him, but he resisted and was shot. His hair-pipe breast plate and quiver were sent to Kicking Bird for identification; his bones are still lying in a little burial cairn on the shoulder of Zodal-tone Peak.[6] Davidson continued west; he lost a wagon in the mud of Rainy Mountain Creek, but killed two more stray Indians. After skirting the edge of the Staked Plains as far south as Red River, he returned on October 16 to Fort Sill, having traveled five hundred miles.

The main body of Indians who attacked Lyman were having difficulty evading the various troop columns which were converging on them from all directions. But they were spry enough to do it. They camped again on the head of Elk Creek, but did not feel safe. In the morning the chiefs did not know which way to go, and the medicine men differed in their prophecies. While they were discussing the matter another heavy thunderstorm broke. It rained hard all day. The bedraggled Indians sat on their drooping ponies waiting for the downpour to cease. Finally in sheer exhaustion they lay down in the mud and water to snatch a little sleep. Toward nightfall there was a false alarm that the

[5] Reports of Lieutenant Colonel Thomas Neill, File 2815.
[6] Colonel Davidson's report, File 2815; Old Files, Fort Sill, 1875; Medical History, Fort Sill; George Hunt to author.

soldiers were coming. One young boy named Sah-maunt refused to get up. He said that he had warmed up his puddle of water, was comfortable at last, and would not move under any circumstances. Then, as the gloom of evening deepened, the ground was covered with a swarm of hairy black tarantulas. The harassed, superstitious Indians scrambled on their horses and sat like roosting turkeys all night. Their hands were so wrinkled from constant immersion in rain water that they named the 1874 campaign the "Wrinkled-Hand Chase."

The next morning the weather cleared sufficiently for them to proceed toward Palo Duro Canyon. They found a trail leading into the gorge from the north bank, by which they all reached the bottom safely. All of the "out" Kiowas were there; also small bands of Cheyennes under Iron Shirt and Comanches under O-ha-ma-tai. The Comanche bands of Mow-way, Tabananica, Wild Horse, and most of the Cheyennes, were far south of the canyon, on the Brazos, where they were having trouble with Colonel Mackenzie's force from Texas.

PALO DURO CANYON

Maman-ti was in general charge in the canyon. He took out his sacred owl skin, inflated it, blew a few toots on an eagle-bone whistle, and made several reassuring prophecies. Poor Buffalo, who recently had inherited one of the tribal grandmother gods, also tried his hand at making medicine. All of the gods seemed to agree that the hideout was a safe one. The Indians turned their horses out to graze, and put up the tepees. The women seized the opportunity to scrape some new cedar lodge poles out of the trees which grew in the canyon.

The Indians were not to be undisturbed for long. Colonel Mackenzie was headed their way. Operating north along the Mackenzie Trail from his old supply camp on the Clear Fork of the Brazos, Mackenzie soon discovered signs of the runaway Comanches and Cheyennes. One night the hostiles fired into his camp. The next morning he had a skirmish with them, killing a Cheyenne who became separated from his comrades.[7] During the next few days a curious thing happened. The troops and the Indians completely lost contact with each other, although each was searching for the other. As a result Mackenzie actually got ahead of the Indians he was supposed to be pursuing, and headed for Palo Duro Canyon, where he thought they might have gone. On September 26 his scouts under Lieutenant Thompson, ranging many miles in advance of the command, came to the south edge of the chasm. Peering down through the mists and cedar trees they saw on the floor of the canyon hundreds of tepees, stretching up the gorge for many miles.

[7] Mumsukawa, a Comanche, furnished a detailed account of contacts between Mackenzie and the Indians, covering the entire campaign; see also File 2815.

Mackenzie, being notified, reached Palo Duro Canyon with his regiment at daybreak on September 27. At first there seemed to be no trail leading to the bottom. The troops marched quietly along the edge for a mile or more, searching for some path by which to descend. As the minutes passed, the long arms of the sun turned the sky from rose to ochre, silhouetting the men and horses black against the yellow heavens. It seemed impossible that the Indians did not see them. Finally a narrow goat trail was found. How the troops made their way down that zig-zag path is remarkable. Each officer and man, leading his mount, stumbled and slid in single file down the face of the cliff. If the Indians had been ready they could have picked off each soldier before he reached the bottom. But once again the lie-abed habits of the Indians, and their lack of organization, played them false. Three companies reached the floor before the camps were aware that soldiers were in the canyon.

K'ya-been (Older-Men), alias Red Warbonnet, was in charge of that family group nearest the foot of the trail by which the troops were approaching. When he saw the enemy coming he fired his gun twice, then rushed into his tepee to don his war paint. The Kiowas in the more distant camps heard the shots, but paid no heed. They thought that the shots were fired by some early-morning deer hunter. In a few moments they heard four more shots. Still they were not alarmed.

Then the firing began in earnest. Thompson's scouts were the first troops to reach the bottom of the canyon. The veteran Beaumont with his troop was not far behind, followed by the rest of the regiment. Each troop, as it reached the bottom, was mounted, formed in line, and sent off at a gallop after the fleeing Indians, all of whom escaped, abandoning lodges, horses, and other equipment in their flight. Only a few of the bolder ones remained to protect the withdrawal, and these scrambled up the sides of the canyon and hid among the boulders and cedars.[8] After Beaumont had gone, the next two troops were formed abreast. Mackenzie took charge of these in person. As the troopers dashed along the floor of the canyon they passed village after village, all empty and abandoned. The ground was strewn with lodge poles, buffalo robes, horse gear, cooking utensils, and clothing. Pack animals were running around with their half-fastened packs dragging under their bellies. Others, tied to trees, were tugging at their halters and whistling shrilly in their fear and excitement.

Soon Beaumont's company came back on the run, driving before them immense herds of captured horses and mules. The other two troops drew aside to let them pass, then halted in line to await further orders. While they were lolling in their saddles the Indians on the sides of the

[8] An excellent description of the Palo Duro Canyon fight is given in an article in the *United Service*, October, 1885. Palo Duro Canyon is a few miles southeast of Amarillo, Texas.

cliff began to shoot at them from the vantage of higher elevation and superior cover. This fire became galling in a few minutes. The cavalry-men could not ride up the precipitous sides of the canyon after the red-skins. They could not go after them dismounted and leave their horses in so exposed a spot. In a few minutes, authority was given to retreat to a sheltered position in which to leave the animals. As the troops wheeled to go, a bullet struck the bugler in the abdomen, knocking him from his horse. They picked the man up, but no one expected him to live. (Within a few weeks, however, he was blowing reveille as hideously as ever.) The wounding of the bugler was the only casualty suffered by the troops during the action. Mackenzie sent one company back to the plateau to cover the rear of the regiment. Three more companies were sent dis-mounted to engage the Indians in a long-range carbine duel. No blood was spilled.

The rest of the soldiers set to work to destroy the villages. About midafternoon Mackenzie was ready to withdraw. His mission was ac-complished. The capture of the horses had dealt the Indians a heavy blow. It meant that when they went to Fort Sill to surrender, as they would be forced to do eventually, they would have to walk. The Indians in the canyon were obviously demoralized. For Mackenzie to push home an attack through a possible ambush, over terrain impossible for a mounted assault, would cause unjustifiable loss of life. So he retired to the top of the plateau and formed the regiment in a hollow square, with the captured animals in the center. Then he returned to the supply train. The following morning most of the captured horses, some fourteen hun-dred, were destroyed. Mackenzie had learned from previous experiences that he could not hold Indian horses.

Part of the Indian story of this fight is as follows: "It was on a clear cold day in the fall of the year. After the firing started the women and children were trying to climb the bluffs on the northwest side of the canyon. Others fled to a side canyon ending in a high cliff, where there was a waterfall. Some of the people were pulling their belongings up the cliff with ropes. My oldest sister was afraid of the bluff and turned back. The firing was getting closer. While I was getting painted and ready to fight, somebody called to me. It was K'ya-been. He had on a buffalo-horn cap. He told me to get on my horse and see what was the matter with the woman who was crying.

"I found this woman so crazy with fright that she was running toward the soldiers. It was my sister. She had a little baby boy on her back. I told her to give me the baby. She said no, let's throw it away. I said that I would rather leave her than the baby. I took her and the child up behind on my horse and went in the direction the other Indians had gone. We came to the place where those who were on foot were climbing the bluffs. I told her to get off and join the men who were climbing.

"Then I went back toward the firing. I met Iron Shirt. As I got closer, the firing slackened. I was afraid I had missed out on getting into the fight. But I went on past saddles and blankets lying on the ground, and saw a grey army horse lying on the ground. An-zai-te, who was behind a tree, had shot the horse of the officer leading the troops. The troops had halted here and were rounding up the ponies. They had Wichita [Tonkawa?] scouts with them. The guns were firing fast. I heard an Indian singing behind a rock pile. I stopped and looked. It was Poor Buffalo. He was singing the Blackfoot Society song.[9] He said that it was a great honor to be killed by an enemy, and that K'ya-been already was asleep.

"When I got there they had the body across a horse. He was shot in the head, but was not scalped. The enemy had cut off his little finger with a ring on it. We took him up the trail to the top of the cliff. The people danced to honor his bravery. His little brother washed the blood from his body. They were afraid to tell his mother until several strong women held her. After they had dressed him all up, Haun-goon-pau called to the mother and said, 'Your son has gone asleep now.' She said to the women who were holding her, 'Turn me loose. I'm not going to kill myself with a knife. Poor Buffalo, I want to say something about your *grand-mother god*. Don't pray to it when I get sick, don't hunt for something to try to restore me, for I would rather join my son. It was a great honor for him to be killed by an enemy.' She kissed K'ya-been and said, 'My life is broken.' Then they carried K'ya-been to a hole in the wall and piled stones over him.

"In the meantime some of the Indians somehow had managed to capture some army pack mules which were loaded with sugar. They were helping themselves and laughing and shouting.

"That night it rained hard. The Indians, all of whom had lost their tepees, slept forlornly on their packs, or lay in puddles of mud and water, like swine. In the morning we continued the flight. The Cheyennes went one way, the Comanches another, and the Kiowas a third. Poor Buffalo and his band went out on the dry plains where there are some marshes with cat-tails growing in them. Another band went toward the Yellow-house country. On the way I saw some Cheyennes who still were vigorously quirting their horses, though they were miles from the battleground. The prairie was strewn for miles with abandoned packs, equipment, fine beaded pouches, moccasins, and elk-tooth garments."

The Kiowas who went toward the Yellowhouse Canyon met other

---

[9] The Blackfoot Society was a fraternity of Kiowa warriors, similar to the Ko-eet-senko and the Sheep Society.

bands, including Poor Buffalo and Big Bow. The latter had been with the Comanches for two or three weeks. Finally they all reached the western edge of the Staked Plains, where they encountered a party of Mexican traders and Navajos. The Mexicans pretended to be friendly, but a few nights later they stole all of the remaining horses owned by the Kiowas. The situation now looked mighty dreary to the Indians. They turned east toward the Wichita Mountains. When they arrived at the eastern edge of the Staked Plains, they came to a place where Mackenzie, on his return to Texas, had attacked a small camp of Comanches and captured a number of women and children. It was on a place they call Trading River—probably the Blanco Canyon where Mackenzie saw caves built by the Mexican traders. Most of the Quohadas were there. Mackenzie had gone south. Some of the Indians followed him in a half-hearted fashion, until they came to a place where there was a deep artesian spring, thought by the Indians to be a bottomless pond. From there a few of the warriors went toward the Pecos, where they robbed a trading post, then returned to the camps along White (Blanco) River.

MOPPING UP

The troubles of the Indians did not end with the campaigns of August and September. Another series of blows was dealt them in rapid succession. On October 9, in what is now Greer County, Oklahoma, the scouts with Lieutenant Colonel Buell's column struck a band of Kiowas. The Indians fled northward, closely pursued by the scouts The main body of troops, following the course taken by the scouts, passed several abandoned camps and destroyed hundreds of lodges. On October 13, near Gageby Creek in what is now Hemphill County, Texas (Panhandle), a detachment of Navajo scouts accompanying the column from New Mexico under Major W. R. Price, Eighth Cavalry, dispersed and scattered a band of hostiles. Four days later one of the cavalry troops from Colonel Miles' force, under Captain Adna R. Chaffee, surprised an Indian camp five miles north of the Washita River, in the western part of the territory. The Indians escaped in great haste while the troops burned their camp. There were no casualties.

The Fort Sill column took the field again on October 21. The march was directed north to a point near the ruins of old Fort Cobb, thence southwest past Rainy Mountain. On the twenty-sixth, while the main body was camped at Elk Creek, a detachment of the Tenth Cavalry under Major Schofield received the surrender of a large body of Comanches under Tabananica, White Wolf, Red Food, and Little Crow. The Indians had with them about two thousand horses and mules, which they gave up to the government. After a delay of one day a detachment

225

of troops under Captain Norvall escorted them to Fort Sill as prisoners of war.

Colonel Davidson moved west to Elk Creek. It was typical Indian-summer weather. The leaves were turning to scarlet and gold. The air was keen and clear. Never had the health and morale of the men been better. Fresh beef was supplied every day from the contractors' herd driven along with the troops. The soldiers also feasted on wild turkey, deer, and antelope.

But uncomfortable days were ahead. Colonel Miles was busy trying to round up the Indians who had fled from the battle of Palo Duro Canyon to the marshes, or *lagunas,* in the Staked Plains. He consolidated his force with that of Major Price, whom he left on the Washita while he himself took the remainder of the command west via Adobe Walls. His plan was to get beyond the hostiles and drive them east into Price's hands. In this he was only partly successful. A portion of his force under Lieutenant Frank Baldwin drove the Indians northwest to the north branch of McClellan Creek.

On November 6 a hundred hostiles ran into a troop of the Eighth Cavalry from Price's force, under Lieutenant Farnsworth. They were too strong for Farnsworth. He called for help. Davidson's column being near-by, two companies of the Tenth Cavalry under Major Schofield were detached and placed under Major Price. The latter did not make very good use of this reinforcement. On the eighth Lieutenant Baldwin overtook the hostiles and charged them in gallant style. Price was within sound of the small arms fire, but for some unaccountable reason did not throw his forces into the conflict, as he had been ordered to do. Instead he grazed his animals for several hours, then turned and marched directly away from the scene of the fight.[10] Baldwin was able to handle the Indians alone, however. His cavalry charged, accompanied by the infantry in uncovered wagons. The infantry shot over the backs of the galloping mules as they swept into view of the Indian village. This was a novel departure in the technique of infantry combat. But it worked. The Indians were defeated.

In their flight they abandoned Julia and Adelaide German, two small captives who had been taken in Kansas several months before when a party of Cheyennes murdered their parents. Two older sisters, who had been captured by the Cheyennes at the same time as the little ones, remained among the Indians until the following spring, when the last bands surrendered. The plight of these four young girls aroused the deepest sympathy among the soldiers, and throughout the country. They were orphaned, homeless, and destitute. The only clothing they possessed

[10] Colonel Miles's report.

226

was that given them by their rescuers. Yet when an appeal was made to Enoch Hoag to take care of the girls, that great humanitarian flatly refused to accept any responsibility in connection with them. He was too busy trying to save the Indians. After a time Colonel Miles adopted them and provided for their upbringing and education.[11]

By November all of the fight was out of the Indians. The troops remained out to keep them on the run and insure that all finally were driven into the agencies. On the tenth the Fort Sill column reached the broken country where the head of the North Fork and tributary streams cut into the edge of the Staked Plains. Here they found the body of Private William Denshaw, one of Lieutenant Farnsworth's men, scalped and mutilated. They paused long enough to bury Denshaw, then continued their search for hostile Indians. The latter had fled north. Colonel Miles saw them, but his horses were so exhausted that he was unable to pursue. He called on Davidson for assistance. Captain Viele was sent with 120 picked men. Viele followed the Indians northwest, skirmishing with their rear guards, and recovering much abandoned property and many horses. Again the savages faded into the wastes of the Llano Estacado. The area was so large that 120 soldiers could only pick them up again by accident. Viele went as far as Muster Creek, then turned back to join his main body.

Davidson marched slowly to McClellan Creek, then north to the Sweetwater. This was the farthest point reached by him during the campaign. He had no auxiliary supply base in the area, being forced to depend on supplies sent from Sill, two hundred miles away. He was now in an inhospitable region consisting of sand dunes, shin oak, and gullies. Most of the water was alkaline; there was no grass for the horses. The troopers did not have a herd of extra horses with them as did the Indians. When their horses gave out they had to walk. By November 18 all forage was exhausted, and food supplies for the men were running low. To add to the discomfort the weather changed suddenly. A norther roared in, bringing sleet and snow. The thermometer fell to zero within two hours. Several animals died of cold and hunger. A number of the men suffered frostbite.

On the nineteenth Captain Viele rejoined the command. He reported that he had not overtaken the Indians, but that they had not escaped punishment. Captain Chaffee and Captain Hartwell found them and dispersed them with a loss of much of their stock. Some of the Indians now turned east and began to make their way to the agencies. A few of the Cheyennes attempted to escape across the Staked Plains into New Mexi-

[11] Hoag to Pope, Lawrence, Kansas, July 13, 1875, File 2815; Old Files, AGO; Miles's *Personal Recollections,* pp. 176-81; Haworth to E. P. Smith, December 3, 1874; and Pratt to Davidson, December 30, 1874.

co, a country they did not know and in which there were no buffalo. They regretted the experiment.

The Fort Sill column moved east slowly, and with great difficulty, over ground covered with ice. They went down the North Fork to the vicinity of Gypsum Bluffs, where they were pleased to find Captain Lawson waiting with a train loaded with forage. From that point they marched east to Elk Creek, thence south of the mountains to Fort Sill. Only one other expedition of any consequence set forth from the post that year. In December a party under Captain A. S. B. Keyes went northwest, captured fifty-two Cheyennes without a fight, and took them to the Cheyenne agency.

Thus in four short months the pacification of the South Plains Indians—long delayed by one noble experiment after another—was finally and completely accomplished. General Sheridan said, "This campaign was not only very comprehensive, but was the most successful of any Indian campaign in this country since its settlement by the whites; and much credit is due the officers and men engaged in it." Few Indians had been killed. Yet they had been deprived of their means to depredate. Their favorite haunts were cleared and occupied, and although they tried by every means to evade pursuit, or to make it impossible by burning the grass, they found no security. They could not even find a place in which to have a quiet night's sleep. Completely discouraged, they began to straggle into Fort Sill and Darlington. First they came in small groups, then in large.

CHAPTER ELEVEN

THE SURRENDER

SUBMISSION OF THE HOSTILES—THE DEATH PRAYER—SURRENDER
OF THE QUOHADAS—THE LAST RAIDS

THE INDIANS, as they came into Fort Sill to give themselves up, saw that things were to be different from what they had been in the past. There was no peace council, no treaty, no granting of forgiveness and annuities. Each arriving band was driven into the stone corral. Horses, mules, and weapons were taken away from them. Many of the bows, arrows, lances, and war shields, together with camp kettles, saddles, buffalo robes, and other camp gear were stored in a warehouse (which has since been torn down). As the Indians claim that none of this property ever was returned to them, what happened to it is a mystery. The other Indian property was piled in a heap and burned. The women and children were placed in detention camps on the flats of Cache Creek east of the post. The most notorious leaders like White Horse, Big Tree, and Woman's Heart[1] were confined in cells on the north side of the basement of the guardhouse. Other warriors, to the number of 103, were confined in an unfinished ice house of which only the stone floor and walls had been completed. It stood at the foot of the hill east of the post, and in later years was used as a blacksmith shop and ice plant. Only the floor is visible today in the tall grass, fifty yards west of Highway 277. Here the Indians lived in "pup" tents furnished by the quartermaster. Once a day an army wagon drove up to the closely guarded door, and a couple of soldiers took from it chunks of raw meat which they threw over the high walls to the Indians. Gotebo says, "They fed us like we were lions."

When so many Indians had surrendered that the ice house could no longer contain them, the new arrivals were turned over to Cheevers, Kicking Bird, Dangerous Eagle and Horseback. The Indian horses and mules were taken out on the prairie west of the post, near the site of the

[1] Guard reports for 1874-75, Old Files, Fort Sill.

present national guard camp, and shot. After about three hundred had been thus killed the evening breezes blowing in from the west made the post commander suspect that a better plan should be adopted. By the time seven hundred and fifty carcasses lay rotting in the grass he was sure of it. Thenceforth he sold the surrendered stock at public auction and credited the funds thus derived to the bands of Indians who had given up the animals. Altogether, counting the animals stolen by horse thieves from Texas, who boldly approached the Indian camps along Cache Creek from the direction of Red River, the Indians lost seventy-five hundred head of horses and mules, worth over a quarter of a million dollars at the least. But the auctions brought only an average of about four dollars a head. The animals were in poor condition, the bidders few and without much capital. Twenty-two thousand dollars was the total sum realized.[2] The faithful Tonkawa scouts were given a hundred horses, and the volunteer scouts were also presented with a large number.

January of 1875 came and went, and still some of the worst Kiowas and Comanches had not surrendered. Kicking Bird, the indefatigable liaison agent between his people and the government, induced Big Bow to come in alone to dicker with the post commander for the surrender of his band. Colonel Davidson promised Big Bow that he would be exempted from punishment if he brought his tribe to the fort. When the time came for him to give himself up, Lieutenant Pratt was sent out to receive the surrender. Pratt was accompanied by Phil McCusker, sixteen of the Indian scouts, Kicking Bird, and Napawat, another Kiowa chief. They met Big Bow's party in the mountains forty miles west of the post. When they reached Fort Sill most of the men, Big Bow excepted, were placed in irons.

It was the plan of Kicking Bird—who had been left in practical charge of the negotiations—to use Big Bow as the head of a scouting party to go out and persuade Lone Wolf and the other hostiles to come in. Big Bow was selected because he was identified with the hostile group and was well acquainted with all the trails and water holes in the country, even far into Mexico. Furthermore, having just come from these hostile bands, Big Bow knew where to find them.

The group of scouts thus organized were: Sergeant, Big Bow (Zip-ko-etc); Corporal, Gotebo; privates, San Diego, Gum-bi, Guot-sai, Tape-day-ah, Po-hau-ah, Se-loh, Tsain-tonkee (Hunting Horse), and Go-ah-te-bo.[3] This group traveled west under Kicking Bird's direction and persuaded the rest of the Kiowas to surrender. On February 26, the fol-

<hr>

[2] Old Correspondence Books, Fort Sill. Complications arose later when a number of Texans submitted claims for animals which Mackenzie had shot or sold, stating that these animals had been stolen from them by the Indians.

[3] Old Files, Fort Sill.

lowing arrived at Fort Sill: Maman-ti, Lone Wolf, Red Otter, To-hauson, and Poor Buffalo, 68 lesser warriors, 180 women and children, 475 horses and mules, and an uncounted number of dogs, ticks, and fleas.

On March 22 Colonel Davidson, with the soldiers of the Tenth Cavalry, who had built the post and garrisoned it during all the Indian troubles, left for Texas. Colonel Mackenzie and the Fourth Cavalry came in. The new commander continued the policy of sending out scouts and Indians to persuade the remaining hostiles to surrender. On April 18, Stilwell and Kilmartin brought in 36 Comanche warriors, 140 women and children, and 700 horses.

Now came the time to send the worst Indians away to seacoast forts where they were to be confined in accordance with the plan General Sheridan and General Sherman had submitted to President Grant. Seventy-four of the worst Cheyennes, Comanches and Kiowas were sent to St. Augustine, Florida, for confinement in the dungeons of old Fort Marion. Kicking Bird, whom the authorities recognized as principal chief of his tribe in place of Lone Wolf, was given the task of selecting which prisoners should be sent. He picked from the Kiowas several who were notoriously guilty, including White Horse, Maman-ti, Lone Wolf; then made up the balance out of obscure young tribesmen and Mexican captives.[4] On April 28, Companies D and L, Fourth Cavalry, and Companies C and I, Eleventh Infantry, left Fort Sill with these prisoners. Lieutenant R. H. Pratt was placed in charge of the Indians and remained with them during their imprisonment. His sympathetic, kind treatment of his charges won their affection and respect. With a few of them as a nucleus he later founded the Indian school at Carlisle, Pennsylvania.

THE DEATH PRAYER

And now came the martyrdom of the great Kiowa chief, Kicking Bird, a fate which saddened the hearts of all who knew him. Kicking Bird is described as a remarkable man, slight in form compared with the burly warriors of his tribe, but tall, sinewy, agile and very graceful. His extremely affable bearing gave him command among his own people, and this, with his other qualities, would have made him a leader anywhere. A prominent military officer said of him that if he had been white he would have been a United States senator.[5] His efforts to keep his people peaceful during the months immediately preceding the last outbreak had finally gained him a powerful group of enemies among the hostile portion of the tribe. In 1873 one of these enemies went among the

[4] James Mooney, *op. cit.*, pp. 214-16; The complete roster of the Florida prisoners is given in Pratt's reports for May, 1875, Old Files, AGO.

[5] A. L. Vail, *Memorial of James H. Haworth* (Kansas City: H. N. Farey Co., 1886), p. 92.

Kiowas spreading the report that Kicking Bird had been carrying lying tales to the agent about the character of leading Kiowa chiefs. Full of rage, they went to the council room for a showdown. Kicking Bird was present, also the agent. Mr. Haworth, in order to make the hostiles feel that they were held by him in equal esteem with Kicking Bird's faction, indiscreetly remarked that he had used the counsels of Big Bow, a noted raider, as the basis for his latest report to Washington, rather than that of Kicking Bird. The latter, not quite subtle enough to comprehend the agent's motive, immediately decided that he had been cast aside, not only by his own people, but by the whites as well.[6]

He said, "I long ago took the white man by the hand; I have never let it go; I have held it with a strong and firm grasp. I have worked hard to bring my people on the white man's road. Sometimes I have been compelled to work with my back towards the white people so that they have not seen my face, and they may have thought I was working against them; but I have worked with one heart and one object. I have looked ahead to the future, and have worked for the children of my people, to bring them into a position that, when they became men and women, they will take up with the white road. I have but two children of my own, but have worked for the children of my people as though they had all been mine. Five years I have striven for this thing, and all these years Big Bow worked against me to keep my people on the old bad road. When I brought in and delivered up white captives to the agent, Big Bow has taken more. Now for a little while he comes on to the good road. The agent has taken him by the hand, and thrown me away after my many years' labor.

"I am as a stone, broken and thrown away—one part thrown this way, and one part thrown that way. I am chief no more; but that is not what grieves me—I am grieved at the ruin of my people: they will go back to the old road, and I must follow them; they will not let me go and live with the white people. I shall go to my camp, and after a while I shall go a little farther, and then a little farther, until I get as far away as is possible for me. When they show me the big chief they select, I shall follow him wherever he leads. When you take hold of my hand today you have taken it for the last time; when you see me ride away today, you will see Kicking Bird no more. I shall never come back to this place."

But his white friends assured him that they had not thrown him away, that he stood as high in their esteem as before. They finally convinced him that his work had not been in vain. He went away in better humor. In the weeks that followed he redoubled his efforts for peace, and with such success that when the outbreak occurred in July of 1874, the majority of the tribe followed his lead. They returned to Fort Sill, while

[6] Lawrie Tatum, op. cit., pp. 187-88; Thomas Battey, op. cit., pp. 294-97.

Maman-ti and Lone Wolf went on the raid to Texas. There is no doubt that Kicking Bird prevented the slaughter of many innocent persons and saved the government thousands of dollars. After the war was over Kicking Bird's policy seemed to have emerged triumphant. His prestige at Fort Sill was almost unlimited. "Washington" recognized him as the principal chief of the Kiowas. The officials gave him great responsibility in the matter of bringing in the remaining hostiles, and in selecting the prisoners to be sent to Florida. When the day came for the prisoners to depart, the authorities brought to the ice-house prison a column of wagons. The Indians were led forth, chained and dejected, to be loaded into the conveyances. Kicking Bird rode up on a handsome grey horse which had been presented to him by one of the officers at the post.

"Brothers," he said to the sullen Kiowa prisoners. "The time has come to say good-bye. I am sorry for you. But because of your stubbornness, I have failed to keep you out of trouble. You will have to be punished by the government. Take your medicine. It will not be for long. I love you and will work for your release. I have done my best to keep you in the right road, and I hope that the time will come soon when you will return to us happy, at peace, and of a different mind."[7]

Maman-ti, the sinister war leader looked at him steadily without smiling. "Ah yes," he replied. "You think you have done well, Kicking Bird! You remain free, a big man with the whites. But you will not live long. I will see to that!"

Kicking Bird made no reply. At a command given by the officer in charge, the wagons pulled out toward Caddo crossing

On the evening of May 3 Neal Evans and Captain Mauck visited Kicking Bird in his rich, immaculate lodge on Cache Creek, three miles south of the post. He seemed well, but mentally depressed. The next morning at breakfast, shortly after a Mexican servant had served him a cup of coffee, the chief was stricken with a sudden and mysterious seizure. Agent Haworth was sent for. A call was dispatched for the agency doctor.[8] It was no use. About ten o'clock Kicking Bird seemed to realize that his time had come. As the end approached he presented his fine grey horse to the agent. "I am dying," he said, "I have taken the white man's road. I am not sorry for it. Tell my people to keep in the good path. I am dying holding fast the white man's hand. . . . ."[9] He was forty years old, in the prime of life.

Mr. Haworth went to the carpenter shops and told the chief mechanic, Mr. Wyckes, to build a walnut coffin, eight feet long and four

[7] Indian informants.

[8] Reminiscences of Neal Evans; Colonel Henry Inman, *The Old Santa Fe Trail* (Topeka, Kansas; Crane and Co., 1916), pp. 181-83.

[9] Lawrie Tatum, *op. cit.*, p. 197; Thomas Battey, *op. cit.*, p. 317.

feet deep. The dead chief had desired to be buried with his most cherished personal effects, in the ancient custom of the Kiowas. When they returned to the wooded glen where the camp was located the Indian women were wrapping Kicking Bird's body in soft clean buffalo robes. Others were cutting themselves on the arms and breasts, as was always done on the death of a close relative. Kicking Bird's weapons—his bows and arrows, his carbine, his war shield, a pair of beautiful silver mounted pistols—and a roll of currency tied with rubber bands, was laid in the coffin with his body. The other property was broken and buried. His horses were killed. Nothing should remain to remind his people of the man who was gone. Then the agent loaded the great box in a wagon and carried it to the Fort Sill cemetery, where a simple funeral service was pronounced. Few persons were present. The grief and lamentations in the camp were heart-rending. A handsome wooden fence was built around the grave. The post authorities promised to erect a marble monument over it. But administrations changed. The matter was forgotten. The wooden markers rotted away. No one remembered the spot except the daughter and niece of Kicking Bird, who came twice a year to tend the grave. Today it is marked simply, "Unknown."

When Kicking Bird died the post surgeon noted in his record for the month: "Kicking Bird, one of the principal chiefs of the Kiowas, died suddenly May 4, supposed to have been poisoned by strychnia, probably through jealousy or anger of some of his tribe. Kicking Bird was far above any of his own nation, or of the Comanches even, in general intelligence; of fine physique, and had a prepossessing countenance. . . . ." One of the Quaker officials wrote: "I feel as if a good and noble man, whom it had been my privilege to know as a friend, had passed away."

The Kiowas attribute the death of Kicking Bird to a different cause than did the hospital authorities. They say that the second night after the prisoners left Fort Sill on their way to Florida, they were having a council. Eagle Chief, a noted medicine man, passed the pipe to the Great Owl Prophet Maman-ti and said, "Do-ha-te, pray that Kicking Bird may die right away." Maman-ti puffed the pipe thoughtfully for a few moments. Then he replied: "It would be a terrible thing to do. The laws of my medicine forbid the killing of one of our own people. My own life would be forfeit if I thus used my power. But I will do it. In four days, a little after sunup, Kicking Bird will suddenly die. But you must realize that I will pay for it." A few days later the Indians en route to Florida heard that Kicking Bird had passed away, and soon after they reached the end of their journey the Do-ha-te too was dead.[10] To this day the Kiowas believe that Kicking Bird was "hexed" or witched to death.

[10] Reports of R. H. Pratt, File 4117, Old Files, AGO; Pratt to AGO, July 29, 1875.

Quanah Parker, last head chief of the Comanches, with one of his wives.

Smithsonian Institution
Bureau of American Ethnology

Evans' trading store, probably the first frame building (other than picket houses) built at Fort Sill.

Grantham's dugout, an early type of pioneer dwelling, near Quanah Parker's house west of Fort Sill.

George Hunt (left) and Hunting Horse at graves of Warren wagon-train victims.

U.S. Army

Hunting Horse describing Lost Valley fight. Left to right, Hunting Horse, George Hunt, Major Barker, Captain Nye, unknown, Captain Larter, unknown.

Wilbur S. Nye Collection

Esa-rosa (White Wolf), Yapparika Nokoni Comanche chief.

Smithsonian Institution
Bureau of American Ethnology

Rainy Mountain Charlie, son of Maman-ti. Soule
photograph.

Wilbur S. Nye Collection

Cheevers (He Goat), Yapparika Comanche chief. Alexander Gardner photograph.

Smithsonian Institution
Bureau of American Ethnology

Pago-to-goodle (Lone Young Man), prominent Kiowa warrior.

Smithsonian Institution
Bureau of American Ethnology

Geronimo and his family on a farm near Fort Sill.

The Red Store, established in 1886 a few miles south of Fort Sill by Colonel Richard A. Sneed, is the trading establishment best remembered by pioneer settlers in the Fort Sill–Lawton area. Since no railroad had been built to Fort Sill in the eighties, the lumber had to be hauled from Henrietta, Texas. Alonzo D. Lawrence purchased the store in 1904 and operated it until 1911, when the licensed Indian trade came to an end. In this photograph, Armsby Dale Lawrence, a son, is leaning against the post. The Indian women are probably Comanches. The two men to the right are Bert Bear and William Fulbright, clerks who spoke Comanche.

Collection of Arthur R. Lawrence

Captain Wyllys Lyman, 5th Infantry.

Collection of Derek West

Jack Kilmartin, scout and interpreter. W. P. Bliss photograph.

Wilbur S. Nye Collection

Horace P. Jones, veteran post interpreter.

Registration Day at Fort Sill, July 26, 1901.

Troops E, F, H, and K of the 7th Cavalry and D and L of the 5th Cavalry on the old parade ground, 1890.

Fort Sill Museum

Lawton, O.T., September 1, 1901.

Fort Sill Museum

Guardhouse at Fort Sill.

Fort Sill Museum

Sherman House today.

U.S. Army

John Murphy, Sheridan's ambulance driver, who helped set the stake marking the site of Fort Sill. Photograph by W. R. Johnson, 1888.

Wilbur S. Nye Collection

Joshua Given, son of Satank.

Wilbur S. Nye Collection

Old Comanches visit the author at Fort Sill in 1935. Back row, left to right: W. S. Nye, Chockapoyah, Timbo (son of Bull Bear), Phil Looking Glass, Master Sergeant Morris Swett; front row: Millet, Mumsukawa, Quasiah.

Ahpeahtone, Kiowa pilgrim to the "messiah."

Smithsonian Institution
Bureau of American Ethnology

Ghost Dance in front of trader's store.

Fort Sill Museum

The return of the buffalo.

Wilbur S. Nye Collection

A hero's return. At the interment of Master Sergeant Pascal C. Poolaw, much-decorated Kiowa killed in Vietnam, his widow, Irene, kisses the flag that draped his casket. Photograph by Bill Dixon, Lawton *Constitution*.

Field Artillery regimental camp, 1905.

Fort Sill Museum

Academic area fire, June 17, 1926.

Fort Sill Museum

Captain Dan T. Moore, founder and first commandant of the Field Artillery
School, Fort Sill.

Fort Sill Museum

General Lesley James McNair. From an oil portrait by Anne T. Stinson.

Field artillery on Mission Ridge, Fort Sill, 1927.

Fort Sill Museum

Motorized artillery, 1919.

Fort Sill Museum

A car and the army's mess truck stuck in the old back road (Fort Sill Boulevard) in 1918. A pair of mules was needed to remove the vehicles.

Fort Sill Museum

World War I trucks. The mechanics and operators were still rated as wagoners.
Wilbur S. Nye Collection

Early parachutist at Fort Sill, his parachute snagged on tail of aircraft.

H-37 helicopters deliver 105-mm. howitzers.

CH-54 flying crane at Fort Sill.

155-mm. howitzer being fired on Fort Sill's West Range.

U.S. Army

Eight-inch howitzer being fired on Fort Sill's East Range.

U.S. Army

The Field Artillery giants—175-mm. guns, on the move and in the field.

James Auchiah, grandson of Satanta, in dress of Kiowa Tia-piah Society.

U.S. Army

Pershing guided missile at Fort Sill.

U.S. Army

A study in contrast—top, "Calamity Jane," 155-mm. howitzer (French), World War I vintage; below, "Atomic Annie," 280-mm. atomic gun, at Fort Sill Museum.

McNair Hall, top; Snow Hall, below.

U.S. Army

Massed colors of Fort Sill units pass in review on the Old Post parade ground on the one hundredth anniversary of the post.

U.S. Army

18th Field Artillery guidon bearers present arms as they pass the reviewing stand.

U.S. Army

Descendants of noted Indian scouts and members of Fort Sill Artillery Hunt recreate a reconnaissance troop of cavalry in the Parade of History at the anniversary celebration.

U.S. Army

Indian leaders in full regalia representing the nine tribes involved in Fort Sill's historic past lead off the Old Oklahoma Cavalcade.

U.S. Army

Aerial view of the old Post Corral.

U.S. Army

In April of 1875 Colonel Mackenzie induced Dr. J. J. Sturms to travel into the Staked Plains for the purpose of contacting peaceably the Quohada Comanches, and persuading them to come to Fort Sill and give themselves up. Sturms was accompanied by Sergeant J. B. Charlton and several Comanches, notably the minor chief Habby-wake. Mackenzie's offer to the Quohadas was that if they would surrender quietly, no harm would be done to them, and they could live in comparative freedom and safety near the agency. If they refused, he would follow them with all his forces until he had exterminated them. Sturms and Charlton found the Quohadas on White River, near Quitaque. They were amusing themselves with horse races and buffalo hunts. They prepared to fight when they saw the Fort Sill party approaching, but the latter displayed a white flag. Isa-tai, Wild Horse, Black Horse, and several other war chiefs were present, but in the negotiations which followed, a young chief named Quanah took the lead. He promised to be responsible for the surrender of the entire band, but asked for a few weeks grace to complete the buffalo hunt on which they then were engaged.

From this time on, Quanah, who was possessed of superior intelligence, shrewdness, and force, seemed to increase his influence over the Comanches. It was not long before he had completely overshadowed the older chiefs, and was recognized by the whites as principal chief of the Comanches. This was something they had never had before. On June 2 Quanah, accompanied by most of the Quohadas, arrived at Fort Sill. There were 100 warriors, 300 noncombatants, and 1400 ponies. The men were disarmed and their ponies were sold at auction.[11]

The surrender of these last bands of Indians from the Staked Plains marked the close of the Indian warfare in the southwestern part of Oklahoma. It ended the day of the Kiowas and Comanches as free, independent savages; it signalized the beginning of their conformance with the dictates and privileges of modern white civilization.

THE LAST RAIDS

In the spring of 1875 six Comanches sneaked away from the camps near Fort Sill and went to Jack County to steal horses. On May 8 they arrived at Loving's Ranch, the scene of much border warfare. Here they stole several animals, including the favorite mount of the owner of the ranch, Mr. Oliver Loving.

It so happened that a detachment of Texas Rangers, under Lieutenant Ira Long, was in the vicinity. They sighted the Comanches near

---

[11] Old Files, Fort Sill.

Spy Knob, that peculiar hill which stands in Lost Valley just north of the town of Jermyn. A running fight ensued, in which all but one of the Indians were overtaken and cut down. Lieutenant Long killed one in a hand-to-hand fight. In examining the bodies the rangers found that one of the Indians was a woman—young, good-looking, and evidently part white. One of the men who was slain had curly hair, of an auburn shade. Since there had been considerable argument in that part of Texas as to whether the stock stealing had been done by Indians or by whites disguised as Indians, the troops at Fort Richardson were asked to verify the fact that these were Indians. The soldiers therefore cut off the heads of the Indians, preserved them in jars of alcohol, and sent them to Washington.[12] It is said that Agent Haworth had given these Indians a pass to go hunting, and was greatly aroused over the fact that they had been attacked by the rangers. The auburn-haired Comanche was named Aycufty, which means "Reddish." The leader was Isa-toho (Black Coyote), and the woman was his wife. Another of the slain was Pea-sea-no-chaman. The names of the other two are not remembered.[13]

The amount of rations allowed the Indians under the terms of the Medicine Lodge treaty was based on the theory that the principal part of their sustenance would be provided by hunting buffalo, or, when the wild game was gone, that the Indians would be able to support themselves by farming and stock raising. Unfortunately the buffalo were exterminated much sooner than had been anticipated, and the Indians in the short period intervening had not become farmers or stockmen. Hence by 1878 they were practically starving. Mackenzie had protested vigorously to Washington concerning the scanty rations being issued the Indians, but no permanent relief was secured.[14]

In the winter of 1878 Sun Boy's band of Kiowas was given permission to hunt buffalo in the western part of the reservation. Escorted by a company of colored troopers under Captain Nicholas Nolan, they went west into what is now Greer County. Game was very scarce, and the Indians were in a pitiable condition from cold and hunger. One day Ah-to-tainte, a brother of Sun Boy, slipped across Red River in pursuit of two deer. With him was another Indian named Buffalo Calf-tongue. They encountered a company of Texas Rangers. Ah-to-tainte was killed.[15] The other Indian ran to camp to report that the rangers were preparing to charge the camp and kill all the Indians, women and children included. Captain Nolan had his men dig trenches for the defense of the camp. Soon the rangers appeared, headed by a man wear-

12 Oliver Loving to author, 1935.
13 Penateka to author, 1935.
14 Old Files, Fort Sill; also File 4608, AGO, 1875.
15 James Mooney, op. cit., 343-44; File 5641, AGO, 1878; Indian informant, Ay-tah.

ing a leopard-skin vest. It looked as though there would be a fight. Nolan told the Indians to get their guns and defend themselves; but they were afraid of being arrested. The commander of the rangers rode boldly up to Nolan and demanded to see his papers. When the officer produced them the ranger threw them in his face and cursed him roundly for allowing the Indians to cross the line. But the fight did not take place. After the rangers departed the Indians buried Ah-to-tainte in the trench. The Texans had cut off his ring finger, but had not scalped him.

In April Pago-to-goodle, a brother of the slain man, organized a revenge raid. His party consisted of thirty-seven men, including Tsa'l-au-te, Lone Bear, Yee-goo, Set-maunte—and one young woman, the wife of Set-maunte. They went to the region in which Ah-to-tainte had been killed; it was their express purpose to slay one white man for him. They spent the night on the northwest side of a low hill which stands a few hundred yards north of the present town of Quanah, Texas, About ten or eleven o'clock on the morning of April 12 they saw a horseman approaching from the south, followed at a little distance by a wagon with two men in it. At a signal from Pago-to-goodle the Indians raced north to cut off the leading white man. Their presence was concealed by a draw. Suddenly they appeared within a few yards of him. Two Kiowas rode up on either side of the man (Joe Earle, by name); one of them seized his horse by the bridle and the other shot the rider. The two men in the wagon were not molested. They unhitched their team, mounted up, and fled eastward. Tsa'l-au-te wanted to take a shot at them to speed them on their way, but the leader would not permit it. Ay-tah (Set-maunte's wife) says that when she arrived on her slow horse the white man was lying on his back with a bullet hole in his forehead. The clothing on his abdomen was on fire; she did not know whether this was from a close gunshot flash, or whether the braves had kindled the fire on purpose. This occurrence led to a report made by the whites that Earle had been tortured. After killing Earle, the Kiowas plundered the wagon, which was loaded with supplies of food evidently destined for some cattle camp. Ay-tah says that she got a small coffee grinder as her trophy. The arrival of several Texans in the vicinity spoiled the fun, and the Indians rode rapidly north. They were pursued, but escaped under cover of a dust storm. The authorities at Fort Sill heard of the affair, but were unable to obtain any details or proof. When the Indians returned to Rainy Mountain they had a victory dance, but kept the matter as quiet as possible. Only recently have they disclosed the details, and somewhat apprehensively, as many of the participants are still alive.

In June a small band of Comanches made the last raid into Texas. Captain Wirt Davis, with Company E, Fourth Cavalry, had been sent from Fort Sill to establish a camp on the North Fork of Red River. His orders required him to send scouting detachments from time to time under a commissioned officer to prevent the Indians from the reserve from going into the Panhandle or south of Red River. This was because various parties of Indians were out on authorized hunting trips at the time and, as the game was scarce, it was realized that they might wander away from the reservation in their search.[16] The buffalo had almost completely disappeared. The Kiowas had been unable to find a single one, and had been forced to kill their horses to keep from starving. The Comanches had no better luck. Black Horse, a subchief who recently had returned from Fort Marion, Florida, went with twenty-five of his people on a buffalo hunt. The Comanches headed south into Texas. Finally they came to a ranch somewhere south of Big Spring where they killed several colts and ate them. While engaged in this forbidden meal they were attacked by seven Texas Rangers, who comprised a patrol from Company B of the Frontier Battalion, the company being commanded by Captain June Peak. The rangers, who had followed the Indians from the ranch, sighted them in a clump of cedars somewhere near the head of the North Concho River.

At first the Indians were superior, and drove the rangers back. Then the fine marksmanship of the Texans forced the Comanches to take refuge in a place where there was a jumble of boulders, surrounded by cedar trees. During the gun fight which followed the Indians captured two pack mules from the rangers, while the latter captured all the horses from the Indians. Two rangers were wounded. The Indians were afoot, night was approaching, but the rangers were in a sorry predicament. The pack mules which they had lost were loaded with their food, blankets, and extra ammunition. The Texans waited through the night, hungry and without water, watching for the Indians to come out. It was anticipated that they would make a sortie in an effort to recover their ponies. But when daylight came they were gone. Their trail showed that nineteen of them had left the cedars. The rangers did not stop to explore the thicket for dead Indians; they followed rapidly after the retreating savages. For miles they rode across hot plains of red sand, thinly dotted with mesquite. Now and then they crossed dry watercourses lined with scrub cedar. The Indians, seeing them coming, prepared an ambush; Black Horse concealed his men in a buffalo wallow and turned the captured mules out to graze. The leader of the rangers, seeing the pack mules, became suspicious. He sent two men forward to investigate. Just as one of them stooped to examine a moccasin which he saw on the ground, the Comanches opened fire at a range of ten yards. The Texan fell, dying. Both horses were killed and the other man was wounded. The

16 Old Files, Fort Sill, 1879.

other rangers rescued the wounded man, but retired without the body of his dead companion. The Indians remained in possession of the field.

Several scouting parties of troops from Fort Concho were out also looking for the Indians who had been reported stealing stock. Lieutenant C. R. Ward, with a portion of Company D, Tenth Cavalry, went to Hollman's ranch, where he heard of the fight between the Indians and the rangers, which had occurred on June 29, the preceding day. He went to Mustang Springs and found the trail of the rangers and Indians. In following this trail Ward came to where the last skirmish had been fought, a few hours before. Here he discovered the body of Ranger W. G. Anglin, which he buried. He picked up several Indian blankets marked "USID."[17]

This was the last Comanche raid into Texas.

[17] Reports of Engagements with Hostile Indians in the Military Division of the Missouri, Old Files, AGO, 1879.

PART IV

THE LAST TEPEE

CHAPTER TWELVE

THE DESPERADOES

BOOT-HILL CEMETERY—DAYS OF THE EMPIRE

AFTER the army completed the subjugation of the Kiowas and Comanches, no more white persons were killed in the vicinity of Fort Sill by Indians. However, the profession of illegal homicide was taken over in an able fashion by Negroes and white men. The Fort Sill reservation was a lodestone for many thieves, cattle and horse rustlers, whisky peddlers, prostitutes, and ordinary scalawags. The military authorities did not have jurisdiction over civilian criminals, and the nearest Federal court was at Fort Smith, Arkansas, a week's journey away. Some of these rascals came in openly, posing as employes of the hay, wood, and beef contractors. Others sneaked across the line at night, stole horses from the Indians, committed murders, and were across Red River before the post was aware of their presence.

On August 27, 1875, Thomas Campbell, an employe of the hay contractor, was shot and killed during a brawl at the hay camp. A few days later a man named Postelthwaite was killed at the Indian agency by a "friend." On September 21 a harmless wayfarer named James Harris, together with his small son, was brutally murdered by a Negro named Aaron Wilson. Mr. Harris was traveling in a covered wagon from Kansas to Texas. As he passed the Penateka camps near the Anadarko agency he was observed by Wilson, a discharged soldier living with the Indians. Wilson followed the wagon, overtaking it a short distance south of Fort Sill. The Harrises had just gone into camp for the night.[1] Wilson asked if he might share their meal and spend the night with them. The old man made him welcome. That night as Harris lay asleep the assassin murdered him with an axe, then shot the small boy, though the latter begged that his life be spared. Wilson robbed the camp, and made his way back to the Comanche camp with his late host's team of horses.

The Indians did not approve such a violation of hospitality. Tosawi saddled his pony, rode to the agency and reported that he suspected that

[1] Old Files, Fort Sill.

Wilson had committed murder. Fort Sill was notified; Lieutenant Mathew Leeper, Jr., with several cavalrymen, went out to investigate. First he went to the Comanche camp and arrested Wilson on suspicion. By threats and intimidation he forced the murderer to confess his crime and lead the way to the bodies. Leeper buried the gruesome remains, and lodged Wilson in the post guardhouse. Wilson was taken to Fort Smith, brought before Isaac Parker, the famous "hanging judge," who promptly tried him; conviction and execution followed with like promptitude.[2]

The killing season of 1876 opened on June 9, when James Yearns shot and killed Charles Cox, four miles west of Fort Sill. Scout Jack Kilmartin was killed in July. He had gone with Sergeant Charlton and Jack Stilwell in search of thieves who had stolen Indian stock. They stopped the first night south of Red River, at Whaley's ranch, in which Kilmartin owned an interest. Kilmartin's wife, a hard-faced woman, was employed there as a cook. Early the next morning she blew out Kilmartin's brains while he lay asleep. It was supposed that her motive was a desire to rid herself of her husband in order to be free to indulge in a liaison with a civilian at the ranch. Kilmartin was one of the best scouts who ever served at Fort Sill. He was quiet, unassuming, and possessed of absolute courage. Had he survived it is likely that his fame would have equaled that of Stilwell and Ben Clark.[3] On September 28, Fritz Niggli, foreman of a Texas cattle outfit, was shot and killed by one William Sherry, a cowboy, in a gun fight which took place six miles north of Sill. The fight occurred at breakfast after Niggli censured Sherry for going to sleep on guard. The unsuccessful duelist was buried in the post cemetery.[4]

For the next four years no homicides are recorded near Fort Sill. On August 19, 1880, several unoccupied hay workers in the camp of Contractor McGarvey, which was located at the crossing of Cache Creek just east of the post, were trying to think up some mischief to pass away the time. William Brown and a man named Moore finally provided the entertainment for the evening by staging a rough-and-tumble fight, in which Brown received a severe beating. As soon as he regained his senses he rushed to the bunkhouse, where someone handed him a pistol. In the gathering twilight he lay in ambush for Moore. A few moments later a man came running toward him. Brown shot several times, killing his best friend, Ralph Tate, who was coming to help him. Judge Parker wrote the final sentence of Mr. Brown's biography.[5]

[2] *Ibid.*

[3] Old Files, Fort Sill; R. G. Carter, *The Old Sergeant's Story* (New York: Frederick Hitchcock, 1926).

[4] Old Files, Fort Sill.

[5] *Ibid.*

The following year two brothers named Davis were lynched under peculiar circumstances, on the east bank of Cache Creek, opposite the present site of the Fort Sill Indian hospital. It is supposed that they were cattle rustlers who had been trailed to Fort Sill from Texas. Masked horsemen took them away from Indian police who had them in custody in a camp just north of the Fort Sill hospital, threw lariats around their necks, dragged them down the creek, and finally shot them. The wife of one of the brothers was in camp near-by, but was unable to prevent the lynching. The whole affair was conducted with such dispatch and such secrecy that the bodies were not discovered until several months later, when Mr. William Quinette happened upon them while hunting quail.[6]

During 1882 there were three rousing murders. In April Robert Massey killed E. P. Clark. In July William H. Finch committed the other two crimes by shooting two Negro soldiers stationed at Fort Sill.[7] The Finch case was a noted one. Old-timers still talk about it. Finch was a mulatto, well educated and a fluent writer. He was employed at Fort Sill as a tailor. For some time he had been "keeping company" with the dusky daughter of the post barber, a Negro who lived in a picket house adjacent to the old Grierson house, at that time known as the Fort Sill Hotel. The barber objected to these attentions. One night he shot at Finch as the latter crawled out of a rear window. This affair reached the ears of Colonel Guy V. Henry, post commander. Colonel Henry called Finch into the office and ordered him to leave the reservation. Finch asked to be allowed to remain until after pay day so that he could collect his bills. This permission was granted, but after pay day had come and gone Finch continued to loiter about the post. He lived in the brush, and rustled food from the troop kitchens. On the twenty-third of July he stole two pistols from one of the supply rooms, then went to Mr. Quinette's stable where he helped himself to a fine pony with saddle and bridle. Later in the day a freighter arrived from Texas with information that a man answering to Finch's description had passed him on the Jacksboro road about ten miles south of the post. Two detachments were sent in pursuit. They came in sight of Finch, opened fire at long range. But the thief galloped into the timber and made good his escape. On August 10 he was arrested at Decatur, Texas. On information wired from Fort Sill, the sheriff turned him over to the military authorities at the camp at Red River Station. Sergeant Bush Johnson and Privates Jerry McCarty and Wash Grimke were detailed to take him back to Sill. The first night they slept little on account of mosquitoes. The next evening they arrived eighteen miles south of the post and went into camp. Johnson and Grimke lay down and were asleep almost immediately.

[6] W. H. Quinette to author, 1934; Andrew Stumbling Bear and George Hunt to author.
[7] W. H. Quinette to author, 1934.

245

They thought that Finch, who was handcuffed, would not make any serious attempt to escape. McCarty went to the creek after a bucket of water. No sooner had McCarty disappeared than Finch took a gun and shot Grimke. McCarty poked his head up over the bank just in time to see him also shoot Johnson. This was all McCarty needed to know; he ran up the opposite bank and hid behind a tree. Presently he heard Finch calling for him to come out, saying that he would not be hurt. But McCarty took no chance. He continued to lie doggo. Presently he saw Finch remove the keys from Sergeant Johnson's pockets, and unlock the shackles about his wrists; then the murderer helped himself to arms and food, saddled one of the horses and rode off, leading a second animal.

McCarty hurried to the spot. Grimke was dead, but Johnson was still alive. Feebly he told McCarty to ride to Fort Sill for help. It was Sunday. McCarty reached the post at 9:30 P.M., just as the people were coming out of church. A detachment was made ready and set out for the scene of the killing. But McCarty lost his way in the darkness so that they did not find the place until early morning. Johnson was dead. Finch was recaptured in Texas and taken to Fort Smith. His defense at the trial was an ingenious invention of the imagination. He declared that McCarty had killed the other two men, but had released him unharmed, telling him to clear out of the country and say nothing about it. "You have nothing on me!" he cried. "It is my word against McCarty's." Judge Parker was unimpressed by this story. Finch was led to the gallows.

On the afternoon of March 26, 1887 a wild-eyed cowboy named William Williams rode into Fort Sill from Quinette's dairy ranch, which was near Hairpin Ford. He dismounted just west of the cavalry stables, rested a gun over his saddle and drew bead on Quinette's foreman, who was standing in front of the trader's store. The shot missed the foreman but struck Private Harris Ansley in the head, putting out his eye. Lieutenant G. A. Dodd collected a detachment of the guard and rode in hot pursuit of the gunman. Dodd was gone all night. He returned in the morning empty-handed, and reported that Williams had disappeared. The post commander commended the lieutenant so warmly in orders that some of the people at Fort Sill entertained the base suspicion that Dodd might have been more successful than he claimed to be. At any rate Williams was not heard of again.[8]

At high noon on May 8, Sim Powel killed Billy Linton and Gibson Lewis at the crossing of Cache Creek (where Hoyle Bridge is now). And so it went. Shootings in the hay and cattle camps were of such common occurrence that they hardly excited comment. Usually the victims were

[8] Old Files, Fort Sill.

buried where they fell, but so many of them were planted in the rapidly expanding post cemetery that it bid fair to rival other famous boot-hill cemeteries in the gun-toting west.

Murderers and horse thieves were not the only unsavory gentry who gave the authorities at Fort Sill sleepless nights. Bootleggers frequented the area in large numbers. The profits of sales to Indians and soldiers were so high that long prison sentences did not deter resourceful, dangerous men from coming into the Indian reservation with liquor. They were hard to catch, and were apt to use weapons when cornered.

Wrattan Creek, formerly called Whisky Creek, was a favorite resort of bootleggers. They came from Texas a few nights before each pay day at the post, and camped in the wooded bottoms of Cache Creek and Whisky Creek. Usually they had a wagonload of prostitutes in addition to firewater. When pay day arrived they drove a line of stakes with bits of white cloth tied to them, from some point known to the customers, leading toward the place of business.[9]

Grierson's old house north of the trader's store was used as a stage relay station and hotel. It was the only place where civilians passing through the territory could stay unless they camped on the prairie. On pay days it was occupied by persons whom the post commander would have preferred to bar from the post, as he was not always sure of their character. The border was infested with all manner of questionable-looking persons of both sexes, but it was not possible for the post commander to determine which of these were scoundrels and which were honest pioneers with rough exteriors.

One day in the eighties the post commander, who will be called Joe Tuttle because, as Alexander Woollcott would say, that happens not to be his name, strode into the trader's store.

"The Fort Sill Hotel is filled with a boisterous crowd of girls. I am convinced that they are prostitutes," he told Mr. Quinette. "I want you to put them off the reservation."

"But Major," protested Quinette. "That is not my affair. Why don't you have your adjutant order them away?"

"I have done so. They won't go."

"Then you ought to write to the United States marshal."

"A good idea. I will do it."

As the major left the store, one of the women, who was standing on the porch of the hotel, called, "Hi there, Joe! Come on over."

Joe marched toward headquarters, looking neither to right nor left.

[9] *Ibid.*

His neck and ears were the color of an artillery guidon. He wrote a hot letter to the marshal, but the "girls" remained for several weeks.[10]

In 1890 a canteen for enlisted men was opened in the building known as Amusement Hall, today used as the post children's school. This enabled the commanding officer to close the bar in the trader's store. As a result, since civilians were not permitted to patronize the canteen, there were fewer pay-day fights between soldiers and civilian desperadoes. Prior to this time it had been necessary for the women and children of the post to stay indoors on pay days. When the bar was permanently closed in the trader's store, the officers' club also was moved to the Amusement Hall. The post library had been there for years. The officers established a small clubroom equipped with books, periodicals, and a billiard table. It was located conveniently to the canteen. Officers who were permitted to be away from home in the evenings spent many enjoyable hours at the club. One member patronized the club so thoroughly, and so frequently, that a wheelbarrow was kept beside the building, in which he was delivered to his door by friends, late of evenings.[11]

[10] Old Correspondence File, Fort Sill.
[11] W. H. Quinette to author, 1934.

CHAPTER THIRTEEN

FROM TEPEE TO CABIN

FIRST EFFORTS TOWARD CIVILIZATION—THE FLORIDA PRISONERS
—TRANSITION—THE CATTLEMEN—INDIANS IN UNIFORM

AS SOON as the Indians were disarmed and subdued, efforts to civilize them were resumed. Colonel Mackenzie made the first experiment. He decided to spend some of the money derived from the sale of Indian horses for the purchase of sheep and goats for the Indians. The idea was that they would become domesticated more quickly if they were encouraged to give up the practice of roaming around after the buffalo and settle down to raising livestock. The sheep would supply meat and wool. The long, fine hair of the goats could be used to make blankets and rugs similar to those manufactured by the Navajos.[1]

In the summer of 1875 Lieutenant A. E. Wood set forth from Fort Sill with a detachment of the Fourth Cavalry; he went to Fort Bascom, New Mexico, where he purchased $22,000 worth of pure-bred sheep and goats. Several Mexicans were hired to escort the herd back to the Kiowa and Comanche reservation. The long trip was hard on the animals, and many of them perished along the way. Those that reached Fort Sill were in such poor condition that Mackenzie held them over until spring to fatten them before issuing them to the Indians. When the day arrived to issue the sheep and goats, the Indians came forth in all their finery, curious to see what would happen. The animals were driven from their pasture and assembled in the field where the Indian school now stands. Each deserving "beef-band" chief was given a small herd. Stumbling Bear got a hundred. So did old man Horseback. Lesser braves received their share. But the nomadic Kiowas and Comanches soon discovered that they did not care for lamb chops or mutton stew. They preferred buffalo meat or beef. There was not a man, woman, or child among them

[1] This project is discussed in the correspondence files of Fort Sill for 1874–75; see also Mooney, *op. cit.*, pp. 339-40, and Medical History of Fort Sill.

who knew how to weave a rug, nor was there one who cared to learn. They chased the animals out on the prairie and practiced shooting at them with bows and arrows. The small boys in particular enjoyed the fun. So did the camp dogs. Wolves and coyotes got what was left.

Mackenzie also gave the Indians some cattle. It would have been better if he had spent all the money in this way. The Indians appreciated the cattle. Their background and natural inclination gave promise that they might become successful cattlemen. It is their great misfortune that they did not. One reason was that they were forced to eat all of their cattle for food, and could not save any for breeding purposes. The Indian agent was allowed $3.00 a month to feed each Indian. This allowance had been based on the assumption that the Indians would supplement their rations by hunting. Unfortunately the buffalo, on which the Indians depended for their principal source of food, were by this time practically exterminated by commercial hunters. Hence the Indians were hungry most of the time. Mackenzie made vigorous protest against this condition, but was unable to do more than effect temporary relief by obtaining permission to issue army rations to the starving Indians.[2]

During Mackenzie's administration of Fort Sill one other step was taken toward weaning the Indians away from camp life. Houses were built for ten leading chiefs who had been friendly to the government during the recent hostilities. These were erected in 1876. Stumbling Bear and Horseback each got one, much to their delight. It increased their prestige in the eyes of their clansmen. But, in spite of the pride the Indians felt in their new dwellings, they would not live in them. They continued to camp in the yards and allow their dogs to sleep in the houses. Mr. Quinette asked Horseback why he did not live in his house. "Hoh!" replied the Comanche. "Heap snakes in house." Andrew Stumbling Bear says that when his father's house was turned over to them the family enjoyed roaming through the empty rooms whooping to hear the strange echoes set up. Andrew asked his mother to build a bed for him in the fireplace so that he might look up the flue at the stars.[3]

THE FLORIDA PRISONERS

The Indians like to recall the summer of 1878 as the time when the Florida prisoners were returned to their homes. Not all of them came

[2] Mackenzie to Sherman, August 31, 1875, File 4608, AGO. Mackenzie wrote, in part: "I have so often been obliged to report such failures [to feed the Indians] on the part of the Indian Department that I am reluctant to report further on the subject, but the emergency is pressing, and unless these Indians are fed and the obligations of the Indian Department to them fulfilled, we may expect certainly a stampede of the Kiowas and Comanches from their reservation."

[3] At least two of these houses are still standing, and in use. Horseback's former house is on Highway 62, about six miles north of Fort Sill. White Wolf's house is on the Medicine Park Highway, just west of Welch Hill.

back. Several had died in captivity, and others had remained in the east to go to school.

The imprisonment of the Indians had not been rigorous. They were allowed considerable liberty within the walls of old Fort Marion. Later, when the people of the near-by town of St. Augustine realized that the Indians were not dangerous, the latter were allowed a certain amount of freedom outside the fortress. Various philanthropists visited them; a few young men were taken away by these kind-hearted people for training and education. At first the prisoners were homesick. The semi-tropical climate did not agree with them. Some of the older ones pined away and died. Captain Pratt tried to keep them entertained by telling them stories of his experiences in the army, or by organizing games and amusements. George Fox, whom the Indians all liked, was there as interpreter. There were many strange sights to see, and many new foods to taste. A few of the Indians acquired an inordinate fondness for tropical fruits.

When they returned to Fort Sill the Kiowa and Comanche prisoners had many interesting and amusing stories to tell their people. One of the favorite tales brought back from St. Augustine was that of the famous bullfight.[4] It seems that the inhabitants of St. Augustine were chiefly of Spanish descent. It was Captain Pratt's good fortune to make the acquaintance of many of them. In the evenings he would visit in the town and talk about his life among the wild animals and Indians on the western plains. He was inclined to boast about his Indians, and in order to impress his auditors he informed them that the Indians were extremely wild and ferocious. He said that one of their accomplishments was to ride headlong into a herd of buffalo and kill the powerful beasts with guns, or even with bows and arrows. His Spanish auditors were not impressed. They pointed out that in Spain their people killed wild bulls —man-killing bulls. The men who performed these brave feats were armed only with a cape and sword and faced the dangerous animal on foot. What had the Indians to offer which could equal this? The argument grew somewhat heated. The result was that young Pratt offered to put on a bullfight, wherein his Indians would kill, without the aid of a gun, any bull the townsfolk could supply. He guaranteed that the spectacle would be as thrilling as any of the *corridas* of Granada or Seville.

The principal thoroughfare in St. Augustine was roped off to form an arena for the event. A huge bull was purchased somewhere and shipped in by freight. He was held in a cage and starved and tormented to keep him in an ill humor. The Indians were promised that if they put on a good show they could have the meat for barbecue. This filled them with joy. They had been living on beans and salt pork, and were pining

[4] Told to author by George Hunt.

for fresh beef. They said they would do their best. When the big day arrived the citizens sat in improvised grandstands, or crowded the grilled balconies on either side of the narrow street. After a fanfare of speeches and trumpets, the bull was released from his crate. He stood for a moment weaving slowly from side to side and shaking his head.

Two Indians mounted on nags from the local livery stable dashed out of a side alley at the opposite end of the arena. One of them was the champion buffalo slayer of the Cheyennes. The other was none other than White Horse, the Kiowa who had raided the corral at Sill in 1870. The redoubtable White Horse, to the consternation of Pratt and the confusion of the ladies, had "dressed" for the occasion by stripping himself to the traditional G-string. He flourished as a weapon only a sharp butcher knife.

The bull focused his baleful eyes on the Cheyenne, who, decked out in turkey feathers and strips of gaily colored flannel, was making an opening address to his admiring fellow-tribesmen. The bull pawed the ground. Then he gave vent to a terrific snort and dashed after the Cheyenne. The latter sat rooted to his horse for a moment. No buffalo had ever acted like that. He hastily wheeled his frightened horse and fled to the other end of the enclosure. Old Toro was after him in a flash, gaining at every jump, and puffing like a locomotive. The spectators yelled. Strong men turned pale. Women fainted. Impresario Pratt lost seven years' growth. But White Horse was equal to the occasion. Like a polo player riding an opponent off the ball, the muscular Kiowa drove his faltering steed up behind the bull until his right knee was touching the animal's rump. His knife flashed high in the air. Down it came in a mighty thrust. It caught the bull above the loin, severing the spinal column. Toro gave an agonized bellow. He dropped to his belly. White Horse was on the ground instantly. He placed his foot on the bull in the best manner of a cinema Tarzan, and let out a triumphant screech. Then he slashed a great hole in the bull's side, snatched out a kidney—smoking hot—and commenced to devour it raw. The blood ran down his chin and chest, which made the picture vividly authentic.

White Horse was not acting. He was hungry for raw meat. The members of the aristocratic audience tumbled open-mouthed from their seats. They were convinced that they had viewed a real wild man in action. The Indians were delighted. At a signal from Pratt they ran out to where the bull lay. Almost before the carcass stopped quivering they had reduced it to a heap of bones.

Finally, in the early summer of 1878, the government, on the recommendation of Captain Pratt, decided to release the prisoners and send them to their homes. They were sent by rail to Kansas, thence conveyed in army wagons to their reservations. When they saw great brown hawks sailing close to the folds of the land like albatross at sea, and heard the prairie dogs chirping in their villages, the Indians knew that they were in their own country at last. It was pathetic to see the joy shining in their faces as they jumped from the wagons and ran ahead, knee-deep in the soft green buffalo grass, to drink in the warm fragrance of their prairie homeland. This was the season when terrapin, a favorite Indian delicacy, was plentiful on the plains. The returning prisoners caught a number of the creatures; at night they sat around their campfires under the starlit sky singing happy songs and roasting terrapin.

TRANSITION

The summer the prisoners returned to their reservations was marked also by a noticeable trend among the warriors to give up close tribal association and community life in order to settle down with their immediate families. Several of the war chiefs abdicated. Among these was Mow-way, who stated that he desired to end his days with his family on a farm south of Fort Sill. Mow-way died there a few years later, and was buried on the southern slopes of Arbuckle Hill, three miles east of the post.[5]

There still was a chance that the Indians could become stockmen. Opportunity was offered for this through association with the cattlemen who were coming in from Texas. Immense herds of cattle were being driven from Texas to the northern markets. One trail ran just east of the Indian reservation, and another skirted the western border, near Tepee Mountain. The cattle drivers used to give beeves to the Indians, especially to influential chiefs, to keep the tribesmen from molesting their herds. A few of the Indians shrewdly commenced saving these cattle to build up herds of their own. Among the far-sighted Comanches were Tabananica, who had a ranch four miles north of Fort Sill, and Quanah, who lived some twenty miles west of the post. The latter formed valuable associations with various cattlemen, and thus, it is said, laid the basis for a modest fortune.

But the Indian agent was determined that the Indians should become farmers. He made special efforts at this time to force them to take up agriculture. It was not an easy task. The Indian ponies were not trained to work in draught. The Indians themselves were inept and not suited to the life. One of their major difficulties was learning to plow a straight furrow. One man solved this problem by tying several lariats together and laying them on the ground as a guide for the plow. The agent also had trouble in making the Indians understand that corn would grow better if the young plants were thinned out. They were greatly offended at the suggestion that they pull up plants which they had worked so

[5] Ti-so-yo, son of Mow-way, to author.

hard to grow. Several flatly refused to do so. Finally the Indian department decided to move the agency away from Fort Sill. Mr. Haworth, who did not approve of the army post in any particular, had recommended this many times. In 1878 he resigned on account of ill health. But his recommendation was carried out under his successor, P. B. Hunt. Colonel Davidson, who had taken command of Fort Sill after Colonel Mackenzie departed, opposed the move, setting forth his reason, in part, as follows: "Major Pollock, an Inspector in the Indian Department, spent *one day* here, and during his visit told the Indians that the agency would be moved at the end of the month. I had a conversation on the subject with Maj. Pollock. He said the movement had been unanimously recommended and would be made. I asked who it was that unanimously made the recommendation and learned that it was a former agent [Haworth] and Mr. Galpin, former chief clerk of the Indian Bureau.

"The former had private reasons for the recommendation and the latter simply knew nothing of the duties of an inspector. . . . It seems strange that knowing, as the head of the Indian Department does, that the main dependence of these people [the Indians] must be in their becoming a pastoral people, effort is being constantly made to make them support themselves by agriculture, and almost nothing done to encourage them to keep stock. . . .

"They have themselves taken one long step towards civilization by establishing settlements scattered at intervals over a country fifty miles in extent, and are asking that the land may be secured to them in severalty. Now the desire is to break up this very desirable condition of affairs and concentrate them on the Washita on the extreme northern boundary of the country, setting them back in their efforts toward civilization, and annoying the neighboring tribes who do not want them in their vicinity.

"The ruin of these people is to be accomplished on the unanimous recommendation of Mr. Haworth, a man who was a total failure as an agent, and who, as I said, had private reasons for the recommendation he made. . . ."[6]

Colonel Davidson inclosed with his letter statements made by Tabananica and Horseback, who objected to being moved. Horseback said that it would be a great inconvenience to the Comanches to have their agency so far away. He expected trouble with the Wichitas over the cattle. He said that he spoke for all the Comanches. "We sometimes like to talk to the Commanding Officer [of Fort Sill]," he continued. "When the agent hears of it he finds fault and says we must not talk with the Commanding Officer. I think that the agent and the Commanding Officer should work together. I do not think that the agent has good sense."

[6] Papers relating to removal of Indian agency are to be found in File 5641, AGO, 1878.

Tabananica said, "I agree with what Horseback has said. There is another thing. The Washita is not a good place for our cattle. When the northers come they will drive our cattle into the mountains, and they will be lost. . . . If the agent does not like the place where the agency now is, why does he not select another place near the center of our country?" General Sheridan placed the following comment on Colonel Davidson's letter: "I fully indorse the above views, and I am satisfied, after an experience of more than twenty years, that the principal objection to troops at Indian Agencies, and the removal of the agencies from military posts, has for its main motive a desire to cheat and defraud the Indians by avoiding the presence of officers who would naturally see and report it." Major Pollock, in his refutation of the arguments of the military, stated that the land, the buildings, and the timber were better at Anadarko. He said that he did not find that the Indians were opposed to moving the agency, and that the influence of large numbers of white men at the army post was demoralizing to the Indians. The Kiowa and Comanche agency was consolidated with that of the Wichitas, Caddoes and other minor tribes, and was moved to Anadarko in 1879.

This same year a number of Indians were afflicted with malaria, contracted during a severe epidemic of this disease, which broke out on the reservation. Several died, including the former principal chief of the Kiowas, Lone Wolf, who was buried in an unmarked grave on the north side of Mount Scott. Only his relatives know its exact location. He was succeeded as principal chief by Mamay-day-te, who took the name of Lone Wolf, conferred at the time of the Lost Valley fight in July of 1874. Two other noted Indians had died the preceding year: Asa-toyeh and Satanta. Asa-toyeh will be remembered as the Penateka Comanche chief who guided Colonel Grierson to the site of Fort Sill in December, 1868. His funeral was attended by the garrison; he was buried in the post cemetery.

Satanta committed suicide in the Huntsville prison in Texas. During the last years of his imprisonment he had lost his old cockiness, grown more and more wistful. He could be seen sadly staring north toward Red River. On October 10, 1878, he asked a deputy marshal if there was any chance of his being released again, to which the officer replied, "No"; Satanta was a lifer. The next day the Kiowa threw himself head first from a second-story balcony to the prison courtyard. He died in a few hours, and was buried in the prison cemetery. Thus perished the man who once had said, "When I roam the prairies I feel free and happy, but when I sit down I grow pale and die." To the last he was the embodiment of the wild spirit of the plains Indian. He left four children: two daughters, both of whom married Fort Sill Indian scout Eonah-pah, one of whom still lives near Carnegie; two sons, the eldest being Tsa'l-au-te, who became a member of the Indian police; and the youngest, Mark Auchia, who enlisted in Troop L, Seventh Cavalry. Mark Auchia died at Saddle Mountain March 2, 1935.

One of the most significant changes in the attitude of the Indians at this time was their willingness to assist the authorities in the arrest and trial of members of their own race who had committed crimes or misdemeanors. In the old days no Indian, with the possible exception of Kicking Bird and Horseback, would make any effort to turn over to the authorities guilty Indians. But Agent P. B. Hunt, shortly after taking office, succeeded in organizing a force of Indian police. At first the Indians were unwilling to enrol. The chiefs were not sure that their young men should arrest Indians. Finally on October 1, 1878, they consented. Sankey-dotey, a Kiowa, was made captain. He had under him two lieutenants, four sergeants, and twenty-two privates. The officers received the munificent salary of $10.00 a month, and the privates $5.00.

The Indian police rendered excellent service, and managed to settle without trouble many cases which might have led to serious consequences had civilian peace officers attempted to make arrests. For example, the ridiculous affair at Fort Sill on July 26 might have been avoided had the Indian police been organized at that time. On that day a deputy United States marshal arrived at Fort Sill with a warrant for a Comanche named Esa-to-it who was wanted for attempting to kill a guard the previous year. Esa-to-it had spent the winter in the mountains, but was brought to Sill in the Spring by Quanah and lodged in the guardhouse. The marshal had a capias for him and for two other Comanches who were charged with being accessories in the assault. These Indians were working on a farm operated by prisoners from the guardhouse. The post adjutant, the post interpreter, and the marshal went to the farm to make the arrest. The small guard stationed there in a tent was turned out to assist, and the combined force went to the Indian camp near-by. The two culprits were in the tepee of a medicine man, who urged them to resist. The adjutant directed a burly Negro teamster to hold the medicine man while the sentries clubbed and handcuffed Esa-to-it and two or three other Indians. But the athletic Comanches were more than a match for the officers in the scuffle which ensued. The medicine man passed knives to his comrades. The adjutant and his friends started firing. The medicine man fell wounded and two of the Indians were killed.[7] A more intimate knowledge of the Indian character and mentality might have averted this unfortunate conclusion. For a while it was thought that the Indians might cause trouble over this incident, but, to the surprise of everyone, they did not exhibit much excitement. This was unusual as

[7] *Annual Report of Commissioner of Indian Affairs,* 1878, p. 59.

being the first recorded case in which the Fort Sill Indians did not feel it necessary to indulge in a revenge raid over the death of relatives.

THE CATTLEMEN

One of the principal duties of the new Indian police force was to watch the cattle trail. In this duty they were assisted by troops from the post. Fort Sill maintained a semi-permanent camp at Otter Creek, called Camp Davidson, and another at Soldier Spring. From these camps, patrols were sent along the North Fork and Red River, to the crossing at Doan's store. The cattlemen were prohibited by law from leasing land on the reservation. But they found it easy to move their herds across the river and allow them to graze on Indian land until they were ejected by the troops.

In executing their orders the army officers found it necessary to exercise a great deal of tact and diplomacy. They had to be careful that they returned all the cattle which had been driven across, to give back to the cowboys any firearms which had been taken from them, and to make sure that no Indian stock was included in the herd. They had to satisfy all—cattlemen, Indians, and beef contractors—that the rights of each were being respected. The cattlemen, on conviction of trespass, were fined a dollar for each head of stock. As this was a low grass rental, they paid it willingly and continued to trespass. The reservation line was so long that the few troops and Indian police found it impossible to keep out the cattle. But they tried day and night. The Fort Sill people who were engaged on this duty found it the most unpleasant, thankless task of their military careers.

The trouble over cattle continued through 1880 and into the following year. In 1881 a shortage of crops, brought about by drouth, together with the insufficiency of government rations, caused Mr. Hunt, the agent, to seek a better arrangement with the cattlemen. He offered to allow them to graze their herds on the Indian reservation without molestation if they would furnish free a certain amount of beef to the Indians. This scheme was made immediately necessary by a near outbreak which occurred in June. On June 2 the Kiowas refused to take their beef ration, saying that it was too small, that they could not subsist on so small an allowance. They obviously were in a bad humor; rumors were rife that they intended to kill everyone at the agency. The Wichitas and Delawares moved their women and children into the brush for safety. Mr. Hunt telegraphed to Fort Sill for help. Major Mizner came with five troops, and remained at the agency until the Kiowas quieted down.[8] Mr. Hunt's agreement with the cattlemen was strictly unofficial. He was roundly abused by his superiors when word of it reached Washington,

[8] Old Files, Fort Sill.

but it already had been consummated, so nothing was done to change it. As a result the Indians were more adequately fed for a time, and the Fort Sill people were given a welcome rest from riding the cattle trails. Unfortunately, however, when the time came for the cattlemen to remove their herds in accordance with the agreement, the troops had to eject them.[9]

Hunt realized, as had Colonel Davidson, that the soil and climate of the Kiowa-Comanche reserve were not well adapted to agriculture. He advocated that the Indians be taught to raise cattle and other livestock; but the plan met opposition from certain groups who preferred that the Indians be consumers rather than producers of beef. Furthermore it was hard to obtain enough cattle to start herds for the Indians. Only a few of the more progressive, like Quanah and Tabananica, were able to provide for themselves in this manner. When the crops failed, and the women and children were crying for food, the Indians could not be blamed for killing the few breeding cattle which had been issued to them. The attempt to make farmers of these people was not a success, and remains a failure to this day.

By 1885 the agent and the Indians saw that it was not possible to keep trespassing cattle off the reservation. They saw that they might as well allow the cattle companies to use the grass, and charge them rental for the privilege. In February, 1885, a delegation of Indians, accompanied by Horace Jones, went to Washington to secure official approval of the proposition of renting grazing privileges to the cattlemen. Chief Howea was one of the members of the party. It was his first trip to civilization. He had heard many stories concerning the great number of white men who lived in the eastern part of the United States; but he had been unconvinced. Before starting, he said that he was going to count them in order to determine whether his informants were telling the truth. As the train passed through village after village, and raced on through cities of increasing size, Howea became confused in his effort to count the white men. He drew his blanket over his head and sat in stunned silence. Later, when the train entered the Allegheny Mountains, and plunged into a tunnel, Howea was so frightened that he went into convulsions and became unconscious.[10] In Washington the President refused to have anything to do with the matter of grass leases for the Kiowa and Comanche land, on account of troubles which the government was having with the Cheyennes over similar questions. The Indians were advised that they

[9] An excellent account of the affairs between the government officials and the cattlemen is to be found in Martha Buntin, "The Leasing of Surplus Grazing Land on the Kiowa and Comanche Reservation," *Chronicles of Oklahoma*, Vol. X, No. 3 (September, 1932). See also *idem*, "History of Kiowa, Comanche, and Wichita Indian Agency" (master's thesis, in University of Oklahoma library, Norman).

[10] W. H. Quinette to author.

might make their own arrangements with the cattlemen if they chose; the government would not handle it for them.

On the return trip the delegation stopped off at St. Louis. Mr. Quinette, the post trader at Fort Sill, who was present in the city on business, met them at the Planters' Hotel. When he entered the lobby Mr. Quinette saw Horace Jones and his Indians sitting disconsolately on the stairway. Jones said that they had been waiting an hour or more for the porters to carry their baggage up to the rooms. Quinette told the Indians to go on up. Jones and the redskins were greatly surprised to find their luggage waiting in the rooms. When it was explained that it had been brought up on an elevator Jones looked very sheepish. He was no more familiar with city life than were the Indians.

A little later Quinette took the whole party out to see the sights of the town. Across the street was a concave mirror of the kind which distorts the image. Jones and the Indians were vastly amused to see themselves first as tall thin men and then, when the mirror was reversed, as extraordinarily squat and fat. A considerable crowd gathered to watch the reactions of the Indians.

That night the Indians were taken to the banquet room of the hotel for dinner. Since they were in native garb, Quinette thought they would feel more at home if they dined in private. When they all had taken their seats Quanah unfolded his napkin and laid it on his lap in the approved fashion. The other Indians carefully followed suit. Horace Jones adjusted his pince-nez spectacles to study the menu. When he had given his order, Saddey-taker (Dog Eater) reached for the glasses. He peered through them owlishly at the bill of fare, which he held upside down; after a long period of concentration he turned to the waiter and boomed, "Whoa-haw!" which is the Indians' word for beef. The other Indians laughed until they cried, and so did Jones. When the meal was over the Indians found that they had eaten so much they were unable to partake of the fine fruit which was placed in bowls before them. They rectified this by filling their blankets with apples, oranges, and bananas, much to the embarrassment of the white men and the amusement of the waiters.

The granting of lease privileges to cattlemen did not stop all the troubles over cattle. Most of the cattle drivers who conveyed herds across the reservation to the rail terminals in Kansas kept the Indians appeased by giving them occasional beeves. One Kiowa named Polant took advantage of this to impose on the stockmen. It was his habit to ride along the trail demanding "whoa-haw." When the cowboys refused, as they did occasionally, Polant would strike them across the face with his quirt. The cowboys submitted to this because they were on the Indian reservation and were fearful of starting a massacre. But complaints were lodged against Polant and another Kiowa named Komal-ty for these acts, and for killing stray cattle. On September 21, 1885, a marshal came to the agency at Anadarko with a warrant for Polant and Komal-ty. Agent Lee Hall, who had succeeded Mr. Hunt, called the Indians into his office and told them that he was going to arrest them. He directed them to wait until he was ready. He was waiting for a detail of troops to arrive from Fort Sill. The marshal sat down outside under a tree. As there were a number of Kiowas loafing around the premises, the marshal and Hall hesitated to take action until the troops arrived. Unfortunately the message sent to Sill went astray and the soldiers never appeared.[11] After waiting three hours to be arrested, the Indians became restive and started to leave the office. Hall rashly attempted to intercept them. There was a strenuous scrimmage. Lone Wolf and several other Kiowas rushed in to participate. Lone Wolf tried to cut Hall's throat but was prevented by Kiowa Bill. In the confusion Polant and Komal-ty escaped. Several days later the two Indians were arrested quietly in the Kiowa camps. Hall, who bore them no grudge, soon procured their release, for he did not consider that they had committed any great crime in killing cattle which were trespassing on the reservation.

Another source of trouble over cattle came from thievery. The stockmen were, of course, the principal sufferers, but they had a protective association and were able to look after themselves. The Indians also lost cattle from rustling, and they could ill afford to lose them. The cattle and other stock stolen from the Indians generally were run into the Chickasaw country, where the brands were altered. In June of 1886 Big Bow lost seventy-five head of horses. He and Ad-la-te (Loud Talker) followed the trail of the thieves, overtaking them near Mobeetie, Texas. While the Indians were showing one of the white men papers authorizing them to be absent from the reservation, one of the thieves treacherously shot at Big Bow at close range, but missed him. Big Bow killed this rustler and frightened the other away. The Kiowa had to stand trial for homicide, but was exonerated.

P. B. Hunt recommended, and so did Hall, that an Indian court be established to try Indians. This court was set up in 1886, and operated successfully until the end of the reservation system in 1901. The judges were Quanah, Lone Wolf, and White Man (a Kiowa-Apache). They served for $10.00 a month, and tried every imaginable kind of case. These judges fully appreciated the dignity of their position. They had a way of driving straight at the truth that would do credit to more sophisticated tribunals.

There is a record at Fort Sill of a case tried before this court, in which an Indian named Mah-kah-do was charged with killing a dog belonging to a man at Fort Sill named Dawson. The accused attempted

[11] Martha Buntin, "History of Kiowa, Comanche, and Wichita Agency."

every means of circumlocution in pleading his case, but the judges, with inexorable directness, kept him to the subject at hand. Finally they fined him $10.00, to be paid to the owner of the deceased canine. The agent, in reviewing the case, stated that he believed that the Indian shot the dog merely in a spirit of amusement. Apparently a jovial spirit covered at least one sin, if not a multitude.

INDIANS IN UNIFORM

After the close of the Indian war in 1875, a detachment of Indian scouts was maintained at Fort Sill. These scouts were used to carry messages from the post to detachments of troops camped on Otter Creek, and to other outposts; they also helped to guard the paymaster, search for outlaws and deserters, and the like. The camp of the scouts usually was northwest of the post, near the trader's store, but sometimes the Indians camped near White Wolf Ford. A number of former warriors—raiders who had been engaged in hostilities against the whites, and even against the troops themselves—were later enlisted as scouts, and performed loyal service. Among these were Eonah-pah, Set-maunte, Pago-to-goodle, Tsa'l-au-te, and other Kiowas. Not many Comanches enlisted.

In 1892 the government attempted the experiment of forming several Indian troops of cavalry at various western posts. At Fort Sill was organized Troop L, Seventh Cavalry, commanded by Lieutenant Hugh L. Scott. It consisted mostly of Kiowas, with a few Apaches and Comanches. Quanah and Tabananica prevented the Comanches from enlisting. Quanah gave as his reason the fact that the missionaries were teaching the Indians that it was wrong to go to war; therefore it was not consistent that the white people should employ the Indians in an organization whose sole business was fighting.[12]

Although Lieutenant Scott, in organizing his Indian troop, used as his principal enlisted assistants Sergeants Clancy and Stecker, I-see-o was appointed first sergeant. Since I-see-o could neither speak nor read English, he was only a figurehead, at least as far as dealing with the whites was concerned. In talking to Scott he used the sign language, in which the latter was as adept as the Indians. I-see-o was a holdover from the scout detachment. He was over the enlistment age, but Scott got him in. When he came to the table to be signed up as a soldier the recruiting officer asked him his name. "I-see-o," was the reply. As I-see-o was well known around Fort Sill under his former name of Tahbone-mah, it is reasonable to suppose that the recruiting officer recognized him. But nothing more was said, and Tahbone-mah, aged about forty-two, was regularly enlisted as I-see-o, aged twenty-nine.

The Indians made good soldiers, within their limitations. Their aver-

[12] George Hunt to author.

261

age in marksmanship was high, their discipline good, and they were proud of the uniform. It furnished them a means of gaining prestige, and even today the veterans of Troop L are among the most respected members of their tribes. The Indians, like other nationalities, needed something to be proud of. The older Indians, the members of the passing generation, had their war exploits to talk about. But the rising generation, being forced to become farmers, had little to look forward to, and no way in which to distinguish themselves. Agriculture is an honorable and ancient profession, and at times a profitable one. But not for the Indians.

One of the duties of Troop L was to provide turkey and deer for General Miles's holiday dinners. General Miles, who was department commander in the nineties, was accustomed to send to Sill for venison and other game. Occasionally he came to the Indian reservation to hunt. On these visits he was met by Scott and Troop L. Perhaps it was partly on account of this association that Fort Sill was not abandoned when the War Department considered vacating some of the frontier posts which had outlived their usefulness. Miles was fond of Fort Sill on account of its history and the excellent hunting which the region afforded.

Troop L was quartered on the flat ground immediately north of the trader's store. Here the Indian soldiers lived with their families in canvas tepees. They spent a good part of their time playing monte, of which the Indians were passionately fond. Their military duties were not onerous.

In 1897 the War Department disbanded all the Indian troops, including the one at Fort Sill, although the latter was considered a success. Since that day a few Indians have served in the army at Fort Sill, but only as individuals. During the World War many of them went overseas with the A.E.F., where they fought bravely.

THE MESSIAH

ONCE there was a Golden Age in which all women were models of grace and loveliness and all men were stalwart heroes. Or so the legend goes—a legend which in various forms may be found among nearly all races. But in later days, when the people groaned under the foot of an alien conqueror, "how natural was the dream of a redeemer, an Arthur, who shall return from exile or awake from a deep sleep to drive out the usurper and win back for his people what they have lost. The hope becomes a faith and the faith becomes the creed of priests and prophets, until the hero is a god and the dream a religion, looking to some great miracle of nature for its culmination and accomplishment."[1]

This messianic urge was part and parcel of the life and hope of the Plains Indians in the '80's and '90's. The military campaigns of 1874–75 and their aftermath left the Kiowas and Comanches disarmed and subjugated—impoverished in goods and in spirit. During the next few years the buffalo, which formerly had roamed the prairie in countless millions, totally disappeared. This phenomenon has few parallels in the annals of natural history; small wonder is it that the Indians, children of nature that they were, and ignorant of the vast forces at work, could not comprehend the reality of so awful a calamity. They told themselves that the buffalo merely had gone into hiding or had been shut up in a vast cavern beneath the surface of the earth, from which they could be released by proper prayer and sacrifice.

In 1881 there arose among the Kiowas a self-appointed prophet and medicine man named Dau-te-kaun. Renaming himself Pau-tape-ty (Buffalo Bull Returns), he announced that he would conduct ceremonies for bringing back the buffalo. The whole tribe was invited to be present at the bend of the Washita, between the present sites of Carnegie and

---

[1] James Mooney, "The Ghost Dance Religion," *Fourteenth Annual Report of the Bureau of Ethnology* (Washington, 1896), p. 657.

Mountain View, where a medicine tepee was to be erected on the high bank of the river. Not all of the Kiowas attended. There were a few skeptics like Stumbling Bear, Sun Boy, and a number of young men, who could not be bothered. But most of them came with their travois, wagons, squaws, and papooses. As old Tay-bodal said, "I like to be where there is a big gathering of men smoking."[2]

Pau-tape-ty chose fourteen assistants, seven men and seven women, whom he instructed to prepare proper costumes and be ready to take part in the ceremonies. One of the girls, Pe-ah-to-mah, describes what happened: "The women had skirts and jackets of green calico, with sleeves made of red bandanas. The men were naked except for their loin cloths and moccasins, and were painted red from head to foot. The medicine man wore a jacket of coyote fur, covered with blue beads. In one hand he carried a red pipe, and in the other a coyote fur. The other men held red fox furs. From the women's small braids blue beads were hanging, and soft white eagle feathers were tied to the back of their hair.

"We put on these costumes before sunrise of the appointed day and assembled in the medicine tepee. Outside were gathered all the rest of the tribe, and we could hear the roar of conversation as they waited anxiously for the spectacle to commence. Pau-tape-ty led a procession around the inside of the tent, circling four times, followed in single file by the men, and then the women. He was praying with his arms stretched out. Then we came out and stood in line facing the sun, which was just peeping over the eastern horizon. After prayers to the sun we faced about. Inside the tepee we could hear the keepers of the *grandma gods*. They were beating old buffalo hides with their sticks and singing:

> '*Hi-yah, he-yah, hi-yah, he-yah,*
> *Ko-la, ko-la, hi-yah, ko-la.*'

"The whole tribe, crying for mercy, joined in the prayer and song. We went inside the tent and the crowd dispersed. Secretly I did not have full faith. But I was very young.

"The medicine man placed two long poles in front of the tepee on either side of the door, and stretched a red blanket between them to serve as a veil to the mysteries to be conducted within. Over his blue beaded jacket he threw a red blanket decorated with eagle feathers. We stayed inside the tepee all day. From time to time the medicine man had us drink seven times from a sacred drinking cup.[3]

[2] Tay-bodal was an old Kiowa from whom Mooney secured much of the material for his *Calendar History of the Kiowa Indians*. Mooney spells the name "T'e Bodal." The succeeding account of the mysteries celebrated by Pau-tape-ty was given to the author by the wife of Hunting Horse, who, when a young girl, was selected as one of the medicine man's assistants.

[3] The sacred drinking cup in this case was an old fruit jar.

"Toward evening his prophecy became very strong. He told everybody to dress up after sundown. 'Tonight is our real time. We are going to do something that we have been wanting to do.'

"He called on me to sit on one side of the door and Amo-tah on the other. Between us was a little round altar-hole dug in the ground. Pau-tape-ty covered this with a round rock, about a foot in diameter, which he took from near the fireplace hole. He told us to grasp the rock and not to let it fly up until he gave the word. If the stone commenced to shake we were not to be frightened. This was the place from which the buffalo were to burst forth, and the rock was a cork to hold them in until the medicine man was ready to release them.

"We laid our hands on the rock and commenced to tremble with fear and anxious anticipation.

"The medicine man said, 'Get ready now. Keep your mind on this. Don't let it wander to other things. Put your real faith in it.' Then everyone picked up their fox hides and commenced to sing:

'Hi-yah, he-yah, hi-yah. . . .'

"We all felt scared and funny. Pau-tape-ty was bawling like a buffalo, and called on everyone to join him.

" 'If my prophecy is a lie,' he said, 'I will pay with my life. You are safe however.' Then he began to dance around inside the tepee, circling it four times. The strain was too much for me. I was getting ready to run if that rock moved. I didn't want to be trampled when the buffalo burst forth. On the other side of the stone was Amo-tah, with tears running down his cheeks. He was holding the rock tightly and shaking and trembling all over.

"Pau-tape-ty stood on the west side of the tent and howled like a wolf. He was trying to imitate Sindi.[4]

"Nothing happened.

"Then he said, 'I have one more chance. Let's sing again.' There was a buffalo robe in the middle of the floor. He lay down on it and tried to drive out the buffalo by grunting and lowing. The robe began to shake and move. A noise came like a cow in the brush. But nothing else happened. Then Pau-tape-ty dived under the robe and said, 'You told me to do this. But you have brought me to shame.' He came out covered with sweat and looking awful.

"This ceremony was repeated and maintained for a night and a day. No buffalo appeared. Finally the medicine man was in despair. He called in the keepers of the grandma gods and made ready for a supreme trial. He intended to make a sacrifice of human skin. He went outside and had one of the keepers strip some skin from his back, cut in the shape

[4] Mythical hero of the Kiowas.

of a buffalo. He wound this bleeding piece around the pole in front of the tepee. Then the seven male associates cut strips of skin like thongs, from their living bodies, beginning at the wrist and running down the arm and body, down the leg to the ankle. These also were wrapped around the poles. It was very painful. Amo-tah has the scars to this day. But it failed."

The ceremonies kept up for ten days and ten nights. The audience outside began to get restless. Criticism of the prophet grew more vociferous. The people stopped making presents to him. Some of them suggested that the fourteen neophytes were concerned mostly with love-making, and that the whole thing was a fake. Pau-tape-ty tried to maintain interest by organizing Indian ball games and other amusements. He claimed that the appearance of the buffalo was postponed on account of acts showing lack of faith, committed by various persons in the tribe. But, in spite of sustained efforts by the prophet, the buffalo herds did not return. The people gradually lost interest. The prophet began to droop; within a year he was dead.

Soon afterwards another false prophet made his appearance among the Kiowas. This was none other than Botalye, of the "He-wouldn't-listen-to-them" fame. Young Botalye set up a medicine tepee on the cap rocks between the present sites of Komalty and Gotebo, where he announced that he was going to bring the sun down from the sky. He placed a sacred object under a blanket in the tepee, and solicited presents for the privilege of feeling the object through the blanket. His business prospered for a time, but fell off rapidly when his brother gave it as his opinion that the sacred object was only a discarded door knob, and that the proceedings were a private speculation on the part of the "prophet."

THE MISSIONARIES

About this same time different Christian denominations began to send missionaries into the Indian country. The first to arrive was the Reverend J. B. Wicks of the Episcopal diocese of New York. He came to Fort Sill with two converted Indians, Zontam and Sait-kop-te, who had been prisoners in Florida. In June of 1881 he preached to the Indians near Fort Sill, then went to Anadarko. Other missions were soon started among the Indians. Later the Baptists opened a church at Rainy Mountain. Mennonites came to Post Oak Creek, a few miles west of Quanah Parker's house. Methodists under J. J. Methvin, and Catholics under Father Isidore came to Anadarko. In the nineties, when the Apache prisoners were at Fort Sill, the Dutch Reformed Church built a mission in what is now the Punchbowl, just north of Medicine Bluff. The pastor there was the Reverend Frank Wright, son of one of the principal chiefs of the Choctaw Nation. Mr. Wright was a charming and talented young man, whose sermons and fine baritone solos in the old chapel at Fort Sill were greatly enjoyed and appreciated by the military personnel. Mission Ridge was named for his mission.

The value of the work done by these missionaries in civilizing and humanizing the Indians cannot be overestimated. Many Indians today are devout Christians, considerably better behaved than some of their white neighbors. A convincing testimonial to the good character of the Indians is given by W. H. Quinette, who states that he and other Indian traders used to ride through the reserve carrying large sums of money, without fear of being robbed by the Indians. The red men bought merchandise from the traders on credit, payment being made in the camps when the Indian agent turned over the quarterly collections of grass-rental money. Quinette says that on these occasions he drove for many miles through the Indian country with as much as $10,000 in his buggy, yet never felt the slightest fear. This sense of security was due in part, of course, to the fact that white desperadoes had been driven to cover by the troops and civil authorities; but it is also significant of the inherent honesty and good will of the Indians. Today, when the country is settled by white men, such a condition does not exist. No man's life or property is wholly safe at any time.

At first, however, the Indians were slow to listen to the teachings of the missionaries. The medicine men played on their superstitions. Old customs died hard. The strange language was a barrier to early understanding. Many amusing incidents are recorded concerning the Indians' early reception of the teachings of the missionaries. A church was established for the Comanches in one of the vacant traders' stores on Cache Creek south of the post. The preacher, curiously enough, was named Gassaway. He was sincere, and preached a fair sermon. But he was an exhorter. The Indians, who had come out of curiosity to hear his first sermon, were dismayed to hear the preacher shout and see him shake his fists aloft. In a few moments they arose and solemnly filed out of the building. "He is mad at us," they said. At first Reverend Gassaway tried to get Horace Jones to interpret for him. Jones was reluctant but said he would try it once. Everything went along nicely until they came to the Lord's Prayer, but when Jones repeated in Comanche the words, "Give us this day our daily bread," the Indians, thinking they were about to get something to eat, stood up in a body and shouted, "Oh-ho! Oh-ho!" It was hard to quiet them.[5]

The first effect of the introduction of missionary teachings was to confuse the Indians in their religious concepts. Many of them got the hazy idea that the Messiah was a man who was coming to deliver the Indians from their enemies and to restore the old order. A few years later,

[5] Reminiscences of W. H. Quinette.

when the Ghost Dance religion came down from the north, they were prepared to believe anything they heard.

P'OINKIA AND THE END OF THE SUN DANCE

In 1887, a new medicine man named P'oinkia arose among the Kiowas. This miracle-worker professed to have powers which would make the Indians invincible against the bullets of the white man, and would enable them to drive out of the country those people who were the cause of all their trouble. P'oinkia told the Kiowas that before he could bestow this magic upon them they must purge themselves of all practices which they had picked up from the whites. They must give up matches and return to the use of flint and steel in starting fires. The white man's clothing must be thrown away, and all children removed from the schools.

It was this latter edict which brought P'oinkia to grief. But in the meantime he caused dissension among his own people by insisting that every bit of food consumed must be blessed by him. The best portions of any game they killed had to be brought to him and any crops which they might raise had to be given his approval before they partook of them. He also prescribed that before they placed any food in their mouths they must hold it up to the sky, then thumb it to the ground. He dressed a dozen or more neophytes in special buckskin garments, and drilled them to move always in straight lines, holding aloft fancy medicine lances and ceremonial forked sticks. At night they sat in a tepee until late hours, smoking a pipe and chanting. He distributed red clay to the people, which they were expected to use for face paint in place of that purchased from the traders.

Doubtless most of this has little apparent significance, but most of the Indians were ready for anything which might bring back the old times. Unfortunately a group headed by Big Tree scoffed at this new prophet. Big Tree calmly ate his meat without waving it in the air or thumbing it to the ground; he thrust it directly in his capacious mouth and chewed away in stolid unconcern over the dire predictions of the medicine man. He even refused to have his food blessed by P'oinkia. On one occasion he and his buddy, Gotebo, visited Quitan. The latter had a fine patch of melons and corn, in prime condition to be eaten. "Come on," urged Big Tree. "Don't pay any attention to that fool, P'oinkia. Let us get a load of melons and fill up." Quitan was horrified. He was a disciple of Maman-ti, and was full of superstition. Big Tree sliced a ripe melon and commenced to eat. Gotebo began to cook some fine roasting ears. Several bystanders joined them. Soon a big feast was in full sway.

P'oinkia was enraged by these irreligious doings. But he could do nothing about it. Big Tree and Gotebo were formidable fellows. They had been warriors in their day, and there was no assurance that they were yet fully tamed. The prophet had to do something to save his face. He predicted that all who did not join him would be destroyed by a tornado which he threatened to produce. He moved his place of business to Elk Creek, and called on the tribe to take their children out of school and follow him. Most of them did so. The few who remained on their farms spent their time watching apprehensively for the promised cyclone. Daily gatherings were held at Elk Creek. P'oinkia told the people that if any white people advanced beyond a hill which stood east of the camp he would bring down a bolt from the heavens to slay them. The credulous Kiowas seemed to believe this.

Tahbone-mah (I-see-o) carried word of all this to Fort Sill. He reported that the tribe was preparing to go on the warpath. Three troops of cavalry were sent to Anadarko and placed under orders of the agent. Joshua Given, the son of old Satank, was there as a missionary. An educated Indian, he realized that in an encounter with the army his people might be exterminated. He asked the agent to hold the troops at the agency until he could visit the camp at Elk Creek and try to persuade the Kiowas of their error. With considerable reluctance the agent consented. Joshua, on his arrival at the camp, found the Kiowas standing around with weapons in their hands, glowering at him. They hated him because he had adopted the ways and religion of the white man.

P'oinkia met him at the door of the medicine tepee, saying, "Tau-koi-te, why do you come to this village?"

Joshua replied, "Don't you realize that you are leading our people into serious trouble? Already the soldiers are at Anadarko. The Kiowas should be plowing their fields, the children should be at school. I have talked with the soldier chiefs and with the agent. They are waiting for my return. You must listen to my proposal. If you do not, I will return to the soldiers, who will come here and destroy you."

"These people are under my control," responded the prophet, sternly. "I rule all of them except a few doubters like Big Tree, who will be killed by a cyclone which I am going to send. What is your proposal?"

"Let us talk privately," said Joshua, drawing him into the tepee. "You ought to test your power before you subject our people to so great a risk. If it fails the soldiers will wipe out the tribe. Let me come here with two army officers. You stand on one side of the tent and they on the other. Let them shoot you through the heart. If on the third day you rise from the dead, we will know that you are the true Messiah. The whites as well as the Indians will follow your lead. It is up to you!"

The medicine man was confounded. He realized that Joshua had outwitted him. Summoning his wits he made answer: "I will extend my time. You may tell the soldiers to return to Fort Sill. I will send the children back to school, and the people back to their farms. But if I call another meeting, I don't want you or anyone else to interfere."[6]

The excitement died away, the troops returned to the post. P'oinkia's influence faded.

After Pau-tape-ty, Botalye, and P'oinkia failed to deliver the Indians from Pharaoh, no prophets appeared for three years. Even the sacred medicine dance was abolished. The last dance was held on Oak Creek in the summer of 1887. The Kiowas attempted to hold a dance in 1889 but were forcibly prevented. The Sun Dance was opposed by the agent on the ground that it took the people away from their farms at the very time the crops needed attention. The missionaries objected to it because they considered it barbarous and pagan. Actually the dance did the Indians no harm. It was pleasantly social as well as religious in character. It was a deep-rooted part of their life; they felt that their health and well-being depended on it. Other tribes have been permitted to continue their ceremonial dances, without hurting anyone; today these dances are recognized as an important part of native folklore and custom.

THE GHOST DANCE RELIGION[7]

The failure of the false prophets to bring back the buffalo, the forced cessation of the Sun Dance, and the growing realization that the end of the old free days was in truth at hand, all combined to produce in the Fort Sill Indians a mental state peculiarly receptive for the Ghost Dance religion. They were ready for a messiah.

In the summer of 1890 the inhabitants of the whole western country began to hear stories of a Jesus who was coming to the Indians. It was not clear whether he was the Christ spoken of by the missionaries, or that mythical hero common to all Indian tribes, or a combination of the two. But he was coming to the Indians alone. He had come to the white men and they had killed him. Now the Indians were to have their chance. The old earth was worn out. The white men had cut down the trees, plowed up the grass, and thus had dried up the streams. They had killed off the buffalo, the elk and the antelope. Now they were killing off the Indians. There seemed to be no end to their thirst for destruction. Hence Jesus was bringing a new earth, which was sliding slowly like a glacier out of the northwest, covering the old land. On this new earth were the wild horses, the elk, and the buffalo. Best of all, there were on it all the resurrected spirits of dead relatives, all of the features of life in that golden age before the arrival of the white man. On it were to be reunited dead and living relatives and friends. The entire Indian race was to live in a life of

[6] Sources principally Mooney and George Hunt.

[7] James Mooney gives a splendid account of the Ghost Dance excitement in the *Fourteenth Annual Report of the Bureau of Ethnology.*

aboriginal happiness, forever free from death, disease, and misery. What was to happen to the white man? It did not matter much, because he was only a bad dream to be forgotten, but he was to be pushed back by this glacier into the sea from whence he came. The Indians were to be lifted up by the magic of the Ghost Dance feathers, and alight on the new earth. They did not need to bother about the white man. Jesus would take care of him. All they had to do was to join in the new dance, watch and pray.

It was all very wonderful. The Fort Sill Indians, when they heard these stories, became greatly excited. The news came from sources in which they had supreme confidence, that is, from their own race. It was so good it had to be true. The more they heard the more they wanted to hear. Soon they were given an opportunity to receive an apostle, one who had visited, seen, and talked to the Messiah himself! The apostle or prophet was an Arapaho named Sitting Bull. He came to the Washita and introduced the Ghost Dance among the Caddoes, Wichitas, Kiowas, and Comanches. The skeptical Comanches were slow to take interest, but the Kiowas and other tribes whole-heartedly adopted the new religion.

News of these goings-on reached the whites. Some of the more ignorant dwellers of the western plains were affected by a superstitious fear. They were not sure but what there might be some truth in what the Indians had to say was in store for them. They were of the type who sit up all night watching a comet and waiting for the end of the world. Others were alarmed lest the Indians organize a general uprising. After all, it was but a few years since the last Indian wars, and the prairies were not yet thickly settled. The authorities were importuned from every side to use military force to suppress the Ghost Dance. In the north this was done, resulting in the tragic and unnecessary battle of Wounded Knee. At Fort Sill a different method was employed. The post commander called in Lieutenant H. L. Scott, who was known to have the confidence of the Indians. He was directed to spend the winter traveling among the Indian camps, keeping an eye on those who might become disaffected. Scott took with him a few enlisted assistants to move and operate his camp, and the faithful scout I-see-o.

Scott recognized that the proper procedure for him was not to oppose the Indians in their dances, but to keep himself informed of all that was going on under the surface so that he could give the authorities timely notice if anything serious developed. He used I-see-o as an agent; the Indian was made to understand that he should do what Scott directed, even though it got him into trouble with his own people. In this manner he would be instrumental in saving the Indians, and eventually he would be set up on a high pedestal above them all.

I-see-o was a simple, kindly fellow without any influence among the Kiowas other than that which resulted from his association with the military. He never learned to speak English, and conversed with Scott entirely by means of the sign language. He was a simple product of the stone age, who knew nothing but what he had learned on the sunswept prairies and at the council fires of the tribal elders. He was totally ignorant of the ways of the white man except as he had observed him at Fort Sill or the agency, and was absolutely unable to understand what the Ghost Dance was all about, or its development elsewhere. He was instructed to visit Indian camps and keep Scott informed as to what was going on. Other Indians at times made reports to Scott, but a definite arrangement was made with I-see-o which the Indian kept with utmost fidelity. "If any Indian was talking bad," Scott said, "I would know all about it in less than twenty-four hours, and I would take steps to put his trolley back on the wire."[8]

The clamor among the white populace and press to use the army to suppress the movement was growing daily. The whole countryside was frightened stiff, according to Scott. But he opposed interference by the army, and his superiors supported him. He took the position that the dance itself was harming no one, any more than a cadet hop. He felt that he had complete control, and could give timely warning in case anything serious developed. To use force would merely incite resistance among the Indians. They believed that Jesus was going to do everything. Scott declared that the prophecy would fall of its own weight eventually. This was exactly what happened. The Indians on the reservation were carried through the whole excitement without any bloodshed and without any increased hard feeling toward the whites.

Meanwhile, Scott was anxious to see Sitting Bull, whom he regarded as a mountebank. Scott, when he succeeded in overtaking the Arapaho apostle, was forced to alter his opinion. Sitting Bull was sincere, and evidently as much deluded as any of his disciples. The Indians followed him around as the crowds did Christ in the Holy Land, striving to touch the hem of his garment. Any Indian who succeeded in getting close to him would grasp his hand and repeat a long and earnest prayer, sometimes aloud, sometimes with the lips silently moving, and frequently with tears rolling down the cheeks, and the whole body trembling violently from stress of emotion.[9]

The dance itself, as organized by Sitting Bull, consisted in the participants' forming a large circle, with hands clasped, and moving slowly around to the cadence of a chant, while the medicine man in the center

---

[8] H. L. Scott to General William Cruikshank, December 13, 1933; *see also* H. L. Scott, *Some Memories of a Soldier* (New York: D. Appleton-Century Company, 1928), pp. 146-55.

[9] Mooney, *op. cit.*, pp. 896-97.

strove to induce a hypnotic trance in each of the dancers. Soon various Indians would succumb to this hypnosis, induced no doubt in part by their own religious frenzy. They would fall on the ground in a stupor and remain there for as much as an hour, while the dance went on. While under this trance they were supposed to have visions in which they met dead relatives, and thus have a foretaste of what was to come when the Messiah arrived. Sitting Bull received many valuable presents from his disciples, especially from the Kiowas.

One of the most deeply affected was a young Kiowa named Ahpeatone.[10] Ahpeatone finally determined to travel north and see the Messiah for himself. Recently he had lost a little son of whom he was extremely fond, and he thought that by visiting the Messiah he could see and talk to his child again. A collection of money for travel expense was taken up among the Indians, and Ahpeatone, in company with another Kiowa, departed for the north. The companion soon returned, but Ahpeatone persevered. He visited the Sioux agency, was told that the Messiah was farther west. Going on to the country of the Bannocks, he was directed elsewhere. But Ahpeatone would not give up. After considerable hardship, tramping the railroads in the winter, working to earn his way, he finally arrived in the Piute country, Mason Valley, Nevada. He was told that Jesus was inside a little hogan, and would see him the following day. In the morning Ahpeatone dressed himself in his best clothes and was admitted into the Presence. Here he saw a man lying on a rude bed, his face covered with a blanket. It was a Piute Indian known as John Wilson, he who had started the whole movement, which now had gone further than he ever had intended it should. In the interview which followed Ahpeatone was completely disillusioned. The Messiah could not show him his dead child. He had no supernatural sight whatever. And, most damning of all to Ahpeatone, the stigmata (signs of the crucifixion) were missing. The Kiowa sadly turned away and took his journey home to his people.

When it was learned at the agency that Ahpeatone was returning from his pilgrimage, the agent had all the Indians assembled to hear what Ahpeatone had to tell. Sitting Bull also was there. The scene was highly dramatic. The Indians sat in tense silence, their faces eager with anticipation. But as Ahpeatone unfolded his story their disappointment was tragic. Their whole world was swept away. Some were simply stunned. Others refused to believe that Ahpeatone was telling the truth. Sitting Bull was called on to speak. He denied Ahpeatone's charge that he wilfully had deluded the people in order to enrich himself. He offered to return the presents which had been given him. The Indians dispersed and went back to their homes. A few continued the dance for a time, but

[10] Ahpeatone was a son of Red Otter and a nephew of the old Lone Wolf.

gradually it was given up. Spring had come, the promised time for the arrival of the Messiah. Summer came and faded. Winter approached and nothing happened. Eventually the Indians realized that their hopes were groundless. Most of them sank into an apathy of despair.

An absurd anticlimax occurred at Fort Sill. When Scott returned to the post he found that many of the officers and their families had not witnessed a ghost dance, and were curious to do so. So Scott called in Poafebitty, a Comanche, and a number of his friends, and asked them to stage a mock ghost dance for the benefit of the post. The Comanches, with considerable amusement, agreed. They invited some Cheyennes and Arapahoes, who were practiced in the dance, down to Fort Sill, promising them several beeves if they would put on a dance. The dance was held for two or three nights in front of the trader's store. Finally the beef gave out and the visiting performers packed up and went home. But the dance went on! Poafebitty and his cohorts, who had started the affair in a spirit of fun, had become seriously interested. Some of them even went into trances! Soon the excitement wore off and they sheepishly retired to their camps. Only a few Indian children remained to dance, in imitation of their elders.[11]

INCIDENT OF THE FROZEN SCHOOL CHILDREN

On January 9, 1891, three Kiowa boys attending the Indian school at Anadarko ran away from school on account of a whipping administered to one of them by the teacher, a Mr. Wherrit. The children attempted to flee to the Kiowa camps on Stinking Creek, some thirty miles west of the agency. But a severe blizzard overtook them, and they were found by the Indians on the side of a bleak hill, frozen to death.

The Kiowas were greatly disturbed. They began to congregate near the agency, and their attitude was thought to be threatening. The teacher hid for two days in the rafters of the school building, then slipped out of the country, never to return.

The agent telegraphed to Fort Sill for assistance. The post commander, Colonel Carlton, desired to send a squadron of cavalry, but was persuaded against this course by Lieutenant H. L. Scott, who told him that he could go with I-see-o and quiet the Indians. This he did, though not without an argument with the agent, the principal of the school, and others, who desired strong action to be taken against the Indians. They wanted to see the arrest of the uncle of one of the boys, who had used his quirt on the principal. But Scott was of the opinion that if force were used it might cause a senseless tragedy. With the aid of I-see-o he succeeded in getting the Kiowas to disperse quietly, though they were grieving over the death of the children.

[11] Informants: Poafebitty, George Hunt, and Mr. Quinette.

A description furnished by the Indians of the discovery of the bodies of the boys illustrates a little-known side of Indian character: A dog owned by one of the children led relatives to a hill southwest of Zodaltone Springs, where the boys were lying. Luther Samaunt, an uncle, drove up in a wagon to carry the bodies home. Members of the family and friends were standing around gazing at the boys and crying. Luther, the tears streaming down his cheeks, jumped from the wagon. As he did so the suspenders on the back of his overalls caught on the brake handle; Luther hung in mid-air, squirming and struggling ineffectually to free himself. The other Indians commenced to laugh heartily at his ludicrous position, and Luther himself was forced to grin sheepishly. For the moment sorrow was forgotten.

THE POLANT INCIDENT

In September of 1891 many of the Kiowas were camped on the east bank of Elk Creek, near its junction with the North Fork of Red River. Bob Polant,[12] a large, heavy-set Indian of about thirty years, was preparing for a peyote festival. He sent several young men to a cattle ranch near the site of Warren to obtain a steer for the feast. The Indians returned with the report that the request had been refused by the cowboys. Polant said that he would see about it personally.

The following morning about eight o'clock Polant mounted his horse and rode to the ranch, which was in Greer County, about two miles south of the battlefield of Soldier Spring. Mr. J. P. Dale, who was living in the area at the time, states that Polant had cut several steers out of a herd, and was starting away with them when he was intercepted by one of the employes of the ranch. Polant was notoriously quarrelsome and a trouble-maker, but the cowboy, a newcomer, did not know this. When Polant made his usual gesture of reaching for his Winchester, the white man swiftly drew his pistol and shot him. Later in the day several Kiowas who were camped at Tepee Mountain crossed the river to visit a trader's store. They heard that a Kiowa had been killed near the ranch house; two of them, Kiowa Bill and Elk Creek Charley, promptly rode to Little Bow's camp at Sheep Mountain, where they repeated the news. A large number of Kiowa men had assembled at Little Bow's camp for a big dinner. They decided that probably it was Polant who had been killed.

About four o'clock Tone-mah, Long Horn, Odle-pau, Set-keahty, Black Owl, Domaunt, and Black Buffalo mounted their horses and rode west to recover the body. When they got within about fifty yards of the ranch house they saw Polant's grey horse tied to an oak tree. All around the house were crowds of heavily armed white men, watching silently. Polant was lying on his side. Tone-mah dismounted and turned him over.

[12] Sometimes called Polang, or Poolant (Creeping Snake).

He had been shot through the head; his loaded carbine was clasped in his arms. The Indians knew that tradition, tribal and family honor, and everything else they believed in demanded that they start a fight then and there. But they restrained themselves. The odds against them were too great. They were faced with the problem of how to carry the body of Polant away. Because of the hot sun it had bloated to almost twice its normal size. Some of the Indians were unwilling to dismount. One or two of the others were weak and small. Finally, a few of the bolder fellows succeeded in balancing the corpse across the saddle of a gentle horse, and they retreated slowly with the unwieldy burden. As they neared the river they were met by some other Kiowas with a wagon. They took Polant across Elk Creek and buried him.

The Kiowas immediately began considering plans for revenge. The white settlers were well aware of this; women and children in the near-by farms were sent to Navajo for safety. A few of the more timorous even proposed that they should appease the Indians by delivering up the cowboy to them, but the majority did not entertain this idea for a moment. For the next two days armed parties on both sides of the line watched each other sullenly. A fine war was in the making. But word of the impending outbreak reached Fort Sill. Lieutenant H. L. Scott made a forced march with a detachment of troops, and succeeded in reaching Big Bow's tepee before daybreak. In the morning he held a council with the Indians, wherein he pointed out to them the folly of beginning hostilities. He reminded them that Polant had only himself to blame, that he was off the reservation without authority when he was killed, and trespassing on private property. Finally the chiefs agreed to settle the difficulty in a legal manner.

The sheriff was induced to arrest the cowboy who had shot Polant. The Indians demanded that he be hanged on the spot, so that they could witness the execution. However, the cowboy, a young man of less than twenty years, was taken to Mangum for a hearing, where he was acquitted. The Indians did not know this, but they suspected it. The owner of the ranch was persuaded to give them several beeves in an effort to appease them.

After the troops departed the Kiowas continued to scout the country, searching for a lone white man for the victim of tribal custom. At length they saw a horseman approaching and raced eagerly for the kill. Just in time they recognized the stranger as a tribesman, an old buck named Skinny. They were forced to console themselves by shooting a few stray cattle. Eventually the excitement died away. This was the last interracial disturbance in southwestern Oklahoma.

CHAPTER FIFTEEN

FORT SILL IN THE EARLY DAYS

A TRIP TO FORT SILL—THE OLD POST—THE ADJUTANT—THE
SURGEON—THE QUARTERMASTER—THE POST
INTERPRETER—THE POST TRADER

SERVICE at Fort Sill after 1875 was not as exciting as it had been during the Indian troubles. But it was not entirely without interest. One way to get a clear picture of what Fort Sill and its inhabitants were like in those days is to travel there[1] with a young officer who, upon graduation from West Point, is assigned to Fort Sill for his first station. The lieutenant is accompanied by his bride of a few weeks; neither of them has been west before.

The newcomers enter Indian Territory on the M. K. and T. railroad, which runs south from Sedalia, Missouri. As they roll along through the pastures and wooded hills in the eastern part of the territory they see their first real Indians Seminoles, Cherokees, and Choctaws—standing beside the track holding up beaded moccasins for sale. They wonder if these are the western savages of which they have read so much in Frank Leslie's *Illustrated Magazine* and in *Harper's Weekly*. The redskins do not look especially wild. The young lieutenant experiences no little difficulty in preventing his lady from spending a month's pay for trinkets each time the train stops.

On the second day the train arrives at Caddo, the eastern terminus of the Fort Sill stage line. Army wagons are waiting there for the baggage, and for a carload of rations which has arrived by the same train. As the "shavetail" steps from the car, dressed in his new blue uniform, he is greeted as "General" by a woolly and poorly-informed frontiersman. This affords considerable amusement to a group of soldiers who are lounging on the station platform, and in their allusions to him, amongst themselves, he is ever after styled "General."

[1] Descriptions obtained principally from: W. H. Quinette (to author); articles in *Army and Navy Journal;* diary of Mrs. W. H. Quinette: Mrs. S. H. Burnside (to author); Old Correspondence Files, Fort Sill.

The lieutenant learns that he and his wife may ride to Fort Sill in the army wagons if they desire, but that the trip will take eight days. As the stage makes it in four he decides to use that conveyance. The stage coach is a trifle disappointing. The young people had pictured themselves as dashing gaily along in one of those high, boat-like affairs generally considered typical of western transportation. Instead they see that the Fort Sill stage is only a canvas-topped buckboard, drawn by a pair of mules. The passengers have to sit with their knees drawn up because the floor of the contraption is piled high with sacks of mail.

After an exasperating delay the stage sets off at the breath-taking speed of four miles an hour. Yet so rough is the road, so full of chuck holes and detours to avoid bogs, that by night the travelers are bruised, shaken to the core, and thoroughly anxious to savor the delights of the wayside hotel. The inn, however, proves to be only a rambling log cabin, chinked with mud.

The inside of the hostelry is more decorative than the unpromising exterior. An effort has been made to brighten the walls by papering them with pages from old magazines and newspapers. Beauties of the stage, with vast bosoms and wasp waists, simper beside stalwart acrobats clad in pink tights, whose jet-black hair and waxed mustachios make them look like seeds in a slice of watermelon. The sweet and the stern visages on the wall are marred somewhat by blobs of flour paste and splotches of tobacco juice evidently bestowed from a distance by guests justly proud of their marksmanship.

Supper is announced. In the center of the room is a table covered with a checkered red-and-white table cloth. In the pale light of a smoking coal oil lamp sticky flies circle greedily over the bent heads of bearded pioneers who sit in shirt sleeves silently wolfing their food. The newcomers' shadows move huge and grotesque on the walls as they take their places, somewhat apprehensively, at the board. A sullen servant slaps before them chipped plates in which pale eggs stare up like jaundiced eyes from a sea of grease. On the side are slices of smoked ham and chunks of corn bread. The coffee evidently is brewed from charred sawdust mixed with quinine.

The bedroom to which the travelers are assigned is as tastefully appointed as the rest of the establishment. The furniture consists of an iron bedstead covered with a begrimed pieced quilt. The head and foot of the bed lean inward at the top in profound discouragement. Strips of gay calico hang limply on either side of the windows. These openings, like the doors, are unscreened, and admit a steady stream of bloodthirsty mosquitoes. But in spite of these discomforts the travelers are so tired that they relax wearily on the beds and stare up through rents in the roof at stars twinkling in the velvet softness of the prairie night. Not far away a coyote howls, answered by the bark of a hound in the yard. The newcomers imagine that they hear tom-toms in the distance. They are thrilled to be in the Indian country at last. Before daylight the host calls them to breakfast. The stage is preparing to leave. This hasty meal is a repetition of supper. It is hard to escape the suspicion that last night's plates of food had been merely set aside for them. The charge is four dollars apiece. It is the only thing which reminds the customers that they have spent the night in a hotel.

Toward evening of the third day the stage arrives at Rush Springs, the last station before Fort Sill is reached. Rush Springs is on the border between the Chickasaw country and the reservation of the Kiowas and Comanches. There are perhaps six or eight shanties, with about half that number of privies. The stage station stands on the rise just west of a fine big spring, and is of the usual slab-and-log construction. It is a combination inn, store, and post office. Strangely enough, the place is crowded. A migration of wild carrier pigeons has settled in the wooded bottoms of Rush Creek and in Keechi Hills. Scores of hunters have been attracted to the locality; it is unusual for the birds to come so far into the southwest plains in their annual migration.

The Fort Sill travelers secretly are glad that there are no vacancies at the inn. They make their beds in a near-by haystack, where they sleep soundly until dawn, blissfully unaware that in a day or two chigre bites will make them miserable.

Toward evening on the following day the stage comes over the high ground several miles east of Cache Creek. The mountains, which have been seen dimly in the distance, now show clearly against the sunset. What appears to be a small, orderly village is nestling at the foot of the hills. There comes the dull boom of the sunset gun, and a tiny flag is drawn down from a white pole set in the village square. The newcomers realize that they are approaching Fort Sill.

It is almost dark when they reach Caddo Crossing, the ford over Cache Creek a few hundred yards east of the post. Recent rains in the mountains have made the water swift and deep. The driver cautions the passengers to hold on tight and lift their feet high. Then he whips his team and dashes through in a cloud of spray. For a moment it looks as if they all would be swept downstream and drowned. Yellow lamplight is streaming cheeringly from the windows of the quarters on the officers' line as the stage comes up the hill past the little stone chapel, and goes along the north line of quarters, by the hospital and the trader's store, to the Fort Sill Hotel.

Weary, but happy, the travelers alight and pick their way through a litter of cow droppings in the yard to the door of the hotel. Here they spend the night, expecting to be assigned quarters in the post on the following day. The hotel is no better than the one in which they stayed two nights before. In fact it is worse, for the beds are infested with bedbugs and fleas. The newcomers are forced to sit up all night in rocking chairs, dozing restlessly.

Daylight shows a row of Indian tepees within a few yards of the hotel door. Aborigines wrapped in colorful blankets or white sheets are wandering around. Their long braided locks are wound with green or scarlet yarn, or with otter fur; in their ears are silver ornaments; their faces are painted. The new arrivals wonder if the Indians have put on these costumes for their benefit.

The lieutenant, after reporting to the adjutant and the colonel, at post headquarters, is assigned to a troop. The captain, a grey-haired veteran of the Civil War, with mustachios nearly a foot long, greets him without enthusiasm. He sends him to the stables to supervise the work of the stable sergeant, who is constructing a new feed bin for the horses.

THE OLD POST

Fort Sill, though built as a bulwark in the defense of the west against Indian attack, had nothing of the conventional fortress about it. There was no moat, no parapet, no embattlement bristling with cannon. The buildings were not connected to form a stockade as at Camp Supply and other western forts. The quartermaster stone corral to the southeast, and a small earth redoubt at the southwest corner of the post, were the only structures which resembled defensive works. This redoubt, built about 1872, was pentagonal in shape. It stood on the brow of the hill now occupied by the post radio tower, and was sited to protect the terrain on that side of the post against a sudden rush on the part of the Indians. This hill is now part of a golf fairway, smooth and covered with grass; however recent airplane photographs show the outline of the redoubt with remarkable clarity. It is interesting also to recall that it was in this locality that the Wichitas killed five Pawnees one hundred years ago.

A visitor at Fort Sill in the eighties would have seen an attractive military village, facing a common square on all sides of which were stone buildings surrounded by lawns and gardens. There was also a church, a general store, and a populace of well-dressed men and women. Standing at the flag pole in the center of the parade ground the visitor would have been able to see almost the entire post. A broad path to the north led to the commanding officer's quarters. A similar graveled walk ran south to post headquarters. On the west, each housing two companies of soldiers, were three barracks. These were long, single-story buildings with wide, covered porches. Like the other buildings they were made of light-grey limestone, and presented a fresh, attractive appearance. The interiors were somewhat grim, unplastered and devoid of decoration, but neat in the geometric arrangement of cots, lockers, chests, and arms racks. The mess halls were especially clean; floors and furniture alike were kept scrubbed white with scouring soap and salt.[2]

Sanitation, however, was not up to present-day standards. Behind each barracks were two stone outhouses. One of these was a latrine; the other was supposed to be a washroom, but was used by most of the company commanders as a storeroom or supply room. The post surgeon made frequent complaints against the inadequate facilities provided the men for washing and bathing, but many years elapsed before this condition was remedied. There was no interior plumbing whatever. Kitchen slops were emptied into a covered wooden drain, which ran parallel to the rear of the barracks and spilled its contents south of the post on the side of the hill. Eventually this crude sewer became clogged with grease, meat scraps, and other kitchen offal, an accumulation which produced such an offensive odor that the post commander was forced to order the drain dug up. Thereafter, until a modern sewage system was installed, an open drain was used. Flies were present in swarms; acute diarrhea and dysentery were prevalent. It was not uncommon during this period for at least one soldier to die each month from these disorders.[3]

East of the sewer outlet was "Soapsuds Row," which was a collection of huts, old tents, picket houses, and dugouts. In spite of strict regulations regarding post police, there was an air of squalor and dirt about the locality. Here lived the company laundresses, together with troops of shock-headed children, prowling curs, and scavenging chickens. The laundress was an institution handed down, along with the Articles of War and various customs of the service, from the British army. Each troop of cavalry or company of infantry was allowed four laundresses, who received government rations and were paid for washing the men's clothing by fixed amounts deducted at the pay table. Usually they did their work well, but sometimes they were a source of trouble, and have been supplanted in modern times by the quartermaster laundry. There are cases on record during the good old days when the officer of the day had to be sent to Sudsville to break up arguments among the laundry "spikes" which surpassed the cigarette-factory scene from Carmen.[4]

Back of the barracks, to the west, were the cavalry stables, which consisted of high stone walls partitioned off for the several troops, and covered stalls for the horses. The new administration building of the Field Artillery School stands today on the site of the picket lines which used to be just west of these stables.

[2] *Kansas City Star,* June 6, 1897.

[3] Medical History, Fort Sill.

[4] By 1874 Sudsville was abolished and the laundresses were housed in stone buildings west of the barracks.

Five sets of officers' quarters—three double and two single—stood on the north side of the parade ground, and six double sets on the east. They have been used as quarters of officers continuously since they were built. The commanding officer's house was a fairly large, two-story building; the major's was nearly as big, but was single storied. Each company officer's set contained originally only three rooms and a hall. The rear room was a combination kitchen and dining room; the front room was the "parlor," and the center room was a bedroom. Officers having large families found the insufficiency of bedrooms a great inconvenience. And those were the days of large families. Like the barracks, the officers' quarters were devoid of plumbing. Officers and their families enjoyed their Saturday night baths in "GI" tubs set in the middle of the kitchen floor for the occasion. Behind each quarters was a commodious stone latrine. These relics of a more inconvenient age were preserved long after the need for them had passed, but in recent years have been torn down, the stone being used to build an addition to the old post chapel. Water for drinking, cooking, and washing was obtained from a large uncovered barrel placed on the porch of each quarters. These barrels were filled daily from a tank wagon, which in turn was filled in Medicine Bluff Creek north of the post.

Each set of quarters was enclosed by a neat whitewashed fence. This was not to keep out the Indians; it was to exclude cattle. Orders frequently warned officers to keep their cows tied at night, and not to allow them to wander on the parade ground. Indians were accustomed to stroll through the post at any time. They used to stand for hours with their noses pressed against the window panes, gazing with insatiable curiosity at the strange doings of the white people. Eventually the residents of Fort Sill became so accustomed to this that they did not even look up when the windows were darkened. The Indians usually made signs requesting food or tobacco. They were not at all abashed or reluctant to ask for what they wanted.

As the post grew older the quarters became more and more dilapidated. For many years no money was allotted for repairs to buildings, because it was thought that the post would be abandoned as soon as the Indians were thoroughly pacified. The floors began to rot and the roofs to leak. It was not uncommon for an officer's wife or her servant to stand in the kitchen astride holes in the floor through which the ground was visible, and cook dinner on a stove over which an umbrella was spread as protection against rain leaking through the roof.[5]

In spite of all this the inhabitants of "the line" contrived to live in considerable comfort and style. It is true that furniture was scarce—it had to be hauled three hundred miles in escort wagons—but then, there

[5] H. L. Scott, *Some Memories of a Soldier*, p. 143.

was not much room in the quarters for it, anyway. Nevertheless dinner parties were gay affairs, with ferns in silver centerpieces, red candle shades, salted almonds on the side, and excellent full-course dinners. Somehow the ladies managed to obtain from St. Louis or New York fairly recent models of décolleté evening gowns; conversation at social affairs was bright, and full of reference to plays or operas seen in New York or Washington, even though a year or more might have elapsed since the narrator had been east on leave of absence.

Officers were assigned quarters in order of rank. A new arrival would select the quarters his fancy dictated and to which his rank entitled him; whereupon everyone below him would have to move. His lady might plant fine rosebushes in her yard, only to have some later arrival rank her husband out of the quarters in time to pick the roses. One officer made clever arrangements by which he managed to retain his quarters for several years, in spite of the fact that he was the junior captain on the post. This officer, who was post quartermaster, lived in the first stone quarters at the southeast corner of the post. In the basement was a small artesian spring which kept the cellar full of water, so that the basement could not be used. To remedy this, the quartermaster capped the spring, and installed a large drain pipe which carried the water away from the post. The cap over the spring was provided with a tap so that the water could again be allowed to run into the basement. When the officer learned that some officer who ranked him was coming to the post he would hurry home, turn on the water, and flood his basement. Then the new arrival would be shown the cellar full of water. "You really wouldn't care for this house, sir." And the new arrival invariably chose some other quarters.[6]

THE ADJUTANT

The official head of the army post was, of course, the commanding officer; but he sat in a sanctum sanctorum at headquarters and conducted most of his business through a sort of glorified secretary called the Adjutant. The adjutant was a low-ranking but powerful personage who had the ear of the "old man." He issued all orders and conducted all official correspondence; he had to be a man of executive ability, for it was he who relieved the commander of many of the administrative details in governing the daily life of the post. It was well to be on the right side of the adjutant, for he assigned quarters, kept the guard and fatigue rosters, and made recommendations for leaves of absence or permission to go hunting and fishing.

It was the prerogative of the adjutant to require, in the name of the post commander, explanations in writing—even of his superiors in rank

[6] W. H. Quinette to author.

—of real or fancied derelictions of duty. This is an actual case taken from the old records of Fort Sill: Lieutenant Blank, who was officer of the day, was absent from morning drill because his presence at the guard-house was mandatory. His troop commander, Captain Doe, did not casually ask him why he was absent. Ah, no; that would have been too informal. He sent him a letter "through channels" desiring to know what he meant by it. This letter reached the adjutant, who, having placed Blank on guard, should have known where he was at the time in question. But he did not mention this to Captain Doe; he indorsed the letter back through Doe to Blank, requiring an explanation "by indorsement hereon" as to why the latter was absent from drill. The explanation, duly made, was passed through Doe to the adjutant; then back to Doe, inviting his attention to the preceding indorsements. Thus everyone was made happy by the dignified manner in which the proprieties were observed.

Naturally the adjutant could not personally write or answer all of the communications passing over his desk. He was assisted by the sergeant major and sundry clerks. Like the adjutant, these men were "in on the know"; if a person wished to hear the latest post rumors, or to learn what was going on in the inner circles of the mighty, he did well to cultivate their acquaintance. It was only by means of their help that the adjutant was able to conduct voluminous correspondence such as, for example, the letter about the can of peaches.

In the middle eighties the sanitary officer at Fort Sill condemned as unfit for human consumption a can of peaches furnished by the commissary. This action infuriated the department quartermaster, who, it seems, was touchy about his peaches. He had the contents of the offending can sent to him for examination; not satisfied, he had them analyzed by government chemists in Washington. Effervescing with indignation, he forwarded the report of these food experts to Fort Sill, pointing out triumphantly that the peaches were wholly up to specifications. He wanted the surgeon at Fort Sill tried by court-martial for stirring up such a furor. This cut to the quick the good doctor at Fort Sill; he had only been performing his bounden duty in protecting the garrison against inferior foodstuffs, he said. The ensuing correspondence acquired thirty-four indorsements (all in longhand), and raised the blood pressure of the participants to a dangerous level. Fortunately it reached the attention of General Sheridan, who quickly ended the nonsense, and smoothed out the feathers of his gamecocks by complimenting all concerned for their conscientious attention to duty.

All of this commotion about peaches was trifling compared to the letter written in October, 1899, concerning a post exchange (post canteen) inventory. This missive reached seventy-two indorsements during

284

its two years' shuttling back and forth. Fortunately post headquarters was at that time equipped with a typewriter.

The adjutant also had to be a man of considerable tact and finesse. It was his duty to see that harmony prevailed among the inhabitants of the military community. One of the most prolific sources of friction was the army dog. Everyone at Fort Sill owned dogs—staghounds, wolfhounds, rabbit hounds, and just hounds. At regular intervals Captain or Major So-and-So would write to complain that Lieutenant Ducrot's dogs were keeping him awake at night with their barking. Twice a year throughout the entire history of Fort Sill the adjutant has issued an order cautioning members of the garrison to keep their dogs tied up at night and not allow them to annoy the neighbors. Through the years this has been a favorite order of each successive post administration. Through the years it had been disregarded with equal cheerfulness by dogs and owners alike.[7]

Where the adjutant really was at his best was at guard mount. When he commanded the band to "sound off," and hoisted his folded arms above a magnificent chest, his resplendence rivaled even that of the drum major. And all of his best faculties were brought into play when he selected the best-looking member of the guard to act as the colonel's orderly. Where the appearance of Private Murphy's super-clean rifle was balanced by the shine on Private Wyzykgwski's black Hessian boots, it required a paragon of judgment to say who should have the honor. Often it was necessary to have the leading candidates strip to their underwear to determine who was the cleanest.

There was no signal officer at Fort Sill in the early days; usually the adjutant performed this function in addition to his other duties. His work as signal officer was not difficult, as it consisted largely in being accountable for the signal property, and in instructing small classes of selected enlisted men in visual signaling. There was a base station on the site of the present riding hall, from which messages were transmitted by flag, heliograph, or signal lamp, to another station on Medicine Bluff, thence to the blockhouse on Signal Mountain or to Mount Scott. Sometimes messages were relayed as far north as Fort Reno.

All this was only for practice, however, because a telegraph line to Fort Reno had been established about 1877. The first telegraph line to Fort Sill was completed June 2, 1875, connecting the post with Fort Richardson, Texas. This line was constructed by soldiers from the Eleventh Infantry, under the direction of Captain Beach. The technical phases of the installation were handled by Lieutenant A. W. Greeley,

[7] In 1936, however, post headquarters finally overtook the dogs at Fort Sill, occasioning much weeping, wailing, and gnashing of teeth. Several hundred dogs were impounded at the veterinary hospital for a period of three months to a year.

who later became famous as a polar explorer and chief signal officer of the army. The first telegraph poles were of wood, and frequently were damaged or destroyed by grass fires or by windstorms; therefore they were replaced by poles made of two-inch iron pipe. A few of these poles are still in use in the Wichita Mountain area.

Telegraph service was furnished by a government subsidiary known as the U.S. military telegraph line. J. G. Hewett was the operator at Fort Sill. In addition to official traffic over the line, he used to receive Associated Press dispatches four times daily, which he posted up in different parts of the post for the benefit of all who cared to read. On October 7, 1879, two Phelps Crown type telephones were received at Fort Sill, to be used by connecting them to the telegraph circuit.[8] This was only four years after the telephone was invented and owing to their unfamiliarity with the apparatus, the operators at first had little success with it. Later, after they had learned how to make the telephone function, the operators at Forts Sill and Reno used to disconnect their telegraph instruments at an agreed-upon time on Sunday afternoons, then connect the telephones for an hour of unofficial conversation. As soon as Hewett was assured that the telephone would work, he invited Quanah Parker and several other Indians to the telegraph office to inspect the contraption. Listening over the telephone the Indians were greatly astonished to hear the bugler at Fort Reno, seventy-five miles away, blow taps.

THE SURGEON

Army doctors in the old days were of three classes: surgeons, who ranked with majors of the line; assistant surgeons, who ranked with company officers; and acting assistant surgeons, who were civilians working on contract. There were never more than two medical officers on duty at Fort Sill, frequently only one, so their lives were busy ones. Sick call in the morning looked like an assembly of the garrison for pay day, so many soldiers were afflicted with malaria and dysentery. When, in 1876, the surgeon insisted that drinking water be obtained from the spring instead of from the creek, there was a noticeable decrease in the latter complaint.

Malaria was not well understood in those days; at any rate it was not known that the mosquito was the carrier. Nevertheless, the doctors knew or suspected that swamps and stagnant water had something to do with the prevalence of the disease. The surgeon at Fort Sill succeeded in having the high water coulee which ran west of the post, from near Quinette Crossing to below the cemetery, drained and kept dry. Considerable labor also was expended in draining several pools which formed on the low ground east of the post when Cache Creek overflowed its

[8] Lieutenant C. A. Tingle to P. B. Hunt, October 7, 1879.

banks. In those times, before the dam was built near Mount Scott, Medicine Bluff Creek also flooded each spring. Sometimes it became a half-mile wide.

A supply of pure drinking water for the post was a major concern of the surgeon. In 1883 Surgeon Morse K. Taylor built a spring house north of the hospital. The spring was cleaned out to a depth of twenty-two feet, lined with masonry, and housed in a small stone building. This spring was ancient and famous, known to the Indians on account of its unfailing supply of pure water, even when the water of the adjacent creek was muddy. Inside the spring house was built a stone trough where people from the post kept melons and fruit during the summer months. The spring was named "Ambrosia," in honor of Mrs. Ambrosia Taylor (wife of Major Taylor), who died before it was completed. From the spring house the water was piped to a pumping plant on the south bank of the creek, thence lifted to a wooden tank on the edge of the bank northwest of the commanding officer's quarters. In later years two modern tanks were erected immediately east of the interpreter's house. From the tank the water was distributed to quarters and barracks. Kitchen sinks were supplied to each building and although it was intended that a system should be constructed to carry the waste water to an outlet below the post, funds were exhausted before this was completed. The waste was allowed to discharge into the creek. No other inside plumbing was installed at this time. The post trader also had a well back of the store, with a large storage cistern. Several attempts were made to sink additional wells, but in each case small quantities of oil were struck instead of water.

Although Major Taylor spent no little time and effort in obtaining a modern water system for the post, apparently he did not profit by it personally. In the old correspondence files of the post may be found a letter written by him to the post commander, extracts of which are: "Of the hydrants sent to this post nine have been appropriated to the use of the Post Quartermaster, his employes and enlisted men, two have been set in the grounds of the captains' quarters, and one in the commanding officers' grounds. The Medical Department has been utterly ignored, though chiefly instrumental in getting the present water system introduced. . . . . I therefore renew my request that one of these hydrants, which in my judgment has been misappropriated, be placed in my yard. I certainly am entitled to as much consideration as an enlisted man or a blacksmith."

Post sanitation continued to cause no little worry. In the fall of 1886 Surgeon Taylor returned from an extended leave of absence to discover that a deplorable state of police existed. The gullies between the hospital and the trader's store, and those running into the creek northeast of the

hospital, were filled with about one hundred and thirty-five tons of gar-
bage, trash, and manure. Taylor wrote a long letter bitterly protesting
this condition. He stated that the seepage from this accumulation was
discharging into the stream, whence it was carried to the Indian camps,
the dwellings of beef and hay contractors, and dairies south of the post.
He blamed this for the prevalence of disease at Fort Sill, particularly
diphtheria and typhoid, on account of milk furnished from the infected
herd. This letter was referred by the new post commander to his predecessor, who explained that he had filled up the gullies to prevent erosion
of the soil. The successor attempted to dismiss the whole matter; he
declared stoutly that it was news to him that the presence of manure
was detrimental to health. He had never heard of such a thing. He intimated that it was wholesome, especially in a cavalry command, to have
a certain amount of manure in close proximity to the post. Such had
been the custom at all posts at which he had served. But the surgeon
persisted, with the result that drill and other garrison duties had to be
suspended for several weeks while the command moved the entire mass
out of the area. The post dump was established east of the post. This
done, the post commander gradually became enthusiastic over post
police. He roughly ordered the trader to cease selling bottled beer to
soldiers and civilians, because the drill ground in front of the store was
littered with broken bottles, and was damaging the feet of the cavalry
horses.

Ice for the post had always been harvested from the creek. But in
the middle eighties several mild winters resulted in a lack of ice. When
the new pumping plant was erected, an ice machine was obtained and
set up in the old ice house in which the Indians had been held prisoner
in 1875. Never had the Indians seen anything which astonished them
more than this marvel of the white man, which "made ice out of hot
water in the summertime."[9]

THE QUARTERMASTER

Although the adjutant and the surgeon were indispensable members
of the post commander's official family, the man who really made the
wheels go 'round was the post quartermaster. In those days only a few
officers in Washington or in department headquarters were permanently
assigned to the QMD (Quartermasters Department). All post quartermasters were line officers temporarily assigned to that duty.

Any captain or lieutenant who was too efficient might find himself
suddenly elevated to the sublime position of acting assistant quartermaster and adjutant commissary of subsistence. Thus his former easy
carefree life came to an end. He became the most sought-after man on

[9] H. L. Scott, *op. cit.*, p. 145.

the post. Everyone wanted him. Children cried for him. The commanding officer sent for him to inquire as to when he had made out that requisition; prepared that estimate; completed those plans; sent that team; written that letter of explanation; hung that gate at the corral. Or the colonel, perhaps, desired to know why the clothing in the warehouse was not of better quality, why that ambulance failed to report, why those stores did not arrive, why some extra duty (now called special duty) man was not at his proper post. Captain Jones did not like the bacon and flour which he issued to the troops. Mrs. Blank disapproved of the sales articles which he sold her; she sent them back with a sarcastic letter condemning the tea as weak, the butter as rancid, the cheese as spoiled, and the commissary sergeant as disobliging. Even when the sun had set, his day was not over. Friends and acquaintances alike waylaid him at dinners or at dances to inquire about new shingles for the roof, new stovepipe for the kitchen, more whitewash for the fence. He was expected to know everything about plumbing, masonry, carpentry, architecture, storekeeping, transportation, bookkeeping, and engineering. He had no assistants except a few sergeants, and no sympathy from anyone.

Lieutenant H. W. Lawton was quartermaster under Mackenzie. Contemporaries testify that he was a good one. Lawton had a brilliant military career, but was killed in the Philippines in 1899. The town of Lawton, near Fort Sill, was named for him. Lawton's successors at Fort Sill did not have an easy time. Almost nothing was issued to them. Even the few hardwood boards furnished for the construction of coffins usually had to be made into furniture. Gradually the buildings were allowed to fall into a state of disrepair, on account of insufficient funds being allotted for their upkeep. Not until about 1887, when Lieutenant H. W. Hovey was quartermaster, was there much effort to repair the quarters and barracks. Hovey built stairways in the officers' quarters, thus making it possible to use the upper floors of these buildings. It was under his administration that the improvements to the water system and post sanitation, instituted by Surgeon Taylor, were carried out. Hovey installed the first (tin) bath tubs at Fort Sill. Each officer's quarters got one, and one went to each barracks.

In April, 1887, a severe windstorm caused serious damage at the post by removing the roofs of many of the buildings. The stone corral was gutted of its wood fixtures; and, most serious of all, the post flag pole was blown down. Hovey at once wrote for money to buy a new one. After fencing at long range for seven months over this question, the department quartermaster ordered Hovey to take a detail into the wilderness and cut a flag pole.

Hovey's successor was an ancient lieutenant, a veteran of the Civil War, whose troubles became unendurable when he was directed to prepare estimates to build a new post. He confessed that this was too much for him, so he wrote a letter asking to be relieved and stating that he felt he had done his share, after eight months as quartermaster. He added that he was getting too old for so strenuous a position, and would like to retire.[10]

In 1890 Lieutenant H. L. Scott, Seventh Cavalry, was assigned the position of quartermaster at Fort Sill. He occupied this office for seven years, during which he did much to save the post from being abandoned. He built foundations under the officers' quarters, and buttressed the toppling walls. He constructed wing bedrooms on several of the quarters, replaced the rotting floors, and reroofed most of the post.

The small steam engine which had been installed, in 1886, to pump water to the water tanks and to operate the ice machine, was obviously inadequate. Lieutenant Hovey had made several efforts to obtain a larger engine to replace it, but had not succeeded. Shortly after Scott became quartermaster the boiler burned out, so that Scott was forced to supply the post with water from a tank wagon, as in the former days. Fortunately he was able to make temporary repairs to the machinery, and soon afterwards received a forty-horsepower engine. Scott further improved the water system by erecting a new water tank. Many of the soldiers on the post had been mysteriously ill. The surgeon suspected the water supply, but could find nothing wrong with it. Then it was discovered that there was a two-foot layer of long-deceased pigeons on the bottom of the old water tank.

The first porcelain-lined bath tubs were received while Scott was quartermaster. Seven of these were of ordinary size, while two were unusually large. One of the big ones went to the post commander, and the other, strange to say, found itself installed in the quarters of the quartermaster. Scott was exceedingly proud of this tub. Many years later, when he was a colonel, he visited Fort Sill. The first thing he wanted to see was his old bath tub; so in company with the veteran post trader, W. H. Quinette, he went to the quarters on the south end of the line and rapped on the door. The occupant appeared, attired in his underwear. "Captain," said Scott, who was somewhat formidable in appearance, "I want to see your bath tub!" Considerably surprised, the captain led the way. There stood the famous bath tub, half full of ice and bottles of beer.[11]

THE POST INTERPRETER

One of the most famous fixtures at Fort Sill in its earlier days was the post interpreter, Horace Jones. Horace was a stately man with a goatee. He had come to the Indian country from Missouri in 1855, and

[10] Old Files, Fort Sill.　　　　　[11] W. H. Quinette to author.

had been there ever since. His education was self-acquired, largely as a result of reading in the post library. Consequently his attempts to employ fancy or unusual words in ordinary conversation afforded no little amusement to his friends. But Horace, being an accomplished raconteur, was welcome everywhere. He occupied bachelor quarters in the small house still standing just north of the old chapel, where he maintained several fine hounds.

More than one complaint was entered at the adjutant's office that Jones's dogs were "making the night hideous with their howling," but during the hunting season Jones and his dogs were prime favorites. The officers and their families used to turn out for these hunts. The ladies rode sidesaddles, and did up their hair in flowing veils. Usually the quarry was a jackrabbit. Rabbits were scarce in those days, for the wolves and coyotes kept their number reduced. "Colonel" Jones claimed that he had several jacks trained to avoid the kill, so that the sport would not be spoiled by the death of the only rabbits in the area. Sometimes the hounds started a wolf or a coyote, and occasionally small parties went into the mountains after wildcats, panthers, or bears.[12] Game was plentiful. Although the buffalo and the elk disappeared about 1880 there were still a few antelope, in the Rainy Mountain area. Deer, turkey, prairie chickens, quail, ducks, and geese abounded. A few beaver lived in Medicine Bluff Creek as late as 1900. The streams were full of fish. Heyl's Hole in Medicine Bluff Creek was named for Captain E. M. Heyl, a member of the Fourth Cavalry, who took many bass from that pool.

Horace Jones also was much in demand at masquerade hops and other social gatherings. One of his haunts was the "clubroom" at the trader's store. This place was maintained by the trader for the officers of the post, and consisted of a large room equipped with billiard and card tables, and reading material. There the officers used to gather over foaming steins. Horace Jones was there nearly every night. Under some post administrations the trader was permitted to sell wine and even whisky in the clubroom. One evening Horace had been especially convivial, and when the time came to close shop, the post interpreter was unable to leave; he had to be put to bed at Evans' house. In the morning Jack Evans invited the old gentleman down to breakfast. In those days the morning meal was a substantial affair and on this particular occasion Evans served steak and, as a special treat, fried mushrooms on the side. Soon it was noticed that Horace Jones was pushing his mushrooms to the side of the plate.

"What's the matter, Horace?" Evans inquired. "Don't you like those things?"

[12] R. G. Carter to author, 1935.

"Hrrmph!" grunted Jones, testily. "In my opinion it is bad enough of you to sell champagne to your friends at five dollars a bottle, without serving the corks fried for breakfast!"[13]

THE POST TRADER

No description of early Fort Sill is complete without mention of the trader's store. Though troops and commanders might change station from time to time, the post trader remained. In spite of the fact that the post trader has been maligned in some quarters, oldtimers testify that he usually was a charming fellow, admitted freely to the best social circles. His establishment corresponded to the post exchange of today. Yet it was more. The trader cashed pay checks, acted as banker and postmaster. The people at the post borrowed money from him, or deposited their savings with him. There were no other banking facilities in that part of the territory. Usually the trader charged interest for this service, but his rates were no higher than those of reputable financing companies. In 1878, when Congress failed to pass the army appropriation bill, the trader carried the accounts of the people at the post, and continued to cash pay vouchers, content to wait for reimbursement.

Evans and Fisher remained post traders at Sill until 1876, when they lost their license as a result of the Belknap scandal. Impeachment proceedings were instituted against Secretary of War Belknap for selling post traderships, including the one at Fort Sill. It was proved that Evans had been paying tribute for seven years. Rice and Beyers succeeded Evans. In a few years Captain Beyers died, and the firm then became Rice and Musser. The post trader chiefly remembered by the older inhabitants of Fort Sill is Mr. William H. Quinette, who in 1878 came to the post as an employe of Rice and Beyers, later purchasing Mr. Musser's interest in the firm. Quinette had many firm friends among officers who served at Sill, some of whom became famous. In later years he was influential in securing governmental aid in expanding the post. Mr. Quinette was intimately associated with Fort Sill for forty-eight years. He died at his home in Lawton in 1935.

The post trader was an active participant in the social and recreational life of Fort Sill. He was a welcome member of the officers' circle in their rides to the hounds, lawn croquet and tennis, whist clubs, and dances. He also helped the enlisted men's activities by offering prizes for the exciting baseball series which were played on a diamond in front of the trader's store. The soldiers then did not have the well-organized

[13] W. H. Quinette to author. Phillip McCusker, who was interpreter at Fort Reno, later occupied the same position at Fort Sill, and for a time there were two interpreters at Sill. In 1885 McCusker lost his life on Deep Red Creek, thirty miles south of Fort Sill; he froze to death in a blizzard, while carrying messages from Fort Sill to Camp Augur.

recreational activities now in vogue in the army. They could play baseball or go hunting; but there were no movies, no near-by town to visit. A big event in their lives, therefore, was the field day held each Fourth of July under the sponsorship of Mr. Quinette, the trader.

The annual field day at Fort Sill was held in front of the store and also on the race track laid out on the site of the present polo field and farther east. Here the soldiers enjoyed fireworks, barbecue, beer, races and other competitions such as greased-pig chases, pole climbing contests, and the like. There were events for the Indians, chiefly foot races and horse races. Every Indian of the Kiowa-Comanche reserve attended, and enjoyed the field day as thoroughly as did the soldiers. Mr. Quinette provided the Indians with free beef, and also donated liberal prizes of cash and merchandise. To this day the older Indians speak with regret of the passing of annual field day at Fort Sill.

The trader's store, being the only institution of its kind in the area—except for small establishments operated south of the reservation as Indian trading posts—was a stopping place for cattlemen, travelers, and transients. Thus many unusual characters were seen at Fort Sill. One of these was responsible for considerable excitement there in the summer of 1881. This man was a wizened prospector from Colorado named Snyder.[14] While at the trader's store Mr. Snyder made a few discreet inquiries about the surrounding country and its natural resources. Interest and curiosity were aroused at once, for persistent legends concerning the presence of precious metals in the Wichita Mountains had been floating around since the days of the first Spanish explorers. Presently Miner Snyder visited the post hospital, where he was closeted with Surgeon Williams. Later that evening Major Williams arrived at the quarters of the commanding officer, Major J. K. Mizner. "This fellow Snyder is an experienced miner," he declared. "He brought me a piece of ore which he picked up on the reservation. I tested it, and it appears to be nearly pure silver!" Mizner and Williams put their heads together. They thumbed through the Federal statutes for laws regulating prospecting on government land. Everything seemed to be in order, so they formed a company to exploit Snyder's discovery. One or two other friends were admitted into the partnership.

But good news travels fast. There were similar gatherings that night in other parts of the post. It seems that Snyder had talked to several. In fact he must have talked to everyone. Before sunrise the next morning numerous little groups could be seen riding quietly toward the hills west of the post. Among the argonauts were Majors Mizner and Williams, Captains Wirt Davis, J. M. Thompson, F. B. McCoy, Dr. Rodman, W.

[14] W. H. Quinette to author; Old Files, Fort Sill, 1881; File 4937, AGO, 1881.

H. Quinette, James Morgan, and others equally distinguished. The leading group got no farther than Medicine Bluff. Here they halted, tied their horses, and commenced to stake out claims. Before sundown all the hills west of the post as far as Mount Hinds had been staked. On the sides of Medicine Bluff could be seen piles of rocks, with pieces of paper bearing such resounding titles as "Old Dominion Mine," "Lucky Strike Mine," and the like. Before the week was out the whole countryside as far as Mount Scott was dotted with rock piles and stakes. It mattered not that the land was on the military reservation or on Indian reserves. They dug shallow holes and used dynamite to blast out samples. After several samples were taken from each claim, the miners would proceed to virgin territory to stake additional claims. Each night they strode into the trader's store, their eyes shining with a peculiar glitter, their pockets bulging with rocks. Samples were labeled carefully and sent to Denver for assay. Military work at the post practically ceased.

All this was not as Promoter Snyder had planned. It had been suggested that it was his purpose to sell stock in a mining company of his own organizing. But why should anyone buy stock from Mr. Snyder when there was a whole range of hills to be staked free? Promoter Snyder should have returned in later years with oil-well stock. Soon the glad tidings leaked out of Fort Sill. As the weeks passed a horde of eager civilians sneaked in from adjoining states. They came with burros, picks, shovels, rockers, dynamite. The Indians were exceedingly annoyed. The prospectors tore up their pastures, stole their watermelons, drove off their stock.

On August 3 Agent Hunt heard about it. At once he telegraphed to the commandant at Fort Sill. With confidence he awaited assistance in expelling the intruders and effecting a cessation of the prospecting. What to his surprise should come but a reply from Major Mizner referring him to Section 2319, *Revised United States Statutes*. The good major announced that he intended to dig in the Indian country as well as on the military reservation, and that the law permitted him to do so. Mr. Hunt wired General Pope at department headquarters. General Pope interpreted the matter differently. Shortly there arrived an order to cease mining operations. Troops must be turned out to eject all civilian trespassers.

Thus ended the Great Silver Rush. Officers returned to the prosaic duty of drilling soldiers, acting on boards of survey, or writing letters explaining why they had not accounted properly for "one mule shot for glanders." So far as is known no one made any money from the exciting metallurgical enterprise except J. H. Musser, junior partner of the firm of Rice and Musser, post traders. That astute gentleman appointed himself registrar of claims and opened a ledger at the store, in which he solemnly entered each mining claim, charging a fee of three dollars therefor. Until a few years ago a memento of those thrilling days remained atop Medicine Bluff No. 3, where there was a pile of rock marking the site of "the Old Dominion Mine."

CHAPTER SIXTEEN

THE CHIRICAHUA APACHES

ARRIVAL OF GERONIMO'S BAND AT FORT SILL
—SPANISH-AMERICAN WAR—GERONIMO

PRACTICALLY the only Apaches who had been seen in the vicinity of Fort Sill were the Kiowa-Apaches, a small tribe of Athabascan stock who had emigrated to the southwestern plains with the Kiowas during the eighteenth century, and who, like the Kiowas, had originated in the far north. In New Mexico, Arizona, southwestern Texas, and along the Mexican border roamed other Indians also called Apaches—the Mescalero and Chiricahua Apaches. Under Mangus-Colorado, Cochise, and Geronimo, they had been the scourge of the border and of the thinly settled parts of Arizona and New Mexico for many years. Successive military expeditions had been conducted against these Indians, but not until 1886 were they finally subdued. After a series of exhausting campaigns conducted by Crooks, Miles, and Lawton, they were induced to surrender to Lieutenant Charles Gatewood.

Since Geronimo and his warriors were credited with twenty-five hundred homicides in Arizona alone, it was thought best to hustle the prisoners out of the territory before the wrath of the populace reached them. They were taken first to Florida, then to Mount Vernon, Alabama. They did not flourish there; they wanted to return to a country "where they could see the sun without climbing a pine tree."[1]

After the Secretary of War had been importuned for some time by humanitarians who wanted the Apaches moved to a more healthful climate, it was decided in 1894 to send them to a reservation west of the Mississippi. Oklahoma was settled upon as the place of their confinement, in spite of vehement protests made by the congressional delegate from that territory. General Miles thought that Camp Supply, then about to be abandoned, would be an excellent place for them, but Lieutenant Scott persuaded him that Fort Sill was better. Scott also had persuaded the

---

[1] H. L. Scott, *Some Memories of a Soldier*, p. 183.

Kiowas and Comanches to allow the Apaches to live on the reservation. Some of the chiefs had objected, as they had no particular love for the Apaches, but Scott promised that they would live only on the military reservation.

The Apaches, under Geronimo and Naiche, were loaded into a special train in Alabama and sent to Fort Sill via Fort Worth and Rush Springs. The attitude of many Oklahomans toward the new arrivals was reflected by the following, taken from the *Minco* (Oklahoma) *Minstrel:* "Geronimo and his band arrived at Rush Springs yesterday. They had a special train of twelve cars, and were escorted by Company I, 12th Infantry, commanded by Second Lieutenant Allyn Capron. On arriving at Fort Sill they will be assigned a place by Captain Marion P. Maus and 1st Lieut. H. L. Scott, after which the latter will assume supervision over them. . . . Yes, here we all go to see the king of murderers and sweet prince of fiery destruction, now made glorious by the sentimental adulation of insane freaks and misguided philanthropists. The old devil [Geronimo] should have been hung fifteen years ago. Of course they were given a royal reception at Ft. Worth, as hundreds of idiots were eager to bow down to royalty no matter in what shape it came. The *Gazette* gives us an account of the ovation that acts as an emetic to one acquainted with savage life and history." Nevertheless when Geronimo and his people arrived at Fort Sill on October 7 they made anything but a regal appearance. In addition to a number of people from the post, there were on hand several hundred curious Kiowas and Comanches to watch them unload from the wagons. The wagon train halted about two miles northeast of the post, where Geronimo later had his village. The Apaches were poor, bedraggled and apathetic. The Kiowas and Comanches noticed that they had no livestock, not even dogs, and little clothing or personal belongings. They tried to converse with them by means of the sign language, which the Apaches did not understand. Finally each side had to produce a Carlisle boy and converse by means of the English language.

Captain H. L. Scott was to be in charge of the Apaches, assisted by Lieutenant Allyn Capron. Scott arranged for the Apaches to camp where they arrived, on the little knoll about halfway between Peach Tree Crossing and Dempsey Bridge. It was too late in the season to attempt to erect houses for them. The Apaches put up wickiups in the brush, which they covered with salvaged canvas. With them was their interpreter George Wratten, who had accompanied the band since their capture in Arizona. Wrattan Creek is named for this man.

The following spring Scott put the prisoners to work cutting pickets and putting up houses. He divided them into small villages, scattered over various parts of the reservation. A head man was appointed over each, and several of the Apaches, including Geronimo himself, were enlisted as scouts and given uniforms. This was to win their loyalty to the government. The idea was an excellent one, and no trouble was ever experienced with these people. Geronimo, however, was reduced in rank and treated like any other man, the purpose of this move being to lower his prestige, in order to put a premium on industry and loyalty rather than on past warlike prowess. The hereditary principal chief, Naiche, was given more authority than Geronimo. But the latter remained a constant source of interest and attraction to the whites. His reputation as a fighter and killer drew crowds wherever he went.

Since the Apaches were under military control they could be made to work. Scott had them cut and bale hay for sale under contract to the post. He introduced kaffir corn, the first brought into the southwest, which the Apaches raised and sold to the government for forage. They also grew melons and other vegetables, the surplus being sold at the post and in the vicinity. Later Scott bought cattle for the Apaches. The herd grew in size and produced a comfortable revenue for the Indians. The Apache herd was a prominent feature of the military reservation, and was the cause of its being fenced in. Scott had the reservation extended in size to approximately its present (1935) boundaries. It was roughly in the shape of a figure seven, which has been said to be significant of the Seventh Cavalry, of which Scott was a member. Under this treatment the Apaches prospered and increased in number. Actually they were better off than their Kiowa and Comanche neighbors. Strict military control did not harm them, and provided a pleasant contrast to the management of the other Indians, who were under another department of the government.[2] After Scott left in 1897, various officers were successively in charge of the Apaches, but Lieutenant George Purington was their supervisor during most of the time from then until they were sent away in 1913. The Apache herd of cattle, when finally sold, brought over $300,000, which was credited to the band.

THE SPANISH-AMERICAN WAR

When the Spanish-American War broke out in 1898 all the troops were ordered away from Fort Sill except a detachment of twenty men under Lieutenant Beach. The last unit to leave the post was Captain W. C. Brown's Troop E, First Cavalry, which left at 2 P.M. on April 18, marching to Rush Springs to take the railroad to Chickamauga Park.

After this troop had departed the post was inflamed by a rumor to the effect that the Geronimo prisoners were going to rise up and massacre all the defenseless persons at Fort Sill.[3] The story evidently originated with an Apache girl, the daughter of one of the prisoners, who had been

[2] Major General J. F. Bell to Secretary of War, July 15, 1907.
[3] Information furnished by General W. C. Brown.

educated at Carlisle and who was a domestic servant at the post. The girl had overheard some conversation in one of the villages which led her to believe that the Indians were planning an uprising. Actually the Apaches had no such idea; the girl heard some of the men say jokingly how easy it would be to break out, now that the troops had gone, but they had given up that sort of thing. She had partly forgotten her native tongue, through long association with the whites, or did not hear all of the conversation.[4] At any rate, when the post trader, Mr. William H. Quinette, rode back through the post that afternoon, returning from his dairy east of Hairpin Ford, he was met by several of the officers' wives, who warned him not to go to his store or he surely would be killed. Quinette did not take the warning seriously. When he reached the store he found that Lieutenant Beach, having been importuned by the women, was issuing arms to the employes at the store, and had wired department headquarters to have Captain Brown's troop sent back to the post at once, as well as several other troops. He considered the post to be in great and immediate danger. Quinette investigated privately and was convinced that the rumor was false. Later in the evening Quanah Parker rode in to offer the services of the entire Comanche tribe in controlling the Apaches. "We will kill every one of them if they start anything," said Quanah, who had received some report of the threatened uprising at his ranch west of the post.

Captain Brown, when he arrived at Rush Springs at midnight, received telegraphic instructions from department headquarters to return to Sill. He at once turned his troop around and made a forced march back to the post. He held an investigation the following day, in which he called in Geronimo, Naiche, and several other Apache leaders, and questioned them. They protested almost tearfully that there was no truth in the report. "I am a U.S. soldier," said Geronimo. "I wear the uniform, and it makes my heart sore to be thus suspected." He left no doubt in Brown's mind but that he was absolutely loyal, and that the trouble lay in loose talk on the part of the young girl and some irresponsible young men.

Captain Brown sent off telegraphic reports to department headquarters to forestall any more troops being sent back. Nevertheless Lieutenant S. R. H. (Tommy) Tompkins' troop from Fort Grant and Lieutenant Gaston's troop from Fort Meade were ordered in. On April 24 Troop B Seventh Cavalry, commanded by Lieutenant Tompkins, arrived; Brown departed once more for Rush Springs and Cuba.

Tommy Tompkins is almost a legendary figure. There is probably no one in the army about whom more tall tales are told, some true and some not. While at Fort Sill he drilled his troops by bugle, the horses

[4] W. H. Quinette to author.

responding perfectly without other commands being given. Tommy was inordinately proud of these horses, and nearly had apoplexy when, on being ordered to Chickamauga, he was directed to leave them at Sill.

In 1898 when the war bulletins commenced to arrive over the telegraph line, it was the custom of the operator to telephone these dispatches all over the post. The commanding officer's wife, the major's wife, the trader's store, and Mrs. Allyn Capron were all on the party line. One evening the operator turned the crank and announced bluntly, "Captain Allyn Capron, killed!" The other three people listening on their instruments heard Mrs. Capron gasp and fall in a faint on the floor. Capron was very popular at Fort Sill and his death was a great shock to all. He was the first American officer killed in Cuba.

GERONIMO

The aging Apache chief, Geronimo, continued to be one of the principal sources of interest at Fort Sill. He made several efforts to have his liberty restored, even visiting President Roosevelt in 1905 to make an appeal. But all such requests were refused. There was no place for him to go. The people of Arizona would never have permitted his being sent back there, and he was better off, except for sentiment, where he was. The other Apaches, or at least a part of them, also wanted to return to their homeland. It was argued that it was not right for the government to maintain in captivity the children of this band, many of whom had been born since their parents left Arizona. But the term "prisoners of war" was merely a piece of legal fiction whereby the government could feed and clothe them, as they were under no restraint other than the ordinary military control, which was beneficent in its effect, preventing them from killing each other in drunken brawls and getting into other trouble. All officers who had charge of the band consistently recommended against a change in their status.

There were many demands for Geronimo as an exhibit at fairs, circuses, and side shows. He had been permitted to visit the World's Fair, and had traveled with Pawnee Bill's Wild West Circus. The old Apache liked this life. It gave him a salary, and gratified his vanity to be stared at by the curious. He sold pictures of himself, which he had been taught to autograph, for two dollars apiece. But when a proposition was submitted to send him to Coney Island and similar places, the authorities drew the line.

In 1902 Pawnee Bill's Wild West Show again requested Geronimo for a seven-month's tour of the country; but the request was refused on the ground that show life was not good for the Indian because he was getting old and was bothered with rheumatism. The following year Cummins' Indian Congress wanted him as a summer exhibit, but was denied the privilege for the same reasons. Later the same year Madison Square Garden asked for him, without success. In 1904 he was requested by the New Mexico Territorial Fair. Finally in 1905 he was allowed to go to the 101 Ranch, near Ponca City, where an association of newspaper editors was holding a convention. Some kind of buffalo hunt and barbecue was staged on this occasion, news of which got into the papers. President Roosevelt wrote a hot letter demanding that whoever let Geronimo indulge in the disgraceful exhibition of a public buffalo hunt, in company with army officers, should be punished. But it turned out that there were only two officers there, on leave in civilian clothes, who were merely spectators.[5]

Finally permission was granted for Geronimo to travel with Pawnee Bill. General Bell, when he visited the post in 1907, made the following comment: "It is recommended that Geronimo be not permitted to return to Arizona. He is now a very old man and has already lost any influence he ever had with these Indians. He is a worthless, thriftless old vagabond, apparently without either pride or self respect. He desires to travel with some show. . . . I think it would be a good idea."

On March 14, 1908, a lawyer in Lawton wrote to the War Department to say that Geronimo, whose grandson had recently died, was very much depressed in spirit and brooding over the loss of his only grandson, who was very close and dear to him, and that a change of scenery for ninety days would be both humane and very advantageous to the old warrior. He recommended that a ninety-day release be granted Geronimo. This communication was referred to the post commander at Fort Sill who made the following remark: "The contents of the within letter have been explained to Geronimo and he says that he does not feel depressed, but he does feel the loss of a grandson as any other man would feel; he also says that he never talked with any person in Lawton about his feelings over the loss of his grandson, and if any person has written to the War Department about him it was without his knowledge. He was asked if he would like to take a trip for awhile, and he said he would, if he could get in some good show where he could make some money. From the tone of the within letter, a person not familiar with the conditions would presume that Geronimo was held in confinement at the post; the contrary exists, he goes and comes at will with nothing to do but eat and sleep."[6]

Occasionally Geronimo got drunk; in fact he was in that condition frequently. Several different times he was confined in a cell in the post guardhouse until he sobered up, usually over a weekend. General Upton Birnie, then a lieutenant, remembers seeing the old Indian, with a towel

[5] File 445841, AGO, relating to the Apache prisoners.
[6] File 445841.

301

wrapped around his aching head, splitting wood at the rear of the guardhouse on Monday mornings. Unimportant and brief in duration as these incarcerations were, they have given rise to the erroneous belief that Geronimo was held as a prisoner more or less continuously in the guardhouse. Hence this historic old building now is commonly known as the Geronimo Guardhouse. Actually it was the prison of the famous Kiowa war chiefs in 1875 for a much longer period than Geronimo was held there.

Geronimo died of pneumonia in a little stone hut back of the post hospital at 6:15 on the morning of February 17, 1909. He was buried in the Apache cemetery on Cache Creek, near where the Apaches camped on first arriving at Fort Sill. There was a story current in later years that relatives secretly had conveyed Geronimo's body elsewhere. The reason for this story was that Quanah's grave in Post Oak cemetery west of Cache had been broken into by vandals, and it was thought that the same might happen to Geronimo's. The closest surviving relatives told Sergeant Morris Swett, however, that this was not the case, and Swett had a monument erected over the grave.

In 1913 the majority of the Apaches were sent to the Mescalero reservation. About a hundred of them, however, preferred to remain in Oklahoma. Their share of the cattle money was used to purchase land from the Kiowas and Comanches, and they are at present living quietly near the town of Apache, seventeen miles north of Fort Sill. The training which they had received at Fort Sill gave them a good start on the road to success as citizens. Typifying this is Arthur Guydelkon, nephew of Geronimo, who, as this is written, is operating a steam roller on the new driveway being constructed in front of Fort Sill's new school and administration building.

CHAPTER SEVENTEEN

LAST CAMP FIRES

JEROME AGREEMENT—OPENING OF KIOWA AND COMANCHE COUNTRY
RETURN OF THE BUFFALO—THE LAST TEPEE

D URING the decade preceding 1892 there had been great and continuous agitation in the adjacent country to have the Kiowa-
Comanche Indian reservation opened to settlement. One of the
arguments was that the land was not being used by the Indians, and
that it was needed for agriculture to support the growing population of
the United States. It was pointed out that many whites were homeless
and without land, while between the Washita and Red rivers three million acres were lying idle. All along the border were thousands of people
gazing greedily at this land of Canaan and yearning for the time when
it would be opened to settlement.

A delegation of government officials called the Cherokee Commission
had visited Indian tribes all over the Territory and had persuaded them
to sell their land to the government so that it might be homesteaded.
As a result most of it was being cut up into farms. Only the Kiowa-
Comanche country remained closed. In the autumn of 1892 the commission visited the Kiowas and Comanches. The conference, which lasted
three days beginning October 4, was held in the open air in front of the
Red Store, just south of the Fort Sill military reservation. Joshua Given
was one of the interpreters. The commissioners wanted the Indians to
sell their land for $1.25 an acre. Quanah and others of the more sophisti-
cated Indian leaders asked $2.50 an acre. The majority of the Indians
did not wish to sell at all. They preferred to live on the open range.
Nevertheless, through some means not fully understood, an agreement
was drawn up and signed, whereby the Indians relinquished their land
at $1.25 an acre. Each Indian, in addition to his share of the proceeds
of this sale, was to receive an allotment of 160 acres. The money and
the land were to be held in trust for the Indians for a period of twenty
years, after which the trust period might be extended if deemed desirable.

303

This agreement became known as the Jerome Agreement; it was not a treaty. As soon as the Jerome Agreement was consummated the Indians began to protest. They claimed that they had been tricked into signing something which they did not understand, that they had not intended to give up their land. They protested that the interpreter had made false or incorrect translations of what had been said and written, and that the commissioners had lied to them and defrauded them. The latter were unembarrassed by these accusations; refusing to reopen the matter, they packed up and returned to Washington. Big Tree told Joshua Given that he would die soon, that men who lied to their people could not live. Strangely enough Joshua did die within a year. His relatives say that tuberculosis was the cause, but many of the Kiowas are convinced that the medicine men prayed him to death. The latter theory was aired in the newspapers at the time.

The Jerome Agreement had to be ratified by the United States Senate before it could become effective. Through efforts of Captain H. L. Scott and three prominent Indians, powerfully supported by Senator Matt Quay of Pennsylvania, ratification was blocked for a number of years. Finally Quay died, Captain Scott was in Cuba, and, in June, 1900, the ratification slipped through the Senate. To this day the Indians are pressing against the government a claim that they have been defrauded of rights guaranteed them by the Medicine Lodge treaty of 1867.

OPENING OF THE FORT SILL COUNTRY[1]

A presidential proclamation dated July 4, 1901, announced the opening of the reservation of the Kiowas, Comanches, Kiowa-Apaches, Wichitas, and Caddoes. The country was divided into two districts of 6500 homesteads of 160 acres each. Instead of allowing the homesteaders to select their land by making a "run" like those when other Indian reservations were opened, the officials decided to register the homeseekers and draw the registration cards from a hopper at random to determine who should receive land.

Prior to the registration the cattlemen were required to remove their herds and pasture fences from the reservation. Then the Indians were permitted to choose their allotments. In assigning land to the Indians the officials profited by experience gained during the opening of the Cheyenne and Arapaho country. At that time there had been a certain amount of lending children from one family to another in order to receive double allotments. Furthermore it was discovered afterwards that

---

[1] Dr. E. E. Dale, "The Opening of the Fort Sill Country" (MS lent to the author by Dr. Dale, University of Oklahoma) ; *'Neath the August Sun,* a collection of reminiscences published in 1935 by the Lawton Business and Professional Women's Club.

some of the Indian women had bundled up small fat dogs and laced them in the papoose carriers which they wore on their backs. Agents who failed to investigate each squirming bundle registered a number of canines as members of the tribe and allotted land to them. Careful work on the part of the officials prevented fraud of this kind during the allotment of land to the Kiowas and Comanches. Some old warriors stubbornly refused to make selections. The agent did so for them. Most of the Indians, however, made wise choices, generally picking land along the creek bottoms where the soil was rich and wood and water plentiful. At this time a number of white men who had married Indian women received allotments, and also the Indians adopted a few of their white friends so that they might receive land. One of the latter was Horace P. Jones, who was given a good farm a few miles southwest of Fort Sill. A number of Indians donated cattle and so did Mr. Quinette, so that presently Jones possessed a valuable herd. Dot Babb and his sister, who many years before had been captured by the Comanches but had been ransomed, now appeared to receive allotments as members of the Comanche tribe. They were sent home discomfited.

The money which the government paid to the Indians for the land was placed to their credit in the United States Treasury. Since that time the interest has been paid to them at stated intervals. In addition to this they receive small amounts derived from oil royalties on land along Red River. A few of them farm their allotments, but most of them rent their land on the crop share basis. At the present time most of them are very poor indeed. Their white tenants are mostly on relief, but the Indians, who own the land but cannot sell it or mortgage it and who are no more able to make it produce a living than their tenants, scarcely know where their next meal is coming from. Few of the Indians were given outright title to their allotments. This was a wise provision, for those who did receive title in most cases quickly fell victims to land sharks. An example of this is furnished by the old white captive Millie Durgan, who because of her race was assumed to be sufficiently astute to look after her interests. Environment, however, proved more potent than heredity and Millie soon lost her land through foreclosure.

The great registration of homesteaders was to begin on July 10—at El Reno for the north district and at Fort Sill for the south (Lawton) district. This registration was to last until July 26, after which the cards were to be sent to El Reno for the big lottery. The new country was divided into three counties, with certain lands set aside for schools and for townsites of county seats. Of course the Fort Sill military reservation of some 45,000 acres was exempted from homesteading, being retained by the War Department. Five miles south of Fort Sill a townsite was laid out for the seat of Comanche County; later it was named Lawton in honor of Major General Henry Lawton. Lots here were to be sold at auction after the drawing for homesteads had been completed.

Free land! When the good news spread through the surrounding country, homesteaders began rushing to Fort Sill and El Reno to register. Just why they were hurrying no one knew; every person stood an equal chance of drawing a lucky card in the lottery, irrespective of the order in which he registered. But no one wanted to be last. During the first part of July the roads and trails leading across the prairies were filled with caravans of homesteaders. Some were in wagons, some in buggies, others on horseback. A few rode bicycles and there were many who trudged along with packs on their backs. It was like the migration of a people. One might see a covered wagon drawn by a team composed of a dispirited pony and a placid cow; wagons piled with household goods, here a crate filled with chickens, there a pig squealing in a box. Clouds of dust rose in the sweltering July atmosphere. The people who had thus come prepared to settle evidently intended to buy land if they could not draw it. As the multitudes arrived at Fort Sill a line formed at the door of the building in which registration was taking place; it stretched across the post and on out into the prairie. Eventually it would have been several miles long, and some of the people might have stood in line for two weeks had not one of the officers at the post conceived a happy idea: It was announced that the homesteaders were to organize themselves into companies of a hundred men each, each company to elect a captain. The captain was to report at the office, where he would be given a serial number for his company. Then by keeping account of the companies registered each day he could determine approximately when his men should form in line. This plan worked splendidly and permitted the people to spend most of the time in their camps.

Fort Sill was the only community (except for Indian camps) within many miles. As there were no hotel accommodations the homesteaders had to camp. This camp extended for miles along Cache Creek. In the evenings crowds gathered around the parade ground to watch guard mount and retreat. Most of the people were in good spirits. In those days life was not geared to so high a speed as nowadays. There was more hospitality, less suspicion. People did not bruise so easily; hardships did not cause great dismay. The soldiers patroled the area, breaking up drinking bouts, fights, and gambling. In general good fellowship prevailed. The whole affair was much like a gigantic picnic. At night thousands of campfires winked along the creek. Blue smoke hung low among the cottonwoods and hackberries. More people kept arriving through the days and nights. Before long at least ten thousand persons were drawing mail at Quinette's store.

Registration closed on Friday, July 26. The drawing took place at

El Reno three days later. This was a public spectacle attended by thousands. The first name drawn was John Woods, a hardware clerk from Weatherford, Oklahoma. The second was that of Mattie Beal, a telephone girl of Wichita, Kansas. As the first few persons to draw would pick land in the vicinity of the prospective county seat, it was recognized that Mr. Woods and Miss Beal held claims worth considerable money. And so it proved.

The auction of town lots took place on August 6. Lawton, as it was soon named, became a great sprawling community of tents and shacks, with the main street—known as Goo-goo Avenue—running east and west along what is now the Frisco railroad. Throngs of sharpers, gamblers, cattlemen, and honest farmers mingled in the dust which lay ankle deep in the streets. Water sold at fancy prices. Sanitation was elementary. All the lively entertainments of a boom town were present in quantity. Nevertheless the better elements among the citizenry quickly took charge. The place became quieter and began to develop into a thriving prairie city.

Thus closed an era in the southwest. The day of the Indian was over. He was now an insignificant minority in a land settled by white people. Rapidly the open range became checkered with cultivated fields and fenced pastures. The house supplanted the tepee. The wild game that remained in the area was quickly exterminated. Fort Sill alone was unchanged. Its old stone buildings, neat little square, and the untouched expanse of its reservation were all that remained to remind the Indians of the country's appearance before the settlement. They lost their old fear of the post. It became to them a pleasant reminder of the days that were gone, a place where they might ride through deep grass and camp in the shade beside clear streams.

The Comanches selected their allotments south of the mountains, the Kiowas to the north, and the Kiowa-Apaches remained with the latter. In 1913 a number of Chiricahua Apaches were given land near the town of Apache. The Indians now are scattered through the counties constituted from the former reservation, and are not segregated in any one place. Although the agency remained at Anadarko, a substation was maintained at the site of the old Fort Sill agency for many years, for the convenience of the Indians who lived south of the mountains.

The opening of the country also brought in two railroad lines. This was a source of great grief to Horace P. Jones, the aged post interpreter. Jones, who during his last few years was a semi-invalid, remained unreconciled to the delights of civilization. In his last sickness he could hear the blows of sledges spiking down the rails as the railroad approached from the north. Jones used to tell Mr. Quinette that he did not intend to live to see the railroad arrive. And indeed he did not. When the line reached Cache Creek, Jones was dead. He died November 16, 1901, in his little house back of the old post, and was buried in the post cemetery.[2]

Fort Sill turned out in a body to see the arrival of the first railroad train. The engineer brought his locomotive to a stop at the station, leaned out of the cab window, doffed his cap ceremoniously to the crowd, and shouted, "Everybody put down your umbrellas and parasols; you'll frighten my horse!"[3] It might be thought that the Indians would be greatly impressed by the train, but they were not. On the contrary, they had become rather blasé, having seen many trains at Rush Springs, Chickasha, and other not-distant towns. In fact, that old Comanche war-chief, Tabananica, had died of heart failure brought on by running to catch a train at Anadarko. What a striking example of the "benefits" brought to the children of the wilderness by the hurry of modern civilized life! A scarcely less interesting instance of this occurred some years before, when Yellow Bear was killed in the Pickwick Hotel at Fort Worth, Texas. Quanah Parker and Yellow Bear, on retiring for the night in their hotel room, blew out the gas light. Yellow Bear was asphyxiated and Quanah nearly perished.

Soldiers at Fort Sill derived much more fun from the arrival of the railroad than did the Indians. It became a standard form of amusement to go to Lawton on Saturday nights and steal joyrides on the station master's handcar. This harassed railroad official tried locking his car up in a shed, or removing the wheels. All without success. The handcar continued to carry hilarious military excursionists into the country on moonlight nights. Finally the agent was forced to appeal to the commanding officer for official assistance.

Mr. Quinette, the post trader, perhaps had as much influence in changing the mode of living of the Indians as did the surrounding settlers. When Quinette sent to St. Louis for a fancy baby buggy for his infant son, the Indians were charmed. Soon Quinette received orders for over fifty similar vehicles. In a short time the proud Indian women could be seen wheeling their papooses around the prairie.

RETURN OF THE BUFFALO

In the fall of 1907 the New York Zoological Society presented to the Wichita National Forest Reserve, in the mountains west of Fort Sill, a herd of fifteen bison. The animals were shipped from New York to Cache, Oklahoma, by rail, thence hauled in wagons to the forest reserve. They arrived on October 18.[4]

[2] J. B. Thoburn, *Horace P. Jones, Scout and Interpreter*, p. 390.
[3] Mrs. W. H. Quinette to author.
[4] New York Zoological Society Bulletin No. 28, January, 1908.

The Indians had been warned of the impending event by their friend Frank Rush, the forest supervisor. For two weeks many of them had camped with their families near the pasture waiting to see the buffalo. When the big day arrived they put on their best clothes and stood with faces against the wire, while "God's cattle" were liberated in the enclosure. It was with deep emotion that the older Indians witnessed the return of the buffalo to the plains country. It brought back poignant memories of the old free days when there were no fences, when the grass grew untouched by plow and the prairie was black with buffalo. They pointed out the big animals to their children and grandchildren, who had never seen them; they told old stories of famous hunts, and of the warpath, when the Indian was master of the country and owed allegiance to no one.

THE LAST TEPEE

On the banks of Cache Creek, east of the old post, stood the tepee of Sergeant I-see-o, sole surviving member of the Fort Sill detachment of Indian scouts. The government had provided for him a comfortable little house east of the railroad station, equipped with a stove, electric lights, and running water. But the old Kiowa preferred to remain in a tent. White soldiers passing by saw the Indian seated on the ground within the dim interior of the lodge, silently smoking a long pipe. They smiled at what they considered the inability of the red man to adapt himself to the modern mode of life. But they did not comprehend that I-see-o had become a priest of the ancient tribal religion, a keeper of one of the ten great Kiowa sacred medicines.

Tribal law demanded that this medicine, "Our Grandmother," as they called it, be kept in a tent, not in a house. And so I-see-o sat before a little altar of buffalo chips above which hung a rawhide pouch containing the sacred objects. As he watched the blue smoke rise I-see-o's thoughts wandered back along the corridors of time. He reviewed again the days when he was a young warrior on the war trails leading into Texas and Old Mexico. . . . great buffalo hunts on the Cimarron and Arkansas. . . . joyous days of the Sun Dance on the Washita above Rainy Mountain. . . . the Medicine Lodge Council in 1867. . . . the bloodshed and starvation of the '70's and early '80's. . . . association with his friend Captain Scott at Fort Sill in the '90's. . . .

I-see-o took out of his uniform pocket a letter recently received from Scott and asked his nephew to read it to him once more:

"You did good work at that time (the Ghost Dance excitement)," wrote General Scott. "You brought things about so there was no one killed. . . . the Indian people of Oklahoma owe you a great deal of thanks. . . . If it had not been for you in those days there would have been great

309

bloodshed. . . . the white people owe as much to you as do your own people."

I-see-o held his status as scout at Fort Sill until 1913, when he gave up the position and went to live with his family on his allotment. But he was utterly incapable of making his living by farming. Stunned by the complexities of modern economic life, a simple product of the stone age, the old Kiowa was soon destitute. In 1915 he went with a delegation to Washington, where he encountered his friend Scott, then a major general and chief of staff of the army. Scott's eyes filled with tears to see the venerable Indian, who had given the best years of his life to the government, now ragged and forlorn. He took I-see-o into the office of the Secretary of War.

"Mr. Secretary," he said. "It long has been the custom of the white man to employ a native against his own people, then when the war or other trouble is over to cast him aside like a sucked lemon, with the rankest ingratitude. Look at this old Kiowa! He is down and out— broken in the service of the United States. There is no more work in him, the Army cannot use him. Yet there are Indians and whites alive today who would not be alive were it not for the fidelity of I-see-o. I want authority to enlist him as a sergeant in the United States army for the rest of his life!"[5]

Orders were issued. The post commander at Fort Sill was instructed to care for I-see-o; the government would cherish the former scout during the remainder of his days, in payment for his one-time services. I-see-o's position became an enviable one: Never to be retired on account of age, never to be reduced in rank, for all the rest of his life to hold the rating of senior duty sergeant in the army, and nothing to do but show up at the pay table once a month. He spent most of his time gazing at the changing expanse of prairie and the changeless mountains, wondering whether he was living in the same world in which he had been born. Automobiles, guns, and tractors roared past his tepee, airplanes circled overhead. The works of the white man were too marvelous to contemplate. Had he seen all these things sixty years before, he would have worshipped them as supernatural.

Occasionally I-see-o visited the office of the post commander. He always wore a uniform coat, but clung to his braids and moccasins. Yet he never lost his natural dignity. He was ever treated with great kindness and politeness. It was, "Here, orderly, get a chair for I-see-o," or "Pardon me, we will take up this matter later. I now am going to talk to I-see-o." When distinguished personages such as General Pershing and General Snow, Chief of Field Artillery, visited the post I-see-o was in-

[5] Morris Swett, *Sergeant I-see-o, Kiowa Indian Scout* (MS, Field Artillery School library, Fort Sill).

vited to help receive them. Truly he had been lifted up high, as on a pedestal, before all his people.

At length I-see-o's wife died. There was no one to care for the tepee. He went to live in the cottage near Quarry Hill, attended by his sons, or by his nephew, George Hunt. The old warrior's eyes grew dim. His campfire had burned to the embers. In January of 1927 he contracted that scourge of the Indian race—pneumonia. One hour after midnight on the eleventh of March his spirit passed out of his mouth and ascended to the Milky Way.

Kiowas and Comanches alike paid a last respect to I-see-o in the funeral held in the mission south of Fort Sill. Silence was prolonged throughout the service, broken only by the voice of the missionary and the interpreters. George Hunt said, "He is like a shock of corn gathered in old age." The service was repeated at the post chapel, attended by all of the military personnel who could gather inside the little building, including three general officers. Large crowds waited outside, and followed the flag-draped casket to the post cemetery. While the post flag hung at half-mast, the coffin was lowered. A bugler sounded taps, and a firing squad fired a volley over the grave. It was more impressive than any other Indian funeral in the history of the country.[6]

After the whites had left the cemetery Indian lamentations rose eerily in the chill March air beside the mound of fresh earth. And every year, on Memorial Day, relatives come to "cry for I-see-o."

THE YEARS PASS. It is January 8, 1969, and in a colorful ceremony on the Old Post parade ground a high-ranking officer from Washington and the post sergeant major re-enact before a large crowd General Sheridan's driving of a stake to symbolize the founding of Fort Sill. The scene carries one back through the hundred years that have passed. The Old Post is much the same, with its quarters and barracks still in use. The commander lives in the same center building on the north "line" where General Sherman narrowly escaped death at the hands of the Kiowas. In the parade, in colorful, authentic costume and uniform of 1869, are riders representing scouts, pioneers, Indians, and Custer's cavalry. Even the cannon that fires the salute is a brass Napoleon muzzle-loader of the Civil War.

But there are differences. The garrison of Fort Sill today is larger than the entire United States Army was in 1869. Lined up in front of the old post headquarters is a display of awesome weapons—self-propelled, long-range guns, howitzers, and a huge missile on its carrier. Overhead powerful helicopters are whirling.

[6] H. L. Scott to W. Cruikshank, December 13, 1933.

What of the Indians? In the crowd of onlookers and in the formation they are there in force—descendants of the chiefs and warriors of the Kiowas and Comanches who were camped about the post when Sheridan was there. The grandsons of two noted chiefs, James Auchiah, grandson of Satanta, and Roland Whitehorse, grand-nephew of White Horse and great-grandson of To-hauson, are standing in front of the old headquarters where, as members of the staff of the museum, they have helped prepare the Hall of Flags for dedication. And there are many such present on this day.

All through the country about Fort Sill live the Kiowas, Comanches, and Apaches, on farms and in town, or serving on the post in uniform or as civilian employees. Elsewhere they are in business, in industry, in school, or in government. At this time when the "copperhead" and the disaffected are abroad in the land, it is good to see that the Indians are utterly loyal to their country, and large numbers of them are in the service here or overseas. Many are winning promotion and decorations. Some are dying for their native land.

But for the Indian in this region the road has taken a new turn, and ahead of him the sky on the horizon is growing brighter.

PART V

APPENDICES

GROWTH OF FORT SILL

EVEN AFTER the Indian country was opened to settlement Fort Sill remained for a number of years an isolated western post. A small garrison of cavalry was maintained there, not to control the Indians, for that need had long passed, but simply because the post provided permanent barracks and quarters. It seemed inevitable that eventually Fort Sill would be abandoned; in fact there was some agitation in Washington to turn it over to the Chiricahua Apaches, who were without land of their own. It was realized that these Indians could not remain prisoners forever, that they would have to be given a reservation of some kind. In furtherance of this project the military reservation was increased, and the consent of the Kiowa and Comanche chiefs was obtained to settling the Apaches permanently in the country.

However on January 9, 1902, there arrived at Fort Sill troops of a branch of the service other than cavalry, which was to change the destiny of the post. This was the 29th Battery of Field Artillery. Before long the idea began to take root that Fort Sill might be valuable as an artillery center. Several years elapsed before any action was taken. In 1905 the Chief of Staff of the Army stated in his annual report: "The reservation at Fort Sill is reported as being especially suitable for the station of a full regiment of field artillery; this owing to its size, its varied terrain, and the availability of the adjoining ground belonging to the government, included in the Indian reservation, which, without detriment to the Indians, can be used for artillery maneuvers." Accordingly orders were issued to organize at Fort Sill a provisional regiment of field artillery to consist of the 2d, 8th, 13th, 14th, 15th, and 21st Batteries of Field Artillery, under command of Colonel Walter Howe. The first of these troops arrived at Fort Sill June 29, 1905. A regimental camp was established under tents located on the flats in front of the trader's store, where Grierson's 10th Cavalry had first camped in 1868 and 1869.

From that time on Fort Sill became definitely a field artillery post. It is true that cavalry units were stationed there for two more years, but it was recognized that the future of the post lay in its availability as an artillery training ground. At that time the field artillery, like the cavalry, was strictly a mounted branch of the service. No one dreamed in 1907 that the red guidon of the artillery or the yellow guidon of the cavalry would be carried across the rolling plains on anything except a galloping horse.

Then one fine day in the spring of that year, the peace and sanctity of old Fort Sill was rudely torn asunder by the arrival of a machine which one day was to revolutionize military transportation. This infernal device chugged up the dusty road from Lawton, entered at the southeastern corner of the quadrangle, and made a complete circuit of the post, leaving demoralization and devastation in its wake. The contraption was innocent enough in appearance—it looked extraordinarily like a buggy without a horse. But may the Lord deliver us from the awful sounds it emitted! It snorted; it banged like a shotgun; it clattered like a boiler works. And to add to the confusion, the human devil attired in linen duster and goggles, who was its master, kept pinching a rubber protuberance on its side, which caused it to squawk angrily.

Like the good people in "The Night Before Christmas," the startled denizens of Fort Sill rushed to the windows to see what was the matter. As the uncouth affair careened past at a sustained speed of better than twelve miles an hour, horses tied in front of barracks and quarters stood on their hind legs and screamed in dismay. Surreys and buggies were overturned. Hitching posts were uprooted. Loose animals fled to the plains. In dark places under buildings could be seen shining pairs of eyes where dogs had taken refuge. In the trees cats arched their backs in horrid repugnance. But in a few moments the Thing came to rest in front of post headquarters and, with a final vicious pop, was still. The post gradually subsided, as after danger of an Indian attack. Post headquarters met the emergency promptly by issing the following order:

"FORT SILL, OKLA.,
April 17, 1907

"*General Orders*
     No. 13.

"Automobiles are hereby forbidden to enter the precincts of the post. For this purpose the precincts of the post are described as the plateau on which all the buildings of the post proper are located."

"By order of Major Taylor.
(Signed) "WM. H. CLOPTON, JR.,
"1st Lieut. & Sqdn. Adjt. 13th Cavalry, Adjutant."

In 1907 headquarters and three batteries of the 1st Field Artillery were stationed at Fort Sill. There was a revival of the perennial project in the Army to concentrate its forces in large posts rather than to have them scattered in small garrisons. One of the pet schemes of the incumbent Chief of Staff, Major General Franklin Bell, was to build up Fort Sill into a brigade or even a division post. It is said that he wanted to spend twenty million dollars to make it the military show place of the country. His idea was to build a new post along the south reservation boundary, extending west as far as Signal Mountain with an electric railway running from Lawton, a hotel on the hill, and various other grand features. Everyone in Washington called it Bell's pipe dream.

It was also proposed to modify the old post in order to provide for the already increased garrison. This met with a storm of protest from members of former garrisons who took delight in the romantic historical associations of the limestone fort. Secretary of War William H. Taft visited Fort Sill to look over the situation. After riding around in a buggy and spending the night in the commanding officer's quarters he remarked to Mr. Quinette: "You need worry no longer. We shall not change a single stone of the old post." With two minor exceptions this promise has been faithfully observed to the present date.[1]

There were several obstacles to the proposed expansion of Fort Sill. First there was the lack of an adequate supply of water. Heyl's Hole was investigated to see if it would supply the additional amount required. A pump was rigged up and sucked the hole dry in order to determine the rate of flow. Heyl's Hole was found to be twenty feet deep but without underground source of water; the bottom of the pit was covered with thousands of condemned rifle cartridges. The town of Lawton was also running short of water. The springs and wells upon which it depended were drying up. There had been no rain for months. The streams were mere trickles. It was only a question of weeks before the city would be entirely without water. The citizens formed a project to dam Medicine Bluff Creek near Mount Scott; but first they had to obtain permission from the War Department to run a pipeline across the reservation. Mr. Quinette was sent to Washington in February of 1907 to secure this permit. He interviewed Mr. Taft and General Bell; the latter gave his approval and promised to visit the post in June after he had attended the graduation exercises at the school at Fort Leavenworth. In the meantime the construction quartermaster at Fort Sill dug a new well north of Ambrosia Spring and connected it to the spring house. It appeared that the question of water supply was solved for the time being.

General Bell, on his visit, selected a site for the new post west of the present Post Field. Later he sent Major Slayden of the Engineer Corps to

[1] One stone warehouse and the old cavalry stables.

make the necessary survey. Major Slayden returned to Washington with the report that the government would have to extend the limits of the reservation on the south, as it would be unwise to construct the post so close to the boundary where the soldiers would be easily accessible to bootleggers and other undesirable persons. General Bell put the matter squarely up to the citizens of Lawton. He told them that if they could secure options on the land and donate it to the government the post would be built where he had stated it would. Otherwise it would be located at the other end of the reserve, near Elgin.[2]

The Lawton chamber of commerce immediately became active. At first they were balked by the attitude of the landowners, who demanded twice as much for the land as the civic committee was willing to pay. Finally, through condemnation threats, the necessary options were secured. Mr. Quinette was sent to Washington with them, where he found that it would be necessary for Congress to authorize the War Department to accept the land. The bill was submitted promptly in both houses by the congressmen from Oklahoma; it passed the House without difficulty, but ran into trouble in the Senate because one of the senators from Oklahoma asked that $40,000 be appropriated to pay for the land. The session of Congress came to an end with the bill not passed. It looked as if the new post project was doomed.

Quinette, greatly discouraged, prepared to return to Lawton. But before he left he met Quartermaster General Humphrey who, hearing of his plight, said that he had $400,000 left in his "jeans" which would revert to the treasury if not spent before the end of the fiscal year. He saw no reason why Fort Sill should not have it. It was only necessary that General Bell let the contracts before July 1, and get the actual work started. Mr. Quinette went immediately to see General Bell, who was just leaving his office to lead Mr. Taft's inaugural parade. He said that he had no time to talk. But the veteran post trader fixed him like the ancient mariner, and told him what General Humphrey had said. Bell walked back to his desk, made a big blue-pencil memorandum, and said that he would attend to it right away. That is the way the money to begin the new post was obtained.

A few weeks later General Bell sent out his engineers to make the

2 Major General J. F. Bell to W. H. Quinette, January 4, 1909. General Bell wrote, in part: "If Lawton wants this post it has probably got to get its skates on and hustle. . . . . We don't *have* to have this post, and there are durned few people here who are in favor of having it at all. . . . . Everywhere thruout the United States people are begging the War Department to establish a post, and are offering any amount of land we need for nothing. Evidently Lawton has concluded we have got to establish this post, and they need do nothing. Well, we'll see.

"I have reliable information that speculators have purchased all the land south of the reservation, with a view to unloading it on the Government at their own price. This is another indication that Lawton thinks this post must be built. There is evidently work for some fool-killer to do in that vicinity."

final selection for the site of the post. The place chosen was on the old rifle range which in 1869 had been Custer's parade ground. Some of the people of Lawton were disappointed that the post was not built nearer the town, but they remained quiet lest the authorities be antagonized and not build it at all. Actual construction commenced June 20, 1909, under the direction of Captain David L. Stone, constructing quartermaster.

THE FIELD ARTILLERY SCHOOL

In 1907 the artillery branch of the United States Army split into the Field Artillery and the Coast Artillery. The Artillery School at Fortress Monroe, Virginia, promptly eliminated from its curriculum all matters not pertaining strictly to coast artillery; hence there existed no school for the instruction of field artillerymen, except the Mounted Service School at Fort Riley, which offered nothing in the way of gunnery or strictly field artillery technique.

There were thirty-six batteries of field artillery in the Army at that time; they had been organized into regiments (on paper), but the batteries were so scattered throughout different military posts that little opportunity was afforded officers to gain instruction and practice in handling masses of artillery or in learning higher staff and command duties pertaining to field artillery. It is true that post or regimental schools were conducted annually, but the character of knowledge imparted depended mostly on the varying professional attainments of the higher commanders, and upon their ability and willingness to impart this information. Hence there was little uniformity of instruction, and some of the junior officers were seriously deficient in proper understanding of their duties.[1] Furthermore, the allowances of ammunition for target practice were so small, and so many officers were on duties which prevented their being present at this practice, that many of the captains and lieutenants had never fired a three-inch battery, and there were a number who had not even seen a target practice. In 1911 the commandant of the School of Fire stated that one of the battery commanders of an instruction battery, who had been in command for four years, did not yet know what a bracket was.[2]

[1] Report of Major General Thomas H. Barry to Major General Leonard Wood, June 5, 1913.

[2] Captain Dan T. Moore to Colonel E. J. Greble, July 28, 1911. Readers who are not

Alert field artillery officers recognized that the situation was serious, that if the nation should be plunged into war the infantry would pay in blood for mistakes of artillerymen who had not been trained properly. The question was raised as to whether it was not essential to establish a school of fire for field artillery. To this school would be allotted a much more generous allowance of ammunition than was available to regiments, whereby officers actually would be taught how to shoot. In this school instruction would be comprehensive, thorough, and uniform. Colonel Edwin St. John Greble was a leading proponent of the idea of founding such a school.

It was believed that European armies, which at this time were actively preparing for an imminent war (though this fact was not generally recognized), probably had ideas and methods which in some respects, at least, were in advance of those in vogue in this country. Consequently the War Department sent an able and energetic officer abroad to study in foreign artillery schools, preparatory to his taking a prominent part in the establishment of a school of fire in this country. The officer selected for this important duty was Captain Dan T. Moore, 6th Field Artillery. He spent the year 1908–1909 visiting the artillery schools in England, Holland, Austria, but especially the German artillery school at Juterborg.

In November, 1910, Captain Moore was sent to Fort Sill to make preliminary arrangements for the establishment of the school of fire. Fort Sill was tentatively selected as the site of this school because the concentration of artillery regiments there since 1905, and the target practice conducted by these regiments, showed that the wide expanse (51,000 acres) and the varied terrain of the Fort Sill reservation offered admirable opportunity for training both in firing and tactical handling of field artillery. With these ideas Captain Moore was in such hearty accord that he wrote that the Fort Sill reservation would be worth its cost many times over to the government.

Shortly after Captain Moore arrived at Fort Sill, a board of officers was appointed to formulate detailed plans for the establishment of the school and for its conduct thereafter. This board consisted of Lieutenant Colonel D. J. Rumbough and Captain Jesse Langdon, both 1st Field Artillery, and Captain Moore. In March, 1911, the 1st Field Artillery was ordered from Fort Sill to Hawaii, and, because Colonel Rumbough was going with the regiment, he was replaced on the board by Colonel Henry M. Andrews. In drawing up the regulations for the school, the board had to settle a number of controversial matters, including the rules for safety in firing on the range, the size and composition of the school

field artillerymen are informed that a bracket consists of two ranges differing by, say, one, two, or four hundred yards, which surely enclose the target.

detachments, and the policy as to whether the post commander or commandant of the school was to have the final word in questions affecting the school, irrespective of rank. There were also many decisions to be secured regarding the amount of funds and equipment to be allotted the school. In all this activity Captain Moore played an important role, for he was able to keep in touch with the War Department through personal letters to his friend and sponsor, Colonel Greble, who was on duty in the office of the Chief of Staff, Major General Leonard Wood. Colonel Greble wrote to Captain Moore almost daily, giving him much valuable advice, and encouraging him to redouble his efforts when he appeared downcast over the many difficulties which continued to present themselves.

In March, 1911, after several months of stout effort, the board submitted to the War Department a set of regulations for the new school. Captain Moore and his fellow members were considerably taken aback to have part of these regulations disapproved, the principal fault found with them in Washington being that they did not safeguard adequately the lives and property of the Indians who were occupying the Fort Sill reservation.[3] The Indians in question were the Chiricahua Apache prisoners of war; it will be remembered that the Kiowas and Comanches now lived on allotments, and that there was no longer an Indian reservation in this part of the country. The small picket villages of the Apaches were scattered over the military reservation in such a way that large areas could not be used for artillery practice without shooting over or near the dwellings. Furthermore, the Apaches, with that love of nature characteristic of primitives, spent much of their time camping in various parts of the reservation, so that cannon could scarcely be fired anywhere without endangering them. Even worse, the Indians owned thousands of cattle, which grazed over so much territory that the part of the reservation east of the railroad tracks could not be used at all by the artillery; and the artillerymen hardly dared fire on other parts of the range during the dry season for fear of setting fire to the prairie grass which the Apaches cut and baled for hay. This hay furnished the prisoners of war with their principal income aside from that which was derived from the sale of cattle; therefore loud protests would have arisen from the Indians and their protectors if an artillery projectile had ignited this grass. The grass really belonged to the government, but the government was not in the hay business, so the anomalous situation existed in which the Indians cut and baled the publicly owned hay, then sold it back to the government at a tidy profit. Following this transaction, quantities of the hay were reissued to the Apaches to feed the government mules which they employed to break up land belonging to the United States on which to raise vegetables to sell to the troops at Fort Sill for further profit.

[3] Greble to Moore, March 13, 1911.

322

Captain Moore, with whom the interests of the School of Fire were paramount, seems to have been unsympathetic toward the Indians, for he wrote, somewhat heatedly: "These so-called prisoners of war have more rights and privileges than free men." He went on to point out that the land used by the Apaches long ago had been declared a *military* reservation, and that the Indians had no property rights there whatever. Colonel Greble agreed with all this, but he warned Captain Moore not to antagonize those in charge of the Indians. "Concerning the question of your regulations for the conduct of fire on the range, let that go," he wrote, soothingly. "The War Department will probably decide what is to be done with the Apache prisoners, and I think they will probably be removed from the reservation, but until this question is settled there is no use giving a weapon to the friends of the Indians. They and their property rights have been protected in the past firings, and they can be protected in the future firings without raising a rumpus." And so the matter was allowed to rest. Two years later, just as Colonel Greble predicted, the Apaches were moved away from Fort Sill.

By the middle of April the problem of the Indians on the range had faded to insignificance compared with another obstacle which confronted Captain Moore and the board. This was a water shortage at the post, which at one time became so serious that the authorities nearly decided to abandon the school, and the post as well.

In June, 1911, the work of the board of officers was finished, and the board was dissolved. General Orders No. 73, War Department, June 5, 1911, authorized the establishment at Fort Sill of "The School of Fire for Field Artillery." This was effected on June 18. Another order dated July 19 designated Captain Dan T. Moore as commandant. Captain Moore planned to start the first class in the fall, but in the meantime he had much work to finish in connection with training the instruction batteries, organizing the school detachment, setting up targets on the range, establishing a range telephone line, procuring a proper topographical map of the reservation, and getting his office in order. He had asked for a colored detachment to serve as orderlies, care for the horses of the students, and act as janitors in the buildings; and a white detachment of specialists to care for the materiel, communication equipment, to assist the instructors and provide the necessary clerical staff. The colored detachment was not granted him, but he was given a white detachment of about forty men, somewhat smaller than he had considered necessary. He also was told that forty-seven horses for students was "very excessive." The white detachment built and installed the targets; and Lieutenant Dawson Olmstead, Signal Corps, was sent to put up the range telephone system. Captain Clarence Deems, Jr., Field Artillery, was ordered to the post to make the topographical map which the commandant desired. Captain

Moore personally trained the two instruction batteries. These units were composed partly of raw recruits, who were rather gun-shy at first. Captain Moore was considerably pressed for time to turn out acceptable gun squads before the first course commenced.

It was planned to provide the following courses at the school: for personnel of the Regular Army: three months for battery officers; one month for field officers; three months for noncommissioned officers. For officers of the militia: a one-month course. Courses were to be held in the fall and in the spring for the Regular Army, but for the militia they were to be held in the summer, when the militia officers were able to be absent from their positions in civil life.

On September 15, 1911, fourteen captains and twenty-two non-commissioned officers arrived to take the first course. Among the former was Captain Henry W. Butner, who in 1936 was major general and commandant of the Field Artillery School. The other student officers were: Captains W. S. Guignard, Brook Payne, Augustine McIntyre, T. W. Hollyday, W. K. Lambdin, G. M. Brooke, A. S. Fuger, G. M. Apple, R. O. Mason, J. B. W. Corey, A. F. Cassels, W. S. Browning, and J. F. Barnes. On November 15 the following field officers arrived to take the one-month course: Lieutenant Colonels A. B. Dyer, G. W. Van Deusen, and S. D. Sturgis, and Majors Ernest Hinds and O. W. B. Farr.[4] (General Hinds returned to serve as commandant of the school, 1919–23.)

At first most of the instructional work as well as administrative duty fell on Captain Moore, the commandant, though he was assisted by Lieutenants R. McT. Pennell, the secretary, R. S. Parrott, the supply officer, and Sergeant Major Lynn Boggs. Later in the year Captain Augustine McIntyre was detailed as an instructor.[5] This officer was highly regarded by Captain Moore and by the latter's successor, and was retained as an instructor for a number of years. He was the only officer whose sole duty was that of instructor; other instructors at first were supplied by the instruction troops and by the school staff. Lieutenant Pennell, also highly regarded, served as secretary until 1915 and again in 1917.[6]

After its beginning the school progressed rapidly; and at the termination of the fall course in 1913 Captain Moore felt that it was in excellent shape. He decided that he had been there long enough, and was making efforts to be relieved; but the only encouragement he received from Colonel Greble was, "I do not blame you for having enough of the School of Fire. I appreciate, however, what you have done there and so will anyone who will think it over, and the extra work won't hurt your

---

[4] Old Files, Fort Sill, F.A.C. Museum.
[5] In 1936 Colonel McIntyre was assigned to Fort Sill as commandant.
[6] In 1944, Major General Pennell was assigned as commandant.

constitution nor your future standing in the army. . . . . Keep a-pushing. It is a different field artillery from what it was when the first draft of order for the School of Fire was drawn."

In spite of this support by Colonel Greble, there was considerable criticism of Captain Moore's methods and considerable opposition to them. On September 15, 1914, his request to be relieved was granted, and he was succeeded as commandant by Lieutenant Colonel Edward F. McGlachlin. The new commandant made radical changes in the curriculum, and by placing in operation an entirely new method of instruction effected a reorganization of the school. During 1914 the work of the school became more comprehensive and prominent. Considerable research was done, and much valuable literature was compiled and issued to the field artillery. The statistical department, under Captain Lesley J. McNair,[7] was active in evaluating data secured by firing and other tests.

From its very inception the school was handicapped by a lack of suitable buildings. At first it was housed in the old post. The office of the commandant, secretary, and sergeant major was in a little frame building (No. 432) at the southeast corner of the old post parade ground, now assigned to the post museum and preserved as the first headquarters of the Field Artillery School. The classroom was in the stone barracks across the street, now also a museum building (No. 435), which was formally opened to the public on Fort Sill's one hundredth birthday as the Field Artillery's Hall of Flags. In the fall of 1911, Captain Moore moved his office to the more spacious old post headquarters building (No. 437, now also assigned to the museum), which had been vacated by the post commander upon completion of the new post. But these facilities soon were outgrown. In 1912, the school moved to one of the new unoccupied barracks in the new post (No. 1616, now used as a mess hall and barracks by the Women's Army Corps Battery, the only WAC battery in the U.S. Army); but two years later an increase in the garrison forced the school to vacate this building and return to the old post. The commandant's office, the secretary's office, the library, and the classrooms were established in the southwestern barracks (No. 441), still used by departments of the Field Artillery School. It was under this last building, it will be recalled, that Satanta, Satank, and Big Tree were confined in May, 1871, after the attempt to kill General Sherman.

All students were quartered in tents; this was so ordered to prevent them from bringing their families. The tents were located not far from where General Custer had camped in 1869, on the ground now occupied by the post's Capehart Housing. Here also was a frame tent accommo-

[7] In July, 1944, Lieutenant General McNair, Commanding General, Army Ground Forces, was killed in Normandy. McNair Hall at Fort Sill is named for him.

dating a mess for thirty-five students. In 1915, the students were permitted to move into permanent quarters, if and when these became available.

In 1913, the Infantry School of Musketry had moved from the Presidio of Monterey to Fort Sill, but on account of Mexican Border requirements remained relatively inactive until 1915. In that year, Colonel Richard M. Blatchford and Brigadier General William A. Mann, Infantry, were its successive commandants, and by virtue of rank took command of Fort Sill. Being senior to Lieutenant Colonel McGlachlin, Blatchford ordered the latter to vacate the stone barracks, in order to make room for the musketry school. The artillery school would have to shift for itself as best it might. Colonel McGlachlin was aghast. However, he stirred around and discovered that he could purchase the old trader's store from Mr. W. H. Quinette for $1,500. Quinette had gone out of business as trader in order to become a banker in Lawton, a step which he later regretted exceedingly. But it was fortunate for the School of Fire, because it saved the latter from taking to the woods for shelter. The purchase price of the old relic of Indian days was secured from the War Department, also an additional thousand dollars to renovate the building. A few days later, while these preparations were in progress, Colonel Blatchford stalked into the office of the commandant of the School of Fire. Captain Fox Conner and several other instructors were there discussing with the commandant the projected move.

"Why aren't you out of here?" growled Colonel Blatchford, by way of morning greeting.

"I have a few more things to straighten out before I can move," answered Colonel McGlachlin.

Colonel Blatchford shook his finger threateningly and shouted, "You get the hell out of here and get out quick!"

Although the next day was Independence Day, it was only July 4 for the detachment of the School of Fire, for they labored all day long under a broiling sun, to move the School of Fire and its appurtenances into the trader's store. Into this old building, where once the Kiowa chief Big Tree dived headlong from a rear window, went the commandant's office, the secretary's office, the statistical office, the library, and the clerical force. A coal shed on the north side of the building offered shelter to the print shop, which was the forerunner of the present Army Field Artillery Printing Plant. Fortunately the school had closed for the summer, and no classrooms were required for the time being. The school detachment moved into tents.

A few weeks later funds were secured to build two long, one-story shacks immediately south of the trader's store. The classrooms, print shop, and photo shop were placed in the north building of the two, and the school detachment went into the other. The library remained in the trader's store. Tents for the students, and the student mess tent, were moved to this same area. In this unattractive establishment the fall course of 1915 opened. The heat was so intense in the low, unceiled shanties, that even the instructors worked in undershirts. Captain Fox Conner sought to relieve the situation by having a false roof built over the classrooms, with an air space between the two roofs. If Captain Conner had studied the habits of the Indians, he would have built brush arbors under which to conduct classes. Although these two buildings were supposed to be temporary, they were used by the school, for one purpose or another, until 1934, when they were torn down to make room for new officers' quarters.

In July, 1915, the first military air unit of the United States, the 1st Aero Squadron, arrived at Fort Sill for station and to conduct experiments in aerial observation of artillery fire. As one of its accomplishments this squadron made the first aerial mosaic, using a Brock automatic camera. Aerial photos, both single views and mosaics, came into considerable prominence in the Army for substitute maps and firing charts during the 1930's when it appeared that few if any accurate maps could be made quickly by other means in the event of war.

The first squadron cross-country flight began at Fort Sill on November 19, 1915, when six Curtiss JN–4's (Jennies) of the first Aero Squadron took off for Fort Sam Houston, Texas, distant 439 miles. In March, 1916, while still assigned to Fort Sill, this squadron became the first U S operational air unit in the field when it began operations with Pershing's expedition into Mexico.

In the spring of 1916 the troubles with Mexico caused all the artillery units at Fort Sill to be sent to the border. The instructors and staff of the school were ordered to join their regiments; the school was closed. At least fifty new officers had been transferred to the field artillery, who should have been trained at once; but the school was closed nevertheless.[8]

THE WAR COURSES, 1917–1918

In July, 1917, the School of Fire consisted of a caretaking detachment of some forty men of the old school detachment, under command of the secretary of the musketry school, who was an infantry officer. On July 10 the post commander, Colonel Blatchford, received a telegram from the War Department announcing that an artillery school would be established at Fort Sill in the near future. This telegram occasioned little excitement; the infantry school was having troubles of its own, preparing

[8] Much of the foregoing material should be credited to the late Master Sergeant Morris Swett, who in nearly forty years as librarian at Fort Sill has preserved a great mass of correspondence and records and photographs that otherwise would have been lost.

to meet the expansion caused by the entrance of the United States into World War I. Five days later Colonel Blatchford received a telegram from Oklahoma City, informing him that seven student officers were on their way to report to the field artillery school, and would arrive that very night.

Sergeant Morris Swett, librarian of the School of Fire, was sent with a quartermaster "float" to meet the 11:00 P.M. train. Not seven but twenty-one students stepped off the train. Swett had put up tents and cots for seven, but he managed to provide for the additional number. Food, however, was lacking. The students were tired and hungry. They wakened the woman who was supposed to run the mess. She had a half-loaf of bread and a jar of jam in her cupboard, which the students ate.

Classes met the following day. School was supposed to have started already. There were no instructors, no plans, no guns, no texts, no quarters, no food—nothing but dismay. There was not an artillery officer on the post. The students were officers of the Regular Army of other branches of the service who had been transferred to the field artillery. The senior student, Captain Maynard, organized the class and conducted the students about for the next few days mooning at the landscape (studying the terrain).

On July 19 the first instructor, Lieutenant Colonel F. E. Hopkins, arrived. He took charge and began delivering a series of lectures based on the 1916 drill regulations. Soon other instructors came in and gradually the course got under way. Early in August a number of French artillery officers arrived, and conferred with the American officers in planning the course of instruction to be given. It was realized that the warfare in France was somewhat different from that for which our service had been trained, it being a variety of siege warfare requiring special methods. The first class, which had reported on the night of July 15, was called the "zero" class, to distinguish it from the first war class, which commenced September 29, 1917.

Colonel William J. Snow, 4th Field Artillery, was designated as commandant. He arrived at Fort Sill July 27, appointed Captain R. McT. Pennell as secretary, and took a few days to size up the situation. On a bare plateau, with a plant consisting of the trader's store, two long frame shanties, and a group of dust-filled tents baking under the summer sun, Colonel Snow was charged with the training of thousands of field artillery officers who were needed by the army in its tremendous expansion. With such an outlook the average man might have been inclined to throw up his hands and consider the situation hopeless. But Colonel Snow was not an ordinary man. He evolved a bold and splendid project for the enlargement of the school. Briefly, his plan provided for increasing the capacity of the establishment from about thirty students graduated each twelve weeks, to 1,200 to be turned out in the same period—an increase of 4,000 per cent! The school staff and faculty were to be enlarged proportionately; three and one-half regiments of field artillery were to constitute the firing units; and the sum of $730,000 was to be spent for construction of the necessary temporary buildings. Colonel Snow made a hurried trip to Washington, where by untiring patience and perseverance he convinced the War Department of the soundness of his plans. The project was approved September 12, 1917.

Contracts for the new buildings immediately were awarded to the Selden-Breck Construction Company of St. Louis. Like magic, wooden buildings began to spring up all over the plateau. The students were forced to move their tents frequently to make room for the foundations of new buildings. By the time two classes had graduated, the school was built. In the meantime classes were held under trees or in the shade of buildings. But there were so many classes and sections that shade was at a premium. It became customary for junior instructors to pray that their seniors would be ordered to other posts, so that they might inherit the trees or sides of buildings.

Colonel Snow, having been promoted to the grade of brigadier general, was ordered away early in the fall. Soon afterward he became the first Chief of Field Artillery. His successor at the School of Fire was Colonel A. S. Fleming, who carried on in able fashion.

By November 11, 1918, the school had expanded to such extent that the personnel totaled 2,220 as follows: staff and instructors, 247; field artillery students, 1,554; air service cadets (observers), 419. The average weekly output of the school during its peak was approximately 200 field artillery officers and 100 air service observers. A total of 3,215 student officers were graduated during the war courses.[9]

CAMP DONIPHAN

Early in May, 1917, it was known that the War Department intended to establish large military cantonments in different parts of the United States, to be used as training camps for the new army being organized to participate in the world war. The citizens of Lawton were anxious that one of these camps be located on the Fort Sill military reservation; in the interest of this project the chamber of commerce and the city council each sent delegations to Washington. Mr. W. H. Quinette, who was a member of this party, felt sure that his friend General H. L. Scott, now chief of staff, would favor Fort Sill as a site for a cantonment. Unfortunately General Scott was in Russia at the time as a member of the Root mission, and the head of the army temporarily was Major General

[9] Old Files, Fort Sill.

Tasker H. Bliss. The Lawton delegations called on General Bliss, but received no encouragement. They then went to see Secretary of War Newton D. Baker. Mr. Baker, having heard much of Fort Sill from General Scott, was sympathetic. He pointed out, however, that there was not sufficient water at Fort Sill for so large a post; and added that the whole matter of selecting sites for cantonments had been delegated to the department commanders. The Lawtonians would have to "make medicine" with the commander of the Department of Texas.[10]

The delegation representing the chamber of commerce promptly took the train for San Antonio, leaving the committee from the city council to continue the discussion with the War Department. Major General James Parker, the commander of the Department of Texas, had served at Fort Sill in 1876–77 as a lieutenant in Mackenzie's 4th Cavalry. This old association, however, did not prevent him from favoring some other post as a site for the cantonment in Oklahoma. The Lawton men were forced to wire their comrades in Washington: "Nothing doing." This did not completely discourage Messrs. Quinette, Ferris, and others. They continued to importune the War Department, urging the advantages of the Fort Sill site. On May 28, Fort Sill was dropped from consideration by the War Department, on account of the inadequate water supply. The citizens of Lawton, being notified, held a mass meeting; they agreed to turn over the city's water to Fort Sill. On May 30, E. S. Gooch, S. I. McElhoes, and W. C. Laird, directors of the Lawton irrigation district, wired Congressman Scott Ferris, withdrawing their water right in favor of the Army. The Lawton business men concurred. Five days later Mr. Ferris notified Secretary Baker that Lawton would furnish 5,000,000 gallons of water daily to the post.[11] This action on the part of the citizens of Lawton brought quick results. On June 11 General Bliss sent a memorandum to the Adjutant General, notifying him that Fort Sill had been selected as the site of a national army cantonment.

In this manner the camp was established, though somewhat at the expense of the people of Lawton, who at first were rather short of water. Later, the dam at Lake Lawtonka was raised, and another pipeline laid, so that eventually there was enough water for everybody. The new cantonment was named Camp Doniphan, in honor of Colonel Alexander W. Doniphan, of Mexican War fame. It was built on the prairie west and south of the new post area. Infantry units of the Oklahoma National Guard, part of the 36th Division (commanded by Major General Edwin St. John Greble), began coming in before the buildings were finished, and were quartered in tents. During the short stay at Camp Doniphan, the men of these organizations were given intensive instruction in bay-

10 W. H. Quinette to author.
11 Old Files, AGO, 1917.

onet and rifle drill. One of the indelible impressions made on them was the time they spent in trying to dig trench systems in the sun-baked soil of the Fort Sill reservation. And few of them will forget the hours they spent standing in line to receive the "shot in the arm" given as anti-typhoid inoculation. After a few weeks at Camp Doniphan these Oklahoma regiments were transferred to Camp Bowie, Texas.

In September the 35th Division, comprising the Kansas and Missouri National Guard, was assembled at Fort Sill, and was trained at Camp Doniphan for the next six months. One member was Captain Harry S Truman, who commanded a battery in the 129th Field Artillery. After the war, when he was senator, and even after he became President of the United States, Mr. Truman maintained his status as a colonel in the Field Artillery (Reserve) and his membership in the U.S. Field Artillery Association. Another celebrity, Captain Dwight Davis, 138th Infantry, was later Secretary of War.

With the departure of the 35th Division for France in the spring of 1918, Camp Doniphan became a field artillery brigade firing center, commanded by Brigadier General Edmund J. Gruber, who many years before had composed the famous "Caisson Song."

Altogether Camp Doniphan housed 50,000 men during the war. In 1919 most of the buildings were torn down and sold, but the area continued to be used as the summer camp of the Oklahoma National Guard.

POST FIELD

In 1917 the Air Service (then a part of the Signal Corps) established an airdrome south of Fort Sill, on the plateau where the Kiowa chief Big Tree had tried to steal Colonel Grierson's cavalry horses in 1870. This "flying field" was named Post Field in honor of Lieutenant Henry B. Post, 25th Infantry, who was killed at San Diego, California, February 9, 1914, while attempting to establish an American altitude record.[12]

The 3d Aero Squadron arrived at Post Field and was followed by several others. In 1918 the School for Aerial Observers, employing balloons and aircraft, and the Air Service School, employing several squadrons of observation planes, were established at Post Field. They graduated hundreds of aerial observers who were officers of the Army Air Service.

THE FIELD ARTILLERY SCHOOL

In October, 1918, the Infantry School was moved from Fort Sill, part of it going to Camp Benning and part to Fort Hancock. On April 21 of

[12] Major I. A. Rader to librarian, F.A.S., December 22, 1924.

the following year the Field Artillery School of Fire was changed, by War Department order, to the Field Artillery School. The short but all-embracing course formerly taught at the school was altered to provide a technical education for battery commanders; a basic course for new lieutenants was opened at Camp Knox, Kentucky, and a field officers' course at Camp Bragg, North Carolina. In February, 1922, a board of officers known as the McGlachlin board recommended a consolidation of all branches of the school, in order to reduce the expense involved in the upkeep of three establishments. The basic course then was moved to Fort Sill and combined with the course there to form the battery officers' course. The field officers' course, also moved to Sill, was renamed the advanced course. Both courses were of approximately ten months' duration.

Thus by 1924 the Field Artillery School was well organized and had fairly well-fixed policies. Nevertheless no decision had been made by the War Department as to its permanent location. Pending this decision the whole post suffered from lack of appropriations for new buildings and even for sufficient money to keep the old ones in repair. Furthermore the school staff had to be ready on a moment's notice to move the school to parts unknown.

While awaiting the decision for such a transfer, the temporary build-ings built in 1917 began to burn, one after another, with suspicious reg-ularity. This started in December, 1923, with the destruction of the Service Club. In 1924 there were fourteen fires on the post. Some of them were in officers' quarters, others in the theater, the school library, motor shed, stables, and other buildings. Soon it was suspected that these fires were the work of a pyromaniac. The suspicion was strengthened when a series of false alarms were turned in at the fire station. Frantic efforts were made to prevent the fires and to apprehend the criminal. Fire hydrants and alarm boxes were greased to obtain finger prints, extra sentinels were placed on duty, every means was taken to increase the efficiency of the fire department. All without avail. Traps were set to catch the criminal, but the only man apprehended was the well-known Sergeant Robinett of the military police, who was out "sleuthing" in an attempt to determine who was turning in the false alarms. The fires continued. On April 30, 1925, fire destroyed two warehouses containing household effects belonging to student officers and the school staff, so stored on account of the crowded conditions of the "tenement" quarters. This fire represented personal losses of hundreds of thousands of dollars, not entirely covered by insurance. On June 17, 1925, eight large apart-ment buildings in the academic area burned. This fire cause a loss of more than $1,000,000. All the students and many of the instructors thereby lost their quarters on the post. From then until 1934 all students were forced to live in Lawton and commute to the post.

It never was proved that any of the fires occurring up to 1925 were of incendiary origin, although it was strongly suspected that such was the case in a number of instances. In 1926 there were ten fires within five months. Some of these fires were extremely malicious in character, such as the blaze set in the theater during a show. The greatest damage occurred when an ordnance warehouse was destroyed, representing a loss of $1,025,400. Finally military police, working under cover, succeeded in locating the pyromaniacs in the fire department itself. The criminals were all young soldiers who were setting the fires merely for a thrill, and they had confederates in the military police force. The military police were unable to obtain individual verification, and called in an operative of the Department of Justice. Detective James Fallon was assigned to the case. Disguised as a tramp, he loitered around the fire station, wormed himself into the confidence of the criminals, and obtained all the necessary evidence. The military police arrested seventeen soldiers involved in the case. Conviction against thirteen was secured in the United States district court, and four others were tried by courts-martial. Sentences up to fifty-two years were given the culprits.[13]

On August 8, 1929, the crowning blow was struck when Snow Hall burned to the ground. This reduced the housing of the school to two frame buildings of wartime construction, a row of shacks which were built for the School of Fire in 1915, and the old trader's store. The school was almost facing the conditions which existed at the time of its origin in 1911.

On December 13, 1930, as the result of a lengthy study made by a board of general officers which included the school commandant, Brigadier General William Cruikshank, Secretary of War Patrick J. Hurley designated Fort Sill as the permanent location of the Field Artillery School. Thus ended twenty years of indecision. However, funds were not immediately available for the new construction which was sorely needed. Money for this purpose was not forthcoming until 1933 and 1934 when, as a part of great construction projects undertaken all over the United States, funds were allotted to build a school and administration building, a new library, quarters for the officers, additional barracks for the troops, and extensive additions to the hospital. The old stone post of Indian days was little changed in general appearance. The interiors of the old officer's quarters were modernized, and are still used as quarters. The old troop barracks were used as machine shops, warehouses, and overflow wards

[13] Data on fires at Fort Sill obtained from current files, post headquarters; report of commandant, F.A.S., 1927; files of provost marshal; and personal reminiscences of Sergeant Henry Nebeling.

for the hospital. The old cavalry stables were torn down to make room for the new school building. The post extended from the edge of the old post on the east to the high ground south of Medicine Bluff No. 1 on the west. With its new buildings of modified Spanish architecture, Fort Sill displayed little of its frontier heritage.

Prior to 1935 the technical library of the school had been housed in the historic trader's store that the government had purchased from William Quinette. But a room had been included in the design of the new school building for the library, so it was moved there in 1935, when that building (now McNair Hall) was completed. The trader's store was then razed to make room for one of the new officers' quarters erected in what was known as the Academic Area—some of the Negro maids were heard to refer to it as the "Epidemic" Area. A bronze plaque marks the site, and at one time the rim of the store's cistern was visible in the driveway—a place where in 1935 earnest seekers from Texas asked permission to dig for the mythical lost treasure of an outlaw gang. A replica of the store has been built in the old Stone Corral, a part of the museum.

The Fort Sill museum, or, as it is officially known, The United States Army Field Artillery Center Museum, was formally opened in the old Geronimo guardhouse on December 11, 1934. The Chief of Field Artillery, Major General Upton Birnie, Jr., who had been stationed at Sill when Geronimo was a tourist attraction there in 1902, came from Washington to participate in the ceremony. At that time the museum had only a modest collection of artifacts, uniforms, insignia, weapons, and the like, but even the local Indians were enthusiastic donors. For example, one of the brass buckets used in the beheading of the Kiowas at Cutthroat Gap in 1833 was presented by Chief Sitting Bear's daughter, Julia Given Hunt. Lieutenant Harry Larter, on duty with the Extension Course, was the curator and founder, and he was assisted by two soldiers who spent a few hours there each afternoon.

During the 1930's, Air Corps activities were continued at Post Field, though on a reduced scale. Several obsolete planes, used for observation and aerial photography were stationed there, mainly to enable students at the school to get instructions in air observation of artillery fire and to provide the faculty with photographs for use as firing charts or to demonstrate the art of camouflaging gun positions. It was noticeable to most students and to the somewhat disgruntled instructors that carefully camouflaged battery positions usually showed up distinctly in the photographs whereas those that were carelessly left in the open, but scattered among shell holes and the occasional bushes and mesquite, were hard to spot. As a result the School concluded, and this was a big step forward, that the best way to conceal a battery was to stagger the guns instead of lining them up abreast and at regular intervals. Since that discovery, staggered gun positions have been standard. Of course, preparation of firing data for staggered gun positions required additional calculations, but the gunnery instructors solved this problem quite handily.

An observation balloon was also stationed at Post Field, and occasionally a student volunteered to make an ascension in it. In 1937 the War Department sent to Sill an experimental observation balloon that was sent aloft at the end of a cable in the usual manner, with an observer in the basket. But for traveling from point to point the basket was detached, and a motorized gondola substituted. A pilot flew the balloon, like a somewhat unwieldy blimp, to its next position instead of towing it with a truck. This method seemed to have promise, but never came into use in combat because, as will be seen, the Field Artillery arrived at a different solution.

An autogyro was also stationed at Sill during this period. This was a conventional winged airplane having an added rotor with blades like a helicopter. The difference was that the rotor was not driven by the power plant but was set in motion from the wash of the propeller and the forward motion of the craft. The autogyro could not hover, but could land in a fairly small field such as the Old Post parade ground. This experiment came to naught, and has been forgotten in the great progress made with helicopters and other craft having VTOL capability.

The decade of the 1930's was perhaps the most important period in the history of the Field Artillery. More vital, significant developments were made than in the whole previous life of the arm. This occurred despite the economy policy of the government, customary after a war, but in this case aggravated by the Great Depression—a policy that permitted only niggardly appropriations for replacement of obsolete equipment and development of new. But at Fort Sill there was a great flowering of new ideas and a broadening and intensification of better concepts in the realm of gunnery, fire direction, and mobility. The faculty of the school, using the student classes as "guinea pigs," brought forth new and sound methods for quickly adjusting fire and massing the fires of several units on a target without physically moving the guns. And in the development of reconnaissance, occupation of position, and march techniques, procedures were developed and standardized that enabled the artillery in World War II to make long, rapid marches in all kinds of terrain and under difficult conditions with a mobility previously unheard of. Tactics and techniques in other aspects of field artillery, such as target location and designation, communications, and other operations, kept pace. As a result, during the war the U.S. Field Artillery was pre-eminent the world over. It could march and it could shoot. It could mass overwhelming fire with amazing speed. Officers who commanded artillery units in the European and Pacific theaters were able to exclaim with delight: "Everything Sill taught us is just right! We have nothing to unlearn, nothing to change!"

THE FIELD ARTILLERY SCHOOL IN WORLD WAR II[14]

The tremendous expansion of the Army and its training agencies brought about in 1940–41 by the possibility that the United States might become involved in the European war caused corresponding changes at Fort Sill. Prior to July, 1940, the facilities at the Field Artillery School were able to accommodate a peak load of only 235 commissioned and 340 enlisted students. By March 1, 1941, this had been increased to a total of 2,000, and by the end of that year some 9,000 had completed the various courses.

This augmentation required additional facilities. Many temporary quarters for students were constructed in the area between Old Post and the railroad station to the east. The garrison was increased by the addition of three observation battalions, which were quartered in temporary barracks on Gunnery Hill. The 18th Field Artillery became a special school-troops regiment with two light, truck-drawn battalions and a medium battalion, tractor-drawn. Additional materiel and equipment were issued to the regiment, including pack artillery and heavy artillery. Incidentally, the ease and skill with which this former horse-drawn regiment handled all these diverse types of equipment shows that a regiment can be as flexible as a group without being deprived of numerous advantages that the group lacks.

The physical plant of the school changed considerably. The reservation was enlarged by the acquisition of extensive tracts of land adjoining the south and west boundaries. The Ketch Ranch was purchased, making the military reservation contiguous on the west to the Wichita Mountains National Wildlife Refuge. This had been desired by the school for at least ten years, to provide needed maneuver room.

The school staff was increased by the addition of an administrative assistant to the commandant so that the latter could more readily discharge his administrative responsibilities in commanding both the post and the school. The Department of Motor Transport, now very important indeed, since the arm was fully motorized, was made separate from the Materiel Department; and the Extension Course was succeeded by the Publications Department. The latter change was really a recognition

---

[14] The sources on which the remainder of the text is based are, first, personal knowledge—I was on duty in the office of the Chief of Field Artillery from 1939 until it was abolished; and second, historical summaries furnished by Gillett Griswold, director of the Museum, and the Public Information Office, in turn based on official records of the post and school.

of the wider responsibilities of the department in producing all types of training literature.

The courses offered at the school were altered and increased in number (though shortened in duration) to provide instruction for far more students than had attended in peacetime. Whereas prior to the emergency there were only the one nine months' course for Regular Army officers and the two three months' courses for officers of the civilian components, plus several specialist courses, now there were instituted a field officers' course, a battery officers' course, and three specialist courses for officers. The duration was from eight to twelve weeks. In 1941, 900 officers were taking these courses, an increase of 300 per cent; and more than 1,000 enlisted men were enrolled in seven specialist courses, with an annual output of 9,000 students.

When, in 1942, the United States was actually in the war, the whole National Army began to grow rapidly according to a carefully prepared plan originating in Army Ground Forces. Four new divisions were activated each month as well as a host of corps, army, and GHQ groups and battalions of field artillery. This meant that the Field Artillery School would have to train replacements, cadres, and officer candidates by the thousands. As each new unit was formed, it was supplied with a cadre consisting of a commander and staff, and Sill gave each cadre a four weeks' refresher and orientation course in the latest tactics and technique of the arm. All these officers were already in the service and had varying degrees of experience and skill; but many had not been with troops for a number of years. This procedure of schooling the cadre before it joined its new unit was invaluable in getting each new artillery unit off to a good start and in disseminating uniformly through the service the latest approved doctrines.

A replacement training center at Fort Sill qualified in basic field artillery thousands of enlisted men, but except for specialists, the bulk of such training was conducted in the units themselves.

The normal suppliers of new second lieutenants—West Point, the ROTC system, and the commissioning of qualified enlisted men of the National Guard and Reserves—could not produce enough new officers during a major mobilization. Therefore the Army on April 26, 1941, authorized the establishment of schools to qualify as second lieutenants selected warrant officers and enlisted men who could meet certain criteria. The first class of such candidates for a commission entered an Officer Candidate School established at Fort Sill on July 10, 1941. This school graduated 79 three months later. During 1942 it had a capacity of 6,600 students; and it continued through the war, finally closing down in December, 1946, after having produced 26,209 field artillery second lieutenants.

Before the office of the Chief of Field Artillery was abolished early in 1942, it was instrumental in bringing about two changes in field artillery equipment and employment that deserve a prominent place in history. The first was the adoption of a 105 mm. howitzer to replace the old French "75" that had been standard for light artillery since 1917. At the same time, medium and heavy howitzers and guns were developed to replace the French-designed weapons that had been our materiel since World War I. These new weapons were vastly superior to the old ones in range and fragmentation effect, were more flexible, and, owing to motorization, were even more mobile. In the developing, testing, and adoption of the new cannon, the Field Artillery School (and the Field Artillery Board at Fort Bragg) played an important part, for it was there that the final field tests were conducted and a place for them made in technique, tactics, and organization.

The second notable advance in field artillery was the introduction of the Piper "Cub" or L4 liaison and observation plane. This replaced the "sausage" balloons of World War I and the Air Corps observation squadrons of the following period. The new concept was that a light, unarmed plane of commercial design, modified for military use only by the addition of short-range two-way voice radio, would become an "elevated observation post" by which field artillery targets would be located and fire adjusted on them. These planes were to be piloted by field artillery officers and the observers were to be simply other officers of unit staffs who had had the usual training in forward-observer methods of fire plus some training with radio communication. Two of these planes were to be organic equipment with each battalion, division artillery head-quarters, and group. Small ground crews and first-echelon maintenance personnel were assigned to each aircraft detachment, and they too were field artillerymen.

To train the pilots, a Department of Air Training was established at the Field Artillery School. On June 6, 1942, it took over the Air Corps facilities at Post Field and set up there an air training center for Field Artillery. This enterprise was headed by Colonel (later Brigadier General) William W. Ford, a pioneer in this activity who for years had been flying his own planes.

Artillery flyers were taught different, more suitable methods than those in vogue with heavier, more powerful planes of the Air Corps. Agility in taking off from and landing in short, uneven fields—often surrounded by obstacles such as trees and wires—became an important feature. The Cub pilots trained at Sill became amazingly adept in this type of flying. For example, I recall a misty day late in September, 1944, when my battalions were about to engage the enemy near Luneville, France. Nothing could be seen from the ground, but enemy tanks could be heard not far away. Our Cubs were still on their improvised landing strip far to the rear and had had no opportunity to locate, by ground reconnaissance, advanced landing areas. A radio message brought up a plane quickly, and the pilot actually swooped down through the murk to land safely in a near-by apple orchard! Soon thereafter the planes were operating from a water-soaked turnip patch.

During the war the light planes made life miserable for the enemy, who could not move in daylight without bringing down upon themselves heavy concentrations of artillery fire.

Army aviation, thus re-introduced and pioneered in by the Field Artillery, was later made organic for all the combat arms, and for some engineer and ordnance units. And until after the war all training for these pilots was conducted at Fort Sill and most of the pilots came from the artillery.

An infantry division was trained at Fort Sill during the war, or just prior to our entry into it. This was Oklahoma's 45th Division, National Guard, which occupied the old cantonment area. This division made a combat record for itself second to none.

SINCE 1945

Fort Sill did not shrink back to its prewar size and functions in 1945 as it had done after World War I. Instead, government appropriations enabled the post and school authorities to embark on a progressive con struction program that has produced a fine complex of buildings for academic instruction, shops, hangars, maintenance and storage, a 250-bed hospital with clinics, and barracks, quarters, roads, and facilities for religious and recreational activities. The post has spread out in all directions, but especially to the south and west. Even the firing ranges have been augmented and improved. There were in 1969 six such ranges, each complete with firing positions, observation points, and impact areas. In the northeast part of the range toward Elgin is a helicopter pad, from which giant helicopters daily take off, frequently with howitzers slung underneath.

The postwar period also saw changes in the school and post administration. These were brought about initially and in part by the amalgamation of the Field Artillery and the Antiaircraft (formerly Coast) Artillery, and the development of rockets and other missiles to augment or replace cannon for air defense and for attack of distant, strategic ground targets. As a part of the reorganization, the United States Army Artillery Center was established at Fort Sill on November 1, 1946, since Fort Sill's mission now included testing of materiel and equipment as well as the operation of schools and other training facilities. The Field

Artillery School was renamed The Artillery School, with a branch at Fort Bliss, Texas, called the Antiaircraft and Guided Missile School. On April 13, 1955, the Artillery Center became the Artillery and Guided Missile Center, while the school was renamed the Artillery and Guided Missile School; the Fort Bliss installation became the Antiaircraft and Guided Missile School. On July 1, 1957, a third change occurred in which the Fort Sill school, with a reduced mission, became the Artillery and Missile School, while the Fort Bliss facility became the U.S. Air Defense Center.

The Artillery Center and School at Fort Sill again underwent a period of expansion and increased responsibilities on June 30, 1950, when the Korean War began. During the first year of that war the student body was enlarged to produce an output of 14,876 graduates. The Officer Candidate School reopened on February 21, 1951, with a 23-week course. From an initial graduating class of 28 second lieutenants, this school produced 12,398 officers during the Korean War.

On May 25, 1953, the artillery entered the atomic age when troops from Fort Sill fired the first round with an atomic warhead, at Frenchman's Flat, Nevada. The 280 mm. gun developed for this role has been replaced by a family of tube and missile weapons having both conventional and atomic capabilities.

Army aviation had been so successful during World War II that in 1945 it was made organic to all combat branches of the Army, and on December 7, 1945, the Army Ground Forces Air Training School, later designated the Army Aviation School was established at Fort Sill. The continued growth and support of Army units in all theaters by Army aviation caused it to outgrow its birthplace. In August, 1954, the Army Aviation School moved to Fort Rucker, Alabama. Fort Sill, however, continues to be the home of many Army Aviation units, particularly those of medium- and heavy-lift capability, and has made many contributions to Army Aviation's expansion.

The most striking part of the postwar construction program at Fort Sill was the completion, in 1954, of a new academic headquarters and classroom building containing also a large auditorium and a much larger and more modern library, recently named the Morris Swett Technical Library. This new school building was named Snow Hall for the late Major General William J. Snow, first Chief of Field Artillery. The Artillery Center Headquarters remained at McNair Hall.

The first troop-served Honest John rocket was fired at Fort Sill on June 22, 1954. With the arrival of a Corporal missile battalion in 1956 and the activation of a Redstone missile battalion in 1957, Fort Sill entered the missile age. To cope with the increased requirements of missile training the military reservation was increased to 94,312 acres.

Since then, cannon units, missile units, and Field Artillery missile warhead support groups and detachments, and artillery aviation companies have been activated, trained, and tested for deployment to U.S. forces throughout the world. In addition, missile crewmen are trained as replacements for surface-to-surface rocket and missile units.

The year 1954 was noteworthy also because it marked the beginning of a substantial expansion of the museum, now called the U.S. Army Field Artillery Center Museum. Mr. Gillett Griswold, formerly with the Historical Section of the U.S. Army in Europe during World War II and the postwar occupation, came to Fort Sill to be director of the museum. He brought with him a wealth of enthusiasm, dedication, and ability, and in the intervening years under his leadership the museum has become the Army's largest military and historical museum. It now utilizes several stone buildings of the Old Post, including the former warehouses, post headquarters, infantry barracks, and the Old Stone Corral (where it operates a gift shop and bookstore). The museum has responsibility for the maintenance of fifty marked historical sites on the reservation, including several Indian cemeteries, and has been instrumental in the reburial in the post cemetery of a number of famous Indians whose exploits are a part of the history of Fort Sill and the Southwest. In 1962 the Old Post was designated a Registered National Historic Landmark.

In 1907, when the Coast Artillery and the Field Artillery were separated, the latter adopted as its insignia the crossed cannon of light field guns.[15] In 1950, when the two artilleries were again consolidated, the crossed field guns were authorized as the official insignia. On January 2, 1957, an Army order approved a new insignia in which an upright missile was superimposed on the crossed cannon.

On May 28, 1968, the Secretary of the Army again separated the Artillery into two branches, Field Artillery and Air Defense. Apparently the Pentagon and its subagencies at last realized that there were two kinds of artillery even though both employed cannon and missiles: One was a tactical arm wholly devoted to the support of the infantry and armor, while the other was a strategic arm existing for air defense and attack of distant strategic targets beyond the zone of ground forces operations. The two artilleries were not compatible, and it was futile to attempt to train officers or men in the employment of both. Under its new mission the Field Artillery retains the use of surface-to-surface missiles for long-range fire, but no longer is responsible for air defense.

On December 1, 1968, the commanding general of Fort Sill, Major General Charles Pershing Brown, marked the rebirth of the Field Artil-

[15] Crossed cannons had been the branch insignia of the U.S. artillery since 1834.

lery as a separate arm in a ceremony in which he exchanged the former artillery standard for that of the new Field Artillery.

A Department of the Army order dated January 1, 1969, redesignated the U.S. Army Artillery and Missile Center as the U.S. Army Field Artillery Center. This new designation stems from the order of May 28, 1968 that separated the artillery branch into two new branches—field artillery and air defense. In addition to its traditional arm, cannon, the field artillery retains the Sergeant and Pershing ground-to-ground missile systems, which are considered an integral part of field artillery.

With the Field Artillery again becoming a separate arm, the missile has been dropped from the insignia, and Field Artillery insignia has reverted to two crossed cannons.

The U.S. Army Field Artillery Center now consists of five major subordinate commands: The U.S. Army Field Artillery School; The U.S. Army Training Center, Field Artillery; III Corps Artillery; the U.S. Army Artillery Aviation Command; and the Reynolds Army Hospital. Also located at Fort Sill and supported administratively and logistically by this installation are the U.S. Army Artillery Board, which had been moved from Fort Bragg July, 1954, and the U.S. Army Combat Developments Command, Artillery Agency.

The following major missions are assigned to Fort Sill:

The U.S. Army Field Artillery School. The school is the "University of Field Artillery" for the entire Army, where annually more than 22,000 officers and enlisted men are instructed by the six departments and trained in more than fifty courses in various phases and aspects of field artillery. The specific mission of the school is to assist in developing troop organizations and training procedures as well as to review, evaluate, and co-ordinate new tactics and techniques for the employment of field artillery guns, howitzers, rockets, and surface-to-surface missiles. These weapons may be used to fire conventional, nuclear, or chemical warheads. Many problems confronting artillery commanders in the field are solved at the school, and training literature is prepared to disseminate this knowledge. The school qualifies both officers and men in the technical knowledge and tactical and command experience of the great Field Artillery arm, which has distinguished itself in all of America's wars. To understand this, we can quote General George Patton, who at the close of World War II said to his artillery officer, General Edward T. Williams: "The Artillery won the war!" Artillerymen know this is an exaggeration, that teamwork was required; but they relish such a testimonial from a great combat commander who was not himself an artilleryman.

As the field artillery officer progresses in his career, he will periodically return to the school for more advanced knowledge and for specialized training. This includes the employment of conventional, nuclear, chemical (and biological), artillery weapons. Noncommissioned officers and other enlisted men also acquire the knowledge, skill, and leadership qualifications to perform their tasks more expertly, by taking specialized courses designed to give them a high degree of proficiency.

The Field Artillery Officer Candidate School. This agency, recently designated the "Officer Candidate Brigade," has the primary mission to train qualified applicants to be second lieutenants of field artillery. This is in line with the best concepts of American democracy, in which a young man of good character who is willing to work, and who can meet certain standards of intelligence and physical condition, can become an officer. The course now lasts twenty-three weeks, and the major portion of the formal instruction is given by the six academic departments of the school. More than 6,000 new field artillery officers were graduated in 1967; over 40,000 have graduated since 1941.

The U.S. Army Training Center, Field Artillery. The mission of this agency is the conduct of advanced individual training for enlisted field artillerymen. The Training Center's objective is to train basic trainees during a period of eight weeks to be cannoneers, rocket and missile crewmen, and fire direction and survey specialists. In 1967 more than 37,000 field artillerymen were graduated from the Training Center. It also operates a Noncommissioned Officer Academy.

III Corps Artillery. This organization, which in early 1969 contained fourteen artillery battalions, has the mission of organizing and training new artillery units. It also provides units and detachments to conduct demonstrations, field exercises and maneuvers, and normal technical and tactical exercises for students of the school. The III Corps Artillery, with a strength of 8,545 officers and men, may be contrasted with the school troops of the 1930's, which consisted basically of two light artillery regiments, one being horse-drawn (18th Field Artillery) and the other (1st Field Artillery) a motorized regiment. Other school troops in those days were a battalion of the 38th Infantry and the white detachment and the colored detachment, each of the latter two having the strength of a field artillery battery, but performing chiefly administrative and maintenance functions.

Also assigned to Fort Sill are one infantry battalion with an attached tank company, two target acquisition battalions, and numerous support units. These units together with the III Corps Artillery provide Fort Sill with combined arms capability.

To summarize Fort Sill's growth, we may say that a century ago it was a typical frontier post built to accommodate six companies of cavalry and four of infantry, or 600 men at average strength, with a regimental headquarters in what is now a part of the post museum. From that modest beginning it has grown to the huge modern complex of today, with a military population of over 31,000 and an added 5,500 civilian employees. Instead of simply protecting and supplying a small Indian agency as it did in the 1870's, it has a nation-wide mission of immense strategic and historic importance. General Maxwell D. Taylor, former U.S. Army Chief of Staff, says: "The artillery is the most explosive force the Army possesses," and another former Chief of Staff says: "Through its long and distinguished history, Fort Sill has been one of our key Army installations, best known as the traditional home of the Field Artillery. Now, as the site of the Artillery and Missile Center, it continues to play an increasingly significant role in the development and dissemination of doctrine for the employment of our modern artillery weapons."

The Field Artillery lost its leader and a real cohesive force when the office of its chief was abolished in 1942. I probably was the last officer to enter the offices of the Chief on the Monday after General Robert M. Danford, the last chief, retired and all his assistants were suddenly transferred away. In the offices all the furniture had been moved out, and all the records of tests, progress, and achievements that had been garnered since 1918 had been dumped out of their filing cabinets into a heap on the floor. A gang of laborers was preparing to haul them away to an incinerator. I made arrangements to have the papers boxed and shipped to the school at Fort Sill, where some remnants are today in the Museum. As I turned to leave the empty offices—plans and training, organization and equipment, personnel, materiel, etc.—in each room the phone was sitting on the floor ringing lustily as various members of the General Staff and supply and procurement agencies were calling to ask technical questions about field artillery. When I reached my uptown office, where I edited the *Field Artillery Journal*, the phone there was also ringing, as these same agencies called my office, the only one listed under "Field Artillery" in the directory, to ask the same questions. I was unable to discover then or since what great good was accomplished by wiping out the Office of the Chief.

Fortunately the Field Artillery School at Fort Sill stepped into the breach, and has since held the arm together and preserved its skill and pride and tradition. Today this is plainly evident when one visits Fort Sill. Everyone there, from the Commandant down to the man in ranks, is on his toes. The place hums with activity. There is an aggressive and confident spirit. The Army and this nation can be assured that under the leadership of its school the Field Artillery will "keep those caissons rolling."

GLOSSARY

NAME	DERIVATION
Adams Hill	Colonel Granger Adams, Fifth F.A., former post commander.
Andrews Hill	Colonel Henry M. Andrews, F.A., member of the board of officers which in 1911 formulated plans for the School of Fire.
Apache Gate	Chiricahua Apache prisoners of war. Cf. Apache Ridge.
Arbuckle Hill	Old road from Fort Sill to Fort Arbuckle in 1870 ran east over this hill. Cf. Arbuckle Road.
Arrow Point	Fancied resemblance of contours to an arrowhead.
Aultman Road	Brigadier General Dwight E. Aultman, former commandant.
Austin Ridge	Major General Fred T. Austin, former chief of field artillery.
Barbed Wire Hill	During the World War this hill was covered with a complete system of wire entanglements used in demonstrating how barbed wire should be destroyed by artillery fire.
Bateman Woods	Lieutenant Colonel Harold H. Bateman, drowned while attempting to save a soldier at Heyl's Hole in 1919.
Beef Creek	Apache prisoners slaughtered their cattle on the flats near this creek. Cf. Beef Flats, Beef Tank.
Buzzard Hill	Second Lieutenant Robert G. Buzzard, S.C. Res., who pioneered in the determination of meteorological data for correcting artillery fire, in 1918.
Cache Creek	French word *cache*, a hiding place. Early French traders ascending Red River found many caches of corn and other foodstuffs dug by Wichita Indians along the banks of Cache Creek.
Caddo Hill	Caddo Indian tribe.
Carlton Mountain	Colonel C. H. Carlton, former post commander.
Chatto Crossing	Chatto, a Chiricahua Apache sub-chief. Cf. Chatto Flats, Chatto Ridge.
Chrystie Hill	Captain P. P. Christie, Three hundred and twelfth F.A., killed at Fort Sill Feb. 6, 1918, by explosion of 155-mm. howitzer.
Comanche Hill	Comanche Indian tribe.

345

Corral Crossing	Near old stone quartermaster corral.
Craig Hill	Brigadier General Daniel F. Craig, former director department of tactics.
Davidson Hill	Lieutenant Colonel John W. Davidson, Tenth Cavalry, former post commander.
Dempsey Bridge	Master Sergeant James J. Dempsey, FASD (W), who supervised the construction thereof.
Dodge Hill	Colonel Henry Dodge, commander of Dragoon expedition, 1834.
Donnelly Road	Colonel E. T. Donnelly, F.A., former commandant.
Elgin Gate	Town of Elgin, northeast of reservation. Cf. Elgin Ridge, Elgin Tank.
Ennis Knob	Colonel W. P. Ennis, F.A., former assistant commandant.
Evans Knob	Messrs. J. S. and Neal Evans, post traders, 1869-76.
Feigel Point	Second Lieutenant Jeff Feigl, F.A. Res., attached to Battery C, Seventh F.A. Killed in action in France, March 21, 1918. At that time erroneously believed to be first field artillery officer killed during World War.
Four Mile Crossing	Four miles west of Old Post.
Frisco Creek	S.L. & S.F. (Frisco) Railroad. Cf. Frisco Ridge, Frisco Tank.
Geronimo Hill	Geronimo, noted medicine man and war chief of Chiricahua Apaches. Died at Fort Sill.
Grenade Crossing	Railroad crossing leading to area used in 1918 for grenade instruction by the Infantry School of Musketry.
Grierson Hill	Colonel B. H. Grierson, Tenth Cavalry, first post commander.
Gunnery Hill	Used by department of gunnery for orientation and survey instruction.
Hairpin Ford	Cache Creek makes a sharp curve at this point.
Hand Hill	Colonel D. W. Hand, F.A., former assistant commandant.
Heyl's Hole	Favorite fishing hole of Captain Edward M. Heyl, Fourth Cavalry, in 1875-76. Cf. Heyl's Hill.
Hoyle Bridge	Brigadier General Eli D. Hoyle
Indian Hill	One of the Apache prisoners had his house on this hill. Cf. Indian Spring.
I-see-o Tank	I-see-o (Tahbone-mah), last active member of detachment of Indian scouts at Fort Sill.
Jones Ridge	Horace P. Jones, post interpreter, 1869-1901.
Kiowa Hill	Kiowa Indian tribe.
Mackenzie Hill	Colonel Ranald S. Mackenzie, Fourth Cavalry, post commander, 1875-76.
March Ridge	General Peyton C. March, chief of staff during World War.
Medicine Bluff	Since early times held in veneration by Indians on account of its peculiar appearance.
Medicine Creek	Named for the bluffs. Correct name, Medicine Bluff Creek.
Menoher Hill	Major General Charles T. Menoher.
Meridian Road	Follows the meridian.

Mission Ridge	Dutch Reformed Church established a mission for the Apaches west of this ridge. Mission abandoned in 1916.
Mount Hinds	Major General Ernest Hinds, former commandant. Hill formerly named Monument Hill.
Musketry Flats	Used by Infantry School of Musketry.
McMahon Woods	Major General John E. McMahon.
Nachez Gate	Naiche, hereditary chief of the Chiricahua Apaches.
Nahwats	Comanche Indian.
Paint Shop Hill	Academic paint shop on this knoll during World War. Correct name of hill is Redoubt Hill.
Peach Tree Crossing	Small orchard of peach trees reputed to have been planted by one of the Apaches.
Pratt Hill	Lieutenant Richard H. Pratt, Tenth Cavalry, in charge of Indian scouts and prisoners, 1874-75. Later founded Carlisle Indian School.
Purington Gate	Captain George Purington, in charge of Apache prisoners.
Quanah's Road	This road formerly led to the ranch of Quanah Parker, Comanche chief.
Quarry Hill	Where stone was quarried for construction of old post.
Quinette Crossing	W. H. Quinette, post trader, 1878-1915.
Rabbit Hill	Correct name is White Wolf Mountain, for Esa Rosa (White Wolf), Comanche chief, whose house still stands north of the hill.
Remount Pasture	Used as pasture for remounts during World War.
Rucker Park	Colonel W. H. Rucker, F.A. Formerly Stewart Park.
Rudd Tank	Master Sergeant G. Rudd, FASD (W).
Rumbough Hill	Colonel David Rumbough, president of board of officers to establish School of Fire in 1911.
Scott Gate	Major General Hugh L. Scott.
Signal Mountain	Blockhouse built there in 1871 to be used as meteorological observatory; also used as signal station.
Simpson Gun	Memorial on west shoulder of Signal Mountain erected by Morris Simpson, friend of many former post garrisons.
Sitting Bear Creek	Set-ankeah, or Satank (Sitting Bear) was killed a short distance east of this creek in 1871.
Snow Ridge	Major General William J. Snow, first chief of field artillery.
Sterling Gate	Town of Sterling, northeast of reservation.
Welsh Hill	Colonel Robert S. Welsh, F.A., killed in action in France, Nov. 5, 1918. Kiowas call this Big Tree Hill, for chief who used it as raid headquarters.
White Wolf Bridge	Old ford where trail ran north to camp of Esa Rosa (White Wolf), Comanche chief.
Wrattan Creek	George Wratten, interpreter for Apache prisoners of war.

INDEX

son, (1859), 26; Palo Duro Canyon, 222–25; Sand Creek, 37; Soldier Spring, 78ff; Stone River, 100; Wichita Village, 22–24; Washita, 60ff
Beach, Lieutenant: 298
Beach, Captain W. C., Eleventh Infantry: 205n, 285
Beal, Mattie: 307
Bear-That-Goes-into-the-Timber: 92
Beaumont, Captain E. B., Fourth Cavalry: 188, 222
Beede, Cyrus: 155ff, 165
Belknap scandal: 292
Bell, Major General Franklin J.: 301, 317–18
Bell, Lieutenant James, Seventh Cavalry: 63, 69
Big Bow: Howard Wells massacre, 152–53; kills horse thief, 260; mentioned, 58, 63, 135, 143, 156, 225; Polant incident, 276; sergeant of scouts, 230; surrender, 230
Big Mouth: 57
Big Spring, Texas: 238
Big Tree: Anadarko affair, 208; arrested by Sherman, 139ff; attack on Lyman's train, 215ff; confined at Fort Sill, 229; imprisoned in Texas, 147; opposes opening of Indian country, 304; paroled, 168ff; raid near Fort Sill, 108ff; skeptic, 268; surrenders, 219; visit to St. Louis, 158; Warren wagon-train massacre, 129f
Big Wichita River: 132, 193
Bird-Appearing: 28, 32
Bird Bow: 191
Birnie, Major General Upton, Jr.: 301, 334
Black, Captain Fred H., Field Artillery: 36
Black Buffalo: 275
Black Duck: 204
Black Eagle: 73, 92
Black Horse: 177, 235, 238
Black Kettle: council at Cottonwood Grove, 43f; council with Hazen, 57; Kansas atrocities, 53; Sand Creek massacre, 37; Washita battle, 63ff
Black Owl: 275
Blackfoot Society: 224
Blain, Samuel A.: 26–28
Blakely, Colonel Charles S., Field Artillery: 36
Blatchford, Colonel R. M., Infantry: 326
Blinn, Clara: 71
Bliss, General Tasker H.: 330
Blue Beaver Creek: 10
Bob-tailed Bear: 67
Boehm, Lieutenant Peter M., Fourth Cavalry: 132, 151
Boggs, Sergeant Major Lynn: 324
Boggy Depot: 77
Boone, Colonel Albert G.: 86, 99
Borthwick, Lieutenant, Sixth Cavalry: 123
Botalye (alias Eadle-tau-hain): 217–18, 266
Box, James: 41
Brazeal, Thomas: 125–26

Brazos River: 150, 153
Broken Hand: see Jack Fitzpatrick
Brooke, Captain G. M., Field Artillery: 324
Brown, Major General Charles Pershing, Field Artillery: 342
Brown, Captain W. C., First Cavalry: 298f
Brown, William: 244
Browning, Captain W. S., Field Artillery: 324
Buck Creek: 168
Buckley: 110
Buell, Lieutenant Colonel: 187, 211, 225
Buffalo: efforts to produce return of, 263ff; extermination of, 187f, 250; near Fort Sill, 50, 76f; regarded as sacred, 187; return of, 308f
Buffalo Calf-tongue: 236
Buffalo Good: 172f, 210
Buffalo Hump: 19, 29
Buffalo Tom: 210
Buffalo Wallow fight: 219
Buffalo-Woman: 67
Bullfight: 251f
Bunger: 25, 29, 30
Butler, Josiah: 111, 112
Butner, Captain Henry W., Field Artillery: 324
Butterfield Trail: 123, 124, 127
Byrne, Captain Edward, Tenth Cavalry: 120f

Cache Creek: Big Tree's raid on, 108ff; Indian camps on, 7, 164, 229; Indian Mission, 267; lime kilns near, 105; murders near, 244ff; named, 13; visit of dragoons, 7ff
Caddo, Oklahoma: 277
Caddo Crossing: 233, 279
Caddo George Washington: see Washington, Caddo George
Caddo Indians: Anadarko affair, 205ff; boy killed by Tonkawas, 30; destruction of Fort Cobb, 29–31; government scouts, 19ff, 28, 32f, 41, 43; trail near Mount Sheridan, 89
California Joe: 60, 87
Cameron Creek: 119, 195
Camp Augur: 187–88, 193n
Camp Comanche: 9
Camp Cooper: 150, 161
Camp Davidson: 257
Camp Doniphan: 329–31
Camp Medicine Bluff: 87n
Camp Napoleon: 38
Camp Radziminski: abandoned by army, 28; base of operations for Van Dorn, 19ff; base of Texas Rangers, 28; confused with Fort Beach, 205n; established, 19; visited by Custer, 95; visited by Grierson, 50
Camp Supply: 59, 94, 214ff, 296
Camp Wichita: 84, 99f
Campbell, C. E.: 175

Campbell, Thomas: 243
Canadian River: 16, 28, 35
Canby, General: 165f
Cannibalism: see Tonkawa Indians
Canyon Blanco (see also White River): 151
Capron, Lieutenant Allyn, Seventh Cavalry: 297, 300
Captives of Indians: Gabriel Martin's son, 11; Koozer family, 112, 116, 117; Lee children, 154; Lizzie Ross, 22; Louella Babb, 43; Martin B. Kilgore, 118; McElroy, 52; Millie Durgan, 36, 37, 305; Mexicans, 8, 24, 132, 162, 182; Mrs. Box and 4 children, 41; Tehan, 214–17; Theodore (Dot) Babb, 43, 305
Carlton, C. H.: 274
Carnegie, Oklahoma: 220, 263
Carpenter, Captain Louis H., Tenth Cavalry: 140, 208
Carson, Kit: 36–37
Carter, Lieutenant Robert G., Fourth Cavalry: 125, 132, 151, 159
Cassels, Captain A. F., Field Artillery: 324
Catholics: see Missions and missionaries
Cattle: 250, 257–60, 298
Cedar Planting: 89
Chaffee, Captain Adna R.: 225, 227
Chandler, Joseph: 29, 109
Chandler Creek: arrival of dragoons, 7; Chandler's ranch, 111; Indian camps, 164; mentioned, 85; Tone-tsain massacre, 33–34
Charlton, Sergeant John B., Fourth Cavalry: 235, 244
Chee-na-boney (Tsee-na-bo-ne): 210
Cheevers: council of 1873, 177; custodian of prisoners, 229; mentioned, 164; registration of band, 204; search for renegades, 177–78
Cherokee Commission: 303–304
Cheyenne Indians: atrocity on Signal Mountain, 305; attack on Fort Wallace, 44; Battle of Washita, 63ff; Custer's North Fork expedition, 88f, 94f; depredations in Kansas, 52ff; German family massacre, 226; Palo Duro fight, 221ff; Sand Creek massacre, 37; skirmishes with Fifth Infantry, 212; treaty, 40; uprising of 1874, 191ff; warlike overtures to other Indians, 165, 188
Chickasaw Indians: 41
Chickasha: 24
Chisholm, Jesse: 40
Chivington, J. M.: 36–37
Cholera epidemic: 17
Chouteau (see also To-me-te): 15
Civil War period: 28–40
Clancy, Sergeant: 261
Clark, Ben: 60, 65, 70, 244
Clark, E. P.: 245
Clous, Captain John W., Twenty-fourth Infantry: 75ff
Co-boy: 191

Cobb Creek: 27, 209
Cochise: 296
Co-hay-yah: 191
Collier, John: 205
Colorado: 36–37, 52
Comanche Indians: allotments, 304–305; at Fort Cobb, 55ff; bands named, 6; Battle of Palo Duro, 221ff; Battle of Soldier Spring, 78ff; Battle of Wichita Village, 19–25; Black Horse raid, 238; camp on Cache Creek, 7–10; captive women released, 166; depredations near Fort Sill, 107; Elm Creek raid, 35; fight with Carson, 36f; fight with Texas Rangers, 28; houses built, 250; last Texas raid, 238–39; population, 17; principal range, 16; raids, 19, 34, 35, 48, 51f, 126, 155, 165, 182, 187, 235; registration of, 204; sheep and goats issued, 249; surrender, 207, 225, 229; Treaty of 1853 at Fort Atkinson, 18; village destroyed by Mackenzie, 161–63; visited by dragoons, 7–10
Commissioner of Indian Affairs: 160, 168
Confederate troops: 29, 31, 33, 35, 38, 40
Conner, Captain Fox, Field Artillery: 326, 327
Conover, George: 116, 134
Cook, Lieutenant W. W., Seventh Cavalry: 63
Cooney, Captain N., Ninth Cavalry: 152
Cooper, Douglas: 26, 38–40
Corbin, Jack: 61
Corey, Captain J. B. W., Field Artillery: 324
Corn, Lee: 196, 200
Cornell: 205
Cornett, Ed: 28
Corpio: 154
Corral, stone, at Fort Sill: 107, 155, 229
Cottonwood Grove (see also Verden): 43, 47
Cox, Charles: 244
Cox Mountain: 125, 128, 130, 194
Co-yan-te: see Ko-yan-te
Coyle, John: 25
Craig Hill: 154
Crawford, Samuel J.: 53f, 60
Crockett County, Texas: 152
Crosby, Lieutenant Colonel J. Schuyler: 73
Crow-Bonnet: 32
Cruikshank, Brigadier General William: 333
Custer, Lieutenant Colonel George A.: 54, 59ff, 88ff, 94f
Cutthroat Gap massacre: see Massacres

Dale, J. P.: 275
Danford, General Robert M., Field Artillery: 344
Dangerous Eagle: 229
Darlington agency: 112, 191, 219, 228
Davidson, Lieutenant Colonel John W., Tenth Cavalry: Anadarko affair, 206ff; conversation with Asa-Toyeh and Asa-Havey, 189; first expedition of 1874, 212; Indian uprising, 201; objects to removal

352

353

Little Crow: 204, 225
Little Raven: 43, 88f
Little Robe: 64, 88
Little Rock: 53, 66
Little Wichita River: 132
Lone Bear: 92, 237
Lone Wolf (Gui-pah-go): captured by Custer, 74f; councils, 116f, 134, 141, 156, 170; death, 255; efforts for peace, 164, 174, 179f; fights, 191, 192ff, 206ff 218; Florida prisoner, 231; junket to Washington, 158f; mentioned, 58, 72, 89ff, 165, 219; outlawed, 204; recovers body of son, 189; revenge raid, 192ff; surrender, 231; succeeds To-hauson, 40; Wrinkled-Hand chase, 213
Long, Lieutenant Ira, Texas Rangers: 235
Long, Nathan S.: 125
Long Horn: 153, 182, 188, 275
Lost Valley: 195ff
Lottery for homesteaders: 305
Loving, Oliver: 235
Loving Ranch: 195ff, 235
Lucans, Levi: 110
Luckett, L. H.: 153
Lyman, Captain Wyllys, Fifth Infantry: 214
Lyon, Lieutenant C. S., Sixth Infantry: 41

McCarty, Private Jerry, Tenth Cavalry:245
McClellan, Captain Curwen B., Sixth Cavalry: 113
McClellan, Captain George B., Topographical Engineers: 17
McClellan Creek: 161, 226f
McClermont, Captain Robert, Fourth Cavalry: 166
McCoy, Colonel: 124
McCoy, Captain F. B.: 293
McCusker, Phillip: at Radziminski, 25; escape from Fort Cobb massacre, 31; Grierson's second reconnaissance, 75ff; interpreter at Fort Sill, 176; Medicine Lodge treaty, 45; mentioned, 27, 201, 205, 212, 230
McElhoes, S. I.: 330
McElroy: 52
McGarvey: 244
McGlachlin, Lieutenant Colonel E. F., Field Artillery: 325, 326
McGonigle, Colonel: 87
McIntyre, Captain Augustine, Field Artillery: 324
Mackenzie Hill: 95
Mackenzie, Colonel Ranald Slidell, Fourth Cavalry: commanding Fort Sill, 231; correspondence with Sherman, 148; destroys Comanche village, 161–63; expedition against Kiowas, 148–49; follows raiders to Fort Sill, 143; issues livestock to Indians, 249f; Palo Duro Canyon, 221; Warren wagon-train investigation, 126ff; White River expedition, 151
McKibbon, Steve: 205

McNair, Captain Lesley J.: 325
Mah-kah-do: 260
Mah-wissa: 70
Majors, Lieutenant James, Second Cavalry: 22
Maltby, Frank: 206
Maman-ti: bewitches Kicking Bird, 233f; death, 234; kills Brit Johnson, 123; Lone Wolf's revenge, 192ff; mentioned, 219; surrender, 231; Wrinkled-Hand chase, 213ff; Warren massacre, 127ff
Mamay-day-te (Mama-dayte, or Lone Wolf): as a judge, 260; assaults Lee Hall, 260; Battle of Soldier Spring, 81; becomes principal chief, 1879, 255; Lone Wolf's revenge, 193ff; raid of 1873, 182ff; recovers bodies of Tau-ankia and Guitain, 189
Mangum: 276
Mangus-Colorado: 296
Mann, Brigadier General William A., Infantry: 326
Marcy, Captain R. B., Fifth Infantry: 16ff, 124ff
Martin, son of Gabriel: 11
Mason, Captain R. O., Field Artillery: 320
Massacres (see also Fights with Indians, Indian atrocities): Cutthroat Gap, 5–6; Elm Creek, 35; Fort Cobb, 29; Hennessey, 191; Howard Wells, 152; Sand Creek, 37; Tonkawa, 31; Tone-tsain, 33f; Wichita-Pawnee, 15
Massey, Robert: 245
Mathewson, William: 101
Mathey, Lieutenant E. G., Seventh Cavalry: 61
Mauck, Captain Clarence, Fourth Cavalry: 233
Maus, Captain Marion P.: 297
Maxey family: 118f
Maynard, Captain: 328
Medicine Arrow: 53
Medicine Bluff: camp established, 84f; rattlesnake den, 88; silver mines, 293–94; visited by Marcy, 17f; visited by Grierson, 75f
Medicine Bluff Creek: dam built, 316; ice harvested, 121; site of Wichita village, 13; water supply for post, 122, 282
Medicine Lodge Treaty: see Treaties with Indians
Medley, Hank: 168
Meers: 89
Menard, Texas: 35
Mennonites: see Missions and missionaries
Methodists: see Missions and missionaries
Methvin, J. J.: 266
Mexicans: captives of Indians, see Captives; guides to troops, 78ff; Howard Wells massacre, 152; killed by Indians, 110, 182; sheep herders, 249; trading contraband with Indians, 115, 190, 225

356

357

Pennell, Lieutenant R. McT., Field Artillery: 324, 328
Perez: 182
Pershing, General J. J.: 310
Pike, Albert: 29, 38
Pike, James, Texas Ranger: 28
Placido: 31
Poafebitty: 9n, 274
Po-hau-ah: 230
Pohocsucut: 153
P'oinkia: 268
Polant: 259f, 275f
Pollock, Inspector: 254
Pone-audle-tone (Paul Zontam): 205, 266
Poor Buffalo: 51, 205, 208, 215, 218, 224, 231
Pope, Brigadier General John: 39, 203, 294
Porter, Mel: 197ff
Post, Lieutenant Henry B., Twenty-fifth Infantry: 331
Post Field: 101, 108, 331
Post Oak Mission: see Mission and missionaries
Post trader: 100, 292ff
Post trader's store: Big Tree captured near, 139; built, 100; gunplay near, 246; used as School of Fire headquarters, 326; registration of homesteaders, 306
Postelthwaite: 243
Powel, Sim: 246
Poy-weh-neh-parai: 8n
Prairie Fire (Comanche): 204
Pratt, Lieutenant R. H., Tenth Cavalry: adjutant, Fort Arbuckle, 43; arrests Big Tree, 139; commands Indian scouts, 210; death of Satank, 144, 145; founds Carlisle School, 231; in charge of Florida prisoners, 231, 251ff; mentioned 230
Presleano: 163
Price, Major William, Eighth Cavalry: 211, 218f, 225f
Prince, Captain: 19, 23f
Punchbowl: 15, 266
Purington, Lieutenant George: 298

Quakers: ask for military aid, 247; assume management of Indians, 102ff; management of Indians deplored, 168f, 200; opposition to discipline of Indians, 111, 112; Peace Policy inaugurated, 99; Peace Policy ended, 200f
Quanah: attack on Mackenzie at Mount Blanco, 151; Battle of Adobe Walls, 190f; cattle ranch, 253; death of Yellow Bear, 308; delivers prisoner, 256; in St. Louis, 259; judge, 260; mentioned, 286, 299, 302, 303; prevents Comanches from enlisting, 261; recognized as principal chief, 235; surrender, 235
Quanah, Texas: 193, 237
Quarry Hill: agency warehouses built near, 102; councils with Indians near, 116, 226;

Indian camps near, 134; stone obtained for Fort Sill, 105
Quartermaster, post: 288
Quay, Matt: 304
Que-an-on-te: 193
Quinette, William H. (see also Post trader's store): discovers bodies of Davis brothers, 245; good character of Indians, 267; horse stolen, 245; mentioned, 247, 250, 259, 290, 299, 305, 307, 308; post trader, 292, 326, 329–30; ranch, 246; securing Camp Doniphan, 323; securing New Post, 317–18
Quinette Crossing: 77, 86
Quirts Quip: 172, 204
Quitan, Esteban: as a farmer, 268; attack on Lyman's train, 218f; farm is site of Kiowa fort, 5n; Lone Wolf's raid, 193; on raids, 123, 132; sold to Kiowas, 24
Quitaque Peak: 151, 235
Quohada Comanches: attack Mackenzie, 151f; defy troops, 103; Maxey massacre, 118f; mentioned, 58, 72, 210; surrender, 234f; villages destroyed, 161–63
Quo-ho-ah-te-me: 19ff
Quo-to-tai: 193, 199

Radziminski, Camp: see Camp Radziminski
Radziminski, Lieutenant Charles, Second Cavalry: 19
Rafferty, Captain W. A., Sixth Cavalry: 119
Rainy Mountain: 3, 142, 225, 237, 266
Rainy Mountain Creek: 3, 72f, 220
Rattlesnake den: 88
Rector, Elias: 26–27, 29
Red Food: 204, 205ff, 225
Red Moon: 60–70
Red Otter: 160, 193ff, 231
Red River: explored by Marcy, 17; Davidson's scout, 168
Red River Station: 143, 245
Red Store: 303
Red Warbonnet: 129, 222, 223f
Redoubt: 205, 280
Registration of friendly Indians: 203f
Richards, Jonathan: 103, 119, 155, 205
Rife, Captain Joseph B., Sixth Infantry: 47ff
Riverside Indian School: 206
Robertson, Walter: 197
Robinett, Sergeant: 325
Robinson, Corporal, Fourth Cavalry: 146
Robinson, Captain George T., Tenth Cavalry: 121
Rock Station, Texas: 112f, 125
Rockwell, Captain A. F.: 105
Rodman, Dr.: 293
Rodrigues: 182
Roman Nose: 44
Romeo: 60, 70
Roosevelt, Theodore: 300
Ross, Charlie: 103
Ross, Findley: 206
Ross, Lawrence "Sul": 19ff
Ross, S. P.: 27

360

361

UNIVERSITY OF OKLAHOMA PRESS

NORMAN

8, 24,

43-
52, 158,
154, 182, 214-

305 1.